Passion and Reason

Making Sense of Our Emotions

RICHARD S. LAZARUS
BERNICE N. LAZARUS

New York   Oxford
OXFORD UNIVERSITY PRESS
1994

Oxford University Press

Oxford   New York   Toronto
Delhi   Bombay   Calcutta   Madras   Karachi
Kuala Lumpur   Singapore   Hong Kong   Tokyo
Nairobi   Dar es Salaam   Cape Town
Melbourne   Auckland   Madrid

and associated companies in
Berlin   Ibadan

Library of Congress Cataloging-in-Publication Data
Lazarus, Richard S.
Passion and reason: making sense of our emotions/
Richard S. Lazarus, Bernice N. Lazarus.
p.   cm.   Includes index.
ISBN 0-19-508757-7
1. Emotions.   2. Affect (Psychology)
3. Adjustment (Psychology)
I. Lazarus, Bernice N.
II. Title.
BF561.L38   1994   152.4—dc20   94-9320

2 4 6 8 9 7 5 3 1

Printed in the United States of America
on acid-free paper

We dedicate this book to our dear family—our son David Lazarus, his wife Mary, and their children Jessica and Adam, and our daughter Nancy, her husband Rick Holliday, and their children Maiya and Ava Rose. We wish that their lives be amply filled with the positive emotions—happiness, pride, and love.

Preface

We wrote this book for a number of reasons. First, very few books have been written about the emotions for a general audience, which is a shame because it is such an important psychological topic and, as such, is inherently of great interest to most people. What our book tries to do is unique. Most existing trade books center on one emotion, such as anger, shame, envy, or jealousy, but they do not provide a comprehensive analysis of emotion and each of the major emotions. The public is therefore denied a readable, yet authoritative, account of a rich subject matter in which it is vitally concerned.

A second reason is that magazines, newspapers, and Sunday supplements invariably patronize the reader by so oversimplifying their treatments of psychological stress, coping, and the emotions that little can be learned from them. We had the conviction that a truly interesting and readable book could be written that would still provide a sophisticated analysis of our emotional experiences. We were also confident that this could be done without obscure jargon and excessively technical accounts.

Third, the field of emotion, which includes psychological, sociological, and biological theories and research, has suddenly expanded greatly in the last decade or so. RL had recently written a technical account of emotion for academics, and in doing so came to believe that there was latent public interest in the topic if presented in a readable way. Since the subject matter was potentially so exciting, early on BL wondered out loud why we should not write about it for nonacademics. The problem was to present the essential subject matter in a way that would appeal to intelligent readers who would have little patience with academic jargon.

Finally, we believe that this readership deserves better than the flimsiest treatment of the emotions. Although such readers would be impatient with an obscure academic treatise, we believe that the self-help genre, with its formulaic treatment of complex problems, does a disservice to intelligent readers. We have tried to offer a balanced approach. Self-knowledge and change—even when desired—don't come easily, as we hope our book reveals.

Our book is filled with many short stories—brief case studies—of people struggling with emotional distress and dysfunction, but it also presents an authoritative account of how to understand our emotions and cope with them. These clinical cases are composites of people, some of whom were seen professionally by RL and some we both have known. Facts and names were changed to protect privacy.

Although not primarily a "how to" book, we describe how people can interpret what lies behind their own emotions and those of their loved ones, and to manage them more effectively. The analysis draws on RL's approach to the emotions, which has never been applied systematically to a treatment of the emotions for the lay public.

We are grateful for the efforts of a number of people who helped us make this book readable and accurate. Foremost in this respect is a non-psychologist friend, Ted Smith, who pored over every page of the manuscript, making editorial comments and suggestions for changes. Wonderful suggestions were also made at every stage of the writing by our editor at Oxford University Press, Joan Bossert. They deserve our thanks but carry no responsibility for the limitations of what we have written, the final version being the result of our own decisions.

Walnut Creek, California   R.S.L.
May 1994   B.N.L.

Contents

Passion and Reason

For there is nothing either good or bad
but thinking makes it so.

Hamlet

1

What This Book Is About

OF ALL CREATURES ON THIS EARTH, humans are the most emotional. Our speech, actions (gestures, body movements, and postures), and our faces, too, are frequently contorted with emotion. We express anger, anxiety, fright, shame, joy, love, and sadness, as well as other perhaps socially more subtle emotions, such as guilt, envy, jealousy, pride, relief, hope, gratitude, and compassion. Everything important that happens to us arouses emotion.

Why should this be so? From our birth to death, we struggle to manage the complex demands imposed on us by our physical and social environments. The many emotions people experience reflect the many physical and social issues we must struggle with to get along.

Many myths exist about emotions, and we will try to dispel them in this book. One is that emotions are irrational and do not depend on thinking and reasoning. Actually, emotions and intelligence go hand in hand, which is why humans, highly intelligent beings, are such emotional animals.

Another myth is that emotions get in the way of our adaptation. Though they often get us into trouble, emotions are a vital tool for getting along in the world. They evolved as they have in our species because they aid us in making our way successfully through life. Our remarkable minds are capable of sensing subtle, abstract, and complicated personal meanings in situations in which we must decide whether we are in danger, safe, or in a position to capitalize on the opportunities these situations offer. Emotions are intimately connected with the fate of our struggles to adapt to life in a world that is not very forgiving of adaptive failure.

Perhaps their enormous importance to the successes and failures of our lives is the reason the emotions have always been big business in the media, as evidenced in the multitude of television soap operas that command

3

very large and regular audiences. Along with the soaps, the television talk show has promoted emotion to the pinnacle of popular entertainment, dedicated as it is to displaying the emotional upheavals of guest and studio audience alike for a voyeuristic home audience eager to watch in fascination.

We have all seen such displays. The talk show host baits all-too-ready guests to reveal their expected emotional stories and comments freely about the proceedings. And there is the ever-present psychological "expert," criticizing some guests for personal failures, empathizing with or mollifying others for being victims of a bad fate, and advising attitude changes or new courses of action. The studio audience and those who call in by telephone pitch in as well.

The guests come forth with diatribes of anger at each other, their relatives, spouses, children, friends. They tell stories of pathos about abuse and so-called addictions, and depression, display tears of distress, express guilt about what they have done to others, reveal anxiety about their personal relationships, and paint themselves as persons with low self-esteem, which is said these days to be the cause of almost every human malaise. Indeed, talk shows, with their huge afternoon audiences, have become all but sadomasochistic exercises for viewer and participant. In all these TV shows, emotional displays seem to hold center stage.

Why are so many of us willing participants in what is often a humiliating experience for the guests? The answer is not clear. Perhaps those who do are seeking public attention for a kind of celebrity status, or believe ingenuously they might resolve some of their own emotional problems in this fashion. And perhaps the rest of us like to look on because, by seeing the misery of others exposed, we are reassured about having ourselves managed to avoid or transcend the worst of life's disasters. Perhaps, too, we hope to learn about our own emotions and those of others with whom we must deal. Or we think we might find out how we ourselves might cope with some particular problem.

But what do we mean when we say someone is "emotional"? Although this is often a putdown, suggesting that the person has somehow lost control and is not being reasonable, we also know that something has strongly touched that person. Perhaps we can recognize a similar experience in ourselves. We understand emotions in others, in part, by an appreciation of our own emotions and by our ability to put ourselves in other people's shoes. When we empathize with their plight, we feel compassion; when they have experienced good fortune, we share their happiness.

In fact, whenever we experience an emotion, it indicates that something personally important has happened to us. What has happened is seen as harmful, threatening, or beneficial. Depending on the particular emotion we are feeling, the reaction commonly manifests itself in psychological and physiological turmoil, and possibly some action to deal with the emotional event follows.

Two interrelated themes echo in the pages that follow. The first is that the emotions are products of *personal meaning*, which depends on what is important to us and the things we believe about ourselves and the world. It is the meaning we give to the events and conditions of our lives that makes us feel angry, anxious, guilty, happy, proud, loving, and so forth. To understand our own or another's emotions is to understand the ways people interpret the significance of daily events in their lives, and how these events affect their personal well-being.

One way to understand emotions, such as anxiety, is to recognize that we live in a confusing world, and to do so with verve and reasonable comfort requires a road map, so to speak, that tells us how to orient ourselves. People are unique in the animal world in being aware of their fate and in sensing a past, present, and future. We construct life meanings for the purpose of creating order where there would otherwise be chaos. When these meanings are threatened, we experience anxiety. And when they are edifying, we experience happiness.

Not all of us are aware of this process of constructing meaning. It is especially common in old age—though it can take place much earlier—to engage in a life review in which we try to make sense of how we have lived, what we have accomplished, and where we are heading. What a strange, ominous thing it is to realize that, having spent most of our lives cultivating a unique personal identity—a set of ideas that defines who we are and where we are heading in the world—our existence will end. Believing we will live on in another life, perhaps in heaven, could help. But the ultimate fate of our existence—whether or not it is addressed formally in religion—remains one of the major issues of our lives. Life and death issues—who and what we are and will be—are the main sources of human anxiety and our emotional life. So the meanings we bring to everyday events are central to our emotional health.

A second theme, to which we will return throughout, is that each emotion has a distinctive dramatic plot we all can readily recognize. The plot defines what we believe is happening to us and its significance for our individual well-being. For example, we might find ourselves in a situation in which we have behaved in a way that fails to live up to our own personal ideals; in this plot we experience shame. In a different plot, when we have achieved something for which we are honored by others, our self or social importance is enhanced, and we experience pride. And so on, for each of the emotions. The plot reveals the personal meaning we have assigned to an event, which in turn arouses a particular emotion.

However, unlike the plot of a story or a drama on stage or in the movies, which a writer constructs, the plot of an emotion and its personal significance is constructed by the person who is living the emotional drama. The plots we construct may well be different from individual to individual, even in the same situation. The emotional patterns of our lives are, in essence, personal signatures that identify us as distinctive individuals with our own personal goals and beliefs. We all know people who are predominantly angry, or anxious, or guilty, or proud. They have constructed their own personal meanings for the events in their lives.

And while we don't actually create our emotions directly (though some actors can either feign doing so or, in their identification with the character they are portraying, might actually feel the emotions), many psychologists now agree that there is a large component of thought and meaning in all our emotional reactions that we construct. Far from being irrational, the emotions have a logic of their own, which is based on the meanings we construct out of the situations of our lives.

Theatrical dramas actually provide a good model for the way emotions work. There is little question that people go to a play or opera, watch movies, or read novels to be personally engaged and moved, because the stories are about familiar circumstances of life, which bring about powerful emotions. If the playwright develops life themes of real importance to the audience and the actors are effective, the play or movie is real, vital, and deeply absorbing, and the stories rise above mere intellectual exercises. They carry personal meanings that the audience appreciates as relevant to their own lives.

The fifteen emotions dealt with in this book are anger, anxiety, guilt, shame, envy, jealousy, relief, hope, sadness, happiness, pride, love, gratitude, compassion, and those aroused by aesthetic experiences.

Except for the last, there is a distinctive drama or unique storyline for each, which conveys the personal meaning the individual attaches to the experience. For each of the emotions, a plot unfolds, each distinct, revealing the way we have characterized a situation. If we are to understand how an emotion comes about, we must study the plotline that distinguishes it from other emotions. Why, for example, anger and not shame or guilt? If we know the plot, we can predict the emotion that the person is likely to experience. And if we know the emotion that a person is experiencing, we can grasp the plot. This book explores the plots of each emotion in the context of a theory that sets some ground rules about how emotions operate in our everyday lives.

If you have picked up this book, you may well be interested in troublesome emotions of your own or those of a loved one. Perhaps you would like to understand why you fly off the handle so easily. Or why you are so jealous in what is apparently a successful relationship. Or why you are anxious so much of the time. The questions are endless, and we hope to provide some enlightenment.

We know, for example, that people who are made angry have interpreted what has happened to them as an unfair slight. Everyone experiences such a slight from time to time and flies off the handle. But if you get angry easily and often, perhaps you are particularly vulnerable to feeling slighted. Though you may not recognize it, you might have doubts about your own worth. Such doubts may prompt you to seek admiration from others, and any indication that you might not be so regarded is deeply threatening to your personal identity, which leads to the emotion of anger. A consistent pattern of emotional reactions points up the pattern of personal meanings we bring to situations, perhaps inappropriately.

We also know that the emotion jealousy stems from the fear that one will lose the affection of another person. So if, despite a good marriage, you frequently feel jealous of someone to whom your spouse shows interest, you may want to examine the meaning you attach to these episodes. Your partner may be an outrageous flirt, and your jealousy is a natural reaction. But if this isn't the case, you might really be reacting in this way because you think of yourself as less lovable than others and, therefore, fear your spouse is losing interest in you.

We can learn much about ourselves if we pay attention to our emotions. It goes without saying that if we learn about our own emotions, we may gain some control over them, especially those that distress us, impair our work, or disturb our social relationships. We may also better respond to others in a relationship, successfully tailoring our responses to the needs of spouse, children, parents, and others we deal with day to day. It takes knowledge and understanding to control our emotions effectively.

We need to recognize, for example, that when we retaliate for what we regard as an offense that has made us angry, it will only escalate the other person's anger and often lead to an impasse, even with those we love. Dealing with anger effectively requires knowing how it is aroused and controlled, and why we and others get angry. We need to recognize why we may have difficulty coping with anxiety or guilt or shame, for example, in order to deal with these emotions more adequately in the future. For each of the emotions, we must become aware of how personal meanings shape how we feel.

We need to understand, too, that no matter how we try to reassure people that there is no reason for them to feel angry, anxious, guilty, shameful, sad, envious, or jealous under the troubling conditions of their lives, this reassurance will not help much. They have been told this many times before, yet they still feel this way. What can be more effective in providing help and support is to grasp the personal meanings these individuals attach to events, which in turn elicit the emotions they feel.

Finally, if we understand the personal meanings that underlie our own emotions, we will be in a better position to accept these emotions in ourselves, control them so that they do not interfere with our relationships with those we care about, and be more skillful in managing our lives. Facilitating this understanding is the basic goal of this book.

All books involve a journey of some kind. So you will know where you are headed and the topics to be covered, we provide here an annotated table of contents, an itinerary for the trip.

We first proceed through a set of five chapters, Chapters 2 to 6, each dealing with several emotions, grouped together because, though they differ from each other, they have much in common. The treatment of each emotion begins with a case study of someone who displays the emotion under discussion. These cases are actually composites of the experiences of real people, with names changed and details that would expose them deleted. They are either clinical patients that R.L. had once treated, or they are people we have both known. In these five chapters, you will see each of the emotions at work.

Chapter 2, *The Nasty Emotions: Anger, Envy, and Jealousy*, provides illustrated descriptions of these states of mind. The nasty emotions, especially anger, create tremendous interpersonal and social problems, which threaten not only our working relationships with others, but our very existence as individuals and members of a subculture, ethnic group, or nation. If we as individuals are unable to learn how to manage these emotions adequately, our world will continue to suffer from individual violence, war, genocide, and social decay, which have remained recurrent and seemingly inevitable tragedies throughout human history.

Chapter 3, *The Existential Emotions: Anxiety-fright, Guilt, and Shame*, examines a group of emotions concerned with the individual and collective meanings that underlie our lives—who we are, and what we believe life and death to be all about. We call them existential—which refers to our existence as beings—because they reveal an essential core of our personal world view and of the way we see our lives. The emotions in this chapter are universal, powerful, and troubling states of mind, which have a significant influence—for both good and ill—on our daily social lives. Quite literally, they make up much of the stuff of our daily existence.

Chapter 4 is titled *Emotions Provoked by Unfavorable Life Conditions: Relief, Hope, Sadness, and Depression*. Relief comes about when a negative situation fails to materialize or ends. We hope that a negative outcome won't happen, but we suspect it might. And we are sad—or perhaps depressed—when we must accept an irrevocable loss.

Chapter 5, *Emotions Provoked by Favorable Life Conditions: Happiness, Pride, and Love,* reveals the positive, uplifting side of our emotional lives. These emotions protect us from melancholy and misanthropy, relieve us of misery, and enhance the quality of our daily lives. As such, they are every bit as important as the negative emotions.

Chapter 6 is titled *The Empathic Emotions: Gratitude, Compassion, and Those Aroused by Aesthetic Experiences.* We experience gratitude when we have received an altruistic gift, and compassion when another person suffers an unkind fate. Why we react emotionally to drama, music, art, events of nature, and religious experiences is a fascinating and important question, which we try to explain. These emotions—especially compassion and the emotions aroused by drama and art—are based on our ability to feel empathy for others. They represent the kinder, gentler side of life.

In Chapter 7, *The Nuts and Bolts of Emotion,* we draw on the concrete descriptions and analyses of the emotions provided in Chapters 2 to 6 to pull together the conceptual ingredients that are the tools for understanding the arousal of any emotion. Six basic ingredients of emotion are considered in this chapter: the fate of personal goals, self or ego, appraisal, personal meaning, the provocation for an emotion, and the impulse to act.

Chapter 8 is titled *Coping and the Self-management of Emotion* and deals with how we manage emotional situations. Coping is given a separate chapter because of its special importance in affecting the kind of life we live. It could also be considered a seventh basic ingredient of emotion. This chapter takes a close look at the most common strategies we all use in managing our emotions, and at how coping works.

Having provided a portrait of each of the individual emotions and the general principles of arousal and control of emotion, a number of fascinating questions remain to be dealt with—namely, the origins and effects of our emotions and how they can be managed. These questions form the substance of Chapters 9 to 13.

In Chapter 9, *How Biology and Culture Affect Our Emotional Lives,* we consider the biological and cultural origins of the emotions. Our emotions stem in part from our biological heritage, which humans acquired in evolution and which reflects what we are as a species. But emotions are also influenced by the culture in which we have grown up. We explore how biology and culture combine to produce our adult emotional propensities.

Chapter 10, *The Logic of Our Emotions*, deals with the dependence of emotion on reason or judgment. Those living in Europe and America have a long tradition of thinking that emotions are independent of reason, of believing that emotion and reason are inevitably in opposition. Emotions are denigrated as a manifestation of the primitive animal in us, "tooth and claw," as it were, while reason is considered the lofty province of humans.

We are going to argue instead that, if we know the personal situation of individuals, their emotions are reasonable and predictable reactions to what is happening to them. Indeed, to put it more strongly, emotion follows an implacable logic that is seldom violated, even if we are mentally ill.

On the face of it, emotions appear to be highly fluid, changeable events, unpredictable and irrational. But when we dig deeper we see how they make sense, and we uncover the personal meaning, perhaps not the meaning *we* would give to these events as an observer, but the meaning that the person who is experiencing the emotion has constructed. To understand why an individual experiences any particular emotion requires that we understand the plot and the personal meaning it contains.

For some time, it has been fashionable to think of the present era as the age of stress. Chapter 11, *Stress and Emotion*, examines what stress is all about and its relationship to emotion.

One of the main reasons we are interested in stress and the emotions is the conviction that these turbulent states affect health and illness. So Chapter 12, *Emotions and Our Health*, deals with how we might understand this complex relationship.

Chapter 13, *When Coping Fails—Psychotherapy Offers a Solution*, comes to terms with the fact that our emotions can get out of hand and do serious damage to the fabric of our lives. Fortunately, the troubled person may seek psychotherapy and is able to choose from a number of different schools of treatment. This chapter surveys the dominant theories and strategies now being employed in the clinical treatment of emotional distress and dysfunction.

Chapter 14, *Final Thoughts*, pulls together the main lessons to be found in the book, relating them to the practical tasks of understanding and, perhaps, even managing and controlling our own and others' emotions.

I

PORTRAITS OF
THE INDIVIDUAL EMOTIONS

2

The Nasty Emotions:
Anger, Envy, and Jealousy

ANGER, ENVY, AND JEALOUSY are among the most powerful and socially troublesome emotions. It is fitting, therefore, that we begin with this trio. We call them the nasty emotions because to some extent all share a desire to harm others, or oneself, and so may lead to all sorts of problems for individuals, their community, and our society at large.

Because anger is such a central feature of our social lives, is so powerful in shaping social relationships, and is so commonly the thread that unifies the nasty emotions, it makes sense to begin the discussion with anger, and to give the most attention to it.

Anger

The best way to see how anger works is to look at it in action. Anger occurs readily in married couples, and in any people who must live or work together closely. Looking at a domestic argument provides a useful and probably familiar picture of an episode of anger, as well as offering a view of the other emotions that arguments frequently arouse.

It began while the couple was making breakfast and getting ready to go to work. The husband usually has fresh orange juice squeezed by his wife. This morning she fills a glass with frozen juice.

The husband wonders out loud why she has not followed the usual routine. She responds testily that she must be at work early, and if he wanted freshly squeezed juice he should do it himself. He takes offense and sulks a bit, making no response when she speaks. She says, "Well, it looks like sulking time. That's all you know how to do—sulk. You have no consideration for me, and I'm sick of doing everything as if you were a spoiled child." His anger is now rising too: "No, it's *me* you don't consider." Getting up from the table, he utters an insulting epithet and walks out.

The wife is now irate and she follows him into the bedroom, noting in an accusatory way that he had been uncommunicative last night when he got home from work. She also suggests that they have been failing to get along. The wife is now saying very harsh things to her husband, and she goes over a long list of character assassinations, most of which she has used in other arguments. The mutual anger escalates. "To hell with you," he shouts, hatefully. "And to hell with *you*," she rejoins in the same vein.

As the husband is putting on his coat to leave for work, he volunteers with evident distress that he learned yesterday at work he would have to take a cut in pay and that a number of employees had been let go. At this admission by the husband, the wife's behavior is suddenly transformed from attack to trying to make amends. She holds out her hand to keep him from leaving and apologizes for her outburst.

The anger has disappeared for the moment. She now feels guilt for what she has said, and anxiety too about his job and their economic plight, which she verbalizes. He sits down and says that he shares her anxiety, his anger also having mostly abated. She pulls him up to her and hugs him, and he responds in kind. She asks why he hadn't told her about this last night, but he shrugs his shoulders. Both seem relieved and even affectionate, though he is not as demonstrative as she, and was more wounded by the interchange. They begin to discuss their reactions to the job crisis, but have to stop talking to go to work, promising to speak about it again that evening.

Psychological Analysis

What has happened here, psychologically speaking? The *provoking* event in the marital argument, at least on the surface, seems to be the wife's failure to squeeze the orange juice as she usually does. Seemingly, a trivial event, but that's what makes it interesting. However, we can take the history of the argument back even further by realizing that the husband's noncommunicative behavior the previous evening had offended the wife for some reason or other. Resentment about this led her to retaliate by punishing him the next morning with the refusal to squeeze the juice. The husband then responded with an inquiry that seemed to the wife to be provocative; in any case, she used the events of the previous evening as justification for her verbal attack. She appears to have been waiting for a good reason to pounce on him.

Why was she offended by her husband's lack of communication the previous night? The wife mentions it as a self-justification following his query about the orange juice. What made his lack of communication a provocation? What is the *personal meaning* that led to the wife's anger?

Remember that the wife accused her husband of sulking and, indeed, this has been a continuing source of annoyance in the marriage. And the husband's seeming indifference has occurred many times before. She took the silence the evening before as an insult because, to her, it reflected his indifference.

Since last evening she had experienced a smoldering anger. She wanted to retaliate, but needed a more legitimate reason. That reason was created by failing to squeeze the oranges for her husband, and she expected him to take the bait. When the husband seemed to complain—we need to hear his words and tone of voice to be confident that it sounded like a complaint—she responded testily to repair her wounded ego. Her assault also offended her husband and the attacks became mutual and escalated in ferocity.

One general principle operating in any emotion is that there must be a *goal* at stake for an emotion to be aroused. In the case of anger, the goal is to preserve one's ego. The wife's most important immediate goal was to repair hers, which she felt had been assaulted by the psychological withdrawal of her husband the previous evening, and many other times. The husband's ego was, in turn, undermined by the wife's overtly hostile response to his inquiry about the orange juice, which was the *personal meaning* that had aroused his ire.

It is also possible that the wife had some hidden motivational agendas that further fueled her anger. For one thing, lying behind the goal of repairing her bruised ego was another powerful and frustrated goal of receiving more love, respect, and attention from her husband. Perhaps, too, she resented that her husband does not do what she considers his fair share in the household and secretly gets annoyed at squeezing the oranges for his juice. The juice becomes symbolic of something else.

The wife's personal appraisal of the noncommunicative behavior of the husband the evening before the altercation was that he had demeaned her, but she suppressed her anger until the next morning. Another person with a different personal and marital history might not have made the same appraisal, or might have tried to draw him out of his silence.

When she lashed out at her husband the next morning, the insult to him was obvious, and so he instantly appraised her action as malevolent. Another man, with a different personality and marital history, might have overlooked the insult or found reasons to excuse it or not to retaliate. The reaction of both married partners depended on how they evaluated what the partner had said or done. Because this evaluation was that there had been a demeaning offense, retaliation followed in an effort to repair their mutually wounded egos.

If either spouse had been more concerned with a competing goal—namely, preserving the relationship instead of restoring a wounded ego—or if they had not sensed injury, anger would not have occurred, or it would have been mild enough for the provoking offense to have been overlooked.

The refusal of the wife to squeeze the orange juice might be considered unreasonable. However, her anger is a logical consequence of the particular personal meaning she has given to her husband's behavior. This meaning stemmed from the importance she attached to his affection, regard, and attention, and frustrated need. She wanted him to be more communicative. So it was almost inevitable that she would experience emotional distress. And given her personality, and assuming she did not guess he was having a job crisis, her construal of what was happening led to anger. In all this, personal meaning was central to the anger that was aroused.

The husband's anger in response to his wife's attack the next morning is also compelling from his point of view. Deeply concerned about his job and failing to grasp his wife's needs, it would have been very difficult for him not to react as he did, though he too might have inhibited the retaliation for what he considered an unwarranted attack. That he should have understood why his wife attacked him does not alter the logic behind his appraisal that he had been demeaned without justification.

We have still to understand the rapid transformation of the marital argument, with its vehement anger, into a different set of emotions—guilt on the part of the wife, then shared anxiety and affection. At the precise moment when the husband confronted the wife with the news of the cut in his pay and the danger that he might lose his job, the wife suddenly changed her behavior and related to him in a dramatically different way. Two things seem to have happened.

First, when her husband spoke of his job problem she instantly *reappraised* his silence the previous evening as a response to this problem rather than as an affront to her. Had the wife been able to make a more charitable interpretation of his silence the night before, she might not have felt offended. Apparently, however, she was too vulnerable to make this more benign appraisal because of her severely frustrated need for affection, respect, and attention. Perhaps it is asking too much that she transcend this vulnerability.

Now, however, she could readily empathize with his plight, which led her to recognize that her hostile behavior toward him had not been warranted. She felt *guilty* because she had obviously hurt him without justification, a reaction that seems appropriate under the circumstances. Reappraisal implies that the personal meaning of the encounter for the wife had suddenly changed from a demeaning offense on his part to a moral transgression on hers. And the emotion was transformed accordingly from anger to guilt.

Second, a pay cut for her husband and the danger of job loss were also a threat to the wife, and to the economic health of their relationship. As a result of this new input and the new relational meaning it generated, she experienced the emotion of *anxiety*. The marital partners now share a common plight and must pull together to deal with it. The need to restore a wounded ego is no longer salient, though some lingering and perhaps suppressed sense of injury might remain, which will probably surface again at a later time.

We could also say the same for the husband. He might have found believable reasons for excusing her assaultiveness toward him—in effect, reappraising the situation more benignly. Indeed, as he was leaving for work, the admission that he had taken a pay cut and felt his job was in jeopardy might be regarded as the first successful coping strategy in this emotional episode, one that might have been fruitfully employed much earlier.

Recognition of their joint problem instantly aborted the painful argument because it resulted in a more empathic (re)appraisal of their shared plight on the part of his wife. So after her apology and the expressions of caring, which emerg d both from her feeling of guilt and the shared anxiety, the emotion of *love* then came to the fore. The couple, after all, had made a strong commitment to the relationship; they love each other and normally get along reasonably well. You can see here how changes in personal meaning led to new emotions, shifting rapidly from anger to guilt to anxiety to love.

Coping is always involved when there is an emotional event, especially when the emotion reflects a personally harmful or threatening situation. Coping refers to what we try to do about the unfavorable situation. The wife's refusal to squeeze the oranges, and her sustained anger, was a way of coping with the feeling of being slighted by her husband. The husband's verbal expression of anger reflected his effort to cope by retaliating for her hostility.

At every stage of this emotional episode, opportunities for coping with the ego threat and the anger by making a more benign interpretation that would have reduced the anger, or not giving vent to the anger, were available to both quarreling parties. Had these opportunities been taken, coping could have dramatically changed the emotional scenario.

The wife could have inhibited her aggression, in which case the argument would probably not have started. She might have done that if she believed the marriage was shaky and wanted to save it by not letting her anger be visible, or by reappraising the situation in a less damaging way. However, she did not.

The same coping strategies were available to her husband. He might have made no mention of the orange juice, trying to avoid getting caught up in an angry moment for what on the face of it is quite a trivial slight. On the other hand, the wife was looking for a fight, so if it had not been the orange juice it might have been something else. He might have refused to take the bait and not entered into the argument, but this probably would have infuriated his wife. It appears as if an argument was difficult to avert unless, perhaps, he understood what was bothering his wife and initiated an effective effort to deal with it.

We can also see in the marital argument that emotional encounters may involve several emotions, which change over time as the personal meaning changes with coping actions and the flow of events. Each of the emotions that took place in this marital confrontation is the result of a different aspect of a complex psychological business being transacted. We can be loving and anxious in the same situation—and maybe even loving and angry—because the aspect of the relationship leading to feelings of love are separated in one's mind from the aspect leading to anxiety or anger. One can say, for example, without any sense of contradiction, "I love you [for your thoughtfulness and kindness to me] and I'm angry with you [for often you let others take advantage of you]."

The Many Faces of Anger

Because it is so important in our daily lives, the English language has many words for anger. Some of these words—rage, fury, wrath, ferocity, and hatred—suggest very strong anger. Other words, such as irritation and annoyance, imply milder versions of anger. Still other words describe different kinds of anger and their provocations. For example, indignation, outrage, and being appalled express a sense of righteousness about one's cause. Gloating expresses pleasure at another person's comeuppance, while pouting is a cautious complaint that not enough attention is being paid. Disdain, scorn, and sarcasm describe a contemptuous attitude. And vengeance refers to actions we might take as retaliation for a severe offense.

The words anger and hostility are often confused in common usage. We often say, incorrectly, that a person is hostile when we mean that he is angry. We can make words mean whatever we want them to, as long as we are consistent in their usage. However, hostility usually refers to a sentiment, not an emotion. To say we are hostile toward a person refers to the disposition to get angry at someone whether or not we are provoked by an offensive action. We are always hostile toward that person (which is a sentiment) but we only get angry (the emotion) when provoked. We do not use the term hostile in our account of anger.

The biggest problem with anger is what to do about it and the situation that provoked it. Usually our impulse is to *cope* with the damage to our ego by retaliating. An attack in retaliation, leading perhaps to a counterattack, commonly results in resentment and provides a poor climate for problem solving and negotiation. In a counterattack against someone who has angered us—a spouse, child, boss, or partner—we may temporarily or permanently prevent a solution of interpersonal problems whose resolution is of great importance to us. Anger, and its expression as aggression, can poison human relationships and impair childrearing and education. The same is true of envy and jealousy.

Nevertheless, the expression of anger does not always have harmful consequences. It is sometimes used effectively in gaining our way. We can control what others do when the surprising intensity of our anger—perhaps combined with threatening gestures—shocks and intimidates others into submission, though there may be repercussions later. Anger can also provide unexpected personal information to another person about how strongly we feel about something; prior to the expression of anger, the other person may have had no inkling that we felt offended. We can learn about ourselves too from the realization that we are angry.

People may also feel righteous and pleased with themselves when angry, as if they are saying to themselves: "Better be angry than demeaned, helpless, or depressed." Anger sometimes feels good and we escalate the feeling in our actions, lashing out at other people—especially when it seems safe to do so, but sometimes without thinking of the consequences.

Anger can also power long-range, constructive striving, as in the attempt to show a critical parent that you are competent and diligent rather than incompetent and lazy. And the mounting of plans for long-term revenge may motivate the acquisition of useful skills and generate impressive accomplishments that survive longer than the anger. Our culture's view is that anger is inevitable in human affairs, and it must be expressed because, if it is not, it will inevitably build up, fester, and result in illness. We will see later that this view is, to some extent, erroneous.

It is no wonder, then, that we are ambivalent about anger and the other nasty emotions. Each has its costs and benefits. But in this ambivalence lies the danger that the feeble gains derived from the aggression that arises from anger, envy, and jealousy will blind us to the far more damaging losses that are more often its harvest.

For example, not knowing the true meanings that we attach to events—for example, that we are acting aggressively without realizing its motive is anger, or attacking in the personal desire to control someone else, but self-righteously regarding what we are doing as selfless or as doing our duty—can be calamitous. Many a parent has forbidden their young adult child to date or marry in an effort to control them and succeeded in pushing them into the very situation the parent was trying to avoid.

And so when we act aggressively and self-righteously without recognizing that it comes from anger, we can end up harming another person—including those we love—on the false belief that we are helping them or serving moral principles. The harm done is as unwanted as the "bad behavior" we may be trying to root out.

If we fail to understand the anger that may lie behind what we are doing, we may not be able to stop the ultimate harmful impact on ourselves and our loved ones. We have created a false reality, a false meaning, and it may catapult us unknowingly toward a personal and social disaster, as in a Greek tragedy—where the hero does not see the means of his own destruction. It is as if our decisions are being controlled by unreason; perhaps we should say they are controlled by the wrong reasons, which we fail to understand, leaving us mystified in the end about what has happened and why.

The Arousal of Anger.   The dramatic plot for anger is a *demeaning offense against me or mine.* When we have been slighted, we all have a built-in impulse to retaliate, to exact vengeance for the slight so that our wounded egos can be restored. This is the way we are built as biological creatures (more on this in Chapter 9). If we demolish or neutralize whomever we hold blameworthy for a slight, our integrity is maintained and a bruised ego is repaired.

We also get angry when viewing an injustice, even when it is directed at a person we do not know—for example, the abuse of a child or another comparatively helpless person. You might wonder what this has to do with a slight to our egos. Does our angry reaction to injustice embarrass the claim that anger has to do with being slighted or demeaned? Is it an exception to the rule?

We think not. Our commitments extend beyond ourselves to others, and to meanings and ideas we cherish. They are extensions of our egos. The commitment to justice[1] and human decency is an important part of who we are and defines a fair world in which we can live. A world without justice and the rule of law is deeply threatening to most of us, and the evidence of such an unjust world is taken by most of us as an attack on our very identity, perhaps as threatening as if it were a direct personal assault.

As we can readily see, the situations that provoke anger are diverse. Some consist of strong and unambiguous assaults. An insulting remark that impugns our character or competence, an obvious effort to injure us, as when we learn that a colleague has denigrated our work to others behind our backs, or a menacing physical action—all these instances are quite obvious provocations to anger.

But some provocations are subtle, mild, or ambiguous. Subtle provocations might not even be recognized as such. Mild provocations are easier to overlook. A remark that could be an insult if we choose to take it that way is an ambiguous provocation. None of these is so clear and so strong that it cannot be taken either way. We are reminded of an unusually perceptive fortune cookie that carried this message: "It is often better not to see an insult than to avenge it."

Whether subtle, mild, or ambiguous provocations make us angry depends more on the person who is the target than on the provocation itself. Consider as an example a compliment that perversely succeeds in denigrating us rather than making us feel good. Some people always compliment us about something that actually makes us feel ashamed rather than proud. They seem to be saying something positive on the surface, but the message comes across as really negative.

It is not surprising that we react with personal anger to people who do this, because we sense the hostile intent behind their good words. A person who never displays more than the phony affectation of being solicitous is another interesting example. There is no obvious offense, but merely the lack of evidence of genuine positive regard makes some people angry, especially those who are needy.

In the marital argument described earlier, the failure of the wife to squeeze the oranges for breakfast is an ambiguous act. It is possible that the only reason for the lapse was that she was truly in a great rush to get to work. When the husband asks about it to clarify what is happening, the wife responds with a verbal attack, which leaves no doubt about her malevolent intentions. Similarly, the husband's silence of the previous evening is ambiguous, but the wife takes it as a provocation to anger. Without knowing the relational history of the couple, or the husband's usual behavior, it is difficult to second-guess this appraisal.

In mild or subtle provocations and ambiguous situations, some people will take no offense, some will get annoyed, while others will be aroused to rage. This suggests that it is something about the people who are the targets of the remarks that influences how easily they get provoked and how intense their anger will be. To understand the diverse reactions to these situations requires that we know something about the personalities of those who are reacting.

What makes people vulnerable to anger? One personality characteristic that explains the readiness to get angry is how secure people are about their identities and the positions they hold in society. Since anger is a reaction to being slighted or demeaned, those easily angered are more likely to have grave doubts about who they are. Their egos are shaky. Insecure people—uncertain of their own worth—are more likely than secure people to be provoked by mild provocations and ambiguous situations. When it comes to displaying their anger, however, insecure people often conceal their anger for fear of upsetting the apple cart or facing retaliation.

People like this are said to carry a chip on their shoulders, measuring every social action directed at them as evidence that they are being given proper respect. Just the absence of evidence of positive regard will make them feel uneasy or demeaned. Their high vulnerability leads them to believe they have been slighted, even when there has been no obvious act to provoke anger.

We all know people who are frequently angry. One explanation could be that they find themselves in provocative situations more often than others. They live with or work for an assaultive boss, or they have a history of being oppressed and view themselves as victims. Although this victim-centered explanation can contain considerable truth, it is too facile. Many people who are not oppressed are, nevertheless, angry persons, and many who are oppressed do not become angry persons. Therefore, it's not just the condition of their lives that explains the recurrent anger. The tendency to be angry indicates something about them as persons.

To be anger-ridden, they must have developed beliefs about themselves and the world that make them appraise others as assaultive or demeaning, even when these others have done nothing to justify this appraisal. They may, for example, believe members of a particular race or ethnic group, or those who are rich, educated, or smart, are prejudiced toward them and their kind. They have grown up with the belief that "life is a jungle," that to obtain their fair share requires aggressiveness. Or they assume that to be admired, and to live up to "macho" social standards, means that they stand for no nonsense and fight at the drop of a hat. Not to do so is to be a wimp, which is demeaning. When something goes wrong, they are inclined to blame others rather than themselves.

How We Cope with Anger and Its Expression.   Because the expression of anger as aggression is so dangerous to us individually and collectively, coping with what has made us angry and with the anger itself is a prime psychological task we all face.

We need no more than to glance at the daily newspaper to be convinced that expressing anger in many instances is risky, and that powerlessness often leads to the *disguise* of its expression. Some of the most fascinating examples of disguised anger are nursery rhymes created in eighteenth-century England. Rock-a-bye Baby, a nursery rhyme that many Western children once enjoyed, was originally formulated as an attack on the tyrannical and feared King James I who had an illegitimate child that he hoped would inherit the throne. The rhyme goes:

> Rock-a-bye-baby
> on the tree top.
> When the wind blows
> the cradle will rock.
> When the bow breaks
> the cradle will fall;
> and down will come baby,
> cradle and all.

While benign on the surface, this nursery rhyme communicates a political threat. If the illegitimate baby on the tree top (indicating the topmost position in the land) became heir to the throne, then the revolutionary winds of change would blow and wreak havoc—the bow would break and the throne (cradle) would fall. An open attack on the royal family would have led to the cruelest of punishments. However, people in King James's time could enjoy this attack on the throne with safety because the seditious message is disguised as a harmless ditty.

It is a truism that when it is risky to display it, the expression of anger will be disguised. Sometimes this is done deliberately, as when we avoid the appearance of anger toward people who have power over us, such as employers, supervisors, teachers, and police. We may also fear retaliation for our anger from those we love, or are distressed by the guilt that our anger can sometimes produce.

People can also attack subtly, expressing their anger safely while still exacting a modicum of harm. Instead of expressing anger directly toward those who have power over them, they may act cooperatively, at least on the surface. For example, aggrieved workers can call in sick to undermine the boss's objectives, slow down their rate of productivity, or manifest stupidity in the conduct of their jobs. They may do this without even being conscious of their malevolent intent.

A common way to avoid the dangers of expressing anger is to *displace* it; rather than aiming it at the powerful person whom we fear, we direct it instead at another person who poses no threat. A helpless or otherwise despised minority can be chosen against whom we can vent our frustration with society or our position in it. Displacement of this kind is a common basis of prejudice and discrimination.

One of the saddest features of such displacement is seen in what is sometimes called scapegoating, in which we often see one weak minority direct its frustrations and anger toward another weak minority—ironically, victims of oppression attacking other victims. Another example, again not a pretty manifestation of such frustration, is seen in the person who is being browbeaten or physically abused, who in turn takes out this abuse on helpless children.[2]

Displacement is widespread in the animal kingdom and is most often seen in dominance struggles, which could represent the evolutionary origin of human status struggles and anger. When animals are defeated in a dominance struggle by a more powerful adversary, it is not uncommon for them to turn on a weaker one below them in the hierarchy. We will have more to say about the animal origins of human aggression in Chapter 9, which looks at the roles of biology and culture in emotion.

Earlier we mentioned *pouting* and defined it as a mild reproach, designed to ward off the danger of withdrawal of support. Pouting nicely illustrates one of the ways people cope with the dangers inherent in expressing anger. The person who pouts fears that a more vigorous attack on a benefactor will prove disastrous. One who pouts feels inadequate and dependent on another person's favor. The pouter's complaint is that the object of this display is not being as attentive as is wished, and so the pouter is disappointed. The complaint must be expressed very gingerly so as not to offend the benefactor too much. Pouting, therefore, is mainly a plea for more attention, in which anger is minimally expressed or disguised.

We also noted earlier that viewing an injustice may make us angry. The commitment to justice creates an interesting paradox. After what we have appraised as a demeaning offense, we want to punish the other person for the injustice that has been done to us. This, after all, is only right. However, vengeance must be meted out without excess, and in our morality the punishment must fit the crime. If our counterattack leads to more harm to our adversary than fits our sense of justice, we are likely to react afterward with guilt or shame.

One way to cope with an injustice we ourselves have produced, and the guilt or shame it provokes, is to become defensive about what we have done. We try to convince ourselves of our moral rectitude and spend large amounts of energy in denial and hypocritical self-justification to appease any guilt we might feel if we have to blame ourselves.

Shakespeare takes note of this process in a famous line from *Hamlet* (Act 3, scene 2, 1) about his mother's complicity with his uncle in the murder of his father, the king. In an effort to trap them into revealing themselves, Hamlet has actors perform a play with a similar tragedy. Hamlet, who is observing his mother as she watches the play, says of her deceptive comments, "The lady doth protest too much, methinks." He recognizes what she says as a denial of guilt because of the excessive zeal with which she has defended the murderous king and his paramour in the play within a play, and he uses it to confirm his suspicion about her guilt.

In fact, you may have also noticed the irony that when reprehensible acts have been exposed to public view, those who committed them often react with vigorous and self-righteous denial. The denial is all the more vehement when people know they are guilty, turning their guilt into an attack on their accusers.

Recently, for example, we complained to a woman who had parked in a spot reserved for a restaurant we were about to visit. The woman was actually heading for the beauty parlor next door, which had its own but more inconvenient parking spaces. But instead of acknowledging the error, the woman became verbally abusive and almost physically threatening at being told that she was in a restricted space, claiming it was none of our business. Of course it was our business, because this kind of action often made parking at the restaurant difficult, sometimes impossible, and we knew the restaurant owner was distressed about the situation. The woman had acted inconsiderately and illegally, and her vehemence on being caught in the act only attested to her need to deny that she had done anything wrong.

Another way of coping with the problem of anger is to *inhibit* its expression as aggression. Anger is not aggression, but the impulse to attack when we are angry is strong and often difficult to inhibit. We may feel angry—and even have the impulse to attack—without actually attacking anyone. Nor does aggression always involve anger, as when a prize fighter demolishes his opponent without feeling any anger and a bomber pilot kills large numbers of unseen people without anger.

Writing about the inhibition of anger, which is really the control of the impulse to attack when angry, psychologist Carol Tavris[3] points out the great damage anger can do when it is acted out. She suggests that before lashing out in anger a person should "count to ten" in an effort to cool off before doing or saying what may later be regretted.

Tavris correctly rejects the idea that bottling up anger necessarily produces psychological or bodily harm. The older view that unexpressed emotion builds up as steam does in a boiler and must be discharged is largely discredited. If anger is inhibited and is not subsequently rekindled by additional provocations, it will gradually dissipate with no harm done. If it is recurrently or continually provoked, the person could be in real trouble, both interpersonally and in respect to her health (see Chapter 12).

It is the interpersonal consequences of anger—the way the other person reacts to it—that can cause damage, not the effort to inhibit its expression as aggression. If, for example, we express the anger and the other person accepts it without retaliation, and attempts to mollify the one who is offended, no harm is done. It could even do some good. However, if the expression of anger poisons the relationship, it could have significant chronic costs, and these costs may contribute to continuing stress and result in illness.

Yet to inhibit the expression of anger does not eliminate it as an authentic emotional state. The anger is apt to remain alive as long as the provocation continues, even if it is concealed. Merely the sight of the other person, or being in a similar situation, may provoke it anew. If the anger dissipates, it will occur again with the next provocation. A more powerful coping strategy is needed to curb the unexpressed anger that keeps recurring. As we have seen, such a strategy consists of reappraising the anger-inducing provocation by empathizing with the offending person's problem and not viewing that person's action as a personal offense. The power of this reappraisal is that it is capable of eliminating the anger altogether.[4] In other words, to remove the provocation, we must change the meaning we gave to it. We will say more about this in Chapter 8 on coping.

It stands to reason that if the provocation of an emotion is based on the meaning construed from events, then coping would also be based on meanings we draw from our day-to-day activities. To understand how anger and aggression are or might be controlled, we must also take into account the ways people cope with threats to their egos to predict whether they will publicly express the anger they feel, and whether their anger will be directed.

Coping can also affect the assignment of blame, the target of one's anger, and the decision about how to act. There are self-blamers who usually accept blame for whatever has happened, almost never laying the blame on others. Even if we say to them "It's not your fault," the reassurance may not change how they appraise the situation. And there are those who seldom accept the blame for what has happened.

Freud[5] regarded anger as one of the two most troublesome instinctual urges, the other being sex. Influenced by the horrors of World War I and II and the constant history of human tyranny, aggression, cruelty, and bloodshed, Freud considered destructive tendencies to be a biological imperative in our species. World War II, with its genocide of Jews and other

Hitlerian atrocities, made him pessimistic about whether anger and aggression could long be controlled by society. Indeed, anyone who follows history must despair of the ease with which people justify killing each other, engage in torture, genocide, and other depredations.

Despite human history, some think there might be reason for optimism about the possibilities for controlling aggression. Observations of nonhuman animals show that, unless it is for food, serious aggression—meaning an attack that leads to severe injury or death—is comparatively rare.[6] Though anger is difficult to control, aggression and violence are volatile states that can change rapidly and can be expressed or inhibited under specific conditions. We still need to learn more about these conditions. Yet any optimism is in marked contrast with Freud's pessimistic view, and seems to fly in the face of our species' history.

Central to the emotion of anger, and to others, is the fact that the personal meaning given to events controls the emotion felt and how well it is coped with. In the case of anger, its control or escalation is up to the person who is experiencing it.

Envy

Now we turn to a second nasty emotion—envy. And we take as our case a person who suffers from a debilitating pattern of envy.

Doris married Rick twenty years ago, and suffers from a nagging envy toward those who appear to her as more fortunate and well off than she and her husband. Not being an attractive "catch," she married a man who was not her first choice. The man she wanted, whom she remembers as wonderful, had no real interest in her, though they dated on occasion. She considered Rick to be barely suitable, but better than nothing.

Rick had some modest prospects as a breadwinner when they first married, but now in his late forties his future offered at best the continuation of his job as a salesperson working for a large retail chain. Doris, as a clerical employee at a local community college, makes about the same pay as her husband. They have two children in their late teens.

Doris and Rick had both graduated from a four-year college, and while struggling to keep up with growing costs, live in modest comfort. They take a low-cost vacation every year, and eat out in expensive restaurants infrequently. About once a week they take their kids out to eat at a fast-food restaurant. Both work very hard at their jobs, and try to provide a solid family setting for their children. They go to movies and ballgames, and have some friends, but to an observer these relationships seem shallow.

Doris is consumed with envy of others, which she seems to have been all her life. When she was a teenager, she envied the brightest, loveliest, and most popular girls, and she looked longingly at the most popular boys, who never gave her a glance. Her younger sister was popular, and Doris envied and tried unsuccessfully to compete with her. Her parents always spoke with pride about her sister but never, she thought, about her.

She resents her husband for being what she considers a failure. Unfortunately, she never has appreciated Rick, who is gentle and considerate of her, helps a great deal at home with the household and children, and regards Doris as a desirable wife. Rick is accepting of her faults, but rankles, mostly in silence, at her dour opinion of him.

Doris envies the expensive cars owned by some of the couples they socialize with. She looks hungrily at diamonds and upscale clothes worn at some of the parties she attends. She is ashamed of her home and enviously notices some of the larger, better furnished homes of the people she visits. She feels ashamed of and cheated by her husband. And she envies her friends who are proud of their accomplished kids, while hers seem unimpressive in comparison.

She speaks resentfully to her husband about the women who have these things and contemptuously of her husband who cannot provide them. "Why is she so well-off?" she snarls. "She's no beauty. She's not bright and never even graduated from college." The unspoken thought is always that she has been unlucky because others have so much more than she.

Doris occasionally gains a modicum of satisfaction when some of those she envies experience personal troubles or tragedies. One of her friends developed breast cancer, and the cancer was removed by a radical mastectomy. Although she said all the right things to express sympathy, she secretly was pleased that this "very uppity and fortunate woman" was having a bad time. When divorce struck another friend's marriage, she commented with scorn about what a lousy wife she had been, and wondered why it took so long for her husband to turn against her. But these moments of hostile satisfaction cannot banish or compensate for her consuming envy. She continues to be an unhappy, hostile person, seemingly miserable with her lot in life.

Psychological Analysis

Doris is in pretty bad shape. If one is consumed by envy, as she is, one is poisoned by it; the yearning and the negative comparison of oneself with others are a constant source of misery. Although she was at one time jealous of the woman who got the husband she had wanted, now, in the main, Doris suffers from almost constant envy. She has been unable to gain much, if any, satisfaction from the things she has.

This seems to have been a feature of her character from childhood for reasons that seem connected to an unsuccessful rivalry with her younger sister. It was fueled, in large measure, by the chronic negative comparison she suffered from the parents of the two girls. She has made envy into a style of life, a manifestation of the self-image of being deprived. She has never gotten over her sense of psychic deprivation.

What is the *provocation* for Doris's envy? The original provocation was the unfavorable comparison with her younger sister. She experienced this as a rejection of herself and was never able to win her parents' positive regard by anything she accomplished. It is not just the good things of life she lacks; what she sees as lacking symbolizes the constant sense of being treated unfairly and not properly appreciated. People with such character-ological envy feel a fundamental deprivation that goes to the very heart of their personal and social identity. It is as if Doris is saying, "As a person I deserve more from the world." This is the *personal meaning* of the envy that defeats her.

Now, as an adult, each time she observes how these other couples live, or thinks about something she feels deprived of, these observations and thoughts become provocations for her envy. They remind her of what happened with her sister. Often when such observations and thoughts are provoked, she has a dream that night of being criticized by her parents in the presence of her sister, who is praised as wonderful.

Although she has better moments in which her thoughts are more positive, because of the frequency of negative feelings about herself she seems to be in a constant state of envy. Envy in her case has become a central part of her character, a litany of recrimination against the condition of her life, which mainly carries the personal meaning of having been rejected as a person.

Objectively speaking, Doris doesn't have it so bad, but she interprets her life as an unfortunate failure to obtain what she wants and believes she deserves. What she wants mostly, though she seems not to realize it, is positive regard from people. But she has too many of her own doubts about herself, which stem from half believing the negative opinions of her parents.

Clearly Doris is coping very poorly. Because of her self-image of personal inadequacy, she has not been able to accurately assess her personal situation. We all indulge in this kind of coping from time to time, experiencing a tinge of envy, some of us more intensely or more often than others. For most of us, however, these moments are few and far between, and we can banish them from our thoughts as unproductive and perhaps even unrealistic. But Doris has not been able to achieve any degree of detachment about what she has and does not have. The failure to be able to accept who she is and what she has, and appreciate it, is her sickness.

Why is it that people—like Doris—who are miserable seem to cling to their misery as if they couldn't live without it? James F. T. Bugental, an experienced existential psychotherapist who has written extensively about his work with patients who are suffering, offers an interesting answer to this dilemma.[7] When one of his patients, Frank, is told in a therapy session to "see whether you can feel what it would be like not to feel miserable," after some difficulty expressing himself, Frank bursts out, angrily, "If I ever gave up my misery, I'd never be happy again." Awed by this insight, Bugental writes:

> How clearly he reveals that the way he has learned to cope with life is essential for him. It is not a source of "happiness" really, and Frank's misery is very real. But to give up his main way of being in the world would be so terrifying that his present misery would seem happiness by contrast.

Bugental is suggesting, in effect, that although Frank's ways of coping with his problems are not adequate, to relinquish them is to face an even greater threat of having to see himself and his conflicts without the protection provided by these ways of coping. Doris too is miserable, but she cannot abandon the pattern of envy without replacing it with something more effective which, in the absence of a solid understanding of what has happened in her life, will leave her dangerously exposed.

Doris must overcome this personally created tragedy by changing the way she thinks about herself and the world—in effect, by giving up the sense of being victimized by fate if she is ever to feel lasting satisfaction in her life. Not an easy thing to do.

When one's own resources for coping fail, as they have in Doris's case, an alternative is to seek professional help. Since her problem began so early in life, a sensible choice of therapist would be one who could help her see how it all started. This would suggest psychoanalysis, but extended treatment is probably too expensive for her meager resources. There are briefer psychotherapies, which might help her find a rationale for giving up the fruitless comparisons with others that are contributing to her misery. She needs to learn and understand why she has become so envious of others and to accept, preferably appreciate, what she has and who she is (see Chapter 13 on psychotherapy).

We wish we could say that, at this writing, Doris was getting control over her envy, or was receiving professional help to do this. But she continues to be consumed by her envy, which is directed at everything she believes makes for a good life. She does not see that what she lacks most is a good opinion of herself and the positive regard of others. Given her history, and her inability to attain a reasonable perspective about herself and her life, we would not be surprised if Doris remained a victim in her eyes for the rest of her life, still beset by envy of others and anger at them.

The Many Faces of Envy

Envy is usually regarded as akin to jealousy and discussed along with it, probably because our language is ambiguous about the important difference between them. In the English language, jealousy can denote *either* jealousy *or* envy, while envy is used only in the sense of wanting something another person possesses.[8] Because their meanings are often confused, but readily distinguished, we discuss envy and jealousy separately.[9]

It is a frequent but incorrect usage to say "I am jealous of you" for having this or that. Envy is a two-person emotion. Jealousy, in contrast, is a three-way triangle in which someone threatens or has taken what we consider ours, most often the affection of a third party. Doris was initially jealous of her sister, but later, when there was no third party, she suffered from envy. We envy the person who has a good job but are jealous of the person who got the good job to which we aspired.

The dramatic plot for envy is simply *wanting what someone else has.* The subjective state of a person who envies is one of yearning for what one feels unfairly deprived of, a painful hunger that is difficult to control.

Why do people construct this personal meaning of feeling unfairly deprived and therefore experience envy? In garden-variety envy, which we probably all experience from time to time, when we want what we see others having, the natural reaction is to envy them. We speak of trying to keep up with the Joneses, by which we denigrate the feeling of envy. In such versions, envy can be a one-time or infrequent occurrence. We get over it quickly and go on with our lives. In this form, the envy is not particularly pernicious unless, like Doris, it stems from a deep sense of deprivation that constantly nags at the person. Not all envy is as intense and pervasive as that of Doris whose personal history made her so vulnerable to feeling rejected as a person.

The usual *provocation* for envy—at least on the surface—is the observation that another person has what we want, either actually or symbolically. The *personal meaning* of envy is that someone has what one wants or needs, perhaps someone less deserving, which is construed as unfair, and so one yearns for it too. This unfairness and yearning for what one feels deprived of are in the consciousness of a person who envies. When the ego is heavily involved, as it was with Doris, the positive regard of others becomes a constant, underlying need, which lies buried beneath the surface. Such pervasive envy is then a character trait; we speak of an envious person.

As in the case of the other emotions, if one feels envious, one must *cope* somehow with the emotion and the conditions that bring it about. Social comparisons between ourselves and others can be positive as well as negative, as when we think of ourselves as better off than others in general or someone in particular. So a way to cope is to make such a comparison, which favors one's own situation. This is the opposite of envy. A judgment that we are better off than others is sometimes a way of coping with adversity and with the destructive envy that we might otherwise experience. Doris couldn't do this. She never wanted to pay attention to those whose lives were less favorable than hers, just those who had more.

For example, when people are struggling with a serious illness, such as cancer, they may gain some modest psychological relief by making the appraisal that others are worse off.[10] When a person we envy is seriously ill, this can compensate a little for their otherwise more favorable status. We may think, "My illness can be controlled by medicine while that of others cannot." Or we see that our illness is less advanced than that of others, or less painful and debilitating. Positive comparisons can sometimes change the personal meaning of a situation enough to mitigate some of the distress.

Another way to cope is to enjoy the miseries of the person whom we have envied. The German language includes a word that is absent in English to express this malicious feeling—*Schadenfreude*, which means joy at another's suffering and comes close in meaning to the English word gloating. It could also refer to pain at another's success. Doris revelled in the comeuppance of those she envied, but was so preoccupied with her own victimization that she got little real satisfaction from this form of coping.

Although envy can be benign in the sense that we may admire another and wish that person no harm, it can also be malicious and cruel, in which case it is fused with anger at the person whom we believe has more than we. So if the other person makes a misstep, we feel a little less envious of them, and a little better about our own situation.

Theologian Solomon Schimmel[11] lists envy as one of the "seven deadly sins," tantamount to an immoral action as set forth in the Old Testament. Most of us know the powerful story that biblically demonstrates King Solomon's wisdom:

> A woman whose infant died was envious of the mother of a live baby, and so she falsely claimed that the child was hers. When Solomon offered to cut the child in half and distribute it between the two, the woman agreed whereas the true mother was horrified at the thought and preferred to lose her child to the imposter as long as it would live. By their different reactions to his proposal, Solomon discovered which was the real mother and which the imposter. Here we see the cruelty of envy. Not only did the envious woman try to deprive the mother of her child, she preferred the child dead rather than allow someone else to enjoy what she lacked.

A poor position in life may be made more tenable by acknowledging that even celebrities are sometimes depressed or suicidal, or victims of personal disasters. This is not unlike Doris's enjoyment of her friends' tragedies. Judy Garland and Marilyn Monroe are famous examples of individuals who died young and tragically despite all their talent and wealth. And there is the reality that we somehow take comfort in this—even they can succumb to stress and unhappiness.

We also blame victims of a bad fate in an effort to expiate our own guilt about the good fortune of having been spared, which contradicts the feeling of envy. We want to believe that in a just world, the good are rewarded and the bad punished. When those we love or care about, or people we know to be good and decent, suffer chronic or terminal illness, or are punished with a harsh life, it deeply threatens our sense of justice and our own security. If they could have a bad fate, it could also happen to us.

Therefore, there is a strong wish to believe that victims have failed in some way and have brought their troubles on themselves. In a just world, this explains why they have been victimized. Doris feels victimized, but this creates the added social problem that others readily blame her for her bad luck; she must have deserved it. This suggests that no matter how envious one is, it might be better to cope by concealing it, since envy lowers our social credibility in the eyes of others.

In the Great Depression of the 1930s, the most popular movies portrayed wealthy people enjoying their opulence, sometimes in satire, but most often in a way that could be savored vicariously by poverty-stricken moviegoers. These movies were referred to as escapist; they provided opportunities to fantasize about how it would be to be rich, and to forget about one's own economic woes. Whether this promoted or undermined envy is not clear. It probably did both.

We can also cope with envy by coming to believe that the things we want, such as wealth, are evils rather than blessings, and cannot make us happy. If we can believe that wealth or fame provides no genuine joy, there is less need to envy the wealthy or famous. Doris does not understand this. Her envy has left her unable to put things in perspective. She is still fighting the earlier losing battle of rivalry with her more fortunate sister.

Those who cope with adversity by philosophical detachment—telling oneself to make the best of what one has—have some control over the tendency to be envious. Detachment breeds the outlook that it doesn't do any good to yearn for what we cannot have. This makes it easier to accept deprivation without distress. We are likely to be much happier if we can graciously accept what we have and even consider ourselves fortunate. The Ancient Greek Stoics as well as the Buddhists suggest that one cannot achieve peace of mind without becoming detached from the typical acquisitive goals people usually strive for—in effect, to be freed of such concerns by renouncing them. We can also be happier if we associate mainly with people in our own circumstances, not those much richer or poorer.

Remember that especially in people who display the character trait of envy, the things desired are not just material; envious people do not feel accepted or positively valued by others as a person. This lack or need, which the person may not clearly recognize, potentiates envy of all sorts of things that symbolize this lack of acceptance and regard. We envy others most who are highly thought of, admired, influential, and successful in their life roles, especially when we ourselves have major doubts about our value as persons.

Jealousy

Consider now a sad case of jealousy in a man who viewed himself as unlovable.

Jack is a pleasant but undistinguished looking man who has always thought of himself as unattractive, unintelligent, and unlovable. His mother constantly raved about his older brother, whom he always envied and thought had everything any woman would admire. His mother was not unkind toward him, but seemed disinterested and distant. Women in general seemed uninterested in him, and while in school he did not date much.

Jack had been an average student in school and now has a modest paying job with little chance for advancement. However, he married a beautiful and popular woman, Marcia, who had a good job and good career prospects. By proving he could attract a highly desirable woman, Jack's marriage served as a defense against his negative assessment of his own desirability. To be sought after in marriage by Marcia was in his eyes a strange but glorious piece of good luck.

Shortly after his marriage, Jack began to be suspicious of his wife's interest in an attractive man at work. The two of them would go to lunch together from time to time, and he began to think that Marcia was no longer interested in him, but had fallen in love with her colleague at work. When he expressed concern about this, Marcia laughingly denied that she had anything more than a friendly collegial relationship with the other man. They had business to handle, she said, and lunch was a sensible occasion for taking care of it. Jack had no particular evidence of anything amiss, but could not get it out of his mind that they were having an affair.

This obsession led Jack to nag his wife to break off the presumed affair. He began to make unannounced visits to her office, and once made a scene at a restaurant where his wife and the other man were sharing their lunch hour. He embarrassed and angered Marcia with his suspicions, kept nagging her, complained to her parents, and generally made both their lives miserable. When he tried to make love to her, he would interrupt their lovemaking with efforts to get her to make comparisons, baiting her to say that lovemaking with the other man was more pleasing than with him. This, of course, ended the lovemaking, made Jack all the more suspicious, angered Marcia, and led to constant bickering.

One day Jack came home after work and threatened to shoot himself if she continued her romance with her peer at work. Though he later claimed he had not intended to use it, the gun went off, missing her narrowly and making a hole in the wall of their living room. Marcia became very frightened of Jack and ultimately sued for divorce. She worried that Jack might one day try to kill himself or, even worse, kill her in a fit of jealousy.

Jack went back to live with his parents and took some college courses to keep busy. He was desolate and depressed by the breakup of his marriage and was even more certain that he was unlovable. He never made any further contact with Marcia who, after a time, began to go out with other men, ultimately marrying one of them.

A few years later Jack started dating another woman. When they went to parties, he would get anxious and angry when she showed any interest in other men. Before long, the same pattern of suspicion that characterized his relationship with Marcia again surfaced. As a result of his distrust, the new relationship never got off the ground.

Slowly Jack began to think that perhaps he had a serious psychological problem, one that required psychotherapy. Eventually, he did seek help and the therapy centered on his low opinion of himself, which had no doubt contributed to his suspicion that women did not like him. This suspicion led inevitably to his conclusion that they would then cheat on him.

Psychological Analysis

In this case, as in the story of Doris with her characterological envy, Jack is particularly vulnerable to jealousy because of a personal history that has led him to believe he was unlovable. Not all jealousy is of this sort and, like envy, we are all capable of jealousy under certain circumstances. Jealousy also can be a one-time emotional occurrence. For example, suppose we find our lover or mate kissing and fondling another person. Even without Jack's neurotic personal history and negative beliefs about his worth as a person, we can all experience jealousy when we have been treated in such a treacherous fashion. This is the garden-variety jealousy we are more accustomed to seeing.

The *provocation* for Jack's jealousy of his wife's male colleague was their relationship at work. Their lunches together suggested to him the idea that there was more going on than a work relationship. One could say that there was perhaps some valid provocation, but he seems to have overreacted.

The deeper *personal meaning* of the events that made him feel jealous, however, was that he was unlovable and that attractive women would quickly lose interest in him and be unfaithful. This is a meaning that he— a person especially disposed to experience the threat of loss—has himself constructed as a result of his history and the ways of thinking about himself he has acquired.

Since the objective grounds for this personal *appraisal* were weak, his jealousy has to be considered at least partly a result of a character (personality) flaw, particularly his low self-regard. The inference of a character flaw is reinforced by the second episode of jealousy soon after his divorce. More than one instance of abandonment in close succession begins to suggest that something more is going on here than meets the eye.

Jack still wants desperately to be loved by a woman who is committed to him, which was the main *goal* at stake in the jealousy that had spoiled his two relationships. However, the negative way in which he saw himself led him to *cope* poorly; nagging about his wife's probably innocent relationship, and confronting them at lunch, was hardly conducive to attaining what he wanted. These ineffective coping efforts ultimately led to the ending of what might have been a promising love relationship.

What can be said about his future? Clearly, Jack has made a mess of things. The reason he copes so poorly is that his efforts, in the form of accusations of infidelity, express his most serious problem, which is that he believes he is unlovable. So he expects a bad outcome in love relationships.

The most important thing Jack must do is to recognize how his low opinion of himself—and the counterproductive jealousy it fosters—has failed in the past and, if possible, come to see himself as the desirable person he is or can be. He can either learn to disbelieve the dour assessment he has of himself, so that he can accept a woman's attentions at face value or, barring this, suppress the faulty coping process tied to his jealousy and avoid acting on the neurotic personal meaning he keeps constructing. Changing one's self-concept is a difficult task because so much of the past has gone into its construction. But it is by no means impossible.

This is exactly what happened, though it took 11 years. Jack returned to school and sought a law degree, convinced he wanted no more of women. He achieved a significant position in a law firm, met a female lawyer whom he fell in love with, and was able to sustain a good relationship. Although he still experienced fits of jealousy, he was able to contain them and put them behind him.

The Many Faces of Jealousy

The personal meaning of jealousy is that one has lost or is threatened with loss of favor, usually another's affection. This meaning calls for coping with the harm or threat, either to prevent the loss, restore what is lost, or enact vengeance against the one who is held blameworthy for what has happened. Though this may not reinstate what has been lost, to the extent that one's ego has been damaged in the process, attack on the person who is blamed often appears a valid solution to the jealous person.

As we've seen, anger is usually built on the premise of having been demeaned, and anger is one of the most prominent emotions in jealousy. When jealousy is based on reality, there is no pathology in it, though we must still cope with the anger. However, when jealousy is not based on reality, but is a basic feature of one's character, it will usually result in disaster, and be quite difficult to overcome.

Jealousy is a more complex emotion than envy. Paraphrasing the dramatic plot of jealousy just a bit, it is *resenting a third party for loss, or threat of loss, of another's favor*. The favor might be affection, but can also be about something another person has gained at one's expense—for example, winning a job, a promotion, a prize, or a high grade in school.

In a zero sum game, which means that if someone else is loved, hired, promoted, or given a prize, there is no room left for you to win, someone else's gain is your loss. In envy, you want what you do not have or never had; in jealousy, you have lost, or are threatened with the loss, of what you once possessed or thought you possessed.

The most common dramatic version of jealousy is the love triangle, which occurs when one is jealous of another person who has "stolen" a loved one's affection. This is well illustrated by the story of Jack and by Shakespeare's tragic drama *Othello*. This accomplished military hero and statesman is convinced by the venomous prodding of his lieutenant, Iago, that his beloved wife, Desdemona, has been unfaithful to him. The drama ends when the hero, Othello, consumed by jealousy, slays Desdemona and then himself. Othello symbolizes the poisonousness and tragedy of jealous passion in which the hero believes he is betrayed and, in blaming the betrayer, is propelled into a violent and self-defeating end.

One of the oddities of Shakespeare's play is that we have trouble understanding how Iago is able to convince Othello so easily of what is so obviously false. It would be easier to understand this if we assumed that his jealousy is pathological. However, this explanation is not adequate because it does not tell us in what way Othello was so vulnerable. Nor is it in keeping with the man and his history. Why is Othello so easily victimized by Iago's scheming? Why does he believe Iago and not Desdemona?

Though Shakespeare never hints at it, one possibility is that Othello is an African Moor in a society of Iberian whites. Perhaps he suffers from the defensiveness about inferiority so common in oppressed minorities. He might have fantasized that Desdemona, his Caucasian wife, is rejecting him because of his color. Nevertheless, he has achieved social eminence, respect, and political power, making this explanation of his personal appraisal seem somewhat forced. Another possibility is that Othello is also a soldier, one who acts rather than ruminates, and this kind of character might be more inclined to quick and decisive action, and to act before thinking.

We are fascinated by jealousy because it contains so many paradoxes and dysfunctional features. It has been suggested, for example, that the jealous person's real message is twofold: First, "Pay attention to me," which—like pouting—is a plea for greater attention by the other; second, "Catch me lest I fall,"[12] which could be interpreted as a cry for help. This, incidentally, is a common explanation for suicide threats or actual suicidal attempts that fail, such as Jack's. They are said to be intended as desperate signals to others to show more concern. In Jack's case, Marcia never recognized clearly what was going on. Maybe she was scared by it.

Notice too that, in Jack's case, the threat of violence that followed from jealousy seemed more self-directed, expressing itself as a threat of suicide, but in Othello's, it was directed externally at his wife, whom he murders, a violence he then turns on himself. One of the awesome features of jealousy—especially when it involves sexual infidelity—is the frequency of aggressive and violent acts. This is another instance of a nasty emotion in which there is arousal of anger, the failure to control the resultant aggression, and the strong urge to exact vengeance to heal a wounded ego-identity.

Although we usually think of jealous people as angry and vengeful, they should also be viewed as seeking (or demanding) succor and protection, self-centered but pathetic persons whose needs are not being met. Freud[13] discussed the pathology of jealousy in a fashion consistent with this observation:

> Normal jealousy . . . is compounded of grief, the pain caused by the thought of losing the loved object, and of the narcissistic wound, in so far as this is distinguishable from the other wound; further, of feelings of enmity against the successful rival, and of a greater or lesser amount of self-criticism which tries to hold the subject's own ego accountable for his loss.

If we are considering a single episode of jealousy rather than a chronically jealous person, we must first consider the nature of the provocation. In the case of Jack and Marcia, there was no clear basis for the jealousy, but merely the possibility—exaggerated in Jack's jealous mind—that his wife's work relationship included infidelity. This possibility was enough in his case to trigger the appraisal that Marcia had lost interest in him.

On the other hand, there can be ample reasons for such a suspicion. For Othello, the provocation is the persistent but fictitious accounts Iago gives him about his wife's infidelity. To provide concrete evidence, Iago even plants an incriminating handkerchief for Othello to find.

Many a husband and wife have such suspicions about each other, and there may indeed be evidence suggesting that a marriage partner is engaged in an extramarital affair. Consider, for example, that on the basis of surveys, we are often told that a large proportion of married partners have outside lovers. However accurate or inaccurate these surveys might be, this widely held background belief makes any tendency to be suspicious more credible, especially in the context of suspicious behavior.

When there is an objective provocation, jealousy does not express a personality trait because the provocation makes it reasonable to respond with this emotion. However, there are people with such jealous natures that there doesn't have to be a provocation to arouse jealousy. Something in their personality makes them chronically suspicious, and likely, therefore, to feel jealous. The most poignant cases of jealousy—such as that of Jack—involve men and women who, without grounds, are sure that their loved one has found someone else on whom to lavish affection.

In attempting to explain what it is about some people that makes them frequently jealous, psychoanalysts have suggested that their jealousy stems from neurotic needs that can never be satisfied. In effect, the jealous person has an exaggerated need for love, which is stimulated when loss of love is feared.

Jealousy and envy, too, are said to arise first in the childhood experience of sibling rivalry. Indeed, siblings are often, if not always, rivals for parental attention and succor. In nursing mammals such as dogs, not every dog in a large litter is able to obtain an adequate supply of milk, and one or several are apt to be undernourished or even die.

The jealous person is said to feel that someone else—for example, another sibling—has taken over or has been given the "good breast." [14] However, we don't need to see sibling rivalry as literally a matter of nursing; nurturing in childhood involves supplies of attention, affection, and other forms of psychological support, for which the "good or bad breast" is merely a metaphor. We find the statement of entertainer Tommy Smothers to his brother Dick, "Mother loved you best," both funny and poignant because it resonates truth and fears in all of us. From the psychoanalytic standpoint, envy, jealousy, and anger, as well as personal deprivation and greed, are closely connected states of mind.

In Jack's case it was his older, more popular brother. Whether the deprivation actually occurred or was merely imagined, the one who believes he is the loser in the rivalry may become, therefore, insatiable in the need for love and reassurance. Jack's low opinion of himself and the idealized image of his brother were not at all accurate, which is something he had to learn. Gaining success in his working life seems to have helped him moderate his low opinion of himself.

The chronically jealous person needs little provocation for the jealousy that is felt, which means that such people readily attach the meaning of loss or threat of loss to a rival, whether or not there are solid objective grounds. The disposition to be so threatened is part of the personality, and low self-regard is a common basis for jealous feelings in the absence of genuine provocations.

So once again we see that emotions are set in motion, not only by the provoking event, but also by the readiness to *interpret* situations in particular ways—in effect, by beliefs the person has acquired, which influence the subjective personal meaning given to what is happening.

3

The Existential Emotions: Anxiety-Fright, Guilt, and Shame

ANXIETY-FRIGHT, GUILT, AND SHAME are existential emotions because the threats on which they are based have to do with meanings and ideas about who we are, our place in the world, life and death, and the quality of our existence. We have constructed these meanings for ourselves out of our life experience and the values of the culture in which we live, and we are committed to preserving them. What is specifically threatened in each of these emotions differs. In *anxiety-fright* the meaning centers on our personal security, our identity as individuals, as well as on issues of life and death, while in *guilt* it is about our moral lapses, and in *shame* it is about our failure to live up to our own and others' ideals.

The similarity between guilt and shame is that both have to do with the perception of personal failure. To experience guilt or shame requires that we have internal standards against which we measure ourselves. In guilt we call it a *conscience*. In shame we call it an *ego-ideal.* Psychoanalysts speak of the *superego* in place of both of these terms.

The source of both guilt and shame can be likened to "the still voice within us"—the inner voice that prescribes the way we think we should act. There are presumably two such voices: one concerned with morality, which arouses the emotion of guilt when we have acted badly, the other with the failure to live up to what we as well as others think we should be as persons, which arouses the emotion of shame. We will speak about the differences later. The clinical cases of guilt and shame that we present should help to clarify the distinction.

Guilt and shame could also be regarded as kinds of anxiety; we experience guilt-anxiety if we have violated a moral code, and shame-anxiety if we have not lived up to a personal ideal. We can be said to feel anxious when we anticipate the harmful consequences of these personal failures.

41

These three emotions are brought together in this chapter because, despite their differences, they have much in common. Let us begin with anxiety and its related emotion, fright, which are hyphenated in the chapter title as anxiety-fright because they are often considered different forms of the same emotion.

Anxiety-Fright

Here is a mild episode of anxiety in an otherwise reasonably sound person.

The anxiety attack was experienced by a graduate student in clinical psychology who is studying at a major state university. He is approaching thirty, is shy and unprepossessing, pleasant looking but not handsome, and slight of build. Yet he comes across as mostly outgoing, competent, and energetic.

As part of his clinical training, he had to conduct hour-long, weekly group therapy sessions with about 6 to 10 patients from the community that is home to the university. He had done this for several months and, after some initial discomfort, which was to be expected in acting out a new role, he was getting to be a skillful therapist. Though often uneasy before the start of a session, he found most of these group sessions challenging, rewarding, often exhilarating.

One day, however, he met with a group of patients who were being seen for the first time and found himself under considerable anxiety throughout the session. The anxiety began when a young male patient who, troubled by shyness at work and in social situations, began to speak about his problems in the group. Our young therapist then discovered he was sweating, slightly nauseous, his mouth very dry. These can be physical symptoms of anxiety, but he didn't quite understand what was happening. He feared his distress would be sensed by the group members, and his comments became uncharacteristically hesitant, confused, and nonauthoritative.

The session seemed to have no direction and was experienced as interminable to the therapist-in-training, who remained uncomfortable and ineffective. The group members were also made uneasy by his awkwardness and visible tenseness. The young therapist was obviously failing to pay attention to what was being said. He had evidently reacted to the situation as somehow personally threatening, though he did not understand why.

When the session finally ended, the group was happy to break up and go their separate ways. The student-therapist was worried about what would happen when they met again next week. He tried hard to put the traumatic experience out of his mind, but it kept intruding so much he couldn't study. He was reacting with a mild but debilitating anxiety.

Psychological Analysis

It is customary, especially with beginning therapists who are seeing patients, to have a follow-up training session with an experienced supervisor from the faculty of the clinical training program. When the novice therapist met with his supervisor, he described with some embarrassment the trouble he had in the group session. The supervisor pressed him about what he thought might have been going on, which could have generated so much anxiety.

At first, he seemed not to know and focused on the sweating, nausea, and dry mouth he had experienced during the session as an explanation of his difficulty. Both he and the supervisor recognized, however, that this explanation was not adequate. These symptoms were undoubtedly connected with his emotional distress. So the supervisor turned the student-therapist's attention to the group session itself to find the *provocation* for the anxiety.

In the effort to recapitulate what had happened, the student-therapist slowly began to recognize what had been threatening him. One of the patients had been talking about a problem the student-therapist recognized as his own. It was the young man who was troubled with shyness.

Normally uneasy and self-conscious with others, the student-therapist's standard strategy of *coping* with difficult social situations was to cultivate effective and controlled ways of interacting. This meant knowing a great deal, paying attention to what others said and meant, and responding to them smoothly and appropriately. This coping strategy usually served him well and made him look competent and in charge of social situations.

The social assets he had cultivated, as well as his personal problems, had influenced him to go into clinical psychology. His chief sustaining *goal* had been to gain mastery over social situations, appear in control, and have the respect of others. When he felt in control and respected, he could be socially adroit; when he felt a lack of interest or respect, he would become anxious and behave awkwardly.

Now, as he listened to the patient's account of basically the same problem in the group therapy session, the student-therapist was forced to reexperience his own shyness and self-consciousness. It was as if the patient was talking about him, the therapist, and drawing attention to his problem.

As the session proceeded, he had become increasingly concerned about the possibility that the members of the therapy group would recognize that he, the therapist, was struggling with the same problem as the patient. Trying to conceal it took all his attention and energy and, therefore, he could not respond appropriately to the conversations that were taking place.

A vicious circle resulted in which the student-therapist felt unable to think about what he was doing, which led him to respond awkwardly. This, in turn, made the group uneasy; spontaneity was lost, and the group interaction turned cold. The student-therapist knew something was wrong, and the idea that group members might cease to respect him was threatening. This was the *personal meaning* that resulted in his anxiety—namely, that he was unable to play out his therapist role adequately and had lost control of the situation. Thinking about this made him defensive, and he tried to mask his distress. But this didn't work. His normal cover of appearing competent and in control had been blown. He didn't know what to do.

Now, in the supervisory meeting, confronting this silent internal struggle with the supportive supervisor made it possible for him to recognize what had been just below the surface of his consciousness; the protective mask and coping efforts he normally used had been penetrated and his personal vulnerability exposed.

He made the mistake of trying to cover up his discomfort at the point at which he began to get uneasy. Instead, had the student-therapist leveled with the group about the similarity between the patient and himself, he might have regained composure and control, and could have garnered the sympathy of the group members. This might have enabled him to function well and remain in control. His own problem also gave him the potential advantage of an intimate understanding of the patient's problem, which he could have used to good effect. However, the potential shame of revealing his problem made him want to conceal what was happening.

In any case, the supervisory session had succeeded in highlighting his problem and provided him with a way of coping with similar situations more effectively in future. For now, he decided that he would try to be more open about his own defects rather than concealing them, so that he could be less self-conscious and pay better attention to what is happening in the therapy sessions. And he might one day be in a position to obtain additional therapy for himself.

In this brief episode of anxiety, we see in the student-therapist's experience three common features of a mild anxiety attack: First, how a concrete

provocation can generate anxiety; second, how *personal meanings* can create threat and a special vulnerability to anxiety in particular situations;
and, third, how anxiety can be aggravated by a failure to *cope* successfully
with the threat.

It is worth adding that people who are recurrently anxious may have
serious doubts about their own adequacy. Even if these doubts are suppressed, they lead such people to feel threatened when demands are made
on them that exceed their resources. When coping efforts fail, things go
from bad to worse.

We all use a variety of *coping* strategies to control anxiety, which may
obscure what is really happening when we fail to manage it. For example,
those who are especially vulnerable to anxiety, like the student-therapist,
may function in what clinicians refer to as a counterphobic style. They try
to confront what threatens them with at least the appearance of courage,
boldness, and masterfulness rather than recognizing and accepting the uneasiness they actually feel. Others avoid such confrontations, sometimes
severely restricting what they will try to attain in their lives.

When counterphobic ways of coping work, there is little or no evidence of any problem to the causal observer or even to the person using
them. However, when they don't work, anxiety mounts. They may then
handle the anxiety by denial, claiming to themselves and others that they
are not threatened, that they do not need the approval or admiration of
others, and so on. The denial has disguised the real problem, which lies
hidden below the surface, but ready to appear under the right circumstances. One can sometimes fail to recognize consciously the source of a
threat, but it has nevertheless registered—the person senses that the situation is threatening—and this explains the anxious feeling.

Why was shyness personally so threatening to the student-therapist?
Or, to ask the question differently, what was its *personal meaning?* Why
did he adopt the counterphobic coping strategy of trying to be and look in
command of things? Is there any way he might be able to overcome the
problem in the long run?

Shyness for the student-therapist was both an obstacle to a fruitful career and an indication of personal inadequacy. He admired those who,
like his father, could relate to others with ease, and be effective in presenting themselves publicly. The shyness was, to a considerable degree, a
result of constant criticism and expressions of contempt from his father,
which made him feel hopelessly inadequate. It was an enemy of all he
wanted to be as a person, a threat to the quality of his existence.

So he fought hard from adolescence on to show his father, and himself, that he was a worthy and competent person, but he never lost the
doubts implanted in his mind. His struggle goes to the very root of his

fears—his negative assessment of what he was and what he wanted to be—
in spite of this shortcoming. His counterphobic method of coping was
inadequate, so he could not completely convince himself of his worth.
But this coping strategy was also valuable because it motivated heroic—
and, by and large, successful—efforts to learn how to be competent and
make other people believe he was.

In all likelihood, the student-therapist's problem will never completely
disappear, though psychotherapy might help him understand it better, accept it in himself, and manage it more effectively, if not lead to fundamental changes in his personality. What makes deep insecurities so resistant to change is not well understood. Although they are difficult to
overcome, they can be coped with in ways that reduce the severity of the
distress and the degree of dysfunction.

One reason for the difficulty of changing a persistent pattern of anxiety
is that the deeper sources of the anxiety—being existential—are vague.
This is why all of us experience anxiety to some extent throughout our
lives, and much of the time we are not quite clear about what it is that
makes us anxious. Some people are better able than others to conceal it.
We can try to understand it, keep it from getting out of control, and tolerate it as best we can. Simply accepting it in oneself and admitting to this
distinctly human trait, saying to oneself "This is the way I am" may be—
for most of us—the soundest way of coping with our defects.

The Many Faces of Anxiety

Synonyms for anxiety include apprehension, unease, concern, and worry.
Terms such as dread, alarm, and panic are somewhat ambiguous in that
they can refer to either anxiety or fright.

When we are anxious, we are unable to relax. We experience the
sense that something is wrong in the situation or in our lives. We are
uneasy, worry, are troubled with intrusive thoughts that we cannot put to
rest, and we want to avoid or escape from upcoming confrontations that
are the concrete manifestations of our concern. In the case example, the
student-therapist suffered from sweating, stomach distress, and a dry
mouth, which are common symptoms of anxiety, though they can stem
from other causes as well.

Anxiety is in many respects a unique emotion. Its dramatic plot is an
uncertain threat. Because we do not know the exact nature of the harm
that might befall us, whether or when it will materialize, and what to do
about it, the underlying threat is abstract, vague, and symbolic of other
issues in our lives, such as who we are and what our future might be.

These are usually referred to as existential issues, and anxiety is, par excellence, an existential emotion.[1]

But we need to say more about these existential issues, which are personal meanings that underlie the emotion of anxiety. We can more easily avoid thinking of existential issues, including our death, when we are young. Death seems a long way off. And while we may give little conscious thought to death until we are old, in all likelihood it is always in the background of our consciousness.[2] Obviously, death is a great threat to the living, and its nature is ambiguous. No one can talk about it from experience, and there is little to be done about it in any case.

Anxiety is provoked when the meanings on which we have come to depend are undermined, disrupted, or endangered. If the threat to these meanings seems great, and the endangered meanings are fundamental to our being, the resulting anxiety can be intense and constitute an important personal crisis. The student-therapist in our clinical case example was not aware at first of what was happening, but had evidently somehow sensed the situation as a threat, which made him anxious. Only later, in his own supervisory session, could he put it into words and, thereby, begin slowly to understand it.

Although the basic threat underlying all anxiety is existential—and, therefore, symbolic and vague—we most commonly experience anxiety as having to do with upcoming, real dangers. These dangers become the concrete embodiments of the existential threats. For the student-therapist, the existential threat was one of failing in his role of therapist, which at that time in his life helped define his identity.

We appraise threat and experience anxiety concretely when we are to take a school exam, are interviewed for a job, perform in front of an audience, meet strangers, travel or move to a new community, change jobs, remain out of work, undergo a medical exam to find out if we have a serious illness, experience symptoms that could signify a heart attack, and so forth. All these situations, and many more, have in common the danger of something harmful waiting to happen, which could well undermine or demolish our sense of who and what we are in the world as well as the very meaning of our lives.

People vary greatly in the concrete threats that make them anxious, though we all share the common problems of human existence. Anxiety is a universal feature of human existence. We all experience it. When one threat has passed, there will always be another one to face. Anxiety comes and goes, is mild and infrequent in some people or strong, recurrent, or chronic in others. In some it is experienced as moments of severe panic.

We can understand the unique quality of anxiety better by considering what existential philosophers have said about it. They emphasize the threat of nothingness or nonbeing as the basic source of anxiety, a kind of psychological death.[3] The inevitability of death, which results in the end of our physical and psychological existence, is the ultimate basis of anxiety. We must cope somehow with this threat. However, coping with it is difficult, since the basic threats are abstract, symbolic, and vague. Except for its concrete daily manifestations in particular settings—as in situations in which we will be evaluated—it is difficult for us to actually pin down the immediate threat.

Ernest Becker won a Pulitzer Prize for a book with the startling theme that the prime motivating force—the main engine of mind—is *The Denial of Death*, which is also the book's title. Becker argued that denial lies behind all human accomplishment.[4] We invest our lives, and our desire for immortality, in the works we might leave behind when we die, and in our children and grandchildren who may remember us favorably. How strange is the human mind that it can still be a comfort to believe we will be remembered with affection, even though we will not be here to see or hear what is thought or said about us after we die.

In the event that there is no literal life after death, the works that we leave behind, and our progeny, serve as monuments that link us to the future—like the pyramids that were the crypts of ancient Egyptian royalty. These imagined links with the future—imagined because we cannot know what the future will be like—help people cope with death anxiety and the existential threat it carries.

The modern psychoanalyst who has most emphasized the threat of life's (translate as the mind's) termination as the key source of anxiety in people is Robert Jay Lifton.[5] The threat arises from the human need for connection with others, first notably one's parents or caretakers, and from the inevitability of separation because of the temporary nature of life. Along with earlier psychoanalytic thinkers, Lifton considers this struggle between connection and separation to be a universal feature of human existence. In defense of this idea, he wrote:

> Death can be made relatively more acceptable by certain cultures, where there is less denial and numbing around it from the beginning to the end of life. But one should not be too quick with these judgments. The psychological struggle around death's irreversibility would seem to be universal, an aspect of the evolutionary emergence of the human mind.

Lifton describes a fascinating and instructive telephone conversation between a ten-year-old girl and her father to illustrate the searching questions children ask about death. The father was away from home on a short trip, and they are discussing the death of their pet dog, Jumblie, his cremation, and the spreading of the dog's ashes on sand dunes near the family's summer home. These events occurred while the daughter and her older brother were away at camp. The telephone conversation went like this:

Daughter: Daddy, Ken [her brother] and I were talking—why did you and Mommy spread Jumblie's ashes without us?
Father: Well, you and Ken were at camp, so Mommy and I thought we should go ahead and do it.
Daughter: What were the ashes in?
Father: They were in a jar.
Daughter: All of them?
Father: Yes, all of them.
Daughter: Well, how big was the jar?
Father: It was round like a bottle and about six or eight inches high.
Daughter: But where was *Jumblie?*
Father: The ashes were all that was left of Jumblie after he was cremated.
Daughter: But what about his bones?
Father: They were all burned down to ashes.
Daughter: But what about the rest of him? What about his ears?
Father: Everything was burned to ashes.
Daughter: Daddy, are you and Mommy going to have your ashes spread out on the dunes when you die?
Father: I think so—that's our plan now. What do you think of that plan?
Daughter: I don't know. Who will spread them?
Father: Well, it depends on who dies first—whoever dies first, the other will spread them, and maybe you and Ken.
Daughter: But what if you die together?
Father: Then I guess you and Ken will spread them. But that isn't very likely. Anyway, we don't plan to die for a while.
Daughter: Daddy, do you believe that when you die you are reborn again?
Father: No, dear, I don't. I believe that when you die, that's the end.
Daughter: I don't think Mommy believes that.
Father: Well, maybe not. But that's what I believe.
Daughter: Then how could it be the *end?* You must feel *something.*
Father: No, not after you're dead.
Daughter: But what happens to *you?*
Father: Well, when you die, there is only your body left—not really you—and you can't feel anything at all anymore.
Daughter: Does it hurt?
Father: Not after you're dead.
Daughter: But you can still *dream,* can't you?
Father: No, not after you're dead. You can't dream either. You just don't have any feeling at all. That must be pretty hard to understand, isn't it?

Daughter: Yeah, it is.
Father: Well, even adults like us have a hard time understanding it.
(Daughter then changes the topic of conversation and begins to discuss Christmas, explaining that she wants only "big presents"—no little ones this year—even though she knows that means fewer presents—and even trying to extract [unsuccessfully] from her father a dollar figure for these big presents.)

Lifton proceeds to interpret what is going on in this dialogue.

An important theme of the dialogue is the little girl's struggle to grasp and participate in family symbolization and ritual around death and continuity. In cagily testing her parents' beliefs about death, she partly looks for an out but more basically seeks a way to assimilate the difficult truth of death as termination. She brings the concrete concerns of a sensitive ten-year-old to her struggle to construct workable imagery around the troubling absoluteness of death; to absorb the frightening shift from vital being to inanimate nonbeing, which involves first her dog and then (in her associations) her parents and (by implication) herself. The details she explores in her inquiry would seem to be those that for her most impressively characterize the living. For a physical characteristic she chooses the ears, so important in evaluating dogs, and so convoluted and protruding in humans. For mental function, she chooses the fundamental capacities to feel and to dream. Through that choice of detail she gives force to her ultimate question: What happens to the *existence*—or self—of the animal or person? How can such a vital entity cease, so absolutely, to exist?

The image of death as termination is by no means new for her, but the dog's death activates it in her with great force. While she experiences considerable pain, she also senses an opportunity, which she grasps, for further exploration and understanding. When she feels she has done enough exploring, at least for the time being, she changes the subject.

The emotion of anxiety and its existential underpinnings can be better understood if we contrast it with fear or *fright*, which is its close cousin. Synonyms for fright include horror (which combines fright with loathing), terror, awe (which combines fright with amazement when it refers to a negative experience, but is almost the same as wonder when the experience is positive), and fear.

We prefer the term fright because fear has become an all-encompassing and ambiguous word. People say, for example, that they fear a guest may not come; however, this is really an almost pro-forma expression of mild anxiety at best rather than honest-to-goodness fright. Contrast this, for example, with the terror produced by lightning in a thunderstorm, or in finding a poisonous insect crawling on one's leg. The dramatic plot of fright is facing a *concrete and sudden danger to our physical well-being*, which signifies the immediate prospect of injury or sudden death.

When we fly in an airplane, the concern we might have for our safety is usually experienced as a diffuse uneasiness (anxiety); we experience acute fright, however, when the plane suddenly falls rapidly in an air pocket, pitches wildly, and seems to be in dire trouble. Fright is an acute, high-intensity, but brief emotion, which disappears when the danger has passed, while anxiety—except in special cases when it mounts to a panic—is of low or moderate intensity, a state of distress that remains chronic or recurrent. As a reaction to a vague, uncertain, existential threat, anxiety is more of a nagging concern, an ache rather than an acute state of alarm.

Horror movies present an interesting example of the distinction between anxiety, fright, and horror. They are often advertised as fright-inducing, but actually our reaction to blood and gore has more to do with horror, which is both repulsive (disgusting) and frightening. Dread is a useful word for this combination, and is closer to anxiety than fright. We dread the things we fear but don't understand. This is why supernatural images threaten what we want to believe about themselves and the world; they remind us of the unknown.

The most anxiety-producing movies are not the ones we see today, which center on horror, but older genres, which do not horrify because they never show bloodied and repulsive images. Instead, they draw more subtly and suspensefully on the sources of our anxiety. They offer a story-line that makes us vaguely uneasy, leaving more to our imaginations than special effects do. It is not what we see that generates dread, but what is implied.

To sum up the plot for anxiety, the *provocation* is some upcoming event whose concrete manifestations are characterized as uncertain threat, such as the outcome of an illness, a performance to be evaluated, a social interaction with the potential for criticism or social disapproval, and so forth. The underlying *personal meaning* of the threat is existential in that it deals with who we are in the world, our future well-being, and life and death. This meaning is constructed by people out of the situation they are facing and the personal goals and beliefs about themselves and the world that are acquired over a lifetime. We *cope* with the concrete threat by trying to prepare for what might happen, by not thinking about it, or by constructing new threat-reducing meanings to manage it. However, coping with an anxiety-producing threat is difficult because of its vague, existential underpinnings, which make us uncertain what will happen, when it will happen, and what can be done about it.

Guilt

We now turn to a second existential emotion, closely linked to anxiety, but separable from it by its distinctive plot. Our discussion begins with the case of a young man who suffers from chronic, debilitating guilt. As with the other emotions we have already looked at, guilt is as much a product of what is going on in our minds as it is about what is happening in our lives.

A 24-year-old patient, named Robert, had experienced severe guilt in World War II, and suffered from it long afterward. Robert was a lieutenant in the infantry and his outfit was slated to go to North Africa after a period of training. However, he was badly injured in a training accident by a defective shell that exploded as it was being rammed into the breech of an artillery cannon. Several men were killed. His injuries necessitated radical surgery, which left him disqualified for combat.

Robert later learned that his battalion had, indeed, been sent to North Africa, where it had been mostly destroyed by Panzer tanks of the Rommel forces. There were few survivors. This event was the *provocation* for his feelings of what is usually referred to as survivor guilt. Although he was grateful to have escaped this terrible fate, he also had an overpowering feeling of guilt about his escape. It was his inability to get this episode out of his mind that brought him to therapy at an Eastern university after the war had ended.

In therapy it was revealed that even earlier in his life, and perhaps even more important in the long run, Robert had been exposed to another circumstance that produced nagging guilt. His brother had been been born with cerebral palsy, which left him severely handicapped. Understandably, his parents centered their attention on the handicapped child at the expense of their three other children. When Robert was six he protested about this vigorously, which was an appropriate way for him to cope, but he was severely reprimanded by his mother who, after that, seemed to withdraw affection from him. This punishment stopped him from trying to redress the imbalance of attention within the family and made him severely prone to guilt. From that time on, he found himself more and more unable to cope with guilt feelings.

Then, when he was eight years old, a terrible event occurred. He watched another boy with whom he had been skating fall through the melting ice and drown. He always believed he was responsible for the other boy's death by not going after him. No matter how much he had been reassured that he could not have saved the boy, and that had he gone into the hole in the ice, he too would have drowned, he had not been able to see things differently.

After the war, when Robert was in college, he finally made the decision to seek help. Robert regarded himself as unworthy, suffered from guilt feelings—suffused with shame—and believed he was a poor human specimen, as he put it. When he described his family situation and the altercation about his cerebral palsied brother, he averred that his mother was right and that he was a narcissistic and selfish person. When he described his failure to save his playmate in the broken ice, which he interpreted as cowardly, he was making the same appraisal of his conduct. His guilt feelings about surviving during the war when his fellow soldiers did not was additional evidence for the same negative self-assessment.

It was difficult to help Robert see how he had distorted what had happened in these tragic events. Most difficult of all was helping him recognize that his mother, on whom he had been extremely dependent, had used guilt and shame as controlling devices. She had been very unkind in seeming to reject him as punishment for his resentment of his handicapped brother.

One of Robert's attitudes, a defense against shame that undermined the treatment effort, was his continuing distrust of those who might examine his conduct, including his therapist. Robert left the university before he had worked through these problems, and was lost track of, but he seemed to have made some progress in understanding what had happened to him.

Psychological Analysis

The *personal meaning* of Robert's survivor guilt is that, in his own eyes, he does not deserve to live while others, such as the boy who fell through the ice and the men in his unit, had died. Like many concentration camp survivors who believed they should have done more to help those who were later killed, Robert too thought he should have helped the boy who died. Just having survived a collective disaster while others did not left Robert with a heavy burden of guilt. Mostly what he did to cope with this unlucky concatenation of events and the powerful feelings it aroused was to proclaim his guilt publicly, and chastise himself.

Although it is only human to want to avoid death, Robert had *appraised* his survival as somehow unjust, a moral lapse on his part. He regarded his desire to avoid the fate of his comrades as cowardice. Though he could not have done otherwise, and the judgment seems irrational, the guilt-provoking underlying meaning was that he is somehow responsible for what happened to those who died.

Surely Robert's psychological history (his cerebral palsied brother, the boy who fell through the melting ice, and his mother's use of guilt and shame) contributed substantially to a personality greatly predisposed to feel guilt. His complaint to his mother about his impaired younger brother is, perhaps, the first hostile act that set the pattern for his later interpretation that he bore moral responsibility for the deaths of others.

For Robert, to have his mother withdraw approval, love, and attention for his expression of annoyance at his brother was a severe emotional blow, and undoubtedly other children would share his reaction. Yet when confronted with emotional withdrawal by their mothers, some children—even very young ones—retaliate by becoming distant from their punitive mothers, sometimes even hostile and alienated from the parent as a way to establish their autonomy.[6] Others become even more dependent, as Robert seemed to.

Robert's reaction was to be traumatized by his mother's disapproval, and to develop a legacy of guilt and shame, which he seemed unable to shake. This is probably the reason he defended himself against recognizing his mother's role in forming his guilt-ridden personality.

There are several *provocations* for guilt in Robert's unfortunate history—the criticism by his mother for resenting the attention paid to his cerebral palsied brother and the death of his companion who fell through the ice. However, the provocation that led to his entering therapy was his escape from death in World War II when his fellow soldiers lost their lives in a battle in North Africa. One might have thought that Robert, like the concentration camp inmates, would have been overjoyed by his escape from an ignominious death. And yet he was haunted by it, as were so many concentration camp survivors because their friends, companions, and loved ones had perished.

Unlike many other soldiers, Robert could never express pride in his role in the military service. This, he believed, could only be justified if he had gone to battle with his infantry company. Later he tried to *cope* with his guilt feelings by contributing to funds for the families of those who lost loved ones during the war. This charity helped him to expiate his imagined sin.

What is likely to happen to Robert? It is, of course, difficult to say with confidence. We think that later on, when he can, he will again seek professional help because he is so impaired by his guilt and shame. Suffering is likely to push him into therapy. He needs to come to understand the role of the terrible trauma of his mother's withdrawal of love, and to recognize that he is not responsible for the unfortunate deaths that dogged his childhood and young adulthood.

Without treatment, it seems improbable that he would have the corrective experiences that could lead him to reorganize his outlook toward himself. He could, for example, experience a religious conversion, leading to a life of self-sacrifice in the service of others in which he would continually be atoning for the sins he feels he has committed. Without major changes in his outlook, he is probably very vulnerable to future emotional crises, probably depression and possibly the risk of suicide. But the future can never be predicted with any confidence, and people often turn out to be far more resilient than they may appear. We hope Robert finds his way.

The Many Faces of Guilt

For reasons that are hard to fathom, our language does not contain many synonyms for guilt. We may include remorse and feeling sorry. But words like repentant and apologetic are not, strictly speaking, synonyms, since they focus on actions rather than the feeling itself. Feeling sorry or regretting an action are ambiguous expressions, since one can feel sorry, or express regret, without accepting blame for what has happened.

To experience guilt, people must feel that they have transgressed a moral code that has been accepted as part of their own set of values. The dramatic plot for guilt is thus *having transgressed a moral imperative*. People who feel guilt have not necessarily done something morally wrong, but they *believe* they have. Many feel guilt simply because they wished for something their conscience prohibits, and their guilt persists even though they have never acted out the wish. In the emotion of guilt, we are not concerned about real guilt—as in a judicial judgment about a crime—but only the subjective feeling of guilt. In feeling guilt the behavior has been appraised as a transgression against moral values, whether or not this judgment is realistic.

In Western society, the Ten Commandments elaborate the moral values most of us believe in. They have to do with believing in and honoring God, not taking His name in vain, keeping the Sabbath day holy, honoring one's parents, not committing adultery or murder, not stealing or bearing false witness, or coveting one's neighbor's wife. In practical terms, these elaborations can get quite complex, as in the moral dilemmas posed by the competition between our personal interests and those of the community. But one need not be religious or believe in God to accept most of these as core moral values.

Although guilt feelings are painful, and some people suffer from excessive and unreasonable guilt, from a society's point of view, guilt is a very useful emotion because it helps promote socially desirable behavior. In short, guilt is a prosocial emotion. It does this because we learn to avoid socially forbidden actions to avoid guilt feelings and social criticism or rejection. If members of society want to behave well, there is less need to police their actions compared with those who care little about social morality. People with strong guilt feelings are good to have around because they are more apt than others to be fair in their dealings. If they are extremely upright, however, they may constrain the extent to which others could indulge themselves in disapproved pleasures.

Most cultures and religions accept many of the same moral strictures as those found in the Old Testament and, indeed, they could be regarded as human universals or what some refer to as natural laws. However, remarkable variations also exist. For example, in India it has traditionally been considered saintly for a widow to choose to be burned on the funeral pyre of her husband, a ritual called "suttee." While people of our culture regard this as barbaric,[7] women who have died in this ritual are regarded as saints and shrines are built in their honor. Yet there is also some current debate in India over this custom.

Women present an interesting example of a gender difference in the readiness to feel guilt. It has been said that women are brought up to feel guilt more readily than men. In those cases where this is true, the result is that in an altercation with husbands or lovers, even if they are not the cause of the trouble, women are particularly likely to assume guilt. It is as if women accept the responsibility for easing their mate's distress and smoothing over disagreements. In our culture, at least in the past, women have been described as being the glue that holds the family together, and they are likely to internalize this cultural idea and live it in their social lives. Nevertheless, plenty of men like Robert suffer from guilt feelings.

How do we develop the capacity for guilt? What makes some of us more prone to guilt than others? Several distinct kinds of social influence are involved in the tendency to feel guilty, and theories about this have emphasized different influences.[8]

Psychoanalysts think of guilt as a reaction to impulses they regard as socially unacceptable. They suggest that a child's hostile and sexual impulses lead to fear of punishment and the threat of the loss of parental love. Parents try to control the child's anger and the child resists such control. When expressing or acting out prohibited impulses, children become anxious about the likely punishment. This fits the situation of Robert who undoubtedly wished that his cerebral palsied brother would disappear or at least be ignored so that Robert could have his share of needed attention.

In order to feel safe, the child represses the proscribed impulse—it is as if the impulse no longer exists—and the child adopts as its own the standards of the parent, which become the child's conscience. The dangerous impulse, therefore, goes underground and becomes unconscious, which is what repression means. This doesn't fit Robert's case because he remained acutely aware of his guilt feelings. However, he seemed unaware of the role his mother's use of guilt and her threats of disapproval played in these feelings when he was growing up, probably because it was extremely threatening for him to acknowledge it.

Other theorists treat guilt as a reaction to the natural, biological tendency to empathize with another's distress which, in the course of development, evolves into the desire to treat others fairly.[9] These theorists center their attention on the fact that humans have always lived in groups. This made it advantageous for hominids (early humans) to cooperate in dealing with problems of survival. In other words, the desire to gain the approval of the group by acting in accordance with their social values is said to have evolved because it facilitated survival. But this doesn't help explain why some people, such as Robert, are especially prone to guilt. We need to look at particular experiences in growing up, which can help us understand the special vulnerability some people have.

Still others have suggested that human babies spend a long time—far more than any other species—in a dependent relationship with their parents or caregivers. Desiring their approval is learned because this dependency is necessary for survival.[10]

Finally, some theorists have emphasized that guilt feelings emerge only after children have learned to perceive and understand the social significance of violations of standards of conduct.[11] Robert was old enough to recognize the needs of his cerebral palsied brother, though he came to resent them, too. And he was old enough to understand that he had some responsibility to the boy who fell through the ice and died.

These different theories about the social development of guilt are by no means incompatible. Each is probably right in some respect, containing important truths about the developmental origins of guilt. Nevertheless, all of them recognize that *transgressing a moral imperative*—which is the dramatic plot for guilt—is the central theme of how guilt feelings are aroused.

Guilt and anxiety, too, are closely linked with other emotions, such as anger. We may feel anxious about the aggression we have directed toward others because they might withdraw support or retaliate. This is called aggression anxiety. We may also feel guilt over an aggressive act—punished by our conscience, so to speak—though for some reason we don't speak of aggression guilt. The guilt is more likely to occur if we have strong moral values against aggression, or if our attack has done injury out of proportion to the provocation. Robert's mother made him feel guilty about resenting the time and energy that was given to his brother. Robert felt deprived but also learned that he would be blamed if he voiced this feeling.

A brief example of guilt over aggression was provided in Chapter 2 in the marital argument that was used as an illustration of anger. When the wife who resented her husband's inattentiveness discovered that his job was in jeopardy, she felt guilty about her unwarranted attack. The guilt stemmed from the realization that by hurting him without justification she had acted against her own moral standards.

How does one *cope* with the bitter pangs of guilt? As we said, feeling guilt potentiates the impulse to expiate, atone, make reparation, or seek punishment for the harm that was done. We blame ourselves when we have done wrong. Robert tried to atone for his survivor guilt by making contributions to families of comrades who died in North Africa. Even though he should not have felt guilty about their fate, doing this made him feel a little better.

Because guilt feelings are painful, we sometimes cope with them defensively by justifying our actions or blaming someone else. If we can put the blame for what happened on another person, our own distressing feelings of guilt can be prevented or minimized. Robert was able to blame only himself for the bad fate of others and his own survival.

The proper social conduct following a moral transgression, especially one that injures another person, is to apologize and make amends. What is interesting about *apologies* is that sometimes they work and sometimes they do not. Some apologies are merely pro forma—that is, they occur without the feeling of guilt. Such apologies express institutionalized social routines. We say we are sorry without having blamed ourselves in the least for what happened, in which case we don't feel guilty to begin with.

It is not always easy to satisfy the victim whom we have injured with an apology. The victim may feel that a few apologetic words are not sufficient in light of the damage that has been done. In the manner in which they are made, some apologies also reveal that the perpetrator of the injury does not truly feel sorry. A pro-forma apology won't ameliorate the victim's distress. To work, the apology must seem sincere, appear abject, or offer some kind of personal sacrifice for it to be accepted by the person who has been injured.[12]

On the other hand, there are people who are always saying they are sorry. They seem to be constantly apologizing for everything, as though they were apologizing for their very existence. This could represent an effort by individuals who have strong doubts about their own social acceptability and feel the need to ingratiate themselves with others. The pattern is really one of social anxiety rather than guilt.

To sum up the plot for guilt, the *provocation* is some thought or action that we interpret as a violation of the code of conduct we believe we should live by. The underlying *personal meaning* is existential in that it relates to our view of our moral responsibilities to ourselves and the world, and what we see as the consequences of violations of these responsibilities. This meaning arises from the way we have interpreted and internalized the moral values set forth by our caretakers, peers, and the society at large, and from our experiences in life. Guilt feelings are easiest to *cope* with when they have to do with particular acts or thoughts of the moment, for which we can atone. They are most difficult to cope with when we believe they express moral flaws in our character.

We saw in the problems of Robert, an account of whom began our discussion, that guilt is sometimes suffused with shame. And although guilt and shame have much in common, they are also quite different from each other—both in the way they are aroused and especially in how they are coped with. Let us now examine the last of the three existential emotions, shame.

Shame

To begin with a real-life illustration, we draw on two distressing experiences of shame in a family we have known for many years.

Abe and Fanny had one son, Charles, whom they doted on. He was a late child, and they were in their sixties when the two episodes of shame occurred. They were first-generation Jews, born in New York, and most of their friends were Jewish, although they were not particularly religious. They lived in a modest apartment in New York City. Charles grew up to be handsome and tall, a good athlete and student, completing college with an engineering degree. The parents felt very proud of their son.

Trouble began in his senior year in college in the early 1930s, but came to a head after he had graduated with a bachelor's degree in engineering. In college, he had begun to date an Episcopal girl from an upscale family living in an exclusive neighborhood in Connecticut. He began to spend more and more of his time with her and her family, playing tennis at their country club.

Abe and Fanny's source of shame was that Charles gradually began to disown his parents. Anti-Semitism was quite prominent in those years, and Jewish engineers were not being offered jobs, so he was anxious not to be taken as Jewish. Their son, who was blond, blue eyed, tall, and even-featured, had managed to overcome what he thought of as his negative heritage by being accepted in this wealthy community and covering up his Jewish origins. Although his background was known to his girlfriend and her family, it was never mentioned.

After Charles and the socialite decided to get married, her father arranged a good job for him, and he was fast rising in an upscale world. He was ashamed of his parents and anxious lest their presence in the community and country club wreck his newly found affluence and social prominence. Charles converted to the Episcopal church, and identified himself with his new social set. He did not want his parents to come to the wedding, nor did his wife and her parents want to visit his parents in New York. So his parents were not invited to the wedding, and only learned of the marriage later. This was a terrible blow to Abe and Fanny.

Charles felt it was necessary to keep a distance from Abe and Fanny and their friends, some of whom spoke with strong Jewish accents. They made him ashamed, exposing his origins, which he wanted to forget. From this point on, he had little contact with his parents.

So Charles experienced both shame and guilt for having betrayed his parents. But mostly he anticipated with dread the shame that would be brought down on him by his parents if they ever came for a visit. We can view Charles's withdrawal from contact with his parents as a way of coping with the potential shame created in him by a societal prejudice.

Abe and Fanny, in turn, were greatly ashamed in front of their friends that their son was, in effect, disowning them as parents and Abe railed angrily at his son. Fanny felt more hurt, but it deeply wounded both of them that they were not permitted to attend their son's wedding. They never spoke of this offense to anyone, and it was a taboo topic among their friends. Abe and Fanny kept their painful secret as much as they were able, but their friends still knew.

The feeling of shame in Fanny and Abe was keenly provoked when one of their friends arranged the wedding of their own daughter and son-in-law, which reminded them of their tragedy. Their friends' conversation was filled with the wedding plans, the people who would come, including Abe and Fanny, and all the details attending such an occasion. But when Abe and Fanny appeared at social gatherings, they would stop talking about the upcoming event because they knew about Charles and his wife. This rubbed salt in Abe and Fanny's wound, but they had to conceal their distress. One usually wants to make shame a private pain.

So we have a case of two different kinds of shame in one family, one experienced by the son and another by the son's parents.

Psychological Analysis

The *personal meaning* in the dual experiences of Charles and his parents is that they have failed in their own and others' eyes, a failure that reveals something negative about their characters. The exact personal meaning for Charles and for Abe and Fanny are quite different.

For Charles the risk was to be shamed in his new relationships by being identified with his parents and their old-country ethnic ways. He might also have felt a bit of guilt at having disowned the good people who were his parents and deserved his loyalty. It is difficult to tell how guilty Charles actually felt; his guilt was evidently less powerful in shaping his behavior than the threat of feeling shamed by being exposed for what he was, and this guilt feeling was less powerful, too, than the threat of being unable to advance himself socially and economically.

For Abe and Fanny, the shame stemmed from having raised a child who treated them so shabbily by rejecting who and what they were; it also stemmed from having their friends see what their son had done. Parents of children who act shamefully tend to suffer by asking themselves what, if anything, they have done wrong. Abe and Fanny ruminated about what had happened, thinking about anything they might have said or manifested in their attitudes that could have encouraged their only son to reject his heritage and, worst of all, his nurturing parents.

Some of their disturbing thoughts implied a sense of blame on their part for what had happened. For example, although they were Jews, they gave their son an ambiguous name, Charles, which could easily be perceived as either Gentile or Jewish. They had verbally denigrated newly immigrant Jews by identifying them as "greenhorns," a name used for those who can barely speak English, if at all, and who still live in accordance with old-country ways. This kind of scorn is common among those who have already made it as immigrants. Furthermore, when Charles was growing up his parents had emphasized the importance of making it within the American culture.

Who can say whether these attitudes contributed to Charles's defection? But to the extent that Abe and Fanny shared some of the ethnic prejudice of the times, they sensed that the cause of their tragedy might have to do with defects in themselves. All the more reason to feel ashamed.

Rejection of parents can come about for many reasons other than those already suggested. Fanny was a gentle woman; Abe cold, aggressive, and domineering. Charles felt a certain amount of hostility to Abe, and disappointment that Fanny did not take his side in the struggle against his father's domination. He had difficulty identifying with his passive and ineffectual mother, and probably wanted to attack his aggressive father who had given him little nurturing and understanding, but mainly drove him to be successful.

The difficult problem in shame is to dissociate what has happened from the way one defines one's character. We can feel shame for some given act that goes against one's personal ideals and exposes us to the scorn of others, but still manage not to include this in our self-definition. We suspect that Charles told himself that he was doing his best to advance himself, to secure his future. He believed his parents should be pleased that he was making it in the world.

By avoiding contact with his parents most of the time, having visited them only rarely before his marriage and not at all after, Charles avoided confrontations with them, especially his father, which would have reinforced feelings of guilt and shame. By not encouraging his wife and her family to interact with Abe and Fanny, he could avoid the shame of being identified with their ethnic origins.

During the years before their death, Abe and Fanny centered their lives on their friends and did their best to accept the torn relationship with their son. Although this loss was a source of sadness, as with most losses, and anger, too, it had to be lived with. The loss was harder on Fanny, who had little hostility in her, than for Abe, who found it galling. Abe was less likely than Fanny to blame himself for what had happened, but he felt shamed in the eyes of his friends. Fanny felt this shame too, but her shame included what she took to be her failure as a mother. She was more distressed than Abe about being rejected by her son. And she worried more that her son would pay dearly for what he had done, and suffer later. She was more likely than her husband to turn blame inwardly rather than outwardly toward others.

After a time they both tried not to think about what had happened, and mostly succeeded. They had little to leave in their will when they died, and donated it to a Jewish charity. Charles didn't need anything anyway. He lived well in his chosen setting, but we know only a little about his inner life. He and his wife raised four children, all of whom went to Ivy League colleges and had families of their own. Abe and Fanny never knew their grandchildren.

Our own impression is that Charles did not actually suffer as much shame as Abe and Fanny did, which might bother some readers who resent his actions. His marriage was successful and long lasting. When his parents died, he attended the funeral and was ostracized by Abe and Fanny's friends. This gave him little distress, however, because he had learned how to distance himself from his troubling past.

The Many Faces of Shame

Synonyms for shame include humiliation, embarrassment, mortification, chagrin, and feeling ridiculous, each with its own connotation. For example, humiliation and mortification convey very strong reactions; embarrassment conveys a much milder reaction. Although some writers treat shyness as a form of shame, we think it is better treated as a type of social anxiety, though akin to shame in the sense that it also involves the threat of personal exposure.

The personal ideals relevant to shame consist of the ways we wish to be known as individuals. They may have little or nothing to do with morality, and can be conveyed by diverse adjectives, such as courageous, clever, decent, tough-minded, a bold warrior, street smart, wheeler-dealer, ambitious, intelligent, kind, and so forth. It isn't particularly moral to be a wheeler-dealer, a bold warrior, or tough-minded, but these values specify social and personal standards, which some people want to live up to all the same. They are what we might want to be said about us in an obituary. The ideals connected with shame, however, show far wider variations from culture to culture, and individual to individual, than do moral values.

The distinctions we see between guilt and shame can be confusing, especially regarding their cultural and individual origins. This confusion stems from the fact that both morality and personal ideals have to do with internal standards that are derived from the society and our early experience with adults—especially those who brought us up. In this way we learn to be a "good" person. Obviously, the word good is ambiguous; what it means is not clear unless the specific values underlying "good" are spelled out.

Another source of confusion is that it is an internal voice, which tells us about whether we have or have not lived up to moral values and personal ideals. To speak of an inner voice, of course, is only a convenient metaphor. These values and ideals exist as features of the society, but they are internalized by the individual, thereby becoming a part of that individual's personal outlook. Freud spoke of the source of both guilt and shame as a single agency of the mind, the superego, which develops in the process of growing up. But to the extent that both moral values and personal ideals are involved, two separate voices, so to speak, with different contents, may be at work.

Our subjective experiences and the behaviors we display when we experience guilt and shame are also different. Although there is inner pain in both, the kind of pain is not the same. In guilt we want publicly to atone for our sins, but we hide our shame from others.

For a long time psychoanalysts—in the tradition of Freud—did not make much of the distinction between guilt and shame. But despite the ambiguity in our language and common usage, which often confuses guilt with shame, the two emotions are not only different in kind but also have different origins. Until recently, shame had received relatively little attention and was usually combined with guilt rather than treated as a distinct emotion. And psychoanalysts emphasized mainly guilt, not shame, in their clinical work. This, however, is beginning to change. [13]

Childhood caretakers have great power to influence the development of our ego-ideals because of our long period of dependency on them. We acquire our conscience and ego-ideals from parental figures and peers when we are young, and these persons set the standards for what we should be like. They criticize or punish us when our behavior and attitudes fail to match these standards. After a while these standards become demanding features of our own egos. Some parents set up very harsh standards and demand perfection, and we may become perfectionists and have great difficulty living up to our internal standards.

According to the psychoanalyst Helen Lewis, [14] who has done the most work with shame, the threat underlying the development of shame is criticism, rejection, or abandonment, which is the punishment the child imagines for not living up to expectations. Charles evidently feared rejection by his new wife, his parents-in-law, and their community more than by his Jewish parents. Abe and Fanny, especially Fanny, suffered rejection by their son and feared the same from their friends.

Most of the time the threat of abandonment is implicit rather than explicit. However, parents sometimes cruelly verbalize it to the child directly by saying, for example, "You should be ashamed of yourself. If you don't behave better, I am going to give you away." A less cruel—but still powerful—version of this statement is "If you don't start behaving right, you're going to put me in my grave. You'll be sorry when I'm gone."

The personal failure in shame is *not having lived up to one's personal or ego-ideal*, which is the dramatic plot for this emotion. Living up to one's personal ideal is a way of avoiding shame. In the patient, Robert, who illustrated guilt earlier, we have an instance in which guilt has been suffused by shame.

It is one thing to feel ashamed in situations in which we act in ways that call our personal ideals into question; it is quite another to be ridden with shame, which is extremely dysfunctional. The same could be said about guilt; it is one thing to feel guilt for a particular moral lapse, but it is another thing to be ridden with guilt because we believe our very character as an individual is unworthy.

It is not merely that Robert felt guilty about something, but that he was deeply ashamed of what he was as a person that made him so difficult to treat. He felt he was a bad person. He regarded his guilt for letting so many people down as an aspect of his reprehensible character.

Often in shame our failure to live up to a personal ideal has been observed by someone whose approval we care about. But we can experience shame without anyone being physically present to see the transgression. Implicitly there is always an observer—for example, a parent or role model—who is the hidden observer, even if he or she is no longer alive.

The Old Testament treatment of sin, as expressed in the biblical account in the *Book of Genesis* about the "fall" of Eve from grace, conveys the idea that humans discovered the emotion of shame in the Garden of Eden, expressed as the self-consciousness of being naked. This form of shame is really embarrassment rather than shame. We are embarrassed by our bodies, especially when naked and exposed.

We all know the story. Eve succumbs to temptation at the urging of the serpent by eating the only food that was forbidden by God, the fruit of the tree of knowledge. In disobeying God, Eve's act resulted in the permanent loss of human innocence, and shame became, presumably, an emotion from which we all suffer.

We should recognize, however, that nakedness is not the real source of shame, though it is often treated as such. Rather, it symbolizes a much deeper and more serious problem, the exposure of our unworthy selves because we have violated our standards.

If people are asked to relate an incident of shame, they are apt to be very selective about what they are willing to describe. Some incidents are so humiliating that a person has great difficulty talking about them. Other incidents, though shameful, are easier to relate. Abe and Fanny never, to our knowledge, told their story to anyone, but we and other friends knew about it.

We often know negative things about people without ever mentioning them. There is a kind of social contract we are implicitly bound to in which we would rather not confront what is embarrassing or shameful to our family, friends, and coworkers. We are also confident that Abe and Fanny's friends would not have faulted them for their son's behavior. We pieced it all together by knowing the family, seeing what was happening, and by the defensive comments they made when we asked about their son.

Those who are particularly vulnerable to shame are also likely to be concerned about social rejection or abandonment for being a bad person. This appears to be the underlying goal that operates in shame, to avoid criticism or rejection. Although the experience of shame is consciously painful and perhaps visible, we are typically unaware of the underlying threat of rejection to those suffering from shame, which is terrible for a child and can remain intimidating to an adult.

What helps with the pain of shame? Are there useful ways of coping with it? We can try to avoid thinking about it, though this is usually difficult. Interestingly, people struggling with shame usually hide themselves from the world, either by putting up a good front or actually removing themselves from social functions. Some people keep shameful and humiliating experiences completely to themselves, never divulging them to anyone throughout their lives. But this way of coping does not ease our inner sense of deep personal failure. This is, perhaps, what makes shame so devastating as an emotion.

A common way of coping with shame is to refuse to acknowledge, to oneself or others, that one has done anything for which to be ashamed. People who do this are, in effect, denying their own failure and externalizing the blame for whatever went wrong. If anyone accuses them of acting shamefully, they become angry and seek vengeance against the person who has observed it or wants to expose it.

The more the potential shame, the stronger the anger. We think this strategy of coping often works because one sees it so often. To the extent the reappraisal of meaning—from "I am ashamed" to "I didn't do anything to be ashamed of," or "It's someone else's fault"—is believed by the person, shame is avoided or transformed into anger. For the most part, anger is more tolerable than shame or guilt. Why, you might ask. Shame makes us feel helpless and a bad person while anger—especially when expressed as aggression—constitutes an active defense of our ego-identity, and implies having some power over our lives and others. The same defensive pattern can also be found in situations of guilt that, like shame, can be dealt with by externalizing the blame for wrongdoing and attacking someone else, as we noted in Chapter 2.

We should close our account of the existential emotions by reminding you that, although anxiety, guilt, and shame share many features, the personal meanings that underlie each are distinctive. Anxiety deals with issues of life and death and is powered in large measure by the struggle to sustain a meaningful connection to others and the world, which is threatened by the transitory nature of life. Guilt, on the other hand, deals with lapses from our moral values, and shame with our failure to live up to personal ideals we have acquired as individuals. These learned values are an integral part of ourselves and shape the personal meanings we construct from encounters with the world. And from these meanings issue our emotions of daily life.

4

Emotions Provoked by Unfavorable Life Conditions: Relief, Hope, Sadness, and Depression

EMOTIONS THAT ARE CONNECTED WITH UNFAVORABLE life conditions, such as major illnesses, pain, and the actual or potential loss of a loved one or of one's personal status, are a mixed group that includes relief, hope, and sadness. We have arranged them in a logical order, with relief first, because it reflects a positive outcome that happily follows an unfavorable situation; then hope, which is the possibility of a positive outcome in an unfavorable situation; then sadness, which is the coming to terms with an irrevocable loss. In our discussion of sadness, we distinguish the feeling of sadness from that of a related state, depression or despair, which conveys utter hopelessness about what remains of life.

Relief

Relief is a relatively simple emotion about which little needs to be said. In place of a case study, we identify a few short scenarios that bring this emotion into focus.

If you have ever undergone a medical biopsy for a suspected cancer, you know the dread that can attend not only the procedure itself but the period of waiting before its results become known. All sorts of terrible thoughts run through your mind as you wait: the malignancy may have already spread and the illness may be terminal; you may have to suffer the miseries of chemotherapy; it may be necessary to quit work and you do not know how you will support your family. You try to avoid thinking about the feared outcome but ruminate constantly about what might happen, and feel chronically anxious. However, the news turns out to be good; the tumor is not cancerous, and you instantly experience relief. The good news bringing the feeling of relief can almost make you feel giddy with joy at having escaped what you have dreaded.

Consider two other quite different examples. In one, you see someone you love showering affection on another person, and as you watch you experience acute jealousy, and struggle with the treachery and what it means. However, a second look reassures you that this is not the person you love, only a look-alike, and you instantly feel relief, and perhaps a little foolish.

In a final example, imagine a loved one who has served for nearly a year in a combat zone during a war, and you are in a state of almost constant anxiety about him. Then, suddenly, you learn that he is on the way home. The danger is over. The emotional experience is great relief.

Relief always begins with the frustration of a goal, resulting temporarily in several distressing emotions, usually anger, anxiety, guilt, shame, envy, or jealousy. But when *the frustrating condition has changed for the better or gone away*, we experience the dramatic plot of relief. Although the troubled life condition may have lasted for some time, perhaps years, the change that precipitated our relief dispels the previous and distressing emotional state in what seems like an instant.

What makes relief unique as an emotion is that it has two stages: one negative, the other positive. It begins with emotional distress of some sort, which is why we placed relief in the group of emotions connected with unfavorable life conditions. But the emotional episode ends with termination of the stressful situation. What was dreaded has not materialized, which is the *provocation* for the positive emotional state of relief.

During the negative stage you are distressed and mobilized, wary about what is happening or about to happen. The goal at this stage is for the bad outcome not to materialize or to abate. The mobilization and wariness you experience have to do with the need to make preparations, or to be ready for action, to *cope* with a negative outcome. You may also try to take an active hand to prevent the dreaded outcome.

The *personal meaning* of relief is that everything is okay again and you can get on with your life. When you experience relief because what you fear has not materialized, coping with a bad outcome is no longer relevant. In the second stage, you experience a kind of decompression in which the distress and bodily tension vanish, and you relax, perhaps giving an audible "sigh of relief."

This reversal of tension and the absence of any need for action are the hallmarks of relief, but lead to a question of whether relief is truly an emotion. It almost seems as if it is the opposite of an emotion, because distress and bodily tension disappear. But the state of mind in relief is neither neutral nor unengaged, as we find in completely nonemotional events.

The intensity of the relief we feel is in direct proportion to the importance we attach to the unfavorable life condition causing us distress. If its importance is great and a negative outcome would be devastating, then the feeling of relief is intense; if it is not so important, and a negative outcome only slightly distressing, then the relief that follows is likewise a mild experience.

What is interesting about relief is that it can be so sudden and brief, especially if we have felt distress about some impending disaster for quite some time. The main psychological interest actually lies in the period before the moment of relief. During this period we are struggling to appraise and cope with what we dread, and perhaps hoping against hope that it will not befall us.

When relief comes, however, our state of mind dramatically turns benign, and what is interesting psychologically at this moment might be the way we interpret what has happened, especially if the situation has a complicated history. For example, though relieved, we might resent the judgment of the doctor who needlessly frightened us about the possibility of a disastrous illness or, on the other hand, be grateful for our good fortune or the emotional support of others through the crisis. Although not much has been written about relief, this emotion—extending in time from the negative stage of dread to the discovery that all is well—is important if only because it is experienced so often in our lives when dreaded events fail to materialize and because it is the occasion for vital coping activity.

Hope

In hope, the individual is confronted with an unfavorable life condition, but, unlike relief, hope is a state of mind in which the positive outcome has not yet occurred. If it does, there is no longer any point in hoping. Here is a brief vignette about a person who is confronted with a "death sentence," but who hopes for an almost miraculous recovery. We can use her real name because she has written a book about the experience.[1]

Alice Hopper Epstein is the wife of a distinguished research psychologist who teaches at the University of Massachusetts at Amherst. We know her husband personally. Alice earned a Ph.D. in sociology and works as a computer consultant. In April 1985, she learned she had cancer of the kidney. It had metastasized, which means it had spread widely throughout her body, extending to one lung. Her chances of survival were very poor. The kidney and lung were removed surgically, but after a month the cancer had spread to the other lung. Surgery was no longer a viable option. She was told that the cancer was spreading so rapidly that she could not be expected to live more than three months.

What makes Alice's story particularly interesting is that after the expected initial period of grieving and dismay about her condition, and on the assumption that she had a cancer-prone personality, she embarked on a campaign to change her emotional life to improve her chances. This called for seeking a better understanding of herself, changing her attitude toward living, and trying to reorganize her personality. It was her fervent hope that all this was possible and would improve her physical condition.

Whether Alice had a cancer-prone personality is controversial since the concept has not been widely accepted among health specialists (see Chapter 12 on emotions and our health). What is central here, however, is that Alice thought she could make changes in her life that would affect her chances against cancer. As a person, she was superficially cheerful, helpful to others, competent, and well liked, but always inclined to sacrifice herself and her own needs for those of others. Her cheerfulness could be said to mask an underlying depression.

Alice undertook intensive psychotherapy, both with her husband, who was a professional, but also with a female therapist in whom she had confidence and who, since she was not personally involved, might remain more detached. After a time, the widely spread cancer began to disappear, and then it was gone altogether. Her inspirational book was published in 1989, and to our knowledge she remains well and active.

Psychological Analysis

The *personal meaning* of hope for Alice Epstein was the possibility that her desperate life condition would improve, with or without any effort. She had, in effect, not given up hope that she might get better, even if the outlook at the moment seemed desperate. But hope is not necessarily a passive state of mind. As well as hoping, Alice was actively doing a number of things to improve her prospects. Though she believed the odds were slim, she was also convinced that it was worthwhile to make a major effort to transform her way of life in order to capitalize on the chance that it would help. One could also argue that hope powered and sustained this effort.

We offer this brief, true life story not to convince anyone that psychotherapy offers a practical cure for cancer or other diseases, nor to argue that there is a cancer-prone personality. Instead, what we want to emphasize is that, aside from the miraculous recovery, this is also a story about the sustaining value of hope. We have known cancer victims who despaired from the moment their illness was discovered and who spent the remainder of their shortened lives in misery and seclusion. It is important for us to understand hope not only because it may sustain life—which is quite miraculous—but because it has the capacity to allow us to make the best of a bad lot, to live with verve and dignity despite the odds.

And as we all know, a single case proves nothing. It is quite possible that favorable biochemical changes could have resulted from the ongoing medical treatments and that Alice Epstein would have gotten well without the efforts to alter her emotional pattern. We will pick up this important theme again in Chapter 12 when we look in depth at coping and personality as factors in physical and mental health.

We should also address the idea of false hope—that is, hope that goes against all realistic odds—in which case it is viewed as an undesirable method of coping with potential disaster. In the introduction to his wife's book, Seymour Epstein, Alice's husband, successfully dispels this negative view of hope.

> Some physicians object to a psychological approach because they fear it will produce "false hope." I have never quite understood what false hope is. All hope is "false" in the sense that what is hoped for may not materialize. At the time of hoping one cannot know the outcome. If the hope serves to improve one's quality of life and does not cause one to avoid taking adaptive action when it is possible, nor be resentful when the hoped-for outcome does not materialize, then it is obviously desirable.

We find what Seymour Epstein says here unassailable. It makes no sense to hope only when the odds are in our favor. It is precisely when our life situation is terribly unfavorable that we need most to hope. To the extent that hoping sustains our ability to cope actively with the way things are and to maintain a positive outlook on life, any claim about its falseness seems to lack wisdom.

The Many Faces of Hope

There are several synonyms for hope—promise, expectation, anticipation—but most do not convey the meaning we have given to hope as a wish for better conditions of life in an ambiguous but difficult situation. Other words, such as faith, trust, security, conviction, confidence, all seem too positive and secure to carry the more tentative meaning of hope. Thus, oddly enough, we find no words except hope that convey the emotion we are describing.

Although it is an extremely important state of mind, relatively little has been written about hope as an emotion.[2] It might seem strange to some readers that we group hope with the emotions connected with unfavorable life situations. People who live in Western cultures are accustomed to thinking of hope in positive terms. But hope is essentially an antidote to despair. With it, negative thoughts and the emotions connected with them are diminished in favor of a less bleak outlook. Nevertheless, hope is usually brought about by situations of dread that are sufficiently ambiguous to leave room for hope and permit the person to avoid giving way to hopelessness. And so the *provocation* for hope is usually that a person is in some kind of trouble.

For example, when you or a loved one are ill, you become anxious—perhaps even alarmed—but you hope that the illness is not serious and that you will soon recover. When you face an important evaluation of your work or knowledge—as in a school examination—you are anxious about a negative outcome but hope that you will succeed. When you sense anxiously that your stamina is failing in a competitive race, you hope to reach the finish line. And when you are angry because someone has acted treacherously, you hope you were misinformed, or that you have somehow misunderstood.

Hope may be sustained when there is some possibility that the outcome you wish for might occur, when you have not given up all hope and become despairing. There are probably great individual differences in the extent to which people are capable of sustaining hope and defeating despair under conditions such as those faced by Alice Epstein and her husband.

The *personal meaning* of hope is that one believes there is a possibility that things will get better, however bleak they may seem at the moment. The dramatic plot of hope is, therefore, *fearing the worst but yearning for better*.

Does hope ever arise from positive conditions of life, as when one views the situation as favorable and hope that it will work out as one would like? Perhaps, but we think rarely. Viewing a situation as favorable sounds a bit too much like *optimism,* and people do not speak of hope when they are optimistic. Optimism is having a positive expectation about what will happen. In optimism one is primed for a good outcome. This is sometimes imprudent because one may have risked too much, and, when things go sour, it is all the more dismaying, costly, and even disillusioning. Mostly, one hopes a bad situation will improve.

Why do we consider hope an emotion? We could, after all, regard it as a major strategy of *coping.* To be hopeful is to see the good sense of mounting efforts that will help us strive to overcome obstacles. Although hope is, indeed, a way of coping, it is seldom cool or detached, which is why we can view it as an emotion rather than merely an aspect of coping.

The ability to maintain hope in the face of despair is also a major coping resource. Those who can hope are less likely to despair, and sometimes their struggle against odds has positive results. People may even hope when disillusioned. And they can be pessimists about conditions in the world, yet never give up hoping that the lot of human beings everywhere will improve.

Historical and cultural traditions are inconsistent about the positive or negative features of hope. For example, the ancient Greek myth about Pandora is ambiguous at best. Averill, Catlin, and Kyum, who have made a fascinating psychological analysis of hope, describe the mythical story of Pandora in the following way.[3]

> When Prometheus stole fire from heaven and gave it to humankind, Zeus ordered that a woman be fashioned who would bring misery to the race of men. She was presented to Epimetheus (the brother of Prometheus) who, ignoring a warning not to accept any gift from the gods, took her as his wife. Pandora brought with her a box containing every human ill. When Epimetheus opened the box, all the ills escaped, save one— hope.
>
> The tale of Pandora is ambiguous. Was hope another ill like the others that had escaped, or was it a benefactor left behind to aid humankind? The Greeks seemed ambivalent about hope; but in general they viewed it more as a bane rather than a boon.

Some of the most influential of the ancient Greeks had negative things to say about hope. Plato spoke of hope as being easily led astray, and Euripedes, the well-known tragedian, considered hope a curse on humanity. Both seem to be referring to "false hope," though Seymour Epstein's thoughts about this suggest that, even when hope is in vain, it still gives the person something to hang onto in place of despair. In some situations, however, the danger is that the person will continue to seek what is denied and, therefore, fail to redirect his or her thoughts and energies toward a more realistic outcome.

In contrast, the Judeo-Christian world regards hope positively as one of the three theological virtues, the other two being faith and charity. Hope is regarded as a morale builder and a sustainer of constructive effort. When it is used to imply faith in the future, faith can be likened to hope

In the English language many metaphors exist for hope, expressing both positive and negative attitudes toward it. For example, on the positive side people say "Where there's life there's hope," "A ray of hope," hope as the "Light at the end of the tunnel," or "Having high hopes." On the negative side, they say "Grasping at straws," "Vain and foolish hope," "Prisoner of hope," or "Hope clouds our eyes." And yet, despite its connection with unfavorable life conditions, hope is certainly a far more desirable state of mind than its opposite, hopelessness or despair. Indeed, most literary giants seem convinced that life is intolerable without positive illusions (see Chapter 8 on coping).

One of the most interesting characteristics of hope is that, as a person's prospects of a better outcome diminish, hope is not necessarily abandoned altogether but narrows in scope to keep alive a modest benefit that may still be possible. This narrowing is a way of coping with the painful reality of loss. For example, in the late stages of a terminal disease, such as cancer, what the patient or the family hopes for shrinks from a remission of the disease and resumption of a normal life to having a pain-free period of mental clarity—perhaps just a matter of days or a few hours—that may make possible some lucid communication with loved ones. Even these limited possibilities are worth hoping for in the absence of a better option.

Again and again under desperate conditions of life, the two poles of hope and despair are juggled as opposing options. For the elderly whose time to live is short and who may be in poor physical condition, one often sees a struggle between the two polar opposites of hope and despair.[4] They oscillate between these states of mind, now feeling hope about what is left of life, now despair about its end and what little they may have done with it.

To sum up the plot for hope, the *provocation* is usually an unfavorable life condition whose outcome is uncertain, yet will leave room still for a reversal of fate and for hope. People generate the feeling of hope as a way of *coping* with the trouble because it is better than giving in to despair. The *personal meaning* is that there is some chance, either by virtue of what one does or merely as a result of good luck, that the outcome we dread—and hope against—will not be as bad as was feared, or that despite what we dread, everything will ultimately turn out okay.

Sadness and Depression

Sadness and depression are illustrated by the story of a 62-year-old woman, Clara, who suffered the sudden loss of her husband.

There had been no sign of previous illness. He simply dropped dead one morning from a sudden heart attack. Clara grieved for over a year, during which she became depressed, but later recovered. Her husband had left her financially well off and she did not have to work. Except for the death of a beloved sister when she was fifteen, for whom she grieved for a long time, her life had been largely benign and uncomplicated.

⋅ Though she had friends of her own, Clara had lived her adult life mostly through her husband. He was a successful, outgoing chief executive who loved his work. She entertained his associates and other friends as the supportive wife of a CEO, and she enjoyed this role. The couple had three children, all married, each with children of their own. Two of these families lived in the same West Coast community as their parents, the third in the Southeast.

Clara had shown no signs of great distress immediately following the death of her husband. She managed the funeral and burial with aplomb, though later she said she felt like a zombie while doing it. Then, after the bustle of attention from family and friends had ended, she began to be at loose ends and feel morose. She ate poorly, losing much weight in the next six months. Her children began to worry about her. She was not taking care of herself and stayed mostly at home. She spent her days alone, in a darkened room, examining her husband's things, failing to dress or bathe, showing no interest in anything else.

When friends or family invited her for a stay with them, Clara complained of sleeplessness and a host of physical ailments, which everyone interpreted as psychosomatic. Her children found her presence trying, but did their best to cheer her. They took her into their homes, believing that she would be better off with the company of a loving family. They were concerned that she could be suicidal.

Although her relationship with her husband had been generally good and occasionally affectionate, it was mainly distant, though they had bickered considerably. Now, however, she began to talk about her husband as though he was a paragon of virtue, whom she had tragically lost. She constantly stated that she should have died with him, that her life had no value with him gone. She was obsessed by the idea that if she had cared more for his physical well-being, for example, forcing him to watch his diet and discouraging him from smoking, he might not have died so young.

To her children Clara was experiencing a profound depression. She complained constantly about her ailments. She did, indeed, suffer repeated infections and had a serious bout with flu and pneumonia. Her children urged her to get professional assistance. Finally, they took her to a psychiatrist, who prescribed drugs, which seemed to help for a time.

Unexpectedly one day nearly a year after the loss, on the basis of a newspaper article, Clara decided to make a visit to a crisis clinic and research center at a medical university in a nearby city. She was treated with psychotherapy, without drugs, for three months. The therapy centered on helping her to understand what was happening to her and to cope with her personal loss. She continued to grieve but began to improve and see her situation more realistically. She took a position as a volunteer at a local hospital.

Little by little she began to show increasing interest in things. She began to cook for herself with pleasure, and even entertained newfound friends from her volunteer work. She took an interest in her children and grandchildren. Her physical health improved and she began to return to the level of energy prior to the depression.

After fourteen months, grieving had mostly ceased. She began to think about how she would like to live, which involved continuing to do volunteer work with older people who were ailing. Her natural competence gave her the opportunity to take charge of some of the work of the volunteers, keeping records, providing for awards for service, and organizing social affairs for the volunteers and patients. She still experienced recurrent periods of sadness—not depression—on anniversaries and other occasions on which she was reminded of her husband, but she was receiving pleasure from life again.

Grief had given way to a new pattern of life, which she began to feel good about. There were still many moments of sadness over her loss, especially when she was home alone reading or watching television, when her thoughts would drift off into memories. But the distress was no longer as acute, and the moments of sadness were fewer and briefer. They were limited mostly to particular occasions when she would remember something she and her husband had done on wedding anniversaries, holidays, and other events that readily brought him to mind. The episodes of sadness grew more wistful, and the hopelessness and despair that had clouded her life had all but disappeared.

Psychological Analysis

Clara had lived her life around her husband's career and had little of her own to fall back on when, without warning, he died. The loss was, therefore, extreme, and she for a time was unable to cope. In the first few days, she used her considerable competence to take care of things. It is common to react numbly and seemingly without emotion right after the first shock of discovery of a loss. Her depression, a relatively mild case, began soon after the hustle and bustle of the initial period of adjustment.

She had lost her usual role and function, but she could not immediately reframe her picture of herself and reorganize her life. Undoubtedly, she despaired of being able to do so at this stage of her life. It all seemed hopeless, which is the *personal meaning* underlying depression. Even the interest shown by her children, which was genuine, did not help much because it was clear to Clara that she could not build a new life on the lives of her children, and she had never been a doting grandmother.

Drugs can help in depressions that have mainly neurochemical origins, but they do not address problems of living that must somehow be dealt with to sustain morale and commitments. The visit to the crisis clinic was a major breakthrough. Unlike traditional psychiatry, which tends to focus on underlying disease or psychopathology, crisis clinics view breakdowns, or near breakdowns, as just what they often are, the result of a terrible trauma or loss, rather than as evidence of basic mental illness. In such clinics an effort is made to address the loss, what it means personally, and how to cope with it. Emotional support is given and the person is encouraged to describe and relive what has happened and the emotions experienced, which provide clues to the personal meanings of the trauma.

Since Clara was a strong, intelligent, and resilient woman, she was able to benefit from this treatment and view her situation more realistically than the despair that characterized her early state of mind. With each step toward renewed interest in things came an ever-widening perspective about how she might revamp her life in light of her new situation. After a while, she saw that a satisfying life was still possible on different terms. She was on her way to doing well, after a rocky start.

The Many Faces of Sadness

Sadness is not depression, though it is often confused with it. And it is rare that sadness would dominate a person's mood soon after a loss. Although there is no absolute rule for all individuals, many or most victims of a major loss—which is the *provocation* for sadness, grief, and depression—struggle for a period of time in which the loss is protested and fought against—perhaps denied—before it is fully accepted. Only when the loss is reappraised as irrevocable does grief turn to sadness.

Although there are all sorts of possible patterns, the *personal meaning* of the loss in early grieving may be covered up by an attempt to deny that the death has occurred and to struggle to restore what has been lost. The bereaved person may imagine that the loved one is still present or may when alone try to visualize the person in the hope that the image doesn't disappear.

The exact meaning of the loss varies from person to person, varies with the time period following the loss before sadness is experienced, and varies with how the loss is interpreted. The personal meaning also depends on the history of the relationship between the loved one experiencing the loss and the person who is gone. To understand bereaved persons' emotions requires that we also understand how they appraise the personal significance of what has happened.

We have centered our discussion of sadness on the death of a loved one. Although this is among the most profound of losses, any significant loss can create a sense of bereavement and grief, such as loss of career, rejection by a lover, loss of one's home in a natural disaster, and so forth. But what provokes sadness is not just any loss, but one that we know cannot be restored. *Irrevocable loss* is, in effect, the dramatic plot of sadness. The victim has to understand that there is no chance of bringing back what is lost. Acceptance of the loss usually takes time.

Grieving and the Ultimate Acceptance of Loss

When struggle and protest occur, the emotion experienced is some combination of anger, anxiety, guilt, and sometimes shame, envy, jealousy, and hope. These are the prime emotions of protest and active struggle against loss or the threat of loss. In grieving, the person actively searches for ways of preventing loss or undoing it when it has occurred. This search, and the effort to restore what has been lost, would not occur if the grieving person had firmly assimilated the loss as irrevocable.

If this seems crazy, consider the following: Bereaved people know that the loved one is dead; they are not psychotic. However, in response to the acute stress of bereavement, they sometimes move between a strange twilight world of wish and imagination and one of reality, which expresses the impractical yearning that the death has not happened, that it was all a dream.

In contrast with anger, anxiety, and guilt, sadness is an inactive state in which a person has given up any idea of being able to prevent or restore the loss. It does not usually appear as a dominant emotion until the futile struggles of protest and denial have been abandoned, and the bereaved person has accepted or become resigned to the loss. Clara did not reach this stage of grieving until well over a year after the death of her husband.

The difference between resignation and acceptance is subtle. When you are resigned, you acknowledge the loss with reluctance or distress; when you accept it, you have come to terms with it and are no longer acutely distressed, though you can still feel sad from time to time. However, the sadness may not be oppressive, which is why we have sometimes referred to it as wistful.

We regard grief, or more properly *grieving*, as the process of *coping* with loss. People grieve over any important loss—their job, role in the world, wealth, and so forth—but mostly they think of grieving in the context of the death of a loved one.

Death of a spouse is among the most stressful of the many possible losses in a person's life. A reason for this is that marriage makes the partners so interdependent that, if the relationship is long lived, then neither can go on without making many stressful adjustments. The death of a child is also highly stressful, partly because of the many hopes and plans that have been dashed, because of the injustice of the early loss of a life so soon after it has begun, and because of the freight of guilt that such a loss often entails.

As we have said, anger, anxiety, guilt, and hope all may play a role in the transformation of grief into sadness. The *anger* of grieving may be directed at the medical system that failed, or at someone who is deemed blameworthy for the death. The list of such persons is endless: the drunken driver, the uncle who carelessly left a loaded pistol on the table which, in turn, killed the beloved child, the National Rifle Association that fought the registration and control of weapons, the governmental agency that failed to provide enough research support for the disease that took the loved one's life, and so forth. Clara had no one to be angry at and was not inclined to manufacture a scapegoat.

Paradoxically, however, one may feel anger at the person who died. Perhaps that person brought on death by carelessness; or perhaps the deceased person had been resented or was inadequate and, therefore, is remembered with disdain. In some instances, the anger reflects the belief of grieving individuals that the dead person deserted them by dying. This belief may be hard to dispel even though it seems irrational.

One knows in most instances—an exception being suicide—that the deceased person did not intend to leave the world. Yet the bereaved person may feel abandoned, and guilty or ashamed of that feeling. Clara showed no such anger. However, her tendency to glorify her husband, rather than seeing him realistically, suggests that she was defending herself against other negative emotional agendas—perhaps she was not as impressed with his business success as others were.

The *anxiety* of grieving is the result of threats to central meanings about life and death, and to one's personal identity. The death of a spouse, for example, reminds us of our own imminent demise. It also deprives a person of a long-standing social identity and requires that a new one be sought. The loss, and the need to find a new identity, frequently involves a severe trauma, which is apt to result in anxiety. This fits the problem Clara struggled with in trying to achieve a new social identity for herself after living her life largely through her husband.

The new identity is needed because one's social and business life as a single person will usually be quite different from what it was before, especially for a widow: Married friends of the past may abandon widows, because the relationship with them no longer seems compatible with their social activities. Sometimes married women fear widows as potential sources of temptation for their own husbands. If a widow is asked by a couple to play bridge, a fourth must now be sought; if asked to go dancing, a widow must bring a partner or else the other men will be obliged to dance with her. It is often more difficult for the now single woman to obtain bank credit. Bereavement may also result in unexpected poverty and the need to earn a livelihood, perhaps for the first time. All these changes, and many more, are likely to result in continuing anxiety.

The *guilt* of grieving might arise from the belief that one did not make every possible effort to prevent the death, to communicate with the person before dying, to appreciate the person sufficiently, or to ease the dying. The bereaved individual may have failed to pay attention to medical symptoms whose prompt treatment might have saved the loved one. Clara struggled with this kind of guilt, and a feature of her depression was the sense that she had somehow failed her dead husband. If one feels angry at the person who died, this is also likely to provoke guilt; what happened cannot usually be considered the dead person's fault and, therefore, the anger seems unjust.

If there is anger and guilt, these troubling emotions must be coped with. The negative thoughts that provoked them must be reconciled with the positive image of the dead person and one's relationship to that person, which the bereaved person wants to remember. This is one of the major reasons for funeral eulogies. The reconciliation helps to facilitate the new pattern of life that should emerge when grief has ended. A major task of grieving is to be able to focus on the future while not disavowing or being embittered by the past.[5]

The *hope* of grieving—especially very soon after the loss—is that the deceased person will somehow be restored to the living, that the death is a bad dream that never really happened. A more realistic hope is that one will ultimately recover from the present deep distress and despair. In the depths of depression, people may not have the presence of mind to recognize that a new life awaits them after the period of despair has ended. Depressions are usually temporary, though often recurrent.

An interesting and tragic sidelight of loss and grief arises when there is ambiguity about the fate of the loved one. How difficult it must have been for the wives and families of American servicemen and women who were classified as missing-in-action! They may still be alive, perhaps captured, or managing secretly to live by evading the authorities.

It would have been easier to deal with the certain knowledge that they were dead rather than with uncertainty. If the family were sure they were dead, the normal grieving process could then take place and the family members could get on with their lives. Not to know whether their loved one is alive or dead results in interminable anxiety and indecision. As the years pass, and hope is all but gone, the family wants to grieve and finally to put the loved one in the grave, psychologically as well as physically, but to do this seems disloyal in light of the uncertainty.

The initial reaction to death of a loved one, as we said, is often one of numbness or shock. There may be no tears; it is almost as if the bereaved person has not fully realized what has happened or is denying it. This happened to Clara. The bereaved person thinks, magically: "My husband (child, parent, or whomever) cannot be gone. It's not possible. Where is he? He will soon walk in the front door as he has always done before."

The rituals of the funeral, such as viewing the body, the gathering of the family, the eulogy, the lowering of the body into the grave or the scattering of the ashes, all can help the bereaved person to assimilate the fact of death, though its personal meanings must still be dealt with through grieving.

Eventually, the bereaved person becomes *resigned* to the loss, or, even more positively, the loss is *accepted* with less and less distress. The person feels sad when remembering the dead person, but the sadness is no longer acute sorrow, or emptiness and despair. The remembrance may take on a warm, wistful glow, an affirmation of a positive—perhaps quite happy—phase of one's life, which can be nourished and cherished without distress. The bereaved person ultimately becomes capable of reestablishing a commitment to life. We saw this very clearly with Clara.

The relationships and life meanings that have been associated with the prior life situation are often profoundly changed in bereavement. Ideally, the coping process must reaffirm the old meanings and pave the way for new ones to emerge. The changes are not only in the daily round of life, but in existential meanings about life and death. When the loss is that of a loved one in a long-standing relationship, it should be no surprise that its impact is existential in many aspects. The same also applies to other major losses, such as a work role at retirement, one's physical health and vigor, or children leaving home and moving far away.

The portrait of grief painted in Clara's case is a somewhat idealized one. Its actual course and detail depend on who is grieving, the ages of the principals, the relationship with the dead person, and the circumstances of the death. For example, the death may have ended a period of terrible suffering, and though the person is still mourned, there is the saving thought that death was welcome.

The sense of great loss is very common in bereavement, but some people get over it easily and others never get over it, which leaves them psychologically vulnerable and unable to make a renewed commitment. Thus, older women especially cannot visualize taking on another close relationship. Even though attracted to men, they may not want to reexperience the trauma of yet another loss or wish to avoid reinstating the pattern of the past because it had been too confining.

Depression and Despair

Depression is emotional, but not a specific emotion. A product of grieving and a sense of hopelessness, it is really a composite of several emotions, such as anger—commonly directed at the self—anxiety, and guilt.

It is clinically fashionable to speak of two kinds of depression—one principally of genetic origin, the other a result of a temporary failure at social living. The biological variety is usually referred to as endogenic (endo means constitutional or from within; genic means cause). The form of depression that develops as a result of a failure of social living is referred to as exogenic (exo refers to external or social). The endogenic variety takes two forms: bipolar (meaning the person cycles between depression and mania) and unipolar (meaning only depression).[6]

The distinction between endogenic and exogenic is somewhat overdrawn, since both biology and social causes probably interact in most cases. However, it is important regarding treatment decisions (see Chapter 13). The primary treatment of endogenic depressions is drugs; the primary treatment of exogenic depressions is psychotherapy. Although there are many who think that psychotherapy has greater staying power over the long run, both treatments used together may have advantages over one or the other alone.

The usual assumption about depression that develops in response to a failure of social living is that traumatic losses in early life predispose people to depression by creating later vulnerabilities. Today, one of the most popular professional conceptions of this vulnerability is that these earlier losses result in habits of thinking about oneself and the world that are pathological or cause pathology.

For example, vulnerable people may regard themselves as reprehensible and, perhaps most important, as helpless to do anything about their situation. To depressives, the world may seem hostile and ugly, and they overreact to negative experiences as catastrophic. For people with such an outlook, it is not hard to see that helplessness about changing a bad life situation degenerates into hopelessness about life itself.

Depression is usually associated with grief, though the depressed person may not think of it in this way or consciously recognize that a major loss has occurred. Depression is the term more often used than despair in professional circles, though their essential meaning overlaps substantially. The best way to think about these words is to regard *depression* as a complex emotional response to loss. *Despair* is the outlook on life that underlies depression.

We usually reserve the word *grieving* for the process of coping with loss. Most often grieving persons realize that they will ultimately feel less distressed, and even get over it completely. Depression (and despair) occurs when the loss signifies to the person that there is nothing left worth living for. The person is despairing about the whole of life.

Hopelessness is another word used in referring to depression. Feeling hopeless (or despairing) about our lives is a much more serious problem than feeling *helpless* about restoring a particular loss. A loss may be extremely distressing, but it doesn't necessarily destroy our reason for living. In depression, however, we feel hopeless about the value of our life and want to die. Nothing seems to sustain our interest or is enjoyable anymore. In severe cases, the person must be hospitalized and cared for, and suicide is a danger.

An important point to remember about sadness is that it is not the same as depression, hopelessness, or despair. One can be sad without experiencing these other outlooks and the emotions associated with them.

Some Oddities About Sadness

Having distinguished sadness from depression and grief, we should now consider some of its odd features. The first has to do with crying. We cry when we are sad—and also when we are depressed or grieving. Crying at unhappy situations is a natural thing for people to do, and humans seem to be the only species that does so.

But people also cry at weddings, which are supposed to be happy occasions. This is a difficult reaction to interpret because the crying could express one's own marital dissatisfaction, though people usually say they do it because they are happy for the couple getting married. They cry, too, when a child graduates, or at wonderfully good news, which we might not have expected. In truth, we are not at all sure about why people cry at events that should be happy ones.[7]

Another oddity about sadness is that we often express it about someone's misfortune without actually feeling sad. How often have you said, for example, "I am saddened by what happened to you," not so much because you truly felt sad but because you wanted to express sympathy and friendship toward that person. It is like an apology for injurious actions that is not genuine because we don't really feel guilty. Though we may truly regret what has happened, we express sadness merely in a polite way to relate to the person who is suffering, not as a true feeling. In doing so, we do not mean to be dishonest, yet we wish to assure the other person of our understanding and support.

A third oddity about sadness is that there are times when a person cannot openly acknowledge a loss and admit to grief or sorrow.[8] This occurs when powerful social sanctions have been violated. Imagine a situation in which a person who has died had a married lover. It would be imprudent for the bereaved lover, who is married, to react publicly with grief or sadness, because it would reveal the clandestine affair. And so the bereaved person cannot afford to express sorrow over the loss, though much sorrow is felt. A similar example is when one of a pair of lovers having an illicit affair decides to end the relationship. The rejected lover must take care to conceal distress over the loss to prevent the relationship from being discovered. The inability to express grief publicly could be very troubling for the bereaved person.

We close this chapter by expressing a major source of uncertainty about the status of sadness as an emotion. Sadness often seems to be more of a mood than an acute emotional reaction. An *acute emotion* arises from an occasion in which something saddening has occurred, which is a specific provocation for the emotion.

The focus of a mood is broad rather than being centered on a single, narrow goal or event. Acute emotions usually are provoked by some event that sets them going, whereas moods express existential concerns that are apt to be diffuse. We might, therefore, ask ourselves when sadness or happiness are acute emotions like anger, guilt, shame, or jealousy, and when they are moods. Like anxiety, sadness and happiness often take on existential features and so, some of the time at least, they should probably be regarded as moods. The difference between an acute emotion and a mood remains an issue that emotion theorists are still debating.

In a sad *mood*, it is usually difficult to specify the particular loss to which we are reacting. Moods have to do with existential issues, such as being a success, having wealth, maintaining a good quality of life, being a good person, being loved or appreciated, and achieving stable meanings about ourselves and the world. Although a specific event can precipitate a sad or happy mood, it does so by pointing toward long-term, existential issues.

We are apt to be in a sad or depressed mood when our life in general seems misshapen, when people appear ugly to us, when life is disorderly and has no meaning, when the fates are against us, when we experience holiday blues when everyone else seems happy. With this dour outlook, we feel sad, depressed, and bad about our life.

The same uncertainty can also be expressed about feeling happy. We are apt to be in a happy mood when we sense that our lives are proceeding favorably, that we are wonderful or masterful, loved and appreciated, when we believe that people are good, that life is meaningful, orderly, just, and that the fates are with us. With this upbeat outlook, we feel happy, lighthearted, cheerful, good.

5

Emotions Provoked by Favorable Life Conditions: Happiness, Pride, and Love

IN THIS CHAPTER we deal with emotions that arise from situations favoring the attainment of our goals. They are happiness, pride, and love. We all want to experience and share these emotions because they are associated with getting and having what we want and, although certain forms of love are notable exceptions, they are mostly associated with feeling good.

Happiness

Let us start with a brief example of an episode of happiness to concretize this emotion.

Joe has been in the army in Korea for nearly three years. As a reserve officer, who had served in World War II, he had been drafted again in the fall of 1950 just after he married Amy. He had earned a bachelor's degree in engineering and was working in his father-in-law's tool and die business. He loved Amy and she returned his affection.

Joe and Amy had high hopes for their future, intending to have a family and settle down. The war in Korea had interrupted their lives, and he resented being recalled. Their hopes for a stable future had been dampened.

He found the separation from Amy and his family very distressing and longed to return home to resume his life and career. In Korea he served in the Army Corps of Engineers building roads and airstrips for combat and supply planes. When China entered the fighting in November 1950, both Joe and Amy were even more uneasy about what was going to happen. The war dragged on in more or less a stalemate for several years.

Suddenly, however, the war ended with an armistice on July 27, 1953, and Joe was discharged and sent home. Joe, Amy, and their families experienced first a great sense of relief. He was well and had not been wounded. They looked forward to his arrival home after nearly three years of being separated.

The homecoming and the first week of his return was the most joyful experience Joe and Amy can remember. There was no sense of strangeness between them, which sometimes happens after a couple endures a long separation. There were numerous celebrations with family and friends. Joe had returned at a time of great hope and optimism in the United States, profiting by a rapid economic expansion after World War II. His father-in-law's business was thriving, and he looked forward to playing an important role in it, and to establishing himself financially. At last, life seemed really good. They were ready to get on with the business of living.

The euphoria lasted about a week, after which it was time to tackle problems of career and family relationships. Trouble first cropped up with Joe's father-in-law, who was extremely controlling and unwilling to grant the son-in-law real autonomy and authority. After a considerable period of tension, which extended into his relationship with Amy, he began a search for a new job at which he could draw more fully on his knowledge and talents.

The intense feeling of happiness at the homecoming had given way to standard life struggles, with their typical ups and downs.

Psychological Analysis

For Joe and Amy, the *personal meaning* of their happy situation was simple and straightforward. They were now permanently reunited and able to begin building their lives together with optimism. Any resentment about the delay in the conduct of their lives was quickly abandoned, and they looked forward to resuming their deferred life plans that included family and career.

Although the ways people think about how to live a good life often differ for marriage partners, both Joe and Amy seemed to have shared the same outlook, an image strongly imprinted on the bulk of their American generation after World War II. If they had any doubts, they never came to mind at this moment of joy.

Doubts, however, began to surface with Joe's need for more autonomy, which was resisted by Amy's father. Amy was distressed at the conflict, but she recognized what was happening and saw that seeds of discontent were being sown because Joe was working for her father. So ultimately she supported Joe in his effort to find a better job.

Luckily, at this time of industrial expansion, opportunities abounded and Joe went to work for the Shell Oil Corporation. Although he knew little about the oil industry, his engineering background made him valuable, and after a number of years in which Joe and Amy lived in different parts of the country and abroad, he became a middle-level executive living in a New Jersey suburb, near New York City. They had four children, three girls and a boy, who completed their educations at various colleges, and now live scattered throughout the country.

There were occasions when they struggled with whether to leave the oil company for other opportunities, but this never seemed a totally attractive idea. Joe remained with the company until he was pressured to retire at 62 and, as anticipated, received a solid pension. He enjoyed his retirement and he and Amy mostly go their separate ways during the daytime, except when they take an extended trip in their RV. They are both physically well and active.

The couple, now alone, travel once a year to visit their children, have had the standard ups and downs of most married couples, but have remained together and live peacefully and generally with satisfaction. There have been many happy occasions, and unhappy ones too, largely reflecting problems with their children and disagreements about what to do about them. They faced the economic pressures of having to pay for their childrens' educations and made some serious mistakes in real estate investments. But generally they have been economically sound.

Amy and Joe are rather typical of a large number of families who became established following World War II. They look back on their lives as unremarkable. They barely remember the great moment of joy when Joe returned from military service in Korea, but recall more clearly Joe's struggle with his father-in-law.

The Many Faces of Happiness

Common synonyms for happy are joyous, carefree, jubilant, exultant, cheerful, playful, amused, glad, gay, gleeful, jolly, jovial, delighted, euphoric, ecstatic, elated, enraptured, and triumphant. But many of these words, such as carefree, cheerful, jovial, and gay, refer as much to a general mood as to an acute emotion aroused by a specific event. Indeed, our language reveals that these words for happiness express many different meanings. Moreover, the words seem to vary in the intensity of the indicated reaction, where joyous implies a more intense state than happy, whose intensity is ambiguous. Jubilant, exultant, gleeful, and ecstatic all convey great intensity. Amused suggests a pleasant but distanced and evaluative state of mind, and glad implies a mild and measured one. Some of the words have other special nuances; for example, playful implies being lighthearted, and triumphant implies succeeding or overcoming a foe or obstacle.

When we ask what makes people feel happy, the answers are varied, suggesting that we don't fully understand this state of mind. Nevertheless, because people have many values and goals in common, there are many common conditions of life that make them feel happy. Although there are plenty of exceptions, most people will feel happy when they are paid a compliment or shown that they are loved, when they are promoted or given an increase in pay, when they see their children do well, and so on. These provocations for happiness have positive *personal meanings* for most people.

Although in the above example Joe was deliriously happy, as was his wife Amy, other men return home after a long, enforced separation and feel anger and apprehension, having now to face marital relationships that have soured, career possibilities that have dwindled, and economic struggles that seem insurmountable. Such variations were artfully portrayed in one of the most popular of post-World War II films, *The Best Years of Our Lives.*

Happiness as an Emotion or as an Estimate of Well-being.   Now we come to the most difficult problem concerning what happiness is all about—namely, that the word is used in two very different senses. If we ask people how happy they are, the answer does not usually refer to the acute emotion of feeling happy, but about their general well-being. Their answer will provide an estimate of how people think they are doing in their lives.

As an estimate of well-being, the word happy, or happiness, does not refer to an emotional state—which takes place at a particular moment and is provoked by a particular event—but it stands for a calculation of how well one is doing at a particular time in one's life. It is a summation of emotional ups and downs in which how well their life circumstances match what they always wanted or did not want is gauged. It is, in effect, a considered judgment about the overall quality of their lives. Researchers use the term *subjective well-being* for this judgment.[1]

Feeling happy, on the other hand, is an emotion that is provoked by a particular encounter in which something nice or wonderful happens. We may feel happy at a given moment, but minutes later our state of mind could change in response to other events. Joe and Amy both felt happy when they were reunited after he returned from Korea. This feeling was facilitated by their belief that their lives were on track again. So feeling happy typically requires both a positive occurrence and a background sense that all is well. We will say more about this later.

Most of what has been written about happiness is unclear because we don't know which of these two meanings apply when the term is used. Sometimes the meaning refers to subjective well-being and sometimes to the emotion. In the remainder of this chapter, we use the expression "feel happy" or "feeling happy" for the emotion, and "well-being" for the generalized judgment. They are related but not the same.[2]

The dramatic plot for feeling happy—the acute emotion—is *making reasonable progress toward the attainment of our goals*, an explanation suggested by Aristotle long ago. He proposed that striving toward a goal and using one's resources well, not the attainment of the goal, has the potential for making us feel happy. This is one theory of why we feel happy, a good one we think.

When, for example, after long years of toil and struggle, a student finally obtains an advanced academic degree, at best only a short period of feeling happy results from this momentous event. The student must soon get on to other things—for example, using the degree to obtain a professional job. Simply basking in the accomplishment does not sustain happy feelings—or even a sense of positive well-being—for very long. It's what is happening now—such as writing this book—and its implications for the future, which count. When this book is finished, we will feel briefly happy, but then get on with other things, perhaps writing another. This is what happened to Joe and Amy when the realities of job and family had to be confronted after their happy reunion.

The Foreground and Background of Feeling Happy.   It will help to see the emotion, feeling happy, as *foreground*—that is, as a reaction to a positive event such as receiving a compliment. In contrast, well-being should be seen as a *background* condition that influences the foreground.

For example, when we receive a genuine compliment, it usually pleases us and makes us feel happy. However, if our life situation at the moment is bleak—perhaps we are ill or have suffered a major setback—the compliment may be pleasing, but is not enough to overcome the negative state of mind lingering in the background. Our well-being may be so low that we cannot take even a small measure of pleasure from it. But if our well-being is positive because life seems to be going well, even a negative event—for example, an insult or an embarrassment, which normally would have aroused emotional distress—might pass without generating the slightest distress.

The profound principle here is that our background state of mind—or what we frequently refer to as a *mood*—and the conditions (of well-being or ill-being) that brought it about are of fundamental importance in how we react to foreground events. While this applies to all emotions, it is particularly the case for feeling happy and feeling sad. The capacity of an event to induce either of these emotional states is enhanced or muted by our overall life situation. What makes us feel happy is more complicated than it seems.

We saw this principle in action with Joe and Amy. For the first week of his return from Korea, the foreground was one of joy at being reunited and able to resume their lives. The background also seemed favorable. This union of foreground events and background mood created the prime conditions for feeling happy.

The dependence of the foreground feeling on the background features of life poses an interesting dilemma. Does it mean, for example, that if our overall life situation is bad we have no chance of feeling happy at any given moment? Suppose, for example, that we have a terminal cancer with only a short time to live. Overcoming such a setback does, indeed, pose great difficulty for most people. But the bad fate can sometimes be transcended. Despite a terminal illness, some people manage to feel happy and be engaged in life at least some of the time, ironically even more perhaps than some whose life circumstances are far more favorable.

We really don't know how such people succeed in *coping* in this way. These days there is a common enjoinder to live one day at a time. Good advice. But doing so is the result, not a method, of coping. The question of how they manage to live one day at a time remains to be answered. We might hazard a guess. It is probably very similar to what people do who are able to keep the troubles of their business lives from spilling over into their family lives, and vice versa. When they are with their family they pay no attention to their business lives, and when they are at work they pay no attention to their family.

Some terminal patients are able to keep the long-term life tragedy out of mind while they attend to and enjoy what is happening at the moment. This kind of gallant coping process in the face of adversity does not necessarily deny the harsh reality of the person's life but, instead, allows these individuals to absorb themselves in daily events.

Others are unable to achieve this solution. Perhaps they could learn. As a method of coping they could construct a different, more positive meaning of their lives from the tragic one they are preoccupied with. This is the very thing we do when we reappraise what is happening in a way that favors positive rather than negative emotions. Still another possibility involves concentrating on the positive aspects of living, deflecting for a time the bad fate we must face.

Approaches to Well-Being

It is a remarkable paradox that only a slight relationship is observed between well-being as it is subjectively evaluated and the way things actually are. A rating of well-being does not necessarily reflect the objective social or economic conditions of an individual's life; it is subjective. We might evaluate our life as favorable even when others might judge the current conditions of our life as unfavorable. And vice versa for those who judge their lives as favorable.

Because of this, inspirational books have long flourished in which people are urged to think positively about themselves and their lives. Norman Vincent Peale, a protestant minister, has written one of the most durable of these books, titled *The Power of Positive Thinking*. In it, he adopts the view that being able to maintain a positive outlook even in the presence of adversity is a valuable resource for effective and healthy living.[3] But such a philosophy seems to encourage denial or the maintenance of positive illusions. Both coping strategies are useful, but do not sustain us over the long haul.

Why don't such books work? They fail because for most readers the coping strategy that is implicit in these books has not truly become the reader's own. Peale was certainly right that the capacity to think positively is a valuable gift. Those who have it are undoubtedly better off than those who do not. Nevertheless, just reading his or any other book, or just telling oneself to think positively, are not enough. Those most in need of the advice are, typically, the least able to use it because positive thinking is alien to the way they naturally appraise their circumstances and cope with their lives.

We can look back in history to another version of the theme of positive thinking, namely, the books of Horatio Alger such as *Sink or Swim* and *Survive or Perish*. These books urged people to lift themselves up by their bootstraps and learn how to be successful. Self-help books abound today too, but there is no real evidence—aside from the shortlived inspiration they provide—that they permanently change lives. Yet people devour such books in the vain hope of finding the secret of a good life.

Perhaps you would like this book to reveal such a secret. But there are no magical answers. We believe the secret is to truly understand oneself, which is a considerably more complex and difficult task. Our book's objective is to help in this. If we understand ourselves, and our emotions, we are much more likely to make wise decisions about our lives, which reflect both the realities we face as well as our hopes, the will to struggle, and a degree of optimism that we can prevail against adversity.

An even older version of this kind of advice is the well-known therapeutic exhortation employed by Emile Coué, a French hypnotherapist of the early 1900s. It goes: "Every day in every way I am growing better and better." But it takes more than reciting such a slogan regularly to lift one's life out of the doldrums, just as it takes more than telling oneself how worthy or wonderful one is to truly believe it. Otherwise, we would have no need for our large industry of professional therapists and counselors, or for the support groups that flourish today to deal with all kinds of personal trauma, from being raped or abused to losing one's pet.

But what sometimes appears as a felicitous state of mind is not necessarily a sign of mental health or well-being. Some people are enthusiastically upbeat too much of the time. They seem constantly to be in high spirits, active and noisy in their enthusiasm, so much so that the pattern becomes burdensome to others and we wonder if it is genuine. If such enthusiasm looks compulsive—in other words, pushed from within rather than reactive to what is happening—it may actually be a defense against depression and despair.

Well-being (or happiness in the vernacular) is also viewed by some as an *elusive goal* in the present but remembered as a condition of our lives that was true only in the distant past, say in childhood. We often speak wistfully of the halcyon days when life, work, social relationships or society were splendid. At what times in your life were you most happy? Can you describe the feeling and what brought it about? If you are like most people, one of the most salient features of the emotion of happiness is that it is elusive and seems to resist analysis.

The personal meaning of happiness stems from your engagement with an important life project, say, your career, raising a family, fixing up the house, writing a book, creating a garden, and so on. Life in general seems good in that you have a warm relationship with others you care about, little economic pressure, good friends, physical health, reasonable safety from crime and assault, an attractive future, and a society that allows you to express yourself in striving as an individual in authentic ways.

This scenario describes one of the oldest and most interesting philosophical dilemmas about happiness and well-being. It is that we cannot successfully seek to feel happy as a goal of life; the feeling is a *by-product* of using our natural capacities well and striving for something other than our own positive well-being. Unfortunately, many people hope "just to be happy," and make that their goal. From what we know of human nature, however, they are bound to be disappointed. Anticipation of some event or goal is apt to be better than gaining the outcome we seek.

How Do We Judge Well-Being?

It is not a simple task to evaluate well-being. Some people hardly ever think of it at all. If questions are asked about it, no easy answer surfaces because there are no clear standards on which to base an evaluation. For this reason, much of the data about this judgment, as made by ordinary people, is apt to be flawed. The most serious problem is that it is not clear whether we should use an interindividual or an intraindividual frame of reference on which to base our judgment.

To use an *interindividual* (between persons) frame of reference, we must decide whether our well-being is greater or less than that of others. But we do not have a reliable basis on which to make this comparison. How positive is another person's well-being, even someone we know well? How positive is the well-being of most people? The answers are not only elusive for people in general, but for any given person we are likely to know.

To illustrate, when people complain about their lives, it is not necessarily a good indicator of their morale. People differ greatly in their tendency to complain, and their complaints are not always related to how they actually judge their well-being. They may complain because they don't want others to think they are well off, which could earn them the envy or hostility of their associates. Perhaps too, they are superstitious. Or maybe they are greedy and want more than they have.

One of the strangest features of the statements people make about their well-being is that they tend to rate it as above average, which makes no statistical sense. How can most people be above the average? Perhaps they truly believe they are better off than most others, whatever this means. On the other hand, perhaps they are merely trying to convince themselves or their colleagues. Such a tendency may come from the cultural belief that good fortune indicates positive things about oneself, while bad fortune indicates negative things. We all prefer to feel pride in ourselves rather than to feel ashamed of what we are. Another important reason for the higher than average rating may be that there are no clear comparative standards about others on which to base judgments about ourselves, so we give ourselves the benefit of the doubt.

All this raises the question of *honesty* in the ratings of well-being. What we tell other people, including our loved ones, may have more to do with how we want them to view us than whether we feel truly good or bad about our lives. There is unquestionably a social stigma attached to being miserable. People who feel positive about their well-being—especially in the face of adversity—are usually easier to be with. We turn away from those who are depressed or always complaining about their lot.

We may also believe that people whose lives are rewarding are somehow better people, chosen by God for goodness or success, which is the view expressed in Calvinist teachings. Success, good fortune, and happiness demonstrate that we have been selected as one of the elect. This outlook resembles political conservatism and social Darwinism, both of which look at good fortune as the fruits of the survival of the fittest.

It is difficult to be brutally honest with ourselves because we have a large stake in protecting our positive self-image. So if we are asked about our well-being and answer honestly, we might undermine important illusions about ourselves and our relationships with others. We may even avoid thinking about well-being unless our lives are in crisis, in which case we may not be able to evade it.

To use an *intraindividual* (within the same person) frame of reference, a person judges his or her life at one time compared to another. This is an easier judgment to make because we know ourselves well enough to have a basis for comparison. An intraindividual framework implies that well-being and feeling happy or sad are not constant states of mind. They change from one time to another, and from one situation to another. Sometimes we are more or less sanguine about how things are going compared with other times.

For example, we might judge that our well-being is more positive in our present circumstances than it was five years ago. At that time we were disappointed about not making career progress, or about problems with spouse and children. Now, however, things are better; we are more satisfied with our lives. We have been promoted at work, changed our job, or our relationship with spouse and children is now warm and respectful rather than cold and critical. If Joe and Amy had been asked about this at his homecoming, they would have rated their well-being as infinitely better than during their separation. Although in no sense unhappy, they would have made a more sober appraisal a few weeks later as problems began to surface.

The answers we obtain from using an interindividual—between persons—frame of reference may not agree with those obtained from using an intraindividual—within persons—framework. For example, we may think of ourselves as being better off than most other people, yet may see ourselves as less well off than usual. This is not inconsistency; the two frames of reference ask quite different questions, and most of us employ both ways of thinking about our conditions of life.

Effects of Well-Being and Feeling Happy

Well-being and feeling happy influence the way we function and relate to other people. There is substantial evidence that when our mood is negative, problem-solving ability suffers, but when our mood is positive, we perform well. Positive moods also make us outgoing, expansive, friendly, more considerate and helpful to others.[4] Our attention is then directed more at others than ourselves. Being in a dissatisfied frame of mind, on the other hand, makes us self-centered[5] and defensive.

When people are treated well and have positive experiences, they are likely to feel safe, secure, and self-confident. This makes them more kindly and helpful to others. Their thoughts flow easily, and their performance is apt to be at a peak. Performers are then challenged rather than threatened,[6] and they become less inhibited and more expansive. They can afford to take risks.

The opposite is the case when people feel threatened and in need of protection. Performing in an atmosphere that is critical or hostile elicits wariness and inhibition and the need to hold back lest one seem inadequate or foolish. Under these conditions, people have trouble thinking of what to say and how to say it. Being anxious involves self-centered thoughts, such as "Why am I having trouble and doing badly? Will the audience sense my uneasiness?" These thoughts interfere with performance. This is why stand-up comics cherish a responsive audience so much. It makes them feel appreciated and effective, and in turn they become expansive and enjoy themselves, making the best of their talents.

To sum up the plot of happiness, its *provocation* is a bit of good news about our lives, which we interpret as indicating that we are making progress toward attaining immediate and long-term goals. This progress is the fundamental *personal meaning* that underlies feeling happy. In effect, we are using our resources to address our goals in life, both small foreground goals, such as handling specific tasks well, and large, background goals, such as advancing in our careers or seeing our family develop in positive ways. And along the way we are *coping* by realistically attending to the next steps that this progress makes possible. Feeling happy is a by-product of the continuing process of being personally involved and committed, for whatever reason, in what we are doing.

Pride

Here we provide an example of a strong feeling of pride on the part of a mother for her son.

Mrs. Maccia lost her husband in a work accident when she was still nursing her only child, Anthony. She and her husband had immigrated to the United States from Southern Italy to improve their economic position, and he became a longshoreman. Upon his death, she had to do odd sewing jobs and take in washing to survive. She struggled with a minimum income to raise her child in a poor Brooklyn, New York, neighborhood during the Great Depression of the 1930s.

She was a quiet woman, disciplined and strong-willed, able and willing to forgo her own pleasures to give her son a better chance in life. She wanted him to be a real American, and to facilitate this goal she refused to speak Italian in Tony's presence. She urged him to avoid the street gangs that proliferated in the neighborhood, to work and study hard to "be somebody," but she was troubled that he had no male model to help him assimilate the American success story.

In due time she met a quiet, unpretentious man who liked her and was interested in intellectual matters. He made a poor living working in a library, but read widely and spoke like a professor. Although she was not particularly attracted to him, when at length he proposed marriage it seemed like a good idea for her son to have a father. Both of them now were bringing in some money. They were able to leave the run-down neighborhood, where she feared the boy's chances would be spoiled by being subjected to bad influences, and find a home in a lower middle-class community.

Mrs. Maccia was enthusiastic when she saw her husband reading to Tony and speaking to him in good English, with no trace of an Italian accent. She would hear him correcting the boy's speech. And she was overjoyed when Tony showed real promise in school. She kept prodding the boy to study and make something of himself. From time to time Tony rebelled at the discipline and she would become angry, but he always felt guilty and did what his mother wanted, with the stepfather's soft-spoken support.

Tony finished college with a bachelor of science degree just before he was old enough to be drafted into the Army in World War II. He served for three years. On visits home in his uniform Mrs. Maccia swelled with pride. He was such a good boy, and he looked so handsome. When he finally came home for good at the end of the war, he had already decided to enter graduate school to study literature and writing at Columbia University, using the GI bill to finance his education. When he finished his doctorate, he received several good offers from substantial universities to become an assistant professor. Some stories he published during his graduate years helped to spark interest from departments of literature and he took a job at Princeton.

Mrs. Maccia and her husband were both present at his graduation. Now aging and ill, she felt such pride that it seemed she would burst. She cried with joy when he received his parchment. The graduation was the joyful and proud culmination of her long struggle to help Tony to make something of himself. She could hardly believe that her son was a professor, and now a member of what she thought of as the elite. And Princeton was one of the most elite of universities, which was also not far from New York.

Her feeling of pride knew almost no bounds. She felt compelled to tell everyone about her son's accomplishment, quietly reserving some additional pride for herself. She felt she had accomplished what she had set out to do against the odds, and took credit for it. She knew her life had been worthwhile. And she imagined that one day Tony would marry and have children.

Psychological Analysis

While Mrs. Maccia clearly sacrificed much for her son, she seems to have experienced considerable well-being during her life and, fortunately, was not disappointed in what became of her son. A poor woman without education, living in a foreign country, her personal options with respect to style of life were not many. She truly didn't want much for herself, but lived her life for and through her son. She managed, nevertheless, to do well, to have a decent livelihood and a husband who was a fine father and mate.

Although our account of Mrs. Maccia centered on the great pride she experienced when her son graduated from graduate school and became a faculty member at Princeton, many experiences of great happiness and pride also occurred in Tony's childhood. These included moments when she saw Tony and his stepfather talking warmly or when Tony would display his intelligence and knowledge when she and her husband had visitors. Most of our lives are punctuated with such experiences, which result in positive states of mind that sustain us through the bad times. Mrs. Maccia was lucky because most of what she did and wanted worked out well, and her son gave her little cause for concern about his future.

What might the future be for Mrs. Maccia in the light of her tremendous self-sacrifice for her son, and the great feeling of happiness, well-being, and pride she experienced about him? Much depends on her son.

Will he continue to give her love and attention after he presumably marries and has children?

As it turned out, Tony married a female professor at Princeton. Within five years, the new couple ultimately moved to another university on the West Coast. Their lives, as must always be true, centered on their own professional enterprises and social circle. And while Mrs. Maccia came to visit them occasionally, this offered only a very limited relationship. Some tension occurred with Tony and his new wife when Mrs. Maccia pressed them to have children, which they seem not to want. Since she had thought she would be involved in raising grandchildren, it was now necessary for her to find new commitments that would be satisfying.

For Mrs. Maccia there was no late life encore to her earlier commitment to her son and his career. Her husband died soon after the young couple moved, and the insurance he left provided for her late years. Tony returned briefly for the funeral. Increasingly, Mrs. Maccia felt useless, looking back on the days during which she lived for her son as the best times of her life.

At sixty-five she seems ready to die. She is torn between wanting to move to the West Coast and remaining where the environment is familiar. Tony and his wife have not encouraged her to move; she believes his wife resists it. Tony phones her nearly every month, but this is not enough for her. Their conversation is also stilted now, a reflection of the tremendous void in interests and outlook that has developed between the two generations.

Feelings of happiness and pride are temporary mental states and cannot be centered on the past. To sustain these feelings, there must be something in the present that calls forth our energies and allows us to use our abilities. Without this engagement there is dissatisfaction and recrimination for the loss of function. Mrs. Maccia will have to cope with this problem as she ages, and as her son and his wife forge their own lives. She has not yet found a way to live happily and seems embittered and depressed. Change is always the order of the day, and, with it, new requirements for experiencing the feelings of happiness, pride, and well-being.

The Many Faces of Pride

There are few synonyms for pride. Triumph could be one, but it has special connotations that complicate the meaning. For reasons that are obscure, the single word pride seems to carry the entire meaning of this common and fairly complex emotion.

Feeling happy is often conjoined with feeling proud, as when we say

"She is my pride and joy." Mrs. Maccia felt both happy and proud at her son's graduation. However, pride has a special meaning that distinguishes it from happiness. The distinction was drawn many years ago by philosopher David Hume. [7]

Hume maintained that what provokes pride is not merely a positive event that makes us feel happy, but one that confirms or enhances our sense of personal worth. This enhancement of ego is the *personal meaning* that underlies pride. Something adds to our personal and social position, a beautiful or well-kept home, an achievement, knowledge of the world, a contribution to society, youthful appearance, fortitude, in effect, any of the things that people have learned to value in our society. The *provocation* of pride is an ego-enhancing event or condition, or the mention or thought of such an event that we remember.

The distinction between feeling happy and proud directs us to the dramatic plot for pride, which is an *enhancement of one's personal worth by taking credit for a valued object or achievement*. The achievement may be our own or those with whom we identify—for example, a child, a member of one's family, a compatriot, a group to which we belong, such as a sports team, our tribe, or nation. Mrs. Maccia's pride in her son at his graduation and in herself for being able to take some credit for his achievement are obvious examples.

As in feeling happy, when we feel proud, we are expansive and want to tell others. Our chest seems to swell. As the 1st Lord of the Admiralty, the Right Honorable Sir Joseph Porter, K.C.B., sings in Gilbert and Sullivan's comic opera *H.M.S. Pinafore*: "When at anchor here I ride, my bosom swells with pride."

Contrast the expansiveness of pride with the impulse to hide when we experience shame. When we feel proud we have lived up to—or even gone beyond—the personal and social standard to which we aspire, in contrast with being ashamed for having disappointed those whose approbation we value.

Pride can be compared to humility as well. When we genuinely feel humble (rather than merely the affectation of humility, which is designed to create a good impression), we appreciate our limitations, just as pride involves appreciating our merits. Humility is much different from shame, however, in that it is an acceptance of our limitations rather than an expression of distress over them. Pride may sometimes betray a certain arrogance, which is obviously not found in the self-denigrating emotions of humility or shame.

Neither pride, humility, nor shame necessarily have to do with the objective truth about ourselves but rather how the truth is evaluated or *appraised*. Here again we see how the emotions depend on the meaning we construct from the events of our lives. Mrs. Maccia believed that she did well in pushing Tony toward the achievement for which she also felt pride in both herself and her son. We think so too. The meaning she constructed for her life centered on her hopes for her son to achieve. This fueled her self-sacrifices, which were rewarded by his stunning success and expanded her own sense of her own accomplishment in having empowered him in this success.

Other mothers, however, who value income more than scholarly achievement might condemn the same life pattern as foolish or the success as unimportant or undeserved. And still others fool themselves into feeling misplaced pride in a child who is, in reality, altogether undistinguished and unaccomplished. The differences in these reactions are the result of very different ways of defining success, of what enhances their own egos, or of unrealistic ways of evaluating the outcomes of their children's life styles.

Our society maintains definite but subtle values about pride. For this reason, we may have to cope with our pride, which sounds strange to our ears. For example, we think of pride in a positive way, yet react negatively to showing off or self-aggrandizement, which puts others in a one-down position. Intending to deprecate, we sometimes say "He has a swelled head." Pride is a competitive emotion because it centers on the need to protect and enhance our personal identity. Therefore, one must tread softly so as not to offend others by what is sometimes called "overweening pride."

Mrs. Maccia wanted to tell everyone about her son and her own role in his accomplishment, but it was also necessary to *cope* with the threats that the expression of her pride might generate. For example, she must not seem publicly, or to him privately, to undermine his real accomplishment. Pride for him, fine, but not for herself.

Because pride is competitive, it can also spell trouble for intimate social relationships. An example is what we call "stubborn pride" in which people find it difficult to apologize, forgive, and make up after a wounding argument. Although it is self-defeating in the long run, the stubbornly "proud" person continues to express hurt and anger, and wants the other person to come all the way rather than halfway toward reconciliation. We describe such people as "cutting off their noses to spite their faces." They are coping with a negative opinion of themselves, which makes them believe that to give in demeans them.

Some of the subtle evaluative nuances of pride are illustrated by the lyrics of patriotic tunes and anthems, which express ambivalence about how loud to blow one's own horn. In the American song "You're a Grand Old Flag," one line boasts that we are "the land of the free and the brave," but a second adds "with never a boast or a brag." So in the same lyric there is a prideful boast and an admonition not to boast.

A derogation of the arrogance of pride can also be found in our culture in the quasi-religious dictum that "Pride goeth before a fall." It carries both a moral overtone and a warning that we should not be boastful lest we receive our comeuppance. Our culture also values humility—a kind of opposite of pride—while at the same time admiring those who thrust themselves forward aggressively.

Excessive pride is defined differently in different cultures. In Japan, for example, if one's child or spouse is complimented, the virtues being praised are apt to be shrugged off, as if to deny the compliment. In reality, it is probably the display rather than the inner feeling of pride that is socially unacceptable. Yet both cultures have the same ambivalence about it. Because pride in oneself implies individual competitiveness, an inordinate display of it is to be avoided in a community-centered society, such as Japan. In the United States, we are supposed to enjoy the pride that comes from evidence of our own virtues or those of a loved one, but always without overdoing it.

Those dependent on public approval, such as celebrities in the entertainment and sports world, must be careful not to be too arrogant about their favorable position in life. The public feels ambivalent about their fame and wealth, admiring it but at the same time envying it. In deference to this, celebrities often present themselves with great displays of modesty to ward off envy and hostile disapproval. They even point with pathos to their misfortunes in public interviews.

Television interviewers often nourish this ambivalence by displaying a curious mixture of positive regard and derogation—sometimes even thinly veiled contempt—that the celebrity puts up with as a way of mitigating the potential for public hostility. The public is also intensely interested in alcoholism, drug addiction, depression, suicide, and psychosis among celebrities. If those we envy can be seen as victims, compassion helps us to be more accepting of their otherwise favorable position in life.

Pride can also be used in defense of a vulnerable ego, in which case it expresses an underlying doubt about one's value as a person. When we have little to be proud of, we can enhance our ego-identities by associating ourselves with important religious, national, ethnic, subcultural, or political groups, even a baseball or football team that is having a winning season. Doing so puffs us up and makes us feel good about ourselves. However, it can also take on the dangerous quality of *ethnocentrism*, which is to make positive evaluations of our own group or society and devalue, denigrate, and exclude others.

To sum up the plot of pride, the *provocation* is that something good has happened that has been associated with us and that carries positive social value. The *personal meaning* of pride is that what has happened enhances our identity as an individual and, therefore, makes us—as well as others—think of ourselves as special. This meaning of a gain in social status distinguishes pride from the closely related emotion of happiness. Since pride has competitive, and sometimes even moral overtones, we *cope* with it by walking a fine line between justifiable pride and overweening pride (hubris), which could lead to social criticism.

Love

Few love experiences are a greater source of emotional distress than unrequited love. Before proceeding, let us examine this type of experience.

Janet was a good-looking and popular college student at a college in California, with an average academic record. She lived in a dormitory room she shared with another girl she liked and admired. Math was the only subject that intimidated her, and a bright but strange young man named Steve, a student at the same college, had befriended her and offered to help her with math.

Steve was socially awkward, very intense and explosive, and did not have many female friends. Janet accepted his help gratefully, and sensed that he needed ego-building. So she took advantage of his help, and also went out with him from time to time out of sympathy for this young man who seemed needy, though she found his attentions off-putting.

In consequence of what seemed to him interest on her part, Steve began to lose his sense of reality about the relationship. He began to spend a great deal of his time looking forward to the visits to Janet's dorm and the weekly instruction in math he provided for her. He also became dependent on her for his social activities and seemed to be enamored of her.

While she behaved circumspectly and carefully so as not to encourage him, she did not wish to undermine his confidence. He, in turn, doted on her, wished that he could make love to her, and his moods rose and fell on the basis of her attentions. One evening, while studying together, he confessed his feelings to her. Her reaction was chilly and uncomfortable. She suggested that she liked him, but didn't reciprocate his affection in that way. His love—if one could call it that—was unrequited.

Steve was devastated by what he took to be a rejection. He thought of Janet constantly, hated any other male toward whom she showed any interest, fantasized that he was courting her, and imagined how he might make himself more appealing to her. On one occasion, he began to make love to her. At first, feeling guilty about rejecting him, Janet allowed Steve to fondle her, which only added to the intensity of Steve's yearning. Finally, she told him that she did not care for him in that way and that he must stop. When he refused and began to force his attentions on her, she became frightened and called out to neighbors, who helped to physically remove him from the dorm.

The rejection was a terrible experience for Steve who seemed to have lost all sense of reality, compulsively believing Janet was the only woman he could love and be loved by. He took to stalking Janet, at first from a distance, watching her when she went to class and at public functions. Janet's friends would often tell her of his presence. He wrote her letters, which became more and more strident and threatening. He would try to enter her dorm room. Increasingly he confronted her, pleaded with her, and implied that he would not take no for an answer.

Janet went to the college administration to complain, but was urged not to make a fuss and to wait for him to cool down and forget about her. She took some of his most threatening letters to the local police, who said that they couldn't do anything unless he committed a crime. (California had no stalking law at the time.) At last, he forced his way into her room one day and attacked her. Janet screamed and fought him off, and a 911 call by one of the dormitory women brought police who kept him in jail overnight, got a judge to order an injunction against being seen anywhere near her, and released him.

Janet remained in distress and fear because Steve seemed unable to control his unwanted attention. He continued to stalk her and she was unable to obtain evidence that might lead to an arrest. Unable to study and feel at ease, Janet quit the college, traveled to her home, and ultimately applied to another school, trying carefully to conceal her movements. Fortunately, in this case, she was not bothered again by Steve, who was a few years later arrested for a similar stalking episode with a prominent television actress in Los Angeles. He is now serving time in jail, but is soon to be released. Janet remains uneasy about the possibility that she will again be attacked by Steve, perhaps with a more violent outcome.

Psychological Analysis

The *personal meaning* of this unsatisfactory relationship is obviously very different for Janet and Steve. Steve wanted so much to be loved by this kind, friendly, and popular young woman, and at the outset Janet misinterpreted his intentions in helping her but became increasingly wary. When someone dotes on another person, it is difficult to take the step of actively turning that person off. One feels guilty about a harsh rejection. However, Steve was ultimately faced with a firm rejection, which seems to have reinforced his poor opinion of himself, and so it was all the more devastating.

Steve, a very unstable—and potentially psychotic—man, could not accept the rejection. In childhood, he was rejected by his parents and left largely to his own devices. He managed on the fringe of society, living more or less as a loner, bright enough to get along, get into college, and manage well enough not to cause any alarm, until the episode with Janet. Still, reference to his childhood rejection is too facile to be very useful, because many boys and girls experience rejection but do not become compulsively attached or violent when turned down later by women in their lives. Psychology does not yet provide an adequate account of what goes wrong in such cases.

Janet, in turn, was dismayed when Steve tried to intimidate her into loving him. Then when she saw his potential for violence, she was frightened. She had no real clue to the severity of his emotional and behavioral dysfunctions. She wanted to profit from his skill in math and to be kind to this lonely young man. She felt guilty about her role in misleading him about her intentions. Guilt, however, was not an appropriate reaction inasmuch as Janet tried to deal with Steve sensitively and considerately. When she was forced to tell him the truth, he just couldn't handle it.

The authorities would not or could not provide her with the protection she felt she needed. The trauma for Janet was to face threatening behavior by someone so unstable that he could be violent. She had heard of other such cases that ended in tragedy and she did not want that to happen to her. She tried in every way to get help from the authorities, but the help continued to be inadequate. Except for a trace of guilt, and her legitimate fear of Steve, Janet has no important psychological problem as a result of this episode of unrequited love.

What, however, will happen to Steve? There is no way to say with any confidence. He appears to be mentally ill, reflected in the inappropriateness of his actions, his inability to turn off his compulsive yearning, his social isolation. Yet he normally makes a presentable appearance and has more than average intelligence and skill. He is badly in need of therapy of some kind, without which he is at risk of doing something that will lead to imprisonment or worse.

Society seems relatively helpless to prevent the potential tragedies that might well befall Steve, the many other persons—both male and female— who live on the margins of the society, and their potential victims. And what is worse, it seems unwilling to invest sufficient funds and talent to try to prevent such tragedies, or deal with them when they occur, preferring to ignore them or believe they will go away.

Aside from the mental aberrations involved, this case is fundamentally a matter of learning how to cope better with desires for love in people who are needy. To do well in the love game, people must come to see themselves favorably enough not to hurl themselves at anyone who is kind to them, or make a hasty advance, much less to threaten or commit violence on behalf of those desires. We must also be wary of assuming that the compulsion to possess someone else or dominate their attention is representative of love as most of us experience it.

The case of Janet and her rejection of Steve is far more dramatic and negative than most instances of unrequited love. While the experience of rejection among the young is common, the extreme and negative experiences of Steve's case are uncommon. They rarely lead to more than disappointment and a temporarily bruised ego on the part of the loser, and some guilt on the part of the person who does the rejecting.[8]

What then went wrong? The seeds were in a past that Steve couldn't shake. The pattern he displayed was a living out of early ways of thinking and feeling about himself and others, as though fate had decreed what would happen, as in an ancient Greek tragedy. Steve began by constructing meanings that were false—first that Janet was interested in him as a lover, and second that when she rejected him it was because he was unlovable. By seeing himself as victim, he could, at least on the surface, deny that there was anything wrong with him or that the debacle was mostly of his own making. This is the sickness of mind that lay in waiting for a provocation that would activate it and bring it to its inevitable denoument.

The Many Faces of Love

Because love has so many different connotations, there is an enormous number of synonyms for it. One group of words, which seem appropriate for our concerns here, includes affection, attachment, tenderness, devotion, amity, regard, adoration, adulation, ardor, and passion.

Another group, which seems less appropriate, includes liking, delight, enjoyment, pleasure, relish, and inclination. These two groups in no way exhaust the list that we could generate.

Which word best carries the meaning of love depends a great deal on the aspect of love we are concerned with. It is worthwhile to recognize how many diverse meanings can be found for the idea of love, and what this says about the importance of love in our society, or perhaps to people in general.

But love is not necessarily the same experience for the two people experiencing it. Put differently, the *personal meaning* of love differs from person to person. Thus, one partner may view love negatively as a sacrifice of independence and autonomy, while the other remains smitten. Some partners connect love strongly with sex, but others do not. For them, the wish of one partner may be to share private thoughts, goals, and experiences, while the other may have little interest in or capacity for such sharing. Intensity of feeling and demonstrativeness may also differ for the partners. For one, there may be a strong commitment to the relationship, while for the other commitment is weak.

Love relationships present an endless variety of patterns and emotions, some a source of well-being, some a source of distress, some lively and conflicting, others comfortable but psychologically dead. Steve has already developed a love history that could well shape future love relationships. He must learn first to view himself as a desirable person, or to shift his focus from seeking love to validating himself through other kinds of social and work commitments. He must cope with his history and the unserviceable personal meanings that have characterized his early relationships with women. It is not clear that he has the strength of ego to do so.

Love is also tangled up with cultural values. Not only do cultures vary in their outlook toward love, but these outlooks have changed greatly in the course of Western history. Love, for example, was once not considered relevant to marriage, which was a social and business relationship, with the main societal business being the raising of children. A marriage was negotiated by parents rather than the young couple, and love did not enter the negotiation. Couples were sometimes told that they would learn to love each other, and this probably happened in some cases. Some readers will remember Tevye and Golde in the very successful musical *Fiddler on the Roof* singing "Do you love me?" Our culture has tended to define love romantically.

We believe that the desire for love may have always been a focus of humanity, even when marriages were arranged and love deemphasized. Human biology and the nature of our social existence probably generated a need in our evolutionary ancestors for romantic love relationships. Above all, love defines a caring relationship between two people, without which there is apt to be loneliness and bitterness.

When people are asked to name the most important human emotions, love (as well as one of its opposites, anger or hate) is usually at the top of the list. The case for love as an emotion is actually somewhat complicated, and not all psychologists would treat it as an emotion, though it is always emotional. Chief among the complications is that there are different kinds of love.

Although romantic love has much in common with nonsexual,

companionate love, which includes both fraternal and parental versions, these kinds of love are also different from each other in important ways. Whether or not romantic love should be defined by sexual interest—heterosexual or homosexual—is uncertain. The main reason for the uncertainty is that erotic interest can occur without love and, presumably, many of the attitudes inherent in romantic love can exist without sexual involvement or passion.

Love as a Positive or Negative Experience

Although we often think of love as a positive experience—which is why we placed it in this chapter—literary treatments give us a clue as to how varied this experience really is. It is sometimes idealized as an ecstatic state of mind, an all-consuming and rewarding passion. But others condemn it as a source of conflict, pain, misery, and unhappiness, a folly, especially when unrequited, something to be avoided if peace of mind is desired, a socially acceptable form of madness.

In Cervantes's *Don Quixote*, we have an idealized, therefore positive, but obsessive example of love. The hero is a self-defined knight-errant, who is slightly mad. He has a fixation—consistent with his irrational idealism and desire to do good—about the purity of a whore named Aldonza whom he meets on his travels. He calls her Dulcinea, which is translated as "sweet dream," and his fixation about her purity ultimately leads her to abandon her old way of life and identify with his idealized image.

In Somerset Maugham's novel *Of Human Bondage*, love is celebrated as a seemingly irrational obsession. Philip, a very insecure man with a club foot, becomes the emotional slave of Mildred, a vulgar, shallow, and thoughtless woman whom he cannot respect. But he is helpless to do anything about his attachment. He lives for the moments he can be with her, yet curses his fate. His bondage to Mildred is his own doing and it makes him miserable most of the time. There is a real sense in which Steve's approach to love is one of obsessive bondage because of his low regard for himself and his desperate need to be loved and appreciated by a woman.

Love as an Emotion or a Sentiment

We need to distinguish love as an acute emotion from love as a sentiment. We speak of the sentiment of love when we describe the love of one (or both) partner for the other; the emotion of love is only aroused from time to time, which is quite normal. We couldn't stand experiencing any strong emotion for long, much less constantly—it would consume us.

The acute emotion of love comes and goes in a loving relationship. It is *provoked* by the sight of the other, a particular interchange, a favorable opportunity, a romantic atmosphere, seeing or hearing the other, and perhaps something more physical like a surge of sex hormones.

Even in the most romantic of courtships, when the lovers must go to work or are parted, they normally become involved in other matters, and are not likely to feel the emotion of love actively, except in special circumstances when alone or when reminded of each other. Otherwise, constantly consumed by love, they could not function adequately. Most stable relationships, marital or otherwise, also include a host of other emotions such as anger, anxiety, guilt, shame, relief, happiness, pride, compassion, and the emotion of love too, depending on the particular case. But love, the social relationship, is not the same as love, the emotion.

Love as an acute emotion is an aroused state in which the love is experienced in a particular encounter with the loved one, whether imagined or real. It happens periodically, as when lovers experience mutual feelings of love and passion, whether or not they make love. When love is dying, the frequency of the occasions when feelings of love are aroused declines or disappears altogether, though it sometimes can be rekindled.

Kinds of Love

Aside from heterosexual and homosexual love, there is more than one kind of love. The most important and interesting contrast is that between romantic and companionate love, which includes fraternal and parental love as subtypes. These variants overlap greatly, as we will see in their dramatic plots, but there are important differences that we should examine.

Romantic Love. Thus far we have been talking mostly about what might be called romantic love. This usually includes sexual intimacy, and is reserved for lovers. Romantic love fits in with our modern Western conception of marriage which, in its ideal form, is supposed to be based on love. Our social ideal for this kind of love views the lovers as having positive regard for each other, seeing themselves as equals, probably—but not necessarily—feeling a degree of sexual passion. It is sexual intimacy that distinguishes romantic love from companionate love.

The dramatic plot of romantic love is clear to most of us: *desiring or participating in affection and physical intimacy, usually but not necessarily reciprocated.* The problematic nature of reciprocity recognizes that one may love without being loved in return, what we referred to earlier as unrequited love. In this case, love is a consequence of the wish to love and be loved, not necessarily the reality of being loved in return.

Love brings with it strong impulses to approach the partner, to touch, and to interact for mutual sexual gratification. In love, we desire warmth and tenderness. We are interested and concerned about the well-being of the other. But what we see as attractive in the beloved is both culturally and individually determined.

Courtship in our society is a complicated matter. It is where the *coping* process becomes particularly important in relationships. The difficult problem that must be faced is the potential for rejection, which can be devastating to some. In most healthy affectionate relationships, courtship is a trial-and-error period, gradually advancing only when there is realistic evidence of a positive response.

The absence of a positive response is apt to be distressing and discouraging to most of us, and may in fact terminate further attempts. This process of courting, and the guardedness that protects a person from experiencing too much ego damage, failed in the case of Steve and in Somerset Maugham's character of Philip in *Of Human Bondage*. Both were in some way especially vulnerable to the dependent attachment that resulted. When it takes this form, such a dependent attachment can be referred to as love, though most of us would reject it as pathological.

For many men and some women, the image of the chase is the main theme of courtship. In pursuit of the beloved, the individual continues sustained efforts to interest the other, at least for a while, despite evidence of disinterest. Ambiguity in our society about the appropriateness of persisting in such cases fuels current debates about how to deal with sexual harassment, assault, and date rape. Playing hard to get is considered fair play, even if the woman or man is interested, thus causing even more confusion over real intentions and motives.

It also happens that some women actively try to encourage a man to show interest and engage in courtship without obviously seeming to. In such cases, the man only thinks he is playing the stereotypical male aggressive role when, in reality, the woman is doing so more subtly so as not to seem the aggressor.

Persistent pursuit when it is rejected by the other is tantamount to mental illness and has been known to be dangerous. Often the word obsession is applied to this behavior, which suggests an inner compulsion more than a reaction to what is actually happening. Stalkers—that is, people who keep making unwelcome contact, sometimes of a threatening or violent nature, with someone they claim to love or admire—fall into this category.

Sexual harassment is a political issue as well as a psychological one. In recent times it has even influenced the selection of a federal supreme court male justice, Clarence Thomas, who was accused by Anita Hill of previously engaging in harassment. The testimony of both parties was watched on television by many millions of people, sparking intense debates about who was telling the truth. No doubt, the social focus on sexual harassment in the United States has probably changed our patterns of romantic expression, especially in the workplace. Some celebrate this, others decry it.

Problems of courtship are particularly acute in those who have a low regard for themselves and are most likely to be inhibited or vulnerable to being demeaned by rejection. We can see in this vulnerability a basis for the close connection between love and anger. In troubled courtships, one or both persons might move too fast toward intimacy without evidence of mutuality. A danger is that a suitor may become entangled in a one-sided relationship that is impossible to consummate. Another danger is resentment on the part of a reluctant partner, and even public humiliation, in the event of an accusation of improper conduct.

Loss of love in an ongoing relationship carries similar dangers of producing hurt and damage to the ego; the response might be dangerous levels of anger, or even depression and grieving over the loss. There is probably no human relationship in our society that is more socially complex and sensitive, and contains more emotional hazards, than seeking and maintaining love.

Commitment has little directly to do with love as an emotion, though it may be a condition of falling in love for some people. Love me, but not just for my body, might be the message directly or indirectly communicated to the uncommitted. Commitment declares that one has a stable concern about the well-being of the partner, which is how society usually defines real love. Commitment is an intention to ignore the inevitable periods in a relationship when the emotion of love is not experienced, or has faded completely.

Our social ideal is to take responsibility for the partner, and for the children, which requires consistent nurturing in spite of emotional flux, even after separation or divorce. The commitment may dissolve if passion seldom or never again appears, or if the relationship is too punishing to sustain in the absence of love. In that case we have divorce, with all the attendant problems of economics, childrearing, and social as well as psychological readjustment.

Attitudes toward love and commitment vary with the culture and historical period. Society is concerned with marital records, protecting the rights of the partners, maintaining their mutual obligations, making sure that they remain in predictable and functional social and work niches, facilitating childrearing, and upholding the values to which the society is dedicated. Therefore, commitment plays an important societal role if not always a personal, emotional role.

Even today in some societies, the decision to marry is an economic and social one rather than an emotional one. Remember, however, that we are considering love as an emotion with diverse qualities and patterns, whether or not it follows a social ideal, and whether or not we admire such an ideal.

Sociologists have pointed out that Americans as a whole have particular hangups about sexuality, which are absent or not as strong among European nations.[9] Advertisements for commercial products draw heavily on sex, and TV soap operas emphasize all sorts of sexual liaisons, titillating audiences with provocative poses, actions, and situations. And yet we moralize hypocritically about sex, refuse to commit ourselves to proper sexual education in the schools, and worry about discussing or demonstrating the use of condoms publicly in an effort to prevent unwanted pregnancies or to combat AIDS and other sexually communicated diseases, lest doing so might encourage sexual promiscuity.

Idealizing romantic love—and linking it to commitment—naturally complicates the expectations we develop about love and its stability. This is one of the most serious mistakes people make as they approach love relationships. Many a marital disappointment has stemmed from romanticized and unrealistic notions about love as a constant state of mind in which the partners never falter in their mutual idolatry.

The problem with love as an emotion is that passion waxes and wanes and cannot be sustained moment by moment over the long haul. Long-term relationships are not conducive to constant passion or the acute emotion of love, but the meanings required for active loving feelings surface from time to time, mainly under favorable conditions, when other considerations in the relationship take a back seat.

Companionate Love.   Companionate love also centers on feelings of intimacy and love, with pleasure stemming from the interaction of positive regard and concern for mutual well-being. Its dramatic plot, *desiring or participating in affection, usually but not necessarily reciprocated,* is very similar to romantic love. Parents love their children, and children their parents. Women can love other women whom they may consider their best friends and with whom they want to be, without any evident erotic component. Men feel love for other men too, though in our society they are sometimes uneasy and inhibited about this kind of love because of their definition of maleness. For many men, it is easier to speak of friendship than love.

The commitment to the child in parenting is apt to be strong and is typically much more one-sided than in romantic love. A mother and father are likely to continue to attend to their child's needs even if the child does not reciprocate their affection. But the parent still desires the affection, and its absence is a source of disappointment, anger, guilt, or shame.

The love of a parent for a child is difficult to analyze because it comes in such great variety. And while we have explanations for it, what we think is often a matter of surmise. Some parents consider it mainly an obligation to have children and care for them, a sort of moral imperative. The emotion of love doesn't really enter into it; it is a matter of responsibility.

Nowadays especially, many women opt not to have children, choosing career over family. Yet while some women may begin their adult lives with this rejection of family, as the number of childbearing years shorten, they may decide they want the experience after all. What is it that motivates this change of heart? Do they yearn for it as one might yearn for love? It is difficult to say. For others, having children is viewed as an important—perhaps even necessary—enrichment of their lives. Some believe that children will provide companionship and care in their old age. Still others, seemingly strongly disposed to love and care for children, have been enthralled with parenthood since their own childhood. As children, they often played the role of mommy and looked forward to it as a natural part of their adulthood.

There is probably something biological in the tendency to want to care for a baby, who will be quite dependent on such care for a long time. We often assume that this tendency arises in women on the emergence of a child from their own bodies. But this belies the strong love that parents feel for adopted children. Perhaps the desire for a child has something to do with female hormones and their influence on the brain. However, not all women seem to feel this way, and men are quite capable of experiencing strong paternal love. Perhaps for males this tendency is built into the species, but in less obvious ways than for women.

On the other hand, we may learn from the society in which we grew up that we should feel in certain ways, that children and family are part of an American dream, a shared illusion capable of holding intact the fabric of society. Or perhaps we search for love because we are very vulnerable and need other people to care about us, to acknowledge our importance and positive qualities as individuals, or to combine forces with us in dealing with the demands and opportunities of life—us against the world. There are probably many complex motives for love.

We have touched on a traditional and vexing question: How much are our feelings influenced by biology and how much by social experience? For that matter, the same question can be asked about romantic love. Is romantic love an emotion or just a case of pure biology and hormones—in effect, lust rather than love, which we make more socially acceptable with the euphemism love. What we explore later is the impossibility of separating biology from social experience as a source of any emotion, including love. Undoubtedly both are involved, as we will see in Chapter 9. Perhaps it is enough to say that humans are capable of an emotion of love, and that it is a powerful influence on our lives, for better or worse.

What is missing in companionate love, which holds center stage in romantic love, is erotic passion. The absence of sexual interest in companionate love, both in its parental and fraternal versions, is a societal rule, expressed as an *incest taboo*.

Psychoanalysts tell us, however, that the relative absence of overt erotic involvement in companionate love, particularly in the parental variety, does not mean that sexual interest is lacking but rather that it is inhibited. In companionate love, the relationship is said to be desexualized, and if erotic interest exists—how frequently we do not know—it is apt to be repressed or hidden. Presumably, the parent is unaware of it, and if it should occur in thought or fantasy, it is said to be quickly put out of mind or disguised lest shame, guilt, and anxiety about what is regarded by society as immoral might be too much to handle. Yet incest and child abuse seem quite common, and we have trouble understanding what has gone wrong. In spite of the great attention these societal and individual problems are being given in the media today, it is not clear whether or not their incidence has increased in recent years. Incest is not a passion that would have been discussed openly in years past.

We end our discussion of the emotion of love with the observation that psychoanalysts view the power and intensity of love in human relationships from the perspective of childhood experiences. Adult love is said to reawaken and rediscover early childhood relationships, especially the symbiotic relationship between child and parent. In adult love there is a fusion of two independent individuals.

We also invest love with some of the same problems and virtues that existed in our relationships with our mother and father, or those who served as substitutes for them. To some extent, we relive these parental relationships in our adult love relationships, sometimes by opposing them, sometimes by duplicating them. It is from our parents, after all, that we first learn about love.

If we have sought to dominate or prevent being dominated by our parents, if we coped by distancing ourselves from them, if we were excessively dependent on them, or if we related to them with ambivalence—for example, by loving *and* hating them—we may reinstate these childhood patterns with later love partners. In doing so, we often make the same mistake in relationship after relationship, divorcing for the same reasons, because we carry the same meanings we have constructed from one instance to another.

Some adults remain forever childish in their relationships; they may be unable to love, do not believe they are lovable, or absorb themselves too obsessively in love without reciprocity. Others are hungry for love, and remain insatiable all their lives. For a healthy adult relationship, the recurring childhood pattern must be somehow broken. Doing so might require the acquisition of insight about our childhood origins of love, which can sometimes be gained in psychotherapy.

Romantic and companionate love are very strong human needs, which arouse powerful, sometimes uncontrollable emotions. Cultural influences on love are, no doubt, considerable, but its biology is also central and enduring, regardless of the way society treats the rituals of courtship and coupling.

6

The Empathic Emotions:
Gratitude, Compassion, and Those
Aroused by Aesthetic Experiences

The three kinds of emotion described in this chapter are closely related because each depends to some extent on the capacity to *empathize* with others. Our knowledge about them is modest, but they are important in our daily lives, and their special characteristics make them fascinating and distinct from other emotions.

Gratitude

We can see an example of gratitude in the following story.

When John was 18 in 1940, he was a junior at the City College of New York. This college offered a first-rate, free education for impoverished students. To manage expenses, such as meals, books, and fees, John needed paid employment, which in those years was very scarce.

He made some money by becoming a barber for the students at the college. He had learned to cut children's hair reasonably well at summer camps where he had been a counselor. He posted ads in various locations at the college, which indicated the hours between his classes in which he was free to cut hair. These were haircuts by appointment only, for which he charged 20 cents, 5 cents below the nearby barbershop. He also personally advertised his services in front of his college classes before the lectures began.

The students at CCNY were very sympathetic to this young entrepreneur and welcomed saving even 5 cents, so before long he had a thriving business. However, one day he was visited by a policeman and told that he must stop because he didn't have a city license. Evidently, the local barber had learned of the competition from one of the students. The license was too expensive for John to afford.

At this time, one of his professors, who knew about his barber business, asked John how things were going. When he mentioned the bad news, the professor asked him if he wanted a job working for him at 50 cents an hour delivering research reports in downtown New York. The offer was a lifesaver, and John felt grateful.

So John went to work for the professor, collating and delivering reports between 5 A.M. and 10 A.M., five days a week, after which he would rush to his first class. Months later, he was offered a better job doing calculations for the research report itself at the same rate of pay for 30 hours a week. He found ways of being more efficient at the calculating task, and began to do the job in half the time. This, of course, endangered his 30 hour a week take-home pay, which would be cut by half were he to inform the professor that he only needed to work 15 hours to complete the job.

John was very troubled about this dilemma. After some thought he decided that he should present it to the professor. The professor told him that he was very pleased with John's innovative procedures and that he appreciated John's honesty. He said that he was only interested in seeing that the job was done. Henceforth, therefore, he would be paid the same as before regardless of how long it actually took to produce the weekly research report. This preserved John's income and gave him much more time to study. He remained at the job until he graduated and was drafted into the Army in World War II.

Offering John the job might not, in itself, have been so generous an act on the part of the professor, since he needed the work done and could see that John was a competent and enterprising young man. However, John was enormously grateful to his professor for his unusual kindness and understanding in changing the terms of employment so much in his favor. He considered this action to have been extraordinarily generous.

The professor had given John a marvelous gift, which allowed him to amass a high grade-point average and qualify later for graduate school. He never forgot the kindness. In the years following his military service, John began graduate study, attained a PhD, accepted a position as an assistant professor, and later became well known and respected in his field.

Fifty years later, when he learned that the college professor who had helped him was celebrating his eightieth birthday, John wrote his mentor warmly about his memory of his generous patronage and what it had meant to him, once again expressing his appreciation and gratitude.

It was one of those wonderfully positive experiences early in life that encourages comparable acts when the recipient of the generosity is at last able to do something for others facing the same struggle to get ahead. Still feeling grateful, John regularly tried to reciprocate for the gift he had received by helping other worthy students. What goes around comes around.

Psychological Analysis

The *personal meaning* of John's gratitude was his warm belief that the professor had gone out of his way to help him by making a positive contribution to his life. The gift had been given without strings or personal gain, and so John regarded it as altruistic. The graciousness with which it had been given, and his genuine need as the recipient, made it easy to accept the gift with gratitude.

Because of the gift's importance to his efforts to establish his own career, John remembered it positively even after he had himself succeeded. By making comparable gifts to his young students when needed, he believed he was, in a sense, paying back his professor for his kindness.

The Many Faces of Gratitude

The synonyms for gratitude are few and seem to miss what we present as its central meaning; these so-called synonyms include being thankful, appreciative, and beholden.

The dramatic plot of gratitude is *appreciating an altruistic gift*. Although it is sometimes strongly felt, most often gratitude is a mild emotion. Its *provocation* is based on being given material help, such as money or being driven to work or the hospital, being offered useful information, or being provided with needed emotional support.[1]

Two people are brought together with every gift, the giver and the receiver, and the gift locks them into a more complex relationship than may be evident on the surface. The relationship, which depends on who the person is, the way the gift is given, and how it is accepted, has important implications for the diverse feelings that are aroused in the act of giving and receiving.

This is where *empathy* comes in. To give a gift graciously means putting oneself in the position of the recipient. To receive a gift graciously means the same, since in reacting with gratitude, one usually senses the donor's positive intention. Therefore, to understand the presence or absence of the emotion of gratitude, we must examine the interaction of those who give and those who receive, and the emotions involved in giving and receiving.

When the recipient senses that something is given for personal gain, gratitude is absent, muted, or ambivalent. In such a case the *personal meaning* is not that of an altruistic gift. If, for example, the donor wants to feel self-important or to expiate guilt, the gift may be accepted without gratitude, the gratitude may be grudging, or the gift may be refused. The gift may also be refused if it implies an unwanted obligation in the future, which in Japan is referred to as an "on" (pronounced as *own*). If the gift is accepted under these conditions, it could easily generate resentment, anxiety, or shame rather than gratitude.

Even when people who provide the gift are only doing their job, as in the case of a nurse, physician, or public employee, if what is done is viewed as going above and beyond the call of duty, the recipient will usually feel grateful. Extra care and thoughtfulness in doing the job is seen as an altruistic gift. This was the way John appraised his professor's decision, which must have cost the professor money he might have used for himself. The decision also had the good outcome of increasing John's loyalty and diligence as a worker, as well as increasing the odds that he would be able to finish his education.

The primary basis for feeling grateful is that one is needy and another person voluntarily helps to supply what is needed. The neediness may involve lack of money, housing, food, attention and affection, or care when we are handicapped or ill. One might assume that the more needy we are the more we are likely to experience the feeling of gratitude. However, the reverse is often true, especially when we believe that our neediness is unjust or a source of shame, in which case the gift may be resented.

Individual differences in outlook are important in gratitude. For example, John did not resent his financial neediness—in those days of the Great Depression it seemed as though almost everyone was poor—and he was able to feel grateful for the kind consideration of his professor. Others might resent their poverty; they blame society, and people who are well-to-do are, therefore, objects of envy. Many regard what is done for them as the right of an exploited victim, and so experience no gratitude.

Needing help is, for many people, a psychological problem, especially in our individualistic society. Not being able to take care of oneself or being a burden to others is painful and damaging to the ego. We admire people who get along on their own and fulfill useful roles in society, and there is a special stigma that attaches to anyone who must take from others.

The values and patterns of action in giving and receiving are quite different. When people give willingly, they usually feel good about it and expect their generosity will be welcome and appreciated. Yet recipients often feel that gifts are given without sufficient sensitivity to their feelings. They may be expected to feel grateful, which—for some—is an unpleasant demand. When donors make a big show of their generosity, recipients are apt to feel patronized. In spite of good intentions, the way assistance is provided may be clumsy and hurtful, leading to tensions that may be poorly understood by people who give.

A good example of donor-recipient problems comes from observations of the ways people provide social support to others, and the psychological effects of this support. As we said, support can be *material, informational,* or *emotional,* such as trying to make a needy person feel worthy and cared about.[2] Of these, emotional support may be the most important and potentially troubling. Spouses and friends often try to give emotional support to a mate or friend who is under stress as a result of illness or personal loss. However, what is intended as emotional support is often poorly crafted and not supportive at all, and as a result the recipient feels worse rather than better.

What are some of the good and bad things people say and do in trying to be supportive when another person has, say, a life-threatening illness? A common reaction is to try to give verbal encouragement that the ill person will recover. Coming from someone who would have no professional grounds for knowing how things will turn out, this is not likely to be helpful and could even be annoying. Imagine also a friend who expresses the common platitude that the ill person should live one day at a time. This statement is not apt to be appreciated; it relegates the ill person to the tragic status of having a terminal illness, and the advice is easier said than done.

Consider also the common statement to someone who is gravely ill, "I know how you feel," which is intended as an expression of caring and sympathy. How could people who have not had the experience know what it feels like to be dying or to have lost someone you love! The actual message in this statement—usually not lost on the sufferer—seems to trivialize the victim's plight.

Much better than either of these well-intended but nonsupportive statements would be merely to listen and be concerned, or to express sorrow about the other person's trouble. To indicate merely that you would be happy to be of some help if needed ("Can I do something to help?") would also be welcome. The recipient will feel grateful for the offer when it seems sincere, is given without unreasonable demands or reservations, and is sensitive to the needs of the person. Here again, appropriate manifestation of empathy for the thoughts and feelings of the person in trouble is the key ingredient in providing useful emotional support, for which gratitude is much deserved.

The quality of emotional support was explored many years ago in a fascinating study of male graduate students facing a crucial oral examination after having invested several years seeking an advanced degree.[3] In many of these cases, their wives would often try to ease the students' distress about the upcoming exam by giving reassurances. One wife said, for example, "There is really nothing to worry about. You have taken exams before and done well. I expect you to pass with flying colors."

Some readers will instantly sense what is wrong with this well-intentioned effort to give emotional support. Why does this statement fail to be supportive and not lead to feelings of gratitude on the part of the student husband? In the first place, the student's legitimate concern has been denied by the wife whose statement challenges the legitimacy of his feeling that his ambitions are in jeopardy. Any student who is addressed in this way is apt to feel misunderstood and undermined, leaving him to struggle alone with the threat he perceives despite the attempt at reassurance.

In the second place, the attempted reassurance, which expresses the expectation that he will do well, actually has the opposite effect. It adds even more pressure to do well in a situation already interpreted as threatening, making the recipient feel more rather than less anxious.

One of the worst things teachers can say to a student who is uneasy about an upcoming exam is that they are confident the student will do well. Although the positive expectation is a compliment, even able students—who may truly believe that the teacher has misjudged them—are apt to fear that their inadequacy will be demonstrated on the exam, and that the mentor's positive regard will turn to disappointment and embarrassment. Even successful people feel that they have been lucky and that their vaunted abilities have been greatly overestimated.

It would be emotionally more supportive for teachers to say that they will continue to hold the student in high regard regardless of how the exam turns out. One great teacher we know personally often tells students that she didn't take exams very seriously since she has found that outstanding students often do poorly and mediocre students often do well. This is, indeed, frequently true. In the light of statements like this, though there may still be plenty of pressure, the students need not be so anxious that they will lose the teacher's respect if they do badly. Instead of adding to it, this teacher's statement relieves some of the pressure.

Consider what a student's wife (or husband) could say that would be helpful in the same situation. She might say, for example, "I am worried too. However, we have always managed before, and if things don't go well, we can certainly manage again. Just do the best you can." This is a wonderfully perceptive and supportive statement. It acknowledges and accepts as reasonable the spouse's anxiety. But it also offers effective reassurance that failure would not be an unmitigated disaster, because the couple can work together to meet the crisis. The message to do your best does not produce the added pressure of positive expectations.

Despite good intentions, the student whose wife said not to worry might well feel resentful rather than grateful at the failure of understanding and the added pressure created by the spouse. The student whose wife, on the other hand, said to do the best he could might well feel grateful for her valuable gift of sensitivity and understanding, which goes beyond what is expected.

Thus we may generate negative reactions if we have not learned how to give emotional support effectively. In addition to these problems of giving, recipients themselves may have personality traits that undermine gratitude or predispose them to resent the harsh conditions of their lives and their need for help. And some people have great difficulty accepting *any* help without resentment because they feel it demeans them. Being able to accept help, like being able to give it graciously, is an important interpersonal skill, which is learned. It too, like giving, involves *coping* with the stresses of being in need.

So we see that giving and receiving, in reality, are far more complicated social interactions than meet the eye. Both are more difficult to do effectively and graciously than is ordinarily supposed. The emotion of gratitude depends on the way the donor gives the gift, and how the recipient appraises it, which provides the personal meaning that both those who give and those who receive attach to the gesture.

Compassion

Like gratitude, compassion is a complex and uniquely human emotion. Here is a short vignette about a person who feels too much compassion in her job.

Judith felt nursing was her calling since she had always wanted to ease others' suffering. Nursing seemed ideal to her. When she finished her training, she became a hospital nurse in a children's cancer ward. At first, she was an efficient and popular nurse, greatly valued by parents and children alike.

But as a few years wore on, Judith became increasingly distressed by what she regularly saw—young children dying of terminal cancer, suffering from their treatments, and parents in emotional distress. And yet many children also benefited greatly from the treatments and were able to leave the hospital. For Judith, however, that was not enough. What began to distress her inordinately were the frequent cases of young boys and girls for whom there was no hope. Often their stoic or positive outlook in the face of a desperate medical condition made her cry bitterly.

She could no longer manage to distance herself from the parents' distress or that of the children, which is a method of *coping* that most successful nurses adopt. Unlike nurses who were able to forget about the suffering when they left the ward, Judith kept reliving all this pathos when she was at dinner, reading, and especially when she would wake up in the middle of the night. She began to lie awake for hours reliving the distress of the day. She began to get irritable and cross with the very patients and families toward whom she had earlier been solicitous, and to do her job poorly. Other nurses told her that she had become too involved in the patients' tragedies.

She suffered greatly from anxiety and depression, had increasing symptoms of intestinal colitis, was unable to enjoy herself, and began to think she was not cut out to be a nurse after all. She was suffering from what is often called *burnout*. Feeling totally defeated, she sought professional help and decided after a number of visits to the therapist that after two years of this work she should quit nursing and find another job.

Judith ultimately found work in a bank and advanced to the position of a vice-president in charge of loans. Even at this job, from time to time she had to steel herself when refusing a loan that was badly needed. But coping seemed easier in a bank because she was not continually exposed to the person being turned down, unlike the hospital where she had gotten to know the children and their families intimately.

Psychological Analysis

The *personal meaning* of compassion in Judith's case is to suffer for another person in misery and be committed to help. What distinguishes her experience from ordinary compassion is her intense suffering. Most of us who are capable of compassion recognize that we must not allow ourselves to wallow in other people's misery or, alternatively, to avoid them if we cannot keep our emotions in check. Most of us know we cannot help those suffering by becoming emotionally ill ourselves. So we learn to cope with the excesses of compassion by distancing ourselves enough so we are not as greatly distressed. Only now and then, perhaps when we are taken by surprise or when another's suffering is too close to our own, are we unable to control our emotional reaction. Judith is unable to gain sufficient distance to feel compassion without too fully sharing the other's misery.

In all likelihood, the defining experience that led to this trait was her mother's slow death from a painful cancer when she was eight. She was protected from the worst of the distress by her father, who managed to ship her off much of the time. She was also not very fond of her mother, which added an important complication to the tragedy.

Because she was able to avoid much of what was happening as a result of her father's protection, and also because she did not feel much empathy for her mother, she failed to react as strongly as she might have. Since she knew what was happening, she experienced considerable guilt over her own indifference. This led her to overlook how vulnerable she was to empathic distress when she made the decision to go into nursing.

Guilt seems focal here and gives us the main clue to understanding her excessive reactions. Guilt over her handling of her mother's tragedy had been repressed. Facing the person who was suffering, which she seldom did in the case of her mother, was terribly difficult for her. We think she felt compelled to suffer as the other person does as a way of denying her indifference to her mother's suffering and the guilt feelings it generated.

Although Judith had evidently chosen the wrong field, when she discovered her vulnerability, she wisely coped with the problem by leaving nursing. The need to share the suffering of others should be less evident in an occupation that doesn't remind her of her mother's suffering and her childhood guilt about her indifference to it.

The Many Faces of Compassion

There are several common words with meanings similar to compassion— for example, sympathy, pity, and empathy—but each has a slightly different emphasis. Sympathy is sometimes defined as being in tune with another person, as in the Spanish word *simpatico*. Mostly, however, we think of sympathy as feeling compassion. Pity is also considered a synonym of compassion, but to many it connotes a more condescending or disdainful attitude in which suffering persons are regarded as inferior, perhaps even responsible for their plight. In pity, one holds oneself apart from the afflicted person. Sometimes we even say "I pity you" in anger.

Another synonym of compassion, *empathy*, takes on a special meaning. In empathy one is said to experience the same emotion as another person, whatever it may be. Empathy is, in effect, not a single emotion whose characteristics are always the same, but any of a number of positive or negative emotions, depending on what the other person feels. In empathy, we copy another person's emotion, so to speak. We imagine ourselves being in their shoes.

Although it is not an emotion, empathy is a very important human capacity on which compassion is based. It begins to display itself in childhood and requires the ability to identify with others and sense their plight. Only if we can put ourselves in another's shoes can we relate to them fully and display our humanity toward them. When we watch the happiness or suffering of people in a play or a movie, we imagine ourselves in their situation and experience some measure of what they feel. This uniquely human tendency is one of the primary mechanisms for understanding others and being able to appreciate their experience.

Unlike empathy, in which we relate to another's emotion, compassion is a single emotional state, which we ourselves generate and experience. Although we can feel compassion, because we are capable of identifying and empathizing, feeling compassion is our own state of mind, not merely a copy of the emotion of another person.

The *personal meaning* of compassion is that one understands that another human being, like oneself, is suffering and deserves help. The provocation is the sight of such a person and the awareness of that person's plight and distress. Compassion may be made more likely and more intense by having had similar experiences of suffering ourselves, which leads us more readily to understand and appraise the problems of others compassionately. The dramatic plot for compassion is *being moved to distress by another person's suffering, and wanting to help*.

Earlier we said that emotions always require a personal *goal*, which is either facilitated or frustrated by our relationship with others. Is there a goal in compassion? In the case of loved ones in trouble, we needn't look far to find it. Since we love them, we are committed to their well-being. Our goal is to see them secure and happy. We are distressed when things go badly for them.

The case of strangers, however, is more complicated. We have already spoken of the wish for an orderly and just world in our discussion of anxiety, and this wish (goal or need) is also relevant to compassion. If people suffer needlessly, the idea of justice is violated. A related goal is the hope that, if we ourselves get into trouble, someone will be there to help. Those who doubt that people are ever altruistic sometimes cite enlightened self-interest as the explanation for proverbial Good Samaritans. There but for the grace of God go I.

The capacity for empathy—and the resulting feeling of compassion—seems to be a natural, widespread, though not universal, human trait. In fact, we speak of a person who has no conscience or empathy for others as a sociopath. Yet the absence of compassion under certain circumstances suggests that the capacity for it can apparently be easily overridden.

One process that helps us override the tendency to feel compassion is our ability to distance ourselves emotionally from someone who is suffering. One way to achieve emotional distance is by dehumanizing others (see Chapter 8). We say, for example, that the poor are lazy, the enemy is sly and cruel—more animal than human. If we can view them in this way, we don't have to feel compassion for their suffering. How else could we go to war so easily and drop deadly bombs to kill others when it is not always clear that they are enemies? Why do some people enjoy torturing others and take pleasure from their suffering? Like other desirable human traits, compassion appears to be a delicate flower that is easily withered by harsh conditions of living, training, and the extraordinary human capacity to overlook or rationalize evil.

Individuals vary greatly in the extent to which they feel and display compassion. Some people, like Judith, are overwhelmed by compassion. We have already interpreted her particular vulnerability as repressed guilt over her indifference to her mother's suffering while dying. In any event, for persons like Judith, suffering is intolerable and intensely distressing.

Others are able to steel themselves against the feeling. Compassion is probably most helpful to others when the person who feels it is not overwhelmed by the emotion, yet not too cold and distant. To be compassionate, and at the same time helpful, requires both considerable sensitivity and self-control.

When nurses and doctors take professional responsibility for sick people, in order to avoid being too greatly caught up in their suffering they must cultivate an emotionally distanced outlook toward their patients. When operating, surgeons center their attention on tissues and organs as objects, not as persons with feelings. Perhaps that is why surgeons are so often distant and unconcerned about the patient before and after surgery. How else could they cut people up to cure them of disease? How else could nurses be able to tolerate the pain and suffering of those they are caring for? How else could paramedics and other emergency teams come to the aid of mangled and bleeding people without inordinate distress of their own? To do so, they must achieve a degree of emotional distance from the suffering they must deal with as a routine feature of their jobs. Sometimes they have to work hard to achieve sufficient emotional distance to do their jobs.

Imagine yourself a rescue worker during the Loma Prieta earthquake disaster in Oakland, California, which occurred on October 17, 1989. A little less than a mile of the Cypress Street viaduct of the Interstate 880 Freeway collapsed at rush hour, killing and burying 42 people and injuring 108. A careful study using detailed interviews was made of the experience of 47 male workers charged with cleaning up the mess, which included recovering bodies from their cars.[4] These interviews illustrate some of the sources of distress and the ways the men coped with the traumatizing sights and smells they had to tolerate. One worker described an attempt to reassure himself that the victims died without suffering. The interview provides an intimate picture of the struggle to cope.

> We pulled other bodies out that night. . . . Looking at it, trying to analyze it in my mind, it was easy to see, again, trying to make myself comfortable with it from the standpoint that he died on impact, he died quick. He probably saw it coming, but he died awful quick. The woman, I always had some grave reservations as to whether or not she died right away. Again, in the back of my mind, it bothered me that if these people didn't die right away, at the time I remember thinking, my God, should we have gotten to them quicker, could we have saved their lives?
>
> She was positioned in the seat almost as if she rebounded that way, fine. If she didn't rebound in it, she was kind of turned sideways looking toward the driver. So I really had a gut feeling, my God, she didn't die right away, she was still conscious and she was trying to talk to her boyfriend, husband, brother, whoever the guy was, and yet you know he died right away because nobody could take a chest blow like that and take out the entire steering column and live through it. So that bothered me for a long time. I'm better with it now.

The psychological problem for the workers was often compounded by the awful smell of decay, the torn bodies, and the need sometimes to cut off body parts to free the victims from their mangled auto tombs. Although the smell in itself was terrible, we think that the most important threat it carried for the men had to do with what it meant to view bodies—their own bodies in a very real sense—decomposing after death. We are normally prevented from being conscious of this decomposition, and all it seems to suggest about death, by our traditions of embalming and cremation. The body viewed in a funeral is made to seem as pleasantly lifelike and presentable as possible. Orthodox Jews, who do not embalm or cremate, bury their dead very quickly. Although the worker quoted below is talking mainly about the awful smell of the decomposing bodies, we suggest that it was this terrible *personal meaning* about the nature of death that he is really reacting to.

> Decaying flesh really stinks, especially when at this point it had probably been more than ten days. It was a really obnoxious smell, just terrible. We put Vicks inside of our nostrils to try and disguise it, and that helped to a certain extent. But basically, it was just something that had to be done, you just get in and do it. I talked to some of the fire rescue guys . . . about the smell and they taught me a trick (now I understand why most firemen have mustaches). They would take Vicks vaporub and rub it in the mustache, and so I always made sure I was around someone who had Vicks.
>
> The smell in there was really bad. Well, we both started gagging. Then, for some reason, when we started gagging, we just started laughing. I laughed, and then Marshall laughed, and we laughed for probably 15 or 20 minutes. We were sitting there in this van laughing away, it is just echoing forever, and there's people down below. I really think that's when people thought that I was really going nuts. They really thought that I had just flipped my lid.

Two more illustrations highlight emotional *distancing* as a successful form of coping. One worker described the experience of handling body remains as follows.

> The tools were really primitive and it was really hard. Here you're up to your elbows in somebody's intestines and you're cutting through a spinal column, and that's not a very easy job. Flesh is flopping all over you and that's gross. That is really gross, and all you can think is that you're doing this and your job is to do it perfect—to get this body out, that loved one, or the mother who has passed away. I think a lot of guys thought that— we all thought that and feel that way now.
>
> We had to decapitate him and drag him out of there. . . . It seemed to me as though it wasn't real. It's like you were just in there working, and it didn't seem like this was happening. We just continued to do that for the rest of the four days, that type of work. I was in my own realm of thoughts. I really didn't pay attention. I had my own job to do and I wasn't really paying attention to what was going on.

Another worker provided the following classic example of emotional *distancing*, speaking about the bodies as if he were a medical scientist, which he was not. Notice his frequent use of the emotionally detached term interesting.

A body's a body. Some of them are more gruesome than others. Some were very interesting to look at from a medical standpoint, from my job standpoint. You know, this is a quite interesting job that has its morbid side, but the scientific reason that we're here to look at is what really caused this person to die and that is very interesting.

You can almost palpably feel these men struggling not to become overwhelmed by distress over the suffering of the victims of this tragedy, and by the realization that what happened could happen to them. The most common method of coping with this problem, which stems from empathy leading to compassion run amok, is to keep sufficient emotional distance. This is what the workers are trying to do in these real-life illustrations.

Emotions Aroused by Aesthetic Experiences

Most people react emotionally to movies, staged dramas—including operas—paintings, sculpture, music, scientific discoveries, the sights and sounds of natural scenes such as sunsets and northern lights, toward which they feel awe or wonder, which can be likened to religious experiences. How aesthetic experiences arouse emotions is a fascinating question.

For emotions to be aroused, people must be actively engaged in sensing the meaning of what is presented to them. We make an effort to relate to the content of paintings, music, drama, movies, and consciously look for the meaning in these art forms. In a drama or movie, for example, we look for the plot, try to make sense of the motive, the implications of what is happening for each of the characters portrayed, and so on. We seem to enjoy this process, and there is no question that the most moving of these stories reveal the main sources of human suffering and joy.

As with empathy, there is no single or unique aesthetic emotion. Aesthetic experiences can arouse any one of the fifteen emotions discussed in this book. The emotion, whether anger, anxiety, hope, sadness, joy, or whatever, depends on the personal meaning of the event depicted. Because there is no single emotion aroused by an aesthetic experience, we offer no detailed case example, exploring instead some illustrations of aesthetic experiences to point out their uniquely human quality.

Let us see how emotions are aroused for each of three main varieties of aesthetic experience, namely, movies and drama, music, and art. We begin with movies and drama because they are the simplest for most of us to relate to. Moreover, we can more easily understand how they arouse emotions compared with other aesthetic experiences.

Emotion in Movies and Drama

Narrative stories of human events—told to or enacted in front of an audience—have no doubt moved people from the very beginnings of human history. Modern movies and TV stories of tragedies and comedies do essentially the same thing. We watch other persons, usually while in a theater or the comfort of our home, struggling with success and failure, loss, conflict, tragedy and triumph.

The plots of theatrical dramas cover the entire range of human emotions and the situations that bring them about. The characters are those we recognize from our own lives—some are weak, others strong, venal, loving and lovable; still others hateful and detestable, heroic, foolish, or comic.

Depending on the story, the audience displays its emotional involvement by becoming absorbed in the characters' actions. If members of the audience are not moved, they would leave, or become bored and inattentive. We see and hear the audience applauding, raging against the characters portrayed, laughing, crying, or silently experiencing happiness or distress. Only when the plot fails to touch the audience is emotion absent. This means that to be popular with audiences a play must portray real-life themes that are personally meaningful to the audience and must generate emotions through one or more of the dramatic emotional plots we have already described.

When a play moves us, the playwright has shown a keen understanding of people and the emotions being portrayed. Playwrights must also be skillful in constructing a plot that has the maximum power to move us. This is not to say that everyone in the audience is equally moved or is necessarily experiencing the same emotions. Each of us has somewhat different personal agendas. But successful movies and dramas usually arouse emotions that are shared by a large portion of the audience.

As we said, the capacity to put ourselves in the shoes of others and to feel what they are feeling—which we call empathy—is a human psychological characteristic, which moviemakers and dramatists take advantage of in arousing emotions. To capitalize on this capacity in drama calls for knowing a great deal about how social relationships work.

Here again we see the principle that *personal meaning* underlies every emotion. What happens in a movie or play touches something in us as we sit in the theater amid the audience whose presence and behavior further potentiates what we feel. It is not just what the people on the stage are experiencing that involves us in the story. What is portrayed must fit our personal circumstances in some way; we must in some respects be like the people being portrayed on stage. If their plight were not like our own, we would not react.

The playwright draws on our fears, wishes, and vulnerabilities. If the playwright is skillful, we get to know each of the characters intimately, their desires, frustrations, troubled history, and the tragic mistakes and flaws that have gotten them into the trouble they are in. We understand them. We all have our favorite plots, which reflect particular features of our own personalities and life experiences.

It is as if we are the pained wife, the tragic husband-salesman, or one of the two troubled sons in Arthur Miller's wrenching play *Death of a Salesman*. The play is like a Greek tragedy in that it moves to its inexorable end as though what happened was foreordained by the gods and could not be changed. For readers who have never seen the play on the stage, or its several movie versions, allow us briefly to describe the plot.

A tired, burned out, aging salesman, Willie Loman, who has lived much of his life on the road, is no longer able to sell his product successfully. Times have changed and the son of an old friend has taken over the business. Willie has idolized one of his two sons, Biff, who was a football hero in high school. In doing so he seems to want to live his own unsuccessful life through the boy. He keeps complaining that Biff is drifting without direction.

Biff, in turn, complains that his father has constructed a heroic image of him that is not accurate. Given the confusing messages from his father, he doesn't know who he is and how he fits into the world. He believes he has little talent, or as he puts it with pathos, "I'm just a dollar a day man." Biff's younger brother, Happy, tends to distance himself from this troubled relationship, is shallow and immature, interested only in a good time, and seems not to be much disturbed about what is happening to the other family members.

The wife of the salesman, and mother of these two sons, Linda, keeps trying to get them to be more concerned with the plight of their father, whom she sees as headed for suicide, and she has found concrete evidence of his intention. Alternately arrogant and pleading, Willie Loman has been ignominiously fired by the new owner of the business. She wants the boys to shape up, to help their father. But given their own confused and aimless lives, they are unable or unwilling to help. The wife and mother is anguished that her sons seem so lacking in compassion for their father, who has always done the best he could. She cries out to them in urgency and desperation "Attention must be paid."

During a flashback, Biff, in high school at this time, travels to Boston to talk to his father on one of his sales trips, but inadvertently interrupts an extramarital affair taking place in his father's hotel room. This is a disillusioning experience, which poisons him against his father whom he had earlier admired. The audience understands that this traumatic experience is a major reason for Biff's later demoralization and confusion. The play ends tragically with the suicide of the father, and with an emotional plea by the mother to her sons to give respect in death to this beaten but decent man.

When we watch the play—one of the greatest in American theater—we identify with the tragic father. We cringe watching him make a fool of himself as he lives in the past in his reveries, or when his impatient young boss demeans him. Or we are Biff, the son who is confused about who he is, who can't live up to his father's romanticized picture of him, and who is unable to pull himself together. Some might identify with Biff's brother, though his role is less critical to the story. And we are moved still differently if we identify with the salesman's wife, who watches with dread the agonizing march of her husband toward self-destruction and suffers with the sense of her helplessness in the face of the impending tragedy.

Whom we identify with depends on whether and how the character relates to the significant features of our own lives. The playwright's genius allows us to see ourselves and our loved ones as one or all of these characters. How real the events seem to be depends on the match between the plot and our own experience, as well as on how effectively the people and their problems are portrayed. Poor writing, plotting, characterization, and acting serve to weaken the emotional impact. Though only a story, imagined by an author and acted by people we do not know personally, it can transport us into what seems like a real world that has intimate personal meaning.

It is not that we have necessarily had the particular experiences portrayed in the drama, but that the experiences and relationships of the actors provide close analogies to our own troubling experiences and life concerns. We don't have to be a salesman to identify with Willie Loman, or a wife or mother to identify with Willie's wife. The play creates life themes we understand, and we react to what is happening as real and experience the suffering of the characters as if it were our own.

In all likelihood the intensity of the emotions we experience in viewing plays and movies is weaker than it is in the comparable events of our own lives.[5] If this were not so, our distress might be too great for us to enjoy the play, and we would rapidly burn ourselves out with the heat of emotion. However, we usually know that we are in the safety of a theater rather than actually living the events being depicted in the play, which is an important reason why our emotional reactions to drama do not get out of hand. When we finally get up to leave, perhaps choked up, tearful, or holding back tears, we soon will rejoin the world of our actual lives as we walk up the theater aisle to make our way home.

Emotion in Music

Musicologists and psychologists recognize that music generates emotions, though how it does so is not clear. Although much oversimplified, we could say that cheerful musical themes seem to arise in part from a fast tempo, light melodic sequences, and chords in the major keys—as in the waltzes of Johann Strauss. Sad and troubled musical themes seem to arise from a slow tempo, ponderous musical sequences, and chords in minor and diminished keys. To our knowledge, with rare exceptions,[6] no one has ever tried systematically to measure the emotions produced by music, or to systematically relate musical structure to the emotions.

The musical backgrounds of movies are designed to follow the plot and enhance the emotions elicited by the action. For example, the background music is designed to be ominous for a movie with a plot that focuses on horror or dread, triumphant for a movie about a military victory, airy and light for a comedy. This suggests that the composer understands intuitively how to orchestrate these moods, even if the principles involved are not identified to a scientist's satisfaction.

One theory about why music arouses emotion states essentially that this is the way humans are designed neurologically, but how this actually works is obscure. When we listen to music, we are said to feel uneasy, happy, angry, or sad on the basis of how our nervous system reacts to the particular patterns of sound. From this standpoint, no learning is involved; it is the way our species is constructed.

An opposite theory is that we learn the emotional meanings from what the music has been associated with in our past. Asian music is not readily comprehensible to Western ears, and vice versa, without special training. When we hear musical patterns that have been connected previously to experiences of anger, anxiety, sadness, or joy, we feel these emotions. It is simply a matter of conditioning.

The problem of how music conveys emotion is more complicated when music and drama are combined, as they are in opera. We can be deeply moved by the aria in Leoncavallo's opera *Pagliacci*, in which a clown sings tragically about his wife Nedda's real-life infidelity—the same infidelity experienced by the character he is himself playing. But are we moved because of the story of his pain, which is emotionally powerful even without the music, or are we reacting to the pathos conveyed in the melody and in his voice?

It is undoubtedly *both* the story and the music that are complementary. They combine to provide the fullest emotional impact. In the most emotional aria of the opera, "Ridi Pagliaccio," translated as "Laugh clown," Pagliacci sings that he must play the comic part of the clown while his heart is breaking. Caruso's voice always broke at the same point in the aria, which effectively expressed his heartbreak and was as affecting emotionally to the audience as if he had shed tears. Yet the long period at the end of the aria without singing also seems to have great emotional power.

Composers of great opera capture the emotions of the audience in their musical dramas, just as playwrights do. How this works is a profound question, for which our answers seem inadequate. In any case, as Pagliacci grows more frantic in real life about the infidelity of his wife, and more threatening to her, the anxiety of the audience over the impending tragedy mounts, and ultimately the fright of Nedda before she is slain is palpable.

Imagine yourself as the actor who is certain his wife has been unfaithful, and you believe your wife and her lover are going to run off together. If you are strongly moved, it is likely to be because something in your own life corresponds to what you are seeing and hearing—say, a previous experience of loss or infidelity, anxiety about that possibility, or knowing enough about classic human conflicts to imagine yourself in one.

If you think of movies or plays that have strongly moved you, you might try out this type of analysis on your own theatrical experience. Just ask yourself with whom you identify and why. What are the emotions you experience? How does the plot conform to your own life and the conflicts you are concerned with? You may find themes that point up sources of vulnerability that you can acknowledge in yourself and learn from.

Emotion and Art

We are also moved by the personal meanings conveyed in the content of representational paintings and sculpture. If you examine, for example, Francisco Goya's famous painting *The Third of May*, which portrays an execution during the Napoleonic wars, to experience it emotionally, you must take your time to involve yourself in it and assimilate the personal meaning of what is happening. What the attentive viewer sees is the final, hopeless gesture of the white-shirted victim in the foreground with arms outstretched, glaring at the faceless firing squad. As historian Kenneth Clark puts it, "his death is absurd, and he knows it."[7] The emotions one may experience in viewing the painting might include despairing anger aroused by evil, dread, anxiety, and compassion, as well as joy over the splendid artistry of the painter.

The personal meanings conveyed by nonrepresentational or abstract paintings and sculpture are not usually obvious to those who view them, and one cannot be confident about their emotional significance. If they do arouse emotions in a significant number of people, it must be because of the symbolic meanings they convey, which are unconscious or barely sensed. Some are merely amusing and cheerful designs that delight viewers. Some use color as their primary means of conveying meanings and moods.

Psychoanalyst Carl Jung[8]—originally a disciple of Freud—proposed that symbols carry universal meanings we are not aware of but that nevertheless influence our emotions. Some of the most obvious examples are the egg, which often is used to symbolize spring or beginnings; ancient statues of women with large breasts, pelvises, and abdomens, which connote the erotic and procreative functions they signify; doors and gates as symbols of the vagina; men and women dining as a symbol of sexual intercourse; and swords, guns, and pens as symbols of male sexuality or aggression.

Today, however, psychologists are more inclined to assume that the meanings of symbols vary somewhat with the individual rather than being universal. For Freud, dreams can reveal our highly personal landscape of symbols, and in psychoanalysis one can gain access to these meanings through free association with the help of a trained therapist (see Chapter 13 for a discussion of the techniques of psychotherapy). In any case, to understand the emotions that might flow from nonrepresentational art, we need to examine the deeper and relatively inaccessible features of our minds.

We have not treated mental states like awe and wonder as emotions, because these terms have more than one meaning and, quite frankly, we are not quite sure how to deal with them. Awe may involve dread or have the positive connotation of wonder and joy over discoveries about the world, its vastness, or the remarkable gifts of life and intelligence. These states, which certainly seem to be emotional, may be blends of other emotions. The words for them also have spiritual connotations.

Imagine, for example, what the scientist might have felt who first peered into a microscope and observed never-before-seen microbes swimming in a spoonful of water. Could anyone remain detached at such an observation, one that forever changed our ideas about nature and life?

In viewing what the artist portrays, or an impressive natural sight, we feel awe, wonder, a sense of mystery, dread about death and the unknown, peacefulness, or a sense of spiritual belonging that could contribute to faith and trust. These emotional reactions remain at the frontier of our understanding of the human mind.

What is particularly striking about the emotions of aesthetic experiences is that, as with all other emotions, the *personal meanings* we construct from these experiences arouse emotion, and doing this comes naturally to us all. They are the same particular meanings that arouse each of the particular emotions we have been exploring in the last five chapters.

Given their importance and emotional power, it is remarkable that so little scientific attention has been paid to aesthetic experience as a source of emotion in our lives. Their capacity to move us is undoubtedly the reason why artistic creations—the Greek and Shakespearean tragedies, the plays and movies of modern times, the paintings and sculpture of the Italian Renaissance, and the music of the classical period—have played such an important role in human affairs. They provoke emotions, which are perennial in human experience. The details of plot and character may change, but the emotions these works elicit are what make them endure in human society.

II

HOW TO UNDERSTAND
THE EMOTIONS

7

The Nuts and Bolts of Emotion

Now that we have looked at the unique plot of each emotion, we turn to a discussion of what these emotions all have in common—the nuts and bolts, so to speak. We have seen how personal meaning, which is constructed by us, shapes the emotion we will experience. Far from being irrational, we have seen how the emotions follow from the thought processes of intelligent beings. What is no doubt now apparent is that emotion and thought are inseparable in humans. How this works, psychologically, is what this chapter is all about.

The Nuts and Bolts

The nuts and bolts of emotion consist of six psychological ingredients. These include: (1) the fate of personal goals; (2) self or ego; (3) appraisals; (4) personal meanings; (5) provocations; and (6) action tendencies. We discuss each in turn. Coping can be regarded as a seventh ingredient. However, because it is unique and so important in human adaptation, we have reserved the next chapter exclusively for it.

The Fate of Personal Goals: What Motivates an Emotion?

Not all aspects of living involve emotion. We can prepare breakfast, walk the dog, drive to work, stop at a restaurant for lunch, take our children to school, chat with colleagues and friends, watch television, and so on, without any perceptible or appreciable emotion. We are, of course, modestly mobilized in order to engage in these actions, and we must have some sort of vague plan.

But these actions are largely uninvolving, though perhaps pleasant and comfortable. They do not, per se, involve emotion. It has sometimes been argued that we are always emotional, if only mildly; however, for the most part, much of our routine experience is without significant emotion. What is crucial to the arousal of an emotion is that there is a goal at stake. Stated differently, in emotional situations we are motivated to gain something or prevent something unwanted from happening, which is not the case in nonemotional situations.

Two motivational factors are necessary to arouse an emotion. First, an event must transform a routine encounter into one that involves personal harm or benefit. In other words, an emotional encounter touches on something that we want or don't want to happen. We are keen to attain a goal and the other person in an encounter either facilitates, threatens, or frustrates the attainment. The more important the goal—that is, the more we want something to happen or not to happen—the stronger the emotion will be. Without a significant goal at stake, an encounter with another person or the physical environment will not be emotional.

Second, the way we *judge* the fate of the goal, whether actual or potential, determines whether the emotion will be positive (for a benefit) or negative (for a harm).

Together these two factors combine to make an encounter emotional and determine whether we will feel positive or negative about what is happening. If you think back over the case examples given in Chapters 2 to 6, you will see that the emotions experienced occurred when there was a personal goal at stake, and something happened either to thwart or facilitate attaining that goal.

The angry wife in the marital argument wanted to gain more attention from her husband and was offended by his seeming disinterest. The young therapist who had an anxiety attack wanted to be perceived as competent and in control, but was threatened by the appearance in the therapy group of a patient with a problem like his own. The depressed widow needed some hope that she could recover old meanings and gain new ones after the death of her husband, which would allow her to reinvest in living. The man who was a victim of unrequited love wanted to be loved in return by the woman he set his sights on. The woman who thought her calling was to be a nurse found she couldn't control her distress at the suffering she saw, and had to give up nursing. And so on for each of the emotions.

Now see what happens to some of the routine encounters we mentioned earlier. Preparing breakfast takes on negative emotional significance if we consider doing it an onerous chore. Perhaps we think our spouse, or an unemployed adolescent who still lives with us, should be responsible for it. If our goal is not to be required to fix breakfast, then we are apt to feel distressed about having to do it.

For others with a different pattern of goals, there may be great satisfaction and even happiness in putting the meal together. Imagine, for example, an aging mother who has always felt good about fixing breakfast for her children and husband, but now the children have families of their own and the husband does not eat breakfast. The occasional opportunity to do this again makes her feel useful and gives her joy.

Or to take another example, going to a restaurant for lunch can make us feel happy when it releases us from boredom and onerous chores, which of course we want to avoid. But the normally pleasing stop at a restaurant brings on a negative emotion, such as anger, if we are given a badly located table and think we should insist on a better one. If we are too shy to do so, the conflict between wanting to say something and wanting to avoid being conspicuous or subject to criticism could generate anxiety or shame. What should have been a pleasantly trivial event takes on the added emotional freight of how badly we are being treated and what this implies about our social status.

The routine drive to work makes us anxious when we have an important appointment and get caught in a traffic jam without having left enough time. The goal that is blocked in this situation is to arrive promptly to pursue the important business at hand. But if we have left home at our normal time and have no appointments booked for the morning, we take our time and get to work as usual without any particular emotion. And if we left early and there is a traffic jam, it probably will not bother us because we have no reason to be in a hurry.

In these instances, we can see that emotional distress occurs when the personal meaning of what is happening is changed by circumstances that lead to harm or benefit. A goal has been gratified, resulting in personal benefit, and we experience a positive emotion. Or a goal has been frustrated, and we experience a negative emotion. Emotions of all kinds flow from the fate of personal goals. So a routine, nonemotional activity becomes emotional because the personal meaning we now construct from what has happened has changed from being a routine event to a harm or a benefit, and we experience either a positive or negative emotion.

The Self or Ego

Another psychological ingredient in emotion is involvement of the self or ego, which is exemplified in the restaurant table scenario mentioned above. We all have the goal of protecting and enhancing our self or ego, so that when we are denigrated or dealt with well, we feel, accordingly, bad or good. In the restaurant, our self-esteem was deflated because we were treated less well than we thought we should by being given the last table near the kitchen.

The term *self* usually refers to the image we have of what we are like, the "me" part of our personhood. We all have some sort of picture of ourselves that, during development and throughout life, is influenced by the impressions others seem to have of us. For example, parents or teachers may have communicated to us that we are intellectually dull or bright, handsome or ugly, lazy or energetic, and so on, which then becomes a basis of our self-image.

Ego refers to the "I," which decides what to do and how to relate to the world, a sort of executive in charge of our affairs. An ego binds together the many, often contradictory, tendencies within us. It keeps us moving forward in our lives, in a more or less constant path rather than flying off in a dozen haphazard directions. It makes us a consistent, integrated person in our actions rather than being constantly or recurrently mixed up, distressed, and dysfunctional.

The terms self and ego are frequently used interchangeably. Here we sometimes refer to self or self-esteem when we quote or cite someone else who uses that term. For the most part, however, we use the terms ego, ego-identity, or identity, which are equivalent in meaning. They identify who we are and what our functional connections are with the social world.[1]

The famous philosopher-psychologist William James[2] used only the term self in his writings and made it a central aspect of his psychology:

> [The] personal self rather than thought might be treated as the immediate datum of psychology. The universal conscious fact is not that feelings and thoughts exist but I *think* and *feel*. No psychology, at any rate, can question the existence of personal selves. . . . The only states of consciousness that we naturally deal with are found in personal consciousness, minds, selves, concrete particular I's and you's.

An integrated, stable ego-identity is an important part of our psychological makeup, and it affects our emotional life. Adult emotions often arise because the goal of protecting and enhancing that ego-identity has been realized, as in pride, or frustrated, as in anger, guilt, and shame. We have only to remember from earlier chapters a few of the emotions to see how important our ego-identity is for the emotions we experience.

We feel angry when our identity has been demeaned by another, as when we are insulted or taken as less of a person than we are or want to be. Again, being placed next to the kitchen in a restaurant reflects a denigrated position and makes us angry.

The most common reason for the response of jealousy is sexual infidelity, which we regard as personal treachery. In our culture, and a number of others, sexual infidelity is, above all, an assault on what we regard as a personal right or privilege. The impulse to retaliate murderously in the emotion of jealousy stems from a wounded ego. Think here of the jealousy of Othello.

Anxiety, on the other hand, is more subtle in comparison. We feel anxious when personal meanings about ourselves and the world—the core of our very psychological existence—are threatened. Think here of the student-therapist in Chapter 3 whose very definition of himself was as a knowledgeable and competent person, but who suddenly was confronted with an inability to remain in control of his therapy group. And so on for each of the other emotions that are aroused by unfavorable life conditions.

On the positive side, we feel pride when our ego-identity is enhanced by an accomplishment for which we are able to take credit. Think here of Mrs. Maccia and her son, the light of her life. Or we feel gratitude when someone makes a voluntary gift without denigrating our integrity in doing so. Recall the impoverished college student whose professor facilitated his career by giving him a generous paycheck. In the case of love we want to attain mutual positive regard from a partner in a relationship. In all these emotions, our egos are deeply involved.

Appraisal

Intelligent creatures perceive and comprehend the world around them. To survive and flourish they need to decide whether events are or are not significant for their well-being, and in what way. Without personal significance, there is no emotion. Appraisal is an evaluative judgment about this significance. It is the main process of reasoning on which emotions depend, the heart of the emotion process. We referred to it often in Chapters 2 to 6. Mammals, birds, and primates—including people—are constantly scanning the environment and themselves for clues about their well-being and what needs to be done to protect and advance it.

Appraisal draws on intelligence and depends on what we know about the way things work in the world. From infancy on, we learn about what is likely to happen when certain events occur and what might be done about them. All living creatures deal with threats to their integrity, whether from predators, disease, accidents, and, in the case of people, social relationships. They also deal with opportunities to flourish.

Humans can anticipate the future and plan for it. We grasp what is in our interests, and influence what we wish and do not wish to happen. And this capacity permits us to have exceedingly complex societies and social relationships—and rich emotional lives.

Appraisal consists of two main kinds of judgment: First, we must decide whether we have anything at stake in what is happening. A stake means that some goal has been engaged. In casino gambling, for example, money is usually the stake. If there is no stake, action to deal with what is happening is not called for and emotion will not be aroused. The situation is then irrelevant to our well-being—at least for the moment—and we remain uninvolved. If, however, there is a personal stake in the outcome, we are involved rather than disinterested, and emotion is aroused.

Second, if we have decided that a situation is important for our personal well-being, we must evaluate our options for doing something about it. What must be done? Will it work? Can we do what must be done? What are the consequences of different courses of action? Are they safe? Which one is best? Appraisal thus includes an evaluation of how we can cope with a problem.

If, for example, a fire awakens us while we are staying in a high-rise hotel, we must rapidly check the location of the nearest exit. We may have read the statement on the door of our room, which advises us about which way to go. Our heads may be chock full of warnings about what to do and not do in such an emergency—for example, take the staircase rather than elevator, open doors carefully, put a wet towel over our nose and mouth and crawl on the floor to help avoid smoke inhalation, and so forth.

Although we will probably be anxious or frightened—we can recall reading about disastrous fires and have appraised fires as dangerous—we will at least be ready to act appropriately. An appraisal—on which emotions depend—is often a complex judgment about how we are doing in an encounter with the environment and in our lives overall, and how to deal with potential harms and benefits.

Appraisal is not just passively receiving information about the environment. It must always actively *negotiate* between our personal agendas—that is, goals and beliefs—and the characteristics of the environment—for example, the kind of person with whom we are interacting. If we pay attention only to what we want, we will react in accordance with our desires, but get nowhere with them because we are out of touch with reality. If we pay attention only to the environmental demands, constraints, and resources, we will remain slaves to the external world and thwart our own desires. Either extreme gets us into trouble and leads to unnecessary distress and dysfunction.

In a complex world, this task of negotiating is by no means easy, and its effectiveness marks the difference between success and failure in any situation, and between an emotional life that is generally sound and one that deviates from reality. One reason this negotiation is difficult is that emotional situations are often ambiguous, leaving us uncertain about what to think, feel, and do. Another reason is that these situations are often so complex that we cannot pay attention to everything that might be relevant. So we have to be selective. But if we pay attention to the wrong things, we are apt to make bad decisions.

Uncertainty about what is happening, incidentally, is one of the main reasons people interpret what is happening in different ways. Because they have diverse goals and beliefs, there is not one reality but many. Here is an example of the same event that is appraised differently. Two women are sitting at a restaurant table and both notice that the husband of a friend is with a lovely young woman, engrossed in intimate conversation. What is going on is ambiguous. One construes the situation as a husband of the friend straying and gets angry. The other, who knows the family better, thinks she recognizes the woman as the husband's niece from out of town, and does not experience an emotion. Same event, two appraisals and two different emotional reactions.

It is not necessarily what is actually happening—that is, the objective reality—that influences our actions and reactions, but how we construe it. To quote Shakespeare in *Hamlet*: "For there is nothing either good or bad/ but thinking makes it so." And we are often told, with good reason, that beauty (or ugliness) is in the eye of the beholder.

Personal Meaning

Personal meaning, which is what arouses our emotions, is the product of an appraisal. The person-environment relationships that arouse emotions are most often those that take place with other people—for example, parents, children, siblings, lovers, friends, caretakers, bosses, subordinates, teachers, students, and competitors. This means that personal meanings are also *relational*—that is, they have to do with how relationships affect our well-being.

Particular people in our lives are tremendously important to us. We have committed ourselves to them or to their causes and, as such, their actions and reactions have great power to affect us. They can help us achieve what we want, but they can frustrate what we want too. In a marriage, for example, we react with many different emotions to the various events that take place in that relationship. The personal meaning keeps changing with the ways the partners act and react to each other and to the events with which they must deal. Think here of the anger of the couple who had a bitter argument at breakfast, but who ended up experiencing a sequence of guilt, anxiety, and feelings of love. Emotion arises from the meaning that each spouse derives from their interactions with each other.

Let us consider more closely what it means to say that emotion is, at bottom, a reaction to personal meaning, which refers to the changing consequences of a relationship. To react with an emotion, a goal we want must be joined with an act that is harmful or beneficial for its attainment. The same act will not upset all people, or affect them in the same way. An insult may be devastating to an individual who is desperate to be viewed favorably, but not bother others who don't care how they are regarded by the person who is insulting them, and who consider the insult as trivial or even laughable.

The personal significance of what is happening depends on the way the other person in the relationship acts. Our goals, and beliefs about ourself and the world, and the actions of the other person with whom we are having a relationship, combine to produce the personal meaning that arouses an emotion.

Let us say you love and want to be loved in return by another person who says something that offends you. If you believe that your inamorata is not expressing negative sentiments toward you that must be taken seriously, but is responding to the stress of an illness or a series of frustrations earlier in the day, the personal meaning is not one of an offense but merely an indication that the loved one needs forbearance and compassion. If you appraise the situation in this way, you do not feel hurt and angry, or you resist this feeling knowing that any retaliation for the offense would not be deserved. You may even sense—perhaps with a trace of guilt—that you might have helped to provoke your loved one's annoyance by being inconsiderate or insensitive.

On the other hand, some people are unable to take such a detached or compassionate view. Perhaps they are too vulnerable or the relationship has been troubled for a long time, in which case the personal meaning is that of an undeserved offense. You feel angry and have the urge to retaliate to restore your wounded ego. What you say to retaliate, however, may turn out to deeply injure the person you love, who begins to cry in distress. This instantly changes the personal meaning from a demeaning offense by the other to one in which *you* have acted badly. This change in meaning leads to guilt, and the original anger vanishes.

So you can see that personal meaning—and the emotions associated with it—keeps changing from moment to moment, situation to situation, and person to person, expressing the altered significance of what is happening. Personal meanings, which easily change with the flow of events, lie at the heart of every emotion and contribute to the fluidity of emotions.

A number of interesting research studies make the point that the meaning in an emotion that occurs in an encounter depends, in part, on what a person wants and believes, and in part on the nature of the situation. We illustrate this point with a classic study of the stress induced by a school examination. The researcher wanted to study how ulcers are produced as a result of the secretion of hydrochloric acid (HCL) in the stomach.[3] Seven male students at Yale University were trained to swallow a stomach tube to measure the HCL. The stomach-tubing test was first done in a benign, nonstressful period during the students' senior academic year, and then again on the day of a seemingly important exam just before graduation.

Five of the students showed large increases in HCL under the stress of the exam. Two students, surprisingly, showed no increase. Careful interviews were arranged with these students to clarify what had happened. It turned out that one of the two nonreacting students had been content to attain what in those days in Ivy League schools was called the "gentlemen's grade of C." This student didn't much care about his grade and was not made anxious by the exam. The other nonreacting student had already been accepted into the medical school of his choice; he too felt that the exam could not harm him.

What this research demonstrates is that, because of the personal goals of these two students and the special nature of their situation, the exam was not threatening for them but merely a pro-forma requirement for finishing school and graduating. All the other students were substantially anxious in connection with the exam, leading to substantial increases in stomach HCL.

You can also see from this why some people do not become anxious in situations in which others do. The personal meaning of the exam and thus the emotional reactions were different for these two students compared with the others as a result of their particular goals and beliefs. Two factors must be taken into account in appraising personal meaning—namely, personal characteristics, such as goals and beliefs, and the environmental situation in which individuals find themselves, such as the nature of the demands, constraints, and opportunities.

This brings us back to the central theme of this book—that each emotion has its own unique and dramatic plot, which reveals the personal meaning we bring, consciously or not. To understand each emotion—for example, anger, anxiety, happiness, pride, and so on—requires that we identify the dramatic plot in which we play a part. We discussed these plots and the emotions they arouse in detail in Chapters 2 to 6.

Provocation

We are now ready to look at the provocation of an emotion, which depends on the first four ingredients already described. A provocation simply refers to an event—involving either the physical or social environment—that is deemed personally significant by the individual who experiences it.

There are four types of provocation:

First, a real event results in a particular harm or benefit, or the expectation of one of these outcomes. When the harm has not yet happened but is expected, it is called threat. Examples include a remark that is taken as a personal or social insult and therefore results in anger; or a job interview that leads one to be hired and consequently results in happiness or pride.

Second, an event fails to remove an existing harm or sustain a benefit that had been hoped for. An example is a conversation designed to get a spouse, lover, or supervisor at work to change in some way—for example, to cease what seems like constant criticism. However, instead of creating the desired effect—perhaps because of the ineptitude or hostility with which the subject is broached, or the stubbornness of the target person— the conversation leads to more criticism and, therefore, results in anger, shame, sadness, and so forth.

Third, an event forecasts a harmful or beneficial situation in the future and, accordingly, results in a positive or negative emotion. Examples include the news that the rent is being raised, which will put a strain on one's budget, or that the company one works for is about to lay off many workers. Both these events are likely to result in anxiety. Another example is the news that an expected job layoff will not occur because the company's profits have increased, resulting therefore in relief or joy.

Fourth, a nonevent can also result in emotion if another person fails to say or do something supportive that had been hoped for. The fact that a compliment does not occur could make us feel angry or anxious, depending on how its personal meaning is appraised. Similarly, when an expression of affection, which could reassure us about our relationship with another person, is not forthcoming, its absence may result in anger and anxiety about not being loved or appreciated.

In effect, the nonevent—the absence of something we expect, want, or need—can really be treated as an event, which serves as a provocation for a distressing emotion. We may not even recognize that we wanted or needed positive feedback from the other person, but the distress and disappointment we feel at its absence is a clue about the unmet need. The emotions we feel in such a situation can teach us something about the psychodynamics of our relationships with others, which we may not have recognized or wanted to acknowledge.

In most emotional relationships, the search for a provocation leads away from the immediate situation to the larger history of the relationship, and to the personalities of the participants. What looks like a provocation may be only the most recent manifestation of a continuing or recurrent interpersonal struggle. When we try to understand why an emotion was provoked solely in terms of what is going on at the moment, we may fail to grasp the important part played by this background history.

In a study of adolescent emotions, for example, anger aroused in adolescents by encounters with parents, and the recurrent thoughts that were generated in these encounters, were found to be strongly influenced by longstanding interpersonal stress in the parent-child relationship. The emotional reaction was as much affected by this past and ongoing pattern as it was by the immediate events of the encounter.[4]

Merely a memory of a past emotional event can serve as a provocation for the same emotion to occur in the present. This seems to belie our definition of a provocation as an event that carries emotional meaning. Ordinarily, we do not consider a memory of the past as an event in the present. However, memories do not arise by happenstance. Something has taken place in the present that serves as a reminder of what happened in the past. Why should this be?

The answer is that most of the troubles and triumphs of our lives are not new but tend to recur.[5] They constitute the basic adaptational themes people have always struggled with—being loved or rejected, powerful or powerless, triumphant or victimized. While we may not be conscious of them, these are apt to have been recurrent patterns in our personal experience. Although the details may differ, a kernel of similarity always connects the present with the past, even if we are not conscious of it.

Therefore, the present event should be considered the provocation, not the memory from the past that was aroused by that event. We tend to be consistent in the way we interpret what happens in our lives, and so replay many of the same emotional plots over and over.

Action Tendency

Many emotions—for example, fear, or fright as we prefer to call it, and anger—engender powerful biological tendencies to act in a particular way. This is something we have inherited from our animal ancestors. The action tendency is defined by what it will do for us *psychologically*—for example, getting away from the danger or giving the aggressive person his or her comeuppance—not necessarily by some physical action.

When we are angry we have a strong, hard-to-resist, impulse to attack whomever we hold blameworthy for the offense on which the anger is based. We want to retaliate, to avenge ourselves, to restore our wounded self-esteem, to put down or demolish the person who has offended us.

And when we are frightened, we have an almost irresistible urge to flee from the danger, especially when we lack the means to overcome it by attack. Fright is often a counterpart of anger, and like a lowly animal that is alternately scared and bravely angry, depending on how things go, we may oscillate back and forth between threatening or attacking and running away. In shame, we want to hide what we have done that makes us feel ashamed. In guilt, we want to atone for the act that violates a moral proscription. When we are happy, we have a strong impulse to be expansive, to share with others our good fortune. In pride, we want to tell everyone about the good news—an apt metaphor for this impulse is captured in the expression "puffed up" with pride.

In some emotions, such as sadness, it is more difficult to observe any action tendency, because in being sad we have accepted the situation as resistant to change. We are helpless, and if nothing can be done, there is no strong impulse to act. Yet our body language could be said to express the sense of loss and helplessness in downcast shoulders and head and the slow pace of our movements. The opposite body language is found when we are feeling happy, which is expressed as expansiveness and the outgoing impulse to share one's good fortune.

Action tendencies are often useful in promoting species and individual survival. For example, the pathetic sight and sound of a monkey baby crying because it has been deserted by its mother (perhaps she has died) encourages other adult monkeys to come to the aid of the helpless baby. Empathic reactions to these cries might save its life. People respond in the same way. Similarly, the impulse to attack and display anger in facial expression or body gestures, or to turn tail and flee when endangered, undoubtedly has also saved the life of many a threatened animal.

Built-in action tendencies could be thought of as a biological analogue of what we mean by coping, which is discussed in Chapter 8. The difference is that, in its biological form, action tendencies occur without thought or planfulness; they are an automatic part of our animal inheritance. Coping, on the other hand, is more deliberate and psychological; it often calls for thinking about what could and should be done to deal with the problem.

Coping with the action tendencies generated by an emotion is clearly important in a complex society where we need to be prudent about acting on our impulses. To attack another person can be dangerous. Such actions need to be controlled—sometimes completely inhibited—based on a concern with what is reasonable and allowable in a particular social setting, or whether or not they are useful for attaining what we want.

Action tendencies can be so powerful that they are difficult to suppress or transform into effective social conduct. To be impulsive is to risk getting into serious trouble, and we often speak disparagingly of acting before we have thought about the consequences. Some people have particular difficulty suppressing the impulses that arise from their emotions. Others are so overcontrolled that they cannot be spontaneous. How to cope with biologically based action tendencies, which are an integral aspect of emotion, is a problem of great significance for our well-being, that of our loved ones, and the nations and families of nations we identify with, and on whose fate we depend. We devote an entire chapter to it.

What an Emotion Is: A Definition

It is time to define emotion. Emotions are complex reactions that engage both our minds and our bodies. These reactions include: a subjective mental state, such as the feeling of anger, anxiety, or love; an impulse to act, such as fleeing or attacking, whether or not it is expressed overtly; and profound changes in the body, such as increased heart rate or blood pressure. Some of these bodily changes prepare for and sustain coping actions, and others—such as postures, gestures, and facial expressions—communicate to others what we are feeling, or want others to believe we are feeling.

An emotion is a personal life drama, which has to do with the fate of our goals in a particular encounter and our beliefs about ourselves and the world we live in. It is aroused by an appraisal of the personal significance or meaning of what is happening in that encounter. The dramatic plot differs from one emotion to another, each emotion having its own particular story.

Let us proceed next to how people cope with their emotions and the situations that bring them about.

8

Coping and the Self-Management of Emotion

THIS CHAPTER IS DEDICATED to coping because it is so central to our health and daily experiences. Coping shapes our emotions, but its most important function is to manage those emotions once aroused, as well as the sometimes troubling situations that provoke them. Coping is what we do and think in an effort to manage stress and the emotions associated with it—whether or not these efforts are successful. In other words, even if we fail at a coping task, a great deal of energy, thought, and action has gone into it. When a goal has been blocked or its integrity threatened, people struggle to prevent the harm from happening or to overcome it. If nothing can be done, they work hard to accept and deal with the reality, and get on with their lives.

If coping succeeds, the person is no longer in jeopardy and the reasons for emotional distress disappear. Even if goals are attained, or people are making satisfactory progress toward them, they still cope in order to sustain their good fortune, prevent unfavorable change, and even make additional gains. So even though one is experiencing positive emotions, such as happiness, pride, or relief, coping remains an important part of everyday life.

For example, if you hoped for a promotion at work and get it, you feel proud and happy. This happy state of mind is a fine antidote to the disappointments of your life, and it is drawn on for respite and emotional renewal. However, no one can bask in the job success for long, but must get on with life and cope with new responsibilities that might be daunting. Besides, the boss could be entertaining doubts about your effectiveness at these new responsibilities and you must continue to prove yourself.

Coping also occurs in anticipation of what may happen. In this respect, it can influence future emotional states, which is why it is an ingredient of the emotion process. For example, suppose you have to face an upcoming stressful confrontation. Perhaps you will soon undergo a job interview, a school exam, give a public performance, or have a meeting with your child's teacher, which is made potentially uncomfortable because of the child's problems at school. You rehearse in advance. For the exam, you try to anticipate the questions and study for it. These preparations—called *anticipatory coping*—help to reduce the anxiety and increase your effectiveness when the event takes place.

What people do to cope depends on the situation being faced, the threats it poses, the kinds of people they are—for example, their goals and beliefs—and the immediate results of their coping efforts. To be successful, coping needs to be flexible and adapted to the requirements of the situation, which often change as the event unfolds. We must learn what to do to cope in a new situation. So coping is not just a fixed set of strategies that are drawn on whenever they are needed, but a changing pattern that is responsive to what is happening.

People employ two main strategies to cope—problem solving and emotion-centered coping—and each includes some subvarieties. The remainder of the chapter deals with them, with the greatest attention directed toward emotion-centered coping because it is less obvious than problem solving and well known as a coping strategy. Let us begin with problem solving.

Coping by Problem Solving

One major coping pattern is directed at mounting an action to change a troubling situation.[1] This action entails *problem solving*. If you have appraised the situation as amenable to preventive or corrective actions, you check things out to find out what is going on, what the problem is, and what to do about it.

The solution may be to change what other people think and do—for example, soliciting love from someone you care about, putting together an effective résumé or impressing those in charge so that they will hire you for the job, finding adequate child care for periods in which you are at work, saying no to people who want too much of your time without offending them, getting friends to stop smoking in your home, or persuading your neighbor to trim his trees so that the autumn leaves will not fall on your lawn. The potential examples of such problems, most of them interpersonal, are legion.

In trying to change the behavior of others, it is usually necessary to consider how to approach them. Instead of bluntly communicating your annoyance to the friend who is too demanding, you might figure out how to approach her more sensitively. If you are able to discuss the problem and convince her about your point of view, your problem is solved and the previous emotional distress disappears.

As another example of problem solving, consider the endemic problem in our society of a mother and father who must leave a preschool child to go to work. Good caretaking for young children is not easy to find and may be difficult to afford, adding to the anxiety and anger inherent in such a situation. If such parents see evidence that their child is being neglected or dealt with harshly by the present caretaker, effective action to change a situation that puts the child at risk becomes urgent and is also emotionally distressing.

Although working outside the home plus managing home and family leave little available time for problem solving, much thought and energy may have to be expended to deal with this situation. If ultimately a good arrangement for child care can be found for the period the parents are at work, an urgent problem will have been solved, at least for the present, with consequent relief from the debilitating anxiety and anger.

Or what if we have just lost our job in an economic recession in which our company discharges many employees. We must now consider how to get another job. What kind of job? How should we try? If we can see that the problem arises from the absence of some skill, an effort to learn it might turn the situation around. On the other hand, if the whole industry is failing, it might be better to seek a different kind of job altogether. Since we believe that something can be done about the problem, we employ problem-solving strategies of coping, and the choice of action requires our considered judgment.

There are, of course, a great many examples of problem-solving coping. The parent struggling with child care might at some point become involved in politics to press for more adequate funds and resources. The person struggling with autumn leaves from the neighbor's yard might try to establish local groups organized to keep the neighborhood attractive. No standard coping strategy is appropriate since each problem is different and calls for a different solution.

What often complicates problem-solving coping efforts are the touchy attitudes of the other people you must deal with, friends who are sensitive to rejection, neighbors who are demeaned if told to change their behavior, people who don't like others to have a say over their dominions, and so forth. Commonly, problem solving may create hurt and anger in others and requires a careful touch.

For example, the problem posed by efforts to get your neighbor to trim the pesky tree each early fall may generate emotions that make the task especially difficult. Just urging your neighbor to trim his tree may arouse his anger, depending on how the problem is presented. You may experience some anger yourself because his inconsideration has placed you in this unpleasant situation, and this anger may lead to an ineffective approach. An overly aggressive complaint could make him want to retaliate with some hateful action, and then not only will the original problem remain unsolved but a new one will have been created.

In some cases, the neighbor may do as you wish by sweeping up regularly or cutting back the tree, yet maintain a continuing resentment toward you. Not a desirable state of affairs for someone who lives next door. You solved one problem but created another. So, trying to avoid excessive aggressiveness, you approach him pleasantly. You explain the problem and the distress it causes you, and solicit his help in cutting the tree back before the leaves fall. If you succeed, the problem disappears, along with the emotional distress it has caused.

On some occasions, of course, an open expression of anger will effectively control a troubling situation. On other occasions, however, such an expression may make you feel better but do no real good. Holding back out of fear of the consequences and not revealing one's anger is not very satisfying, though it is often the best thing to do under the circumstances. Thoughtful people realize that a calm and nonthreatening approach rather than a hot-headed one is likely to lead to better continuing relationships.

On the other hand, the most serious negative consequence of not revealing anger, especially when dealing with an intimate or loved one, is that you are really misleading the other person by concealing how you feel. You will have failed to communicate information that is important to the health of a long-term relationship, namely, that certain things are offensive to you and the other person should try to avoid doing them. And not doing so will make you feel less honest and authentic. Which way to go in problem solving in any particular situation is not an easy judgment to make and, given how diverse and complex interpersonal relationships can be, the solution often seems murky.

If you have no other alternative, you may be unable to avoid making an open attack. If doing this produces a bland, cooperative, and apologetic reaction, which you did not expect, you experience a feeling of triumph about the courage you displayed and the success of the action. You may have even gained respect just by speaking out. But don't be too sanguine that this is apt to be the usual case. If you decide to issue a challenge, threatening to take direct action say, cutting back the tree yourself—some people have been known to take matters into their own hands—be sure that this is what you want to do and that you can accept the negative consequences.

If you trust the other person, say, in the scenario with the friend who wants too much time, one of the best strategies might be to wait until you collect yourself, then say something to the effect that you have a problem that's making you uneasy. You would be grateful if the friend would do something about what is bothering you. Actually, saying this is hardly provocative, though you will have learned over time whether or not the other person is likely to react to it as an offense. And, if so, maybe it should be explored anyway.

By all means, however, you should refer only to the specific provocation and refrain from making an attack on the other person's character. Character assassination is bound to provoke anger in almost everyone. Keep to the specifics of what is upsetting you. The more the focus is on your own distress, as distinguished from external blaming, the more reasonable your enjoinder will seem, and the more effective this confrontational strategy is likely to be.

So we see that when problem-solving coping involves other people, the task of coping becomes more complicated because of the emotions that crop up in the relationship. Few interpersonal problems are devoid of emotions that can poison the relationship if they are not dealt with effectively. This means that in most situations calling for coping, problem-solving and emotion-centered coping are usually conjoined. Not only do we have to deal with the problem, but we must also manage our own emotions in the interchange, which brings us to emotion-centered coping.

Emotion-Centered Coping

What if problem solving fails to work, or cannot even be tried because the problem is resistant to change? If we can't change the actual situation, we can subdue or otherwise manage the distressing emotions it causes. *Emotion-centered* coping strategies, which are internal and private, are mounted to control distress and the dysfunction it might cause when there is little or nothing else we can do. Emotion-centered coping consists of what we tell ourselves in the effort at such control. It changes the way we think about what is happening from a threatening to a more benign or positive appraisal.

Consider a problem that is difficult to do much about. Let us say we have a serious neuromuscular disease that is somewhat incapacitating. Can this be changed? What does it mean for the future? Is the disease likely to be fatal or can it be controlled? What can we do to improve our chances? To find out requires that we seek the judgment of experts. We need a medical evaluation. We may require medication to allow us to function, and the good sense to know how to use it.

Because of uncertainty about the nature of this problem, *both* problem-solving and emotion-centered coping are needed. The problem-solving aspect involves seeking a full diagnosis and careful trial and error in the use of medicines to increase the quality of one's functioning. The emotion-centered aspect involves keeping up one's morale, retaining hope, and dealing with the inevitable emotional distress when things don't go well.

Suppose that, as a result of the full diagnosis, we learn that we are suffering from a terminal illness and do not have long to live. This is the circumstance that best highlights the need for emotion-centered coping, because we can do little to change our medical circumstances. Emotion-centered strategies are required for managing the emotional distress, such as anxiety over how much suffering will be involved, anger over a bad fate, depression over loss of full functioning—and soon life itself—depending on the way we have appraised what is happening. We need to keep up our self-esteem and morale in some way. Shortly we will detail some of the specific emotion-centered strategies to use in situations in which we can do little to alter the objective problem.

But before doing this, we should consider the problem of judging whether we can or cannot do something about a stressful situation. The difficulty of judging the truth—that is, whether the situation can be changed by action or must be accepted because nothing can be done—brings to mind the serenity prayer used by Alcoholics Anonymous, which was borrowed from prelates who lived during the Middle Ages: "God grant me the courage to try to change what can be changed, the serenity to accept what can't be changed, and the wisdom to know the difference." To know the difference indeed poses an agonizing dilemma.

In all stressful situations, the more information we have, the better we can cope, since we can then assess our situation and monitor our reactions. We must first try to understand the troubling emotions we are experiencing and the conditions that bring them about. To misapprehend the conditions provoking anger, anxiety, guilt, shame, and so forth, is to be unable to recognize what is really going on when these feelings arise, and not to know what to do. Burying the emotion thwarts the opportunity to learn what it tells us about ourselves and our life situation. It also prevents us from working through the social and personal problems these emotional reactions express and gain insight into them so that we can resolve to react differently next time.

One of the best ways to gain insight into our emotions is to talk about them to someone we trust. Telling others provides the opportunity to review what has happened, why it happened, what is distressing about it, and how it might be dealt with. There is something wonderfully therapeutic about a trusted friend's understanding and accepting reaction.

Research evidence indicates that suppression, especially of very troubling emotional experiences, feeds on itself and sustains the distress, while verbalizing it seems to be a useful way to cope. Extensive research by one health psychologist, James Pennebaker, and his associates[2] strongly suggests that coping with recent traumatic experiences is facilitated by confronting and working through the threats they produce.

These researchers evaluated the effects of writing about or verbally sharing the traumatic experience on later emotional distress and illness. When, for example, students wrote about their homesickness and anxieties resulting from going to college, they subsequently made fewer visits to physicians than a comparison group of students who wrote about unimportant, benign topics. So the first thing a wise person might do in the presence of recurrent dysfunctional and distressing emotions is to recognize that they are occurring and make an effort to evaluate what is going on.

This is probably one of the reasons why support groups can be helpful to people who have experienced a common traumatic experience or personal problem. Such experiences include life-threatening disease, the death of a child or spouse, divorce, rape, assault and burglary, caring for ill and aging parents, and natural and manmade disasters. Talking about what is troubling to receptive people who understand can also help one realize that others have experienced similar traumas and survived. With the insights these conversations may produce, destructive thoughts about what happened can be replaced by more constructive ones, with some consequent amelioration of the distressing emotion.

Two rules of thumb are operative: First, we should not avoid, bury, or close off the episode or condition that promotes the distress, at least not for very long. It is important that it be faced, looked at, learned from, and worked through constructively. According to our best knowledge, this rule applies whether the effort to work over the trauma is engaged in privately, in a group, or with a therapist.

Second, we should be flexible but wise about the people to whom we pour out our feelings. These feelings will turn off many people and lead to frustrating social consequences, even criticism or ostracism. It is valuable to know who our friends are, and who will respond helpfully in a crisis. They are often not the people we think will be helpful; people on whom we counted will often disappoint.

Coping that centers on our emotional reactions can be divided into two types, avoidance and reappraisal of personal meaning. Let us examine each to see how they work.

Avoidance

In avoidance, we try not to think about what is troubling us. When at work, for example, we need to concentrate on what we are doing, so we try to put what is troubling us out of our minds lest it interfere. And when we retire at night, troubling thoughts are put out of our minds in order to get to sleep. Some people can easily do this when they first go to bed. They fall asleep quickly. However, they may awaken during the night and spend the next several hours ruminating instead of sleeping.

People draw on all sorts of emotion-centered strategies to facilitate avoidance. They drink or use drugs, engage in sports or exercise, which can distract them from what is troubling, or they may indulge in fancy meals at home or in restaurants, all of which may help them temporarily. They may even avoid being with people in order not to have to talk about their troubles. Some sleep more than usual, evading as much of life as possible, while others cannot get a full night's sleep. Relaxation techniques and meditation may help. (See Chapter 13.)

Some people are more capable than others of avoiding troubling thoughts. They are better able to concentrate on the task at hand. Consider, for example, people who leave their work at the office when they come home to their families, or their family troubles at home when they go to work. Yet in many other instances, stress at work disturbs family relationships, and stress at home disturbs work. And athletes, such as professional tennis players, who become preoccupied with a string of bad timing and strokes, risk losing their concentration and, therefore, the match. They must learn to avoid ruminating about the poor performance during the match to have a chance of winning.

What makes avoidance a weak and temporary coping strategy is that, although worries may appear less daunting for a time when problems are avoided, they do not go away until the problems are actually confronted and resolved.

Reappraisal of Personal Meaning

The second subtype of emotion-centered coping involves changing the personal meaning of what has happened by reappraising it in a more benign and less threatening way. Reappraisal is a far more powerful emotion-centered strategy of coping than avoidance. In the long run, it may be the most effective strategy.

If you have been offended by your spouse, who provoked you to anger, the natural first impulse is to retaliate in kind. But let us suppose you do not want to endanger the relationship. As we noted in Chapter 2, psychologist Carol Tavris[3] has suggested that counting to ten is one way to cool off before impulsively counterattacking and maybe doing great damage. There is, however, an even better way of coping in this kind of situation because it changes the emotion itself.

This, as we have said, is to make excuses for your beloved spouse, which changes the personal meaning of the situation. You might realize that she has been ill, and so is tired and irritable; or she has been having a bad time at work because of an inconsiderate supervisor. Who could then blame her for being irritable? She didn't think before she spoke. The revised personal meaning is the recognition that your spouse had not intended to offend you, but her understandable distress and irritability led to an unintended expression of anger. So there is really no legitimate reason to be angry. And an empathic and gentle response can produce great dividends in the long-term relationship.

We don't wish to suggest that one can simply tell oneself anything at all to change the personal meaning, thereby totally ignoring the reality of what is happening. To do this is called denial, which we discuss at length later. To make a new appraisal stick requires that there be a believable basis for it.

The principle of changing personal meaning to reduce distress applies to emotional states, such as anxiety, guilt, shame, and depression. Let us see how changing personal meaning might work with these emotions.

To begin with *anxiety*, you might say to yourself, "I am fully capable of handling a threatening upcoming demand when it arrives." If you believe you can cope with the threat effectively, the anxiety is apt to be either overcome or less severe. Such a belief is not denial if it is realistic and what you truly believe. Denial takes place when the attitude is manufactured to relieve the anxiety and has little or no basis in reality.

Reappraising a threat, and the anxiety it arouses, is apt to be less effective in those who view the world dourly or themselves as inadequate. Since anxiety is based on the anticipation of a future harm, we prepare for the confrontation by examining the nature of the threat and increasing our capacity to handle it through preparation as we await the upcoming event. This preparation can greatly augment the sense of control we have over the situation and the actual ability to manage it when the threatening event occurs.

The process is well illustrated by what happens to those who are public speakers. As most people who must speak publicly tell us, anxiety—sometimes quite severe—is likely to occur just before giving the speech and, to some extent, in the first minutes of every speech. "Will I remember what to say?" "Will the audience like me?" The anxiety, however, usually disappears after the performance gets going.

And yet most public speakers believe that anxiety is an important spur to doing a good job. Believing this helps diffuse the anxiety somewhat. But some, however, may not experience any anxiety at all. Ethel Merman, a consummate stage and movie performer, said she never was anxious about a performance. She certainly looked comfortable on stage—perhaps she was just successful in hiding it. It is sometimes difficult to tell.

We had a friend in graduate school who coped with anxiety by preparing carefully for exams, checking out everything he could about the questions that might be asked, reading extensively, taking notes, rehearsing ideas and going over them with other students and his wife. Then, the evening before the exam, believing he had done all that he could, he would go to a Western. He said he chose Westerns because they were light yet absorbing movies, so he could forget his anxiety for a time. Then he would go to bed and sleep soundly, while his wife would stay up anxiously all night.

The emotion of *guilt*, too, can be transformed by coping if we reappraise the personal meaning of the guilt-provoking situation. Normally, if we accept our moral lapse, we try to atone for what we have done.

An interesting historical example is the way the American government coped with the Japanese threat during World War II. The illegal and immoral decision to intern Japanese-Americans in California during the war was justified on the basis of the mistaken idea that an immigrant people from a country that was as ethnocentric as Japan could not be trusted. The justification served as a denial of the impropriety of the action. Half a century later came the belated realization that interning Japanese-American citizens during the war was illegal and wrong. This reappraisal after the damage had indeed been done led to establishing monetary payments to the citizens who were interned, in effect publicly atoning for the wrongdoing.

The only reason to hide guilt feelings would be to avoid acknowledging that one has acted badly. This had been the approach taken for many years in the case of the Japanese-Americans. Atoning for a moral lapse provides the personal benefit of showing publicly that one wishes to live in accordance with the moral strictures of the society. Atonement provides a durable method of coping with guilt feelings. We punish ourselves by acknowledging our sins and going to the trouble of making up for them.

In absolving guilt feelings, much depends on whether apologies or expressions of guilt seem authentic to others as well as ourselves, and whether our efforts to atone are balanced adequately against the magnitude of our moral lapse. If our efforts are not sufficiently weighty, they are apt to be criticized or rejected, and they may fail to mitigate the feelings of guilt. Some people are extremely hard on themselves in this regard, displaying the deeper problem of being guilt-ridden. As such, this is an emotionally troubled pattern that might require professional help to overcome.

Shame, we said in Chapter 3, is a very private emotion because to expose what makes us feel shame only deepens the private sense of having failed. Shame is, therefore, difficult to acknowledge to others, and easier to deny in an effort to change our personal meanings about an event.

In our fantasies, those who view our shame and its causes will reject and abandon us. It is difficult enough to live with our private shame, but it is far more difficult to have it exposed to the world, or to those we most care about. The result, of course, is a vicious circle. If we cannot cope with shame by readily speaking of it to others, we will never be in a position to discover that they would have probably acted similarly and would find what we did easy to understand.

Therefore, it might be useful on occasion to cope with shame by acknowledging it to others. This would leave room for a gracious, empathic response. If support is actually given, then the childhood basis for shame—fear of rejection—is undermined. The strategy always seems risky, however, since graciousness may not be forthcoming, as might have been learned from overdemanding parents. It takes substantial courage to live with the dual distress of disapproval by oneself and others. This is why shame is such a lonely emotion.

Another way to cope with shame is to justify oneself righteously and defensively by denying that we did anything bad. If we are aware of the game we are playing, we must also accept ourselves as manipulative and dishonest. Self-justification is apt to be more successful if we are not aware of what we are doing and believe the denial. To the extent that we believe we have acted in accordance with our ego-ideals, there is no reason for feeling shame.

We suspect that this strategy of coping with shame—whether ingenuous or disingenuous—is very common, and explains why the more legitimate the feeling of shame, the more what has been done is denied afterward. It is a method of stonewalling, toughing it out, which, we suspect, feels better subjectively than abject acknowledgment of the shameful act.

Another emotion-centered way to cope with shame is to abandon some of the unreasonably high standards of personal conduct we have internalized from our parents early in life. This undermines the tendency to be shame-ridden, but is easier said than done. Related to changing our standards is the step of coming to realize, emotionally as well as intellectually, that we don't have to be perfect to be acceptable and even loved. We can learn that our standards are unreasonable, and that life can be happier and more fulfilling if we accept ourselves as we are.[4]

People sometimes use an emotion-centered coping process to deal with *depression* or joylessness in their lives. We pointed out in Chapter 4 that depression is not a single emotion but involves a combination of emotions, such as sadness, anxiety, anger, guilt, and shame. But it is a highly emotional and distressing state of mind, so to change its personal meaning is a viable strategy for overcoming it.

Modern views of depression, when it is a problem of living rather than the consequence of a biochemical anomaly, emphasize mainly helplessness and deep discouragement—indeed, hopelessness—about one's life circumstances, the tendency to blame oneself, and to magnify the dour implications of negative life events and circumstances that are appraised as devastating losses. It is hopelessness that connects depression with joylessness. There is nothing to make life worth living, nothing about which to feel happy or take some measure of pleasure.

If we are to change such dour feelings, we must change the way we see ourselves and our life circumstances. We must learn to think differently—no easy task—because without professional help we are forced to pull ourselves up by our own bootstraps. Some people seem to be able to do this to some degree as a matter of will, depending on how severe their depression is. For a while they wallow in self-pity, complain constantly, annoying their families and friends, resisting more positive assessments of their personal realities by concerned others, and withdrawing into their private hells. The more their friends and loved ones urge them to reappraise the basis of their negative outlook, the more they resist and proclaim what is wrong about their lives.

At some point, however, they seem to say to themselves, "Enough of this," and literally force themselves to shut off the misery. They reassess their circumstances, avoid the dour thoughts, go back to work and planning, and willfully banish their misanthropic outlook. It is as if they are denying that the reasons for their depression should be given any credence. And for these people, this works, at least for a time. And when the next episode of depression seems imminent, they speak of fighting it off, implying that they can prevent themselves from succumbing once again to a depressive outlook.

One of the interesting features of depression is that it tends to be comparatively short-lived but recurrent. The tendency to depression also seems to be a well-entrenched part of people's makeup. What worries their loved ones is that hopelessness could lead to suicide or self-destructive decisions before the depression passes. The conviction that it, too, will pass fuels the conviction of telephone hotline workers to dissuade the caller from an unwarranted suicide, because it is likely that the caller's enthusiasm for life will, in time, return.

Although they do not exhaust the range of emotion-centered coping devices, two such devices are especially important in changing personal meanings, and they work in different ways. They are called distancing and denial. Let us examine them in some detail.

In *distancing*, we remove ourselves emotionally from the distressing meanings of a situation. One way to distance is to perceive a horror without assimilating its full emotional significance. It is as if we are seeing without really seeing. We do this automatically without conscious intent, but precisely how it is accomplished is quite obscure.

In this connection, one of us (RL) remembers doing some research in which participating subjects had to watch a very stressful silent movie while their psychological and physiological reactions were being measured. The film portrayed a series of crude operations on the genitals of young males of an Australian aboriginal tribe. The procedure initiates boys into manhood and is called subincision. The cutting of the underside of the penis into the scrotum is done with a crude stone knife, and maggots are placed in the wound. The boys undergo this willingly as part of their heritage, but they are obviously pained by it. Some of you may have heard about such rituals but few of us have actually seen them.

My (RL) first reaction to this film was that it was very difficult to watch without experiencing considerable distress, undoubtedly based in part on empathy and shock at something so bizarre and hurtful. Once the movie started I had nothing further to do but to watch along with the subject. As subject after subject went through the research procedure, though it had originally bothered me greatly, I became increasingly bored by the film. I even began to wonder why others considered it so distressing.

What seems to have happened is that repeatedly watching the movie made me turn it off psychologically; I simply stopped paying close attention to what was going on, seeing the events but not assimilating their personal meaning. I had somehow managed to distance myself emotionally from what I was seeing.

Then one day with a colleague I initiated another experiment with this film.[5] I now wanted to alter the subjects' appraisal of what was going on in the movie by means of a sound track that would be played along with the film. So I was obliged to run the film over and over again as I tried to craft suitable statements about what the film was all about (see also Chapter 11). As I did this, my detached attitude suddenly disappeared, and once again I found the movie distressing to watch. What had happened to renew my distress?

The answer is that in the process of writing a sound track for the film, I was obliged to watch carefully what was happening, with all its emotional connotations, in order to insert appropriate interpretive statements. And so, once again, I began to relate personally to the film's meaning and react with distress. The psychological cover produced by my earlier emotional distancing had now been blown.

Distancing must have been the process that occurred when the public watched the tragedy of Vietnam unfold on television, the first time a war was fought, so to speak, on public airways. After repeatedly seeing mangled and bleeding bodies, human corpses lying on the ground, and real people—not actors—being shot and killed, watching this could be accomplished by the public without emotional distress. We had become so inured to the sights of suffering that we were seeing without really seeing, having distanced ourselves from the emotional meanings of death and suffering.

The simplest way to gain emotional distance from suffering people is to *dehumanize* them. If we can view them as the enemy, we can think of them as less than human, as animals rather than real people who warrant empathy. In World War II, we did this to the Japanese and the Germans. We called the Japanese "japs" or "nips" (for Nipponese) and the Germans "krauts," short for those who ate sauerkraut. In the Vietnam War, we called the North Vietnamese "gooks." Notice the lowercase letters in these names, which further belittles and dehumanizes the soldiers.

And, of course, our enemies did the same to us. We could enjoy each other's comeuppance, and watch the evidence of their battle losses without compassion because the enemy was dehumanized. Long after these wars ended, however, when we had ceased to be enemies and were now allies of Germany and Japan, we could again view them as people like us, with fears and hopes, and could more easily allow ourselves to feel compassion when they suffered.

Certain occupations seem to favor a distancing style for dealing with other people. We mentioned medical personnel earlier as an example, but there are others, too. You may have perhaps noticed that officials and administrators tend to present a detached, nonreactive demeanor whenever subordinates approach them with a request. It is seldom possible to know on the spot what they think. Their faces show no emotion, and their words are the epitome of cool detachment. Though perhaps pleasant and polite, they show disinterest, no matter how important the matter is to the supplicant.

Administrators distance themselves emotionally and become dispassionate to protect themselves from making what might be taken as a positive commitment before they have thought through its implications or consulted with their peers or superiors. Such consultation might lead them to change their minds. They know that it will be much more difficult to deal with a supplicant's anger if they must renege on what they have implied or said earlier.

Psychotherapists, particularly those who engage in the practice of psychoanalysis, use emotional distance as a routine professional style, which sometimes extends even to their social lives. Talk with them on the phone or in person, and they seem guarded or neutral, which is apt to be sensed as coldness. This pattern could be the result of what they are like as persons, which may have led them into their occupation in the first place. On the other hand, they could just be following what they consider the appropriate professional role to play with patients. In psychoanalysis, the therapist listens to the patient without indicating approval or disapproval, and without making too many interpretive intrusions. Hence the blank-faced demeanor.

This raises the question of whether people who regularly distance themselves are really dispassionate in their relationships with others or are merely displaying a detached manner that is skin deep. Most of us are capable of achieving emotional distance on occasion as a means of coping with stress and emotion. If, however, distancing becomes habitual, it may lead to a constantly overcontrolled, detached style of relating to others. The complete flattening of the emotional life as a result may be too much of a price to pay for a temporary surcease from distress. So much for distancing.

In *denial*, examples of which we have already seen, we change the personal meaning by refusing to acknowledge what we find threatening. We do this by telling ourselves that there is no reason to be threatened. We are not angry, we insist. There is no wrongdoing, we say, in a punitive act in which we are engaging. We are not dying of a terminal illness, but are getting well. Denial, which is the disavowal of reality, is not the same as avoidance; in avoidance, we try not to think of what is happening, but we can still acknowledge the threatening reality.

We dwell on denial at considerable length here for two reasons. First, our views about what is mentally sound have changed considerably in recent years—as will be seen shortly—and the change can be nicely illustrated with denial. Second, we want to know whether some coping strategies are inherently harmful or beneficial. The answer could be used to help people choose beneficial strategies and reject harmful ones. Research on the consequences of denial is fairly plentiful and tells an interesting story.

Based on a view that originated with Anna Freud,[6] the daughter of Sigmund Freud, psychiatry and clinical psychology have followed the tradition that denial is an immature from of coping. The young child uses denial, but gives it up as maturity and a greater grasp of the realities of life set in. Since reality is distorted in denial, an adult who uses denial was presumed to be mentally ill and said to be employing a desperate way of dealing with intolerable situations.

Earlier we mentioned making excuses for loved ones as a way of diffusing an offense. When this coping process fails, most of the time it is because of the inability to find believable excuses for the other person's words or actions. We would like to believe that our wife, husband, or lover is trustworthy and loving. The inability to believe what we wish stems from the reality that the other person does, indeed, harbor hostility, and displays it frequently. To excuse this pattern is to disavow the reality, and so it is denial.

The failure of excuse-making may also arise from personal vulnerabilities, which make it difficult to overlook even the most minor or ambiguous affronts. In the marital argument described in Chapter 2, the wife's unmet need to feel loved and cherished by her husband made it difficult for her to find excuses for what she took to be his offenses against her. Only when the husband stated that his job was threatened was there a believable excuse that the wife could draw on to explain his behavior in a benign fashion. Her anger vanished instantly when she could reappraise his actions on the basis of the excuse. This appraisal was not a denial because it was realistic.

The disavowal of reality can be dangerous because it promotes poor life decisions. However, not all denials are blatant disavowals of reality, especially in the arenas of life that are ambiguous. Denial shades into *illusion*, which is a common human response to the terrors of an ugly, unjust world. By believing in fictions, life is made more tolerable.

Most of us accept many convictions about ourselves and the world without necessarily being aware that these convictions are fictions. If we were aware of their illusory quality, most of us would reject them. The fictions seem believable because they are shared by many others. The people with whom we are familiar—a particular religious group, subculture, community, or family—are apt to be taken as a microcosm of the whole world. Because they have the same convictions that we do, our illusions are seldom challenged, but if they are, we are greatly distressed. Without some illusions, we would probably become cynical or misanthropic.

We believe that our country is glorious and without stain—the Nazis believed this too—and that presidents are, and should be, totally honest; that we never act deceitfully; that good people—including ourselves—don't lie; that there is justice in our society for everyone (or anyone); that we exercise control over our lives.[7] Many would say that the idea of life after death is another illusion. There is a joke about dying in which it is said that death couldn't be so bad, since no one comes back to complain. Joking, incidentally, is a way of coping with threatening ideas and is a form of emotional distancing; you don't have to take so seriously what you can joke about.

Anyway, the notion that denial—or its softer side, illusion—is always harmful, and that we must face reality no matter how painful, is an extreme point of view. Yet the disavowal of reality is surely dangerous. In contrast with the view of traditional psychiatry and clinical psychology that denial is a sign of mental illness, the great writers of literature and drama maintain in their stories that life is intolerable without illusion, and many great dramas deal with this theme. We will have to reconcile these two sensible positions.

The literary example we like best brings home the human need for illusion. It is a story by the psychoanalyst-writer Allen Wheelis called *The Illusionless Man*. Henry, a man without any illusions, marries Lorabelle, a woman for whom illusion is everything. Speaking of their forthcoming wedding, Henry says:

> God won't be there honey; the women will be weeping for their own lost youth and innocence, the men wanting to have you in bed; and the priest standing slightly above us will be looking down your cleavage as his mouth goes dry; and the whole thing will be a primitive and preposterous attempt to invest copulation with dignity and permanence, to enforce responsibility for children by the authority of a myth no longer credible even to a child.

But when Henry and Lorabelle are near the end of their lives, Wheelis clearly tells us that illusion is the only workable way of life. He writes:

> Henry could see himself striving toward a condition of beauty or truth or goodness or love that did not exist, but whereas earlier in his life he had always said, "It's an illusion," and turned away, now he said, "There isn't anything else," and stayed with it; and though it cannot be said that they lived happily ever after, they did live. They lived—for a while—with ups and downs, good days and bad, and when it came time to die Lorabelle said, "Now we'll never be parted," and Henry smiled and kissed her and said to himself, "There isn't anything else," and they died.

Many other famous plays and stories also draw on the theme of life as intolerable without illusion—O'Neill's *The Iceman Cometh*, Ibsen's *The Wild Duck*, Cervantes' *Don Quixote*, Dürrenmatt's *The Visit*, and almost all of Pirandello's plays toy with themes of illusion and reality in wonderfully complex ways. It is an inescapable theme in literature.

Because for so long we have assumed denial is harmful, it may come as a surprise that there are times when it is actually beneficial. In recent decades researchers and clinicians alike have begun to recognize that denial—especially as illusion—is used as a coping strategy by most of us. Denial is most common when we are traumatized by the conditions of our lives and can't cope adequately with them. Sometimes denial is adaptive and sometimes it is maladaptive, so it is important to pay attention to the kind of denial and the circumstances under which it is a beneficial or harmful form of coping.

There are numerous circumstances in which denial actually has been shown to have a favorable outcome. For example, when a patient must face minor surgery, those who deny the danger and show low levels of anxiety have a more rapid recovery and fewer postsurgical complications than those who are vigilant about the dangers and anxious about the upcoming surgery.[8]

Why should this be so? The best guess is that the hospital setting forces surgical patients to be passive and to have little or no control over their actions. There is nothing to do but allow the surgeon and nursing staff to take care of you. Being concerned about every pain or symptom has little adaptive value in the hospital. You will usually get well regardless of anything you do.

If people maintain a positive outlook, believing, even against the evidence, that their surgeon is the best to be found, they will do better than patients who are vigilantly attentive to what is going on. Even the surgical wound seems to heal faster. If you can, the best thing to do under the circumstances is, ironically, to relax and enjoy being the center of attention and count yourself lucky to have a vacation from responsibility.

Recent research also suggests that the positive or negative consequences of using denial depends on the stage of a life-threatening illness. For example, although denial is dangerous when patients are trying to decide what to do about symptoms of a heart attack, it is useful during the recovery period in the hospital because it calms excessive anxiety, which has sometimes been referred to as a cardiac neurosis. If postcoronary patients are frightened of following a therapeutic regimen of modest exercise, it will slow or impair their rate of recovery. However, denial is again harmful when patients go home to resume their normal lives because it increases the likelihood that they will deny danger and take on too much work or physical activity.[9,10]

A parallel illustration, which also reveals the importance of different stages of an illness, is the use of denial in patients with a spinal cord injury resulting from a sudden accident. The patient wakes up in a hospital to find himself paralyzed, sometimes from the waist down (paraplegia) and sometimes in all four limbs (quadriplegia). It is a shocking condition for anyone, and disastrous for morale. Right after the accident, denial leaves room for some temporary hope that sensation and motor functions will return. At that time the reality may be too devastating for the patient to deal with; better to remain numb or hopeful.

After the passage of time, however, the patient begins to assimilate the terrible truth about the handicap and learns that there will be no recovery of function. When denial becomes untenable, depression is a common reaction. There is also another reality to be confronted, namely, that the patient must begin to learn how to deal with the paralysis through rehabilitation training, which could make possible a relatively new and independent lifestyle. If denial were to continue beyond the early stages following the accident, it would prevent the patient from taking the necessary rehabilitative steps.

Many women who discover breast lumps deny the potential of cancer, thereby delaying getting medical attention and risking the spread of a potential malignancy. They are endangering their lives, and this is a clear case in which denial has high costs. Another example of the harm done by denial occurs in men, especially those who are having chest pains and other symptoms that mimic indigestion. Those who deny they are having a heart attack fail to get early medical help at what could be the most crucial, early stage of a heart attack. Cases are reported in which heart attack victims did pushups and climbed flights of stairs, believing that being able to do this proves that they couldn't be having a heart attack. They were, indeed, having a heart attack and survived to tell the story. They were lucky. Others didn't live to tell the story.

So the rule about when denial is adaptive or beneficial and when it is maladaptive or harmful is that it—or any other emotion-centered coping— has negative consequences primarily when it prevents people from taking actions that are necessary to survive or flourish. If something useful or lifesaving can be done, but is not done because of the denial, this strategy of coping can result in harm. However, if nothing can be done, denial often helps make the person feel better without serious costs.[11]

We have thus far given a guardedly positive account of denial as a coping strategy by pointing out that, although it is sometimes beneficial to deny the reality of one's situation and feelings, doing so can also have harmful consequences. We have also likened some denials to a milder kind of self-deception, which is referred to as illusion. The facts show that both truths—that denial is both harmful and valuable—apply, but not equally under all conditions.

Let us now examine one major negative consequence of denial that is not widely recognized and deserves special attention. Imagine you have a terminal illness or a severely handicapping physical condition. Many people who suffer from this kind of malady try to maintain a positive outlook on their own, and some succeed. To be able to think positively about one's situation, and about life overall, is a great blessing and it should not be denigrated. Such thinking helps to make the harsh conditions of life, such as imminent death, less despairing for both themselves and their loved ones. Most people, however, cannot succeed in doing this. It is more usual for people in this situation to experience anger, guilt, shame, and depression.

The patients' plight presents their loved ones with a severe emotional trial. When dealing with a loved one who is dying, friends and family, as well as professionals who are apt to be offended by the idea of death, are made terribly uncomfortable in confronting it. They are apt to put dying patients under subtle pressure—even without directly complaining to them—to deny the inevitability of their death and engage in positive thinking. This pressure *trivializes* the patients' own emotional distress.[12]

Patients who are dying are not only struggling to cope with their own deaths, but they are also threatened by the prospect of another loss—namely, the continuing attention and concern of their loved ones. This is a terrible dilemma. As death grows more imminent, they may sense that their families have begun to write them off, to distance themselves emotionally from their dying loved one in order to cope with their own anticipated loss. Patients can feel the growing gulf that separates them from their loved ones, and can hear the stilted and unrealistic conversation that fails to accord with the patient's emotional needs.

Terminal patients often feel that there is an unstated conspiracy to prevent them from complaining or displaying personal distress. They are being asked to engage in something akin to denial of their plight. They are made to feel that to be open is to drive away those from whom social support and the comfort that comes from caring are needed.[13]

This subtle pressure to be upbeat forces dying patients to present themselves in a way that seems to them phoney rather than authentic. It is as if they cannot continue to be loved for their legitimately distressed selves, but must protect others from having to confront the unhappy truth.

This dilemma for many patients who are dying drives a wedge between them and those they love at the very time when they need each other most. Denial in this instance is the very opposite of what is needed.

Are There Good and Bad Coping Strategies?

Are certain coping strategies inevitably good or bad? One candidate for a bad coping strategy is *wishful thinking* in which the bad reality is accepted but wished away. It makes a person feel better in the short run, but does not change the long-run realities.

Wishful thinking is different from denial—and more similar to avoidance—because the negative reality is acknowledged. However, like denial, wishing or living in a fantasy undermines efforts that could be made to address the problem directly through action. It prevents the person from doing what might help to eliminate or moderate the problem. If we believe we cannot alter the negative situation and merely wish that things would get better, we will not have the will to do something constructive. Wishful thinking is often connected with poor outcomes because the bad situation does not usually go away by itself.

As in the case of denial, the damage done by wishful thinking depends on whether there is anything constructive that can be done. Wishing or fantasizing that things will get better is harmful only when it gets in the way of constructive action, but probably does no harm when there is nothing that could be done.

The same principle applies to emotional distancing, which is a useful strategy of emotion-centered coping under certain conditions but not others. If, for example, we have undergone a biopsy for a possible cancer and do not know the result, there is nothing that can be done for the time being but wait. Waiting in a continual state of alarm has no value—the outcome might be positive. Being able to distance oneself while waiting results in a better emotional state and can do little or no harm, since there is nothing to be done while waiting anyway.

On the other hand, if we are awaiting a stressful confrontation in the near future—say, a job interview or a report that we must give at a business meeting—then distancing during the waiting period could be harmful because we will not be mobilized to make the necessary preparations. The waiting period could be better spent thinking, preparing notes, and planning for the upcoming event. Many people like to prepare vigorously and only then relax for a time before the confrontation.

So another rule of thumb is that a strategy of emotion-centered coping that works in one situation may not in another, depending on whether or not something constructive can be done to solve the problem. It is not possible to say that certain strategies of coping are always or usually effective, while others are always or usually ineffective or counterproductive. What works depends heavily on the conditions of life as well as on the kind of person one is.

How about problem solving as a coping strategy? Europeans and Americans have a tendency to consider that direct action to change things is best. We are a people who believe in controlling and changing the environment in which we live rather than living in harmony with it. Our traditions are those of natural science. We assume that problem solving is the healthy way to cope and emotion-centered coping is unhealthy.

Nothing could be farther from the truth. If we keep trying to change situations that are stressful, but there is nothing to be done but accept them, distress and its symptoms are apt to be greater than if we adopt emotion-centered coping strategies that permit us to live with the problem. This is precisely what was found in a study of coping by those living near Three Mile Island.[14] You may remember the atomic energy plant in Pennsylvania that almost came to meltdown. Having to live near the plant was a source of severe anxiety and depression, but in most cases, people there could not manage financially to move.

Those who kept struggling in futility to force the authorities to close the atomic energy plant showed much greater anxiety and distress later on, and had a much higher incidence of symptoms of illness, than those who used emotion-centered coping to ameliorate their distress by accepting the situation as it was. In effect, persisting in problem solving in a situation they couldn't control was counterproductive to their well-being.

So we conclude that the best coping calls for a mixture of problem-solving and emotion-centered coping. The task of theorists and researchers studying the process of coping is to determine which patterns work and which do not, under which conditions, and for whom. Since our answers are still fragmentary, this remains an important agenda for future research.

We now turn to how biology and culture influence our emotional lives.

9

How Biology and Culture Affect Our Emotions

EMOTIONS SEEM IRRESISTIBLE and difficult to control at times, triggered whether we want them or not. And each emotion seems to have its own distinctive and recognizable pattern, regardless of who is experiencing it. All this suggests a strong biological component.

If emotions are a biological characteristic of our species, then from an evolutionary point of view we must have inherited many of our emotional tendencies from simpler animals. It is difficult to say whether nonhuman animals experience guilt, shame, envy, or hope. A good argument could be made, however, that they experience something akin to anger, fright, anxiety, jealousy, and happiness.

When we walk our dog and she has been playful and in no hurry to come home, we really can't be sure whether the dog is happy. Dogs don't have facial expressions for happiness, as people do when they smile. And they can't tell us in words what they feel. However, the way they act gives us some clues.

We are confident that our dog feels something like happiness, but again it is difficult to tell whether this happiness is anything like ours. Similarly, we are confident that our dog feels something like jealousy. Many of you have no doubt observed how your dog will growl or try to interact with you if you show affection to someone else, including another dog. Is the dog being possessive or showing jealousy? It certainly looks like rivalry, but it is hard to say.

A similar problem of interpretation applies in a situation in which the dog seems to exhibit guilt when it misbehaves. The dog knows it has violated the rules and shows it by cowering. Here too it is hard to say what the emotion is, however. Perhaps it is not guilt that you are observing but

fear of disapproval or punishment. But the reaction does look like an emotion of some kind.

Do animals experience the subtle differences of meaning conveyed by
righteous anger, or gloating, or pouting, or hurt anger? Probably not. It is
reasonable, nevertheless, to wonder whether animal versions contain the
rudiments of human anger, even if the experience of that anger differs
because of the greater complexity of the meanings we bring to emotional
situations.

Most likely, some degree of emotional response occurs across species,
and certainly across different cultures. Animals are far more limited intellectually and more rigid in their thinking than people, so there are bound
to be differences in the experience among species. Nevertheless, all mammals are made up of cells that contain mostly the same biochemicals, and
they have many similar brain structures, adding to the impression that
there must be some degree of sharing of emotions. Sharing, even if what
is shared is limited, would imply common biological roots.

On the other hand, within our own species we know that not every
person reacts to similar events with the same emotion or with the same
intensity. Some people seldom seem to get angry, while others do so at
the drop of a hat. People also differ in the emotions that overtake them
regularly; some repeatedly react with anger, others with anxiety, still others
with guilt, or shame, envy, or jealousy, each person having somewhat
distinctive emotional tendencies. Such differences reflect our diverse goals
and beliefs, which influence the personal meanings we construct from
similar circumstances.

Not only do people differ in their emotional patterns, but those living
in different cultures display patterns that reflect their unique cultural outlook. For instance, some cultures have few or no words for anger; they
seem to discourage anger or its expression. Others are dominated by anger.
The variations apply to other emotions, too. How culture might influence
the arousal and regulation of emotions is an important issue, which we
will examine later in this chapter.

It is not surprising that scientists whose main interests center on physiology, evolution, and the brain are particularly interested in biological
universals, which means that all people, and perhaps all mammals, share
common properties. For them, biology shapes the emotional reaction.
Push the right button in the brain, so to speak, and we get the anger
pattern, or the anxiety pattern, and so forth. Nor is it surprising that cultural anthropologists, who are interested in diverse social patterns, explain
emotions on the basis of culture. For them, culture shapes the emotional
reaction.[1]

Both points of view—biological and cultural—are, to some extent, correct. The great challenge is to reconcile them and learn how both, together, shape emotions. Psychologists, who are interested in individuals and groups as well as in the human species, have a foot in both camps, the biological and the cultural. Therefore, psychologists sometimes feel obliged to take on the task of reconciling both extreme positions, which is our main task in this chapter.

Let us look at the biological side first to see what it tells us about universals in the arousal and regulation of the emotions, after which we examine cultural sources of emotional variability and then try to put them together.

What Are the Effects of Biology?

Evolution, as conceived and described by Charles Darwin in *The Origin of Species*,[2] has had a profound influence on the way we understand similarities in emotion among different mammalian species, peoples, and individuals. Despite scientific controversies about evolution, it is all but impossible to consider universals in emotion without reference to evolution and how it works.

Darwin's seminal idea was that biological (and, therefore, psychological) traits evolved and changed as a result of the process of natural selection. The meaning of natural selection is often expressed by the phrase "survival of the fittest." This phrase, however, is bothersome to many scientists because it is something of an exaggeration—there are many ways to be fit, and to survive one does not have to be the fittest—but the phrase communicates something of general importance and validity.

Not only did Darwin write the preeminent work on evolution, he also published a major but less well-known treatise on the evolution of the emotions, *The Expression of the Emotions in Man and Animals*.[3] In it, he described the main characteristics of human emotion and proclaimed that they are inherited by all individuals in our species.[4]

That different species adapt to their environments in characteristic ways is now a well-established tenet. A distinguished modern ethologist (one who studies animal species in their natural habitats), Eibel-Eibesfeldt, offered a clear statement of this principle when he wrote:[5]

A blue whale swims with fully coordinated movements immediately after birth. A newborn gnu trots or gallops after its mother when danger threatens, and a freshly hatched duckling waddles into the water, swims with no prior practice, sifts through the mud for food, drinks, and oils its feathers without requiring any model or instructions for these behavior patterns. Hatching the duckling's eggs among those of a hen's brood would not alter any of these typical duck behavior patterns. A duckling that hatched with a brood of chicks would, quite contrary to its foster mother's behavior, go straight into the water.

Species that survive and flourish, which means that they multiply sufficiently to preserve and expand their numbers, have acquired traits that are useful in adaptation. This applies especially to mating and reproduction, which is the way genetic traits are passed on to the next generation. Some of these traits increase the likelihood of mating, which propagates the genes of the fittest animals within the species. If those who mate are particularly fit to survive, this increases the chances that more of their offspring will also survive and reproduce, since these offspring share the same genetic endowment as the parents.

In fact, in comparing the brain structures of different animals, neuroscientists find that humans and animals share numerous portions of brain anatomy.[6] These portions have control over many of the physiological changes that take place in an emotional reaction. Indeed, we still think of the bodily changes in emotions as primitive reactions, which are not under voluntary control.

For example, we cannot directly influence our heart rate or blood pressure; these bodily processes work automatically and are controlled deep inside the brain—in an organ known as the hypothalamus. We can only influence these vital functions indirectly by mobilizing physical effort, seeking a less stressful environment, thinking calm thoughts, and making efforts at relaxation. But even animal emotions, as well as those of people, involve evaluations of the significance of what is happening for well-being.

Primitive animals respond automatically with innate, fixed action patterns that are stimulated by specific environmental stimuli. For example, without any experience or opportunity to learn, baby fowl automatically react with fear to a hawklike figure. This was demonstrated by a brilliant ethologist, Nikko Tinbergen.[7]

Tinbergen did a fascinating experiment in which he created a cardboard shape that looks like a goose when moved in one direction but a hawk when moved in the opposite direction. When fowl saw the hawklike shape, they showed fear; when they saw the gooselike shape, they remained calm. The ability to discriminate the two shapes and react selectively is built into their nervous systems. The inborn ability to distinguish between the different outlines, and the emotion of fear created when faced with the predator, helps save their lives.

Although emotions also save the lives of people, and help them get along in the world, people do not depend on these inborn tendencies to distinguish between what is safe and what is dangerous. Our emotions depend mainly on learning. We need to be sensitive to what is going on and interpret what it means for our well-being. We have to learn what is dangerous or benign in a complex society—for example, when a friendly smile disguises a hostile intent, or when our actions will result in a favorable or unfavorable response from others. Many complicated social meanings are subtle, abstract, and require considerable intelligence and experience to recognize.

As higher species evolved, new portions of the brain were added to the old, and this "new brain" made more complex forms of adaptation possible, which had not been available to earlier species. These new forms of adaptation require reasoning, a sense of self, and will power. The portion of the primate brain that was added to the more primitive animal brain governs the capacity to recognize the personal interests that are at stake in an encounter with others, interpret what is happening, anticipate it, plan how to deal with it, and regulate expression. Emotions and intelligence are important features of this evolution.

For example, people often communicate emotionally relevant but contradictory messages, such as "I love you, but not in that way" (meaning erotically). This is a type of message we won't want to misunderstand because getting along in the world depends on it. Thus, understanding the message could lead the person to abort a fruitless struggle to attain what is not possible and could even be socially damaging or physically dangerous.

The brain is an enormously complicated system estimated to contain 100 billion neurons—all carrying signals to each other through complex networking. These neurons are organized into neural regions and patterns, which have specialized functions. Emotion, for example, is said to be governed by primitive brain centers that were originally found in less advanced animals. The new parts of the brain that evolved in humans are where reason—not emotion—is said to be governed.

Nevertheless, though there is some degree of specialization in the parts of the brain, it is not accurate to say that reason occurs only in some neural networks and emotion in others. Both emotion and reason are represented widely throughout the brain and operate together as a result of the complex and fluid interconnections existing among its various parts.

This interconnectedness and fluidity may be one of the reasons why, when we have had brain damage, as in a cerebral stroke, which leads to motor paralysis and the inability to recognize and label common objects, it is often possible to retrain ourselves to move and speak. The lost functions seem to be taken over by other portions of the brain. It is as if the brain circuits have gotten rewired, suggesting that the networks are change-able to some extent rather than permanently fixed.

Until recently, physiologists focused their attention on the relatively primitive portions of the brain that regulate body temperature, breathing, heart action, metabolism, and so forth.[8] But little attention was given to the parts serving intelligence and will. And relatively few physiologists were interested in emotion.

Gradually, however, the idea that reason played a role in arousing and controlling the emotions gained acceptance, and physiologists began to turn their attention to the portions of the brain that had emerged later in evolution—namely, the cerebral cortex.

The cerebral cortex is the area of the brain where abstract thought mainly occurs, which makes possible foresight, planning, and the complex strategies that help us cope with the stresses of living. We are now confi-dent that the frontal lobes of the cerebral cortex play a major role in the emotions, and that emotion and reason are interdependent—in effect, that there is extensive networking between the older, primitive brain and the newer, advanced brain.

How Emotions Help Us to Survive and Flourish

Emotions—and the capacity to think intelligently—evolved because they facilitate survival and help us flourish. They do this in three ways:

First, our emotions mobilize us, providing added strength and endur-ance in emergencies. For example, in anger and fear the blood supply is increased to the brain and large muscles of the body, but reduced to the digestive tract whose activity is not needed in an emergency. Heart rate and blood pressure rise in these emotional states, making it easier to fight or flee. Powerful hormones are secreted into the bloodstream, which markedly change our metabolic activity, helping us to sustain energy over the period when it is needed.

Second, when we experience an emotion, our mind concentrates its attention on the emergency and what might be done to cope with it. Our attention becomes riveted on the danger and how to evade or otherwise deal with it. We become inattentive to everything else, including what we had previously been doing in order to concentrate on what is now the most salient concern in the struggle to survive and flourish.

In other words, there must be some mechanism that allows an animal to turn instantly from what it was doing to deal with emergencies and mobilize its physical resources. As Darwin saw it, emotions serve this need in mammals. They give urgency to making distinctions quickly among safe, dangerous, and opportunistic situations, and make possible the extra energy and stamina needed to deal with emergencies. Emotions have to be smart to facilitate survival, and thus intelligence and emotion evolved together in our species.

You can see how mobilization and the concentration of attention work in a familiar example. Because mothers become fearful of the dangers faced by their children—which they understand but their inexperienced children do not—they often have a problem about how to prevent fatal accidents to their children on today's urban and suburban streets. Imagine finding your two-year-old running into a street where automobiles are speeding, oblivious of the danger. What do you do? Typically, you rush after your toddler in panic, grabbing the child and shouting admonitions.

Parents who do this—and I think it is nearly universal—have shown their intuitive understanding of the importance of emotion for survival when they frighten their young children about crossing the street. Better to scare the child about traffic than to leave his or her survival to trial and error where one error could be fatal. When, in turn, the child becomes fearful, its body and mind also undergo the mobilizing neurochemical changes and increased attention to the danger. This could help it survive next time by making it wary or avoiding the dangerous setting altogether.

Third, emotions signal our state of mind to others. For example, emotions are expressed by muscle-movement patterns of the face, as in a smile, the posture of the body, or a downcast head. These expressions can reveal whether a person or animal is angry and likely to attack, or frightened and likely to flee. The awareness of another's intentions, interpreted on the basis of these emotional signals, makes it possible to be more attuned to social dangers and opportunities. The awareness also increases the effectiveness with which dangers and opportunities are handled.

What we are saying is that intelligence and emotions evolved together because of their value for survival, and they are interdependent in serving adaptation. Emotions are governed as much by the newer portions of the brain that serve reason as well as by the older portions. Emotions depend on an evaluating mind that can discriminate what is good or bad for us. However, once aroused, an emotion—especially when its expression is uncontrolled or badly used in social relationships—can also get us into trouble.

Intelligence, which includes the ability to learn from experience and make quick and accurate decisions, was one of the great adaptational advances as species evolved and grew more complex. As later species gained in intelligence, more elaborate and flexible ways of adapting to social situations came into being. Intelligence helped a species to be selective in responding to what is dangerous or not dangerous, and to make use of opportunities to thrive.

The potential to survive and flourish is also facilitated by being able to predict the future on the basis of clues in the present, which is one of the advantages of intelligence and the ability to judge the future consequences of actions. The ability to learn enough to plan and make things happen in the future is a great advance for our species, which frees us from the tyranny of the present. As far as we know, this ability is most developed in humans.

If we wish to grasp how biology influences emotion, we must also examine the manifestations of emotion that are universal within and between species. The most obvious are the ways emotions are expressed in the face and body, and the physiological changes connected with them.

Facial and Bodily Expressions That Reveal Our Emotions

When an emotion occurs, we are apt to show it in our facial expressions and our body postures and movements. There was a time when the dominant view was that the face mirrored only cultural rules of expression. The breakthrough, which demonstrated universal patterns of expression in a number of emotions, was the result of the work of several research pioneers in the 1970s.[9] Some of these pioneers took motion pictures of facial expressions and carefully mapped the muscle-movement patterns displayed during the enactment of different emotions.

In the course of the next few decades, this work, and that of a growing group of other research workers, revealed that when certain—but not all—emotions were occurring essentially the same patterns were displayed on the face of people from markedly different cultures. In effect, there is an anger face, a disgust face, a fear face, a happiness face, and so on.

Despite the innateness of the facial muscular response in these emotions, we are capable of concealing or disguising what we feel on the basis of social imperatives. For example, we may smile to suggest we are pleased or happy. But there is evidence that some smiles are not happy smiles and look different from those that occur when we are truly happy. Even when we feel angry, anxious, disgusted, depressed, or in pain, we may smile to express our fortitude, because we wish others to think we are happy, or perhaps we wish to mislead an enemy.

Typically, in a happy smile, the mouth turns upward and the muscles of the eyebrows show a correspondingly appropriate motor pattern. However, in a mixed or deceptive smile, the eyebrow muscles that create crows-feet wrinkles react differently.[10] We may or may not notice the difference or recognize precisely what it is about the face that makes it less convincing.

Although there is considerable debate about how this works—as is always true at the frontiers of knowledge—there seems little doubt that facial expressions serve as social clues about what a person is feeling. People differ considerably in how well they can read these clues. Some are more perceptive than others, or know better what to look for. No doubt, these clues—which serve as social signals about what another person's intentions are—were useful for survival in our past, which is, presumably, why they evolved and may still be evolving.

Nonverbal communication, which includes gestures and vocalizations as well as facial and motor expressions, is found in animals as well as people. The closer on the evolutionary tree that animals are to humans, the more similarities there are in these nondeliberate modes of communication. A psychologist who has long been interested in the evolution of human emotions, Robert Plutchik,[11] wrote this about nonverbal communication:

> It is in considering non-verbal communication that the most extensive similarities to human behavior are found. Chimpanzees hold hands, touch and pat each other, embrace, kiss, bite, punch, kick, scratch and pull each other's hair in contexts that are similar to those seen when humans demonstrate the same behavior. Greeting patterns are similar, as are aggressive behaviors. The chimpanzee also has a wide range of vocalizations, and each appears to be related to a specific emotion; screams are associated with fear, barks with aggression, etc. . . . These various detailed observations show many behavioral similarities between chimpanzees and human beings and are consistent with their similarities in chromosomes, blood proteins, immune responses and DNA.

So social signals of all kinds—from gestures to vocalizations—seem a part of our evolutionary heritage. But imagine the importance of such social cues if one is potential prey. It is always surprising in films of herd animals to see zebras and wildebeests standing calmly in close proximity to a pride of lions lying in the tall grass. Why would an animal that is the prey of another remain seemingly calm so close to its predators? The fact is that herd animals can tell when the lions are not interested in hunting; whether by smell or the configuration of the pride, these animals of prey "read" the situation correctly and react accordingly. They probably learned some of this from past experience. And some time in their evolutionary past, their brains incorporated the signals given by lions about their immediate intentions. Vocalizations, too, are seen in humans as well as other species, and they appear closely linked to emotion. As Plutchik has observed:[12]

> Vocalizations are a means of communication in lower animals as well as in humans. Certain distinct sounds appear to be associated with pain, fear, anger, courtship and sex. For example, observations of cebus mon-

keys indicated that they expressed anger by shrill screams. In addition, as fear tends to cause the muscles of the body to tremble, the sounds connected with fear tend to be tremulous. Pigs grunt when satisfied and scream shrilly when distressed. Such screams are considered by Darwin to be calls for assistance and their intense, high-pitched quality tends to make them heard over a long distance. Darwin believed that similar patterns of vocal expression of emotions can be heard in humans as well. Recent research has largely confirmed this.

Useful information about emotions and intentions is provided in an animal's face, and its overall demeanor, just as it is in the expressions of the human face.[13] We know more about facial expressions in emotion than we do about bodily movements and gestures, but the same kind of social signaling seems to be taking place. When we are sad, for example, our bodies seem to have a characteristic look—hunched over, downcast eyes, and drooping shoulders. When we experience embarrassment, an emotion that falls within the shame family, we may display a kind of amused, shy smile—as if to say, "You caught me"—while half turning away from others, head down. There is also the familiar reaction of the blush, an involuntary physiological reaction that gives away our momentary embarrassment.

Physiological Changes in Emotion

When we are emotionally aroused, extensive and profound changes occur in our bodies, which can be measured by modern technology. Early on, the changes that attracted the most attention were the result of action by the *autonomic nervous system* (ANS), sometimes referred to as the involuntary nervous system, because we cannot control it directly.

There are two antagonistic subsystems of the involuntary nervous system (ANS)—one called sympathetic, the other parasympathetic. These are particularly important in our emotions. Activity in one suppresses the effects of the other. The easiest way to understand this antagonism is to remember that the sympathetic nervous system excites and mobilizes us to deal with the world under conditions of danger, and parasympathetic activity turns off these alarms.

In the 1930s, interest began to turn also to the hormones secreted by the endocrine glands, which also become active when we respond emotionally. Foremost among these are the adrenal glands, which secrete two kinds of hormones, adrenaline and noradrenaline. They are produced by the inner portions (or medulla) of the adrenals. Their secretions are stimulated by the sympathetic nervous system at the first sign of an emotion.

When an emotion is aroused, these hormones are poured rapidly into the blood. They make you feel a rush of excitement or nervousness and act on the body in ways very much like those of the sympathetic nervous system. The heart rate goes up, as does blood pressure, and blood is shunted from the visceral organs, such as the stomach and intestines, to the hands and large muscles of the body. The body is being prepared for "fight or flight" by these changes, which is the way the distinguished physiologist Walter Cannon first put it.[14]

The outer portions (or cortex) of the adrenal glands produce a different set of hormones, which are also important in emotion. These hormones are referred to as *corticosteroids* (steroids that are made by the cortex). Corticosteroids have profound effects on metabolism and help in sustaining action in an emergency. However, when too much of any hormone is secreted into the bloodstream, or if these hormones remain in the body for too long, they can result in harm to the tissues, producing what are often called stress disorders.[15]

How Biology Affects the Arousal of Emotions

Now we come to the most fascinating possibility of all, which is that the dramatic plot or personal meaning that defines each emotion is universal in the human species. In Chapters 2 to 6, we discussed the dramatic plot for each emotion. There we said that anger results from a demeaning offense against me and mine, anxiety from uncertain, existential threat, sadness from an irrevocable loss, hope from fearing the worst but yearning for better, and so on. And we focused on how people construe meaning from events, which lead them to emotional responses. What we did not consider was why a particular meaning, or plot, which we detected led inexorably to a specific emotion. For all we know, this is simply how we are built as humans.

How could this be? If we turn to evolution, we can see that the emotions of the modern human adult are a distillation of the wisdom of the ages, a wisdom that derives from the same emotional dilemmas our ancestors experienced. We react emotionally more or less as they did as a result of the way we evolved as a species.

These emotional dilemmas include having our status demeaned or put down (anger), experiencing uncertain threat (anxiety), facing a sudden danger to life and limb (fright), having violated the social mores of our tribe (guilt), acting like a less ideal person than we aspire to (shame), having undergone an irrevocable loss (sadness), and so on, for each of the other emotions. The personal meanings these emotional dilemmas express have been reported in thousands of years of human history—and in most, if not all, cultures.

Because they are inevitable in social existence, by the time we become adults all of us have experienced most if not all of the relationships identified in these dramatic plots. Regardless of culture, no competent person fails to understand strong emotional events, such as human treachery, threat, triumph, loss, hope and despair, love and its vicissitudes, and a joyful gain or stunning success. These experiences and the relationships that provoke them express and reveal the human condition. Given what we are as beings, it could not be otherwise.

Animal Origins of Human Emotions

Could there be nonhuman origins for many of our human emotions? If so, it would add weight to the evolutionary argument about how human emotions came about. Although we should be wary of attributing our own emotions to animals because it is unlikely they comprehend meanings as we do, some striking parallels do exist.

More than any other emotional phenomena, aggression and anger have been looked at from the point of view of their animal origins. Nonhuman animals display a number of different types of aggression. One type, predation, consists of attacking other species for food. Another type is defensive aggression; for example, when young offspring are threatened by a predator, the mother will, in turn, threaten or attack the predator if she believes it might endanger her babies. A third type is the fighting that goes on within a species in order to attain or preserve a rank in the dominance hierarchy. Humans show all three of these aggressive patterns.

In these varieties of aggression the provocation varies, the pattern of behavior looks different, and the physiological reactions differ too. For example, a cat stalking an animal for food displays a tautly controlled stealth until an attack is mounted, while a mother cat protecting her young presents a picture of furious rage. In all likelihood, dominance hierarchies offer the best parallels with human aggression, so let us look at them closely.

A *dominance hierarchy* takes time to be established, but once it is, it remains quite stable under normal conditions and permits a degree of peace. The stability is apt to break down, however, when food is scarce and during the mating season, when there is frantic competition.

The privileges of dominance in animals include better access to food—the dominant animal eats first or controls a food-bearing territory—and mating preference. There may also be some responsibilities. In some species, for example, baboons, one or several dominant males not only control the movements of the group but also fight off attacks by other species that endanger the group.

Under normal circumstances, young males typically challenge the older, larger, dominant males in an attempt to move up in the hierarchy. Initially, they threaten without fighting, but in a full challenge a fight ensues, usually ending when the loser retreats. It is relatively rare in these dominance struggles for an animal to be killed. When a challenged, dominant animal loses, he is relegated to an irrelevant position—no longer competitive and no longer a threat. Because of the importance to animals of the privileges of dominance, including access to food, the loss of a dominant position is extremely stressful for the loser, who may become isolated, sicken, and die.

In the context of dominance struggles, we could look at fright in the same way we analyzed anger, and in many ways, fright is the other side of the coin. When an animal threatens, the threatened animal may withdraw in fear, but it may display threatening behavior as well. When either animal senses that it is outmatched by the other, it will withdraw. Unless an animal is trapped and must fight, what happens is apt to reflect the animal's appraisal of risk and probable outcome. Fright or anxiety probably accompanies withdrawal, just as anger is probably linked to an aggressive attack.

Research with macaque monkeys has indicated that being dominant affords rights to copulation.[16] Only high-ranking males become the main companions of females who conceive babies. In one macaque group the three highest ranking males managed nearly three-quarters of all copulations with such females. Males who rose in the hierarchy spent increasing amounts of time with high-ranking females, who were those that conceived. Presumably, this increased the fitness of their offspring, since more were likely to survive if they came from these high-ranking matings.

Dominance hierarchies appear to be universal in human society as well. They are expressed as social status. Women seem to be attracted to men who display dominance with regard to skill, achievement, money, and power. Interest in dominance has usually been considered a strongly male trait, associated with male sex hormones. However, it may be a well-kept secret that women too struggle for and enjoy dominance in their own way. With changes in sex roles in recent times, it is not clear how dominance patterns will change, if at all. In some animal species, there are also dominance struggles among females.

A good case can be made that dominance struggles are a precursor of status struggles and anger in human societies. If we view the cause of human anger as a "demeaning offense against me and mine," the parallels are obvious. A threat to social status and ego-identity, which provokes human anger, seems much like the situation in which an animal's position in the dominance hierarchy is threatened. Aggression, however, is one thing; anger quite another. Remember that anger is an inner state that can only be inferred from actions and threat displays, or what people say about their state of mind.

Are the animals that engage in dominance struggles angry? The main feature of such struggles are threat displays—that is, efforts to intimidate the other animal. These threats certainly look like anger, but they may represent only aggressive displays and not the emotion of anger. The truth is that we simply do not know for sure.

Are animals angry when they engage in *predation* or killing for food? Alas, we cannot ask the creature. But if we think about human analogues, predation may be akin only to the cool, nonemotional aggression humans employ when they destroy a business competitor, drop bombs anonymously on an enemy they may never see, pummel an opponent in the boxing ring whom they respect and even like, and body check or tackle an opposing ice hockey or football player. Hating an enemy may make a person more ready to attack or even kill, but it is not necessary. Not all aggression involves anger.

The rage displayed by a mother cat protecting her young seems superficially like human rage. Yet if the threatening predator departs the scene as a result of her threatening display of anger, she will not follow. This indifference isn't the stuff of typical human anger and aggression. There isn't enough keenness for revenge in animal aggression once the threat has passed to be the same as what happens with people. Only humans vow to avenge themselves against their enemies.

The difference is probably the result of the human ability to remember, to have a past, present, and future, and to sustain long-term plans. If we have harmed another person, especially in a humiliating way, the victim, if still alive, could represent a constant danger. The humiliated person may return another day and do us in. The history of conquest and revolution is filled with examples of killing a deposed ruler and his family rather than leaving them alive lest they return to murder the new ruler.

The further out we go along the evolutionary tree, and the more mature the human child, the more the patterns we observe seem to resemble the human adult variety of anger. Consider, for example, the case of anger in the chimpanzee, an animal that shares more human DNA than any other, making it perhaps our closest primate ancestor. If on the stage or in the circus you work with chimpanzees, which can be dangerous animals, you need to know whether a chimp is angry or chronically malicious if you want to handle it safely. Adopting an evolutionary perspective, Hebb and Thompson[17] wrote:

> The causes of aggression [notice they speak of aggression, not anger] are
> more varied than in the rat, and far more varied in the chimpanzee than

in the dog . . . the period of emotional disturbance following a brief
stimulation also increases from rat to dog to chimpanzee (the chimpanzee
Fifi, for example, sulked for three weeks over not getting a cup of milk,
first showing outright anger, then refusing to accept milk from anyone
for a day or so, and continuing for three weeks to refuse it from the one
who had denied it to her).

Notice that Fifi, the chimpanzee, remembers her deprivation, on
which her sulking over three weeks must have depended. In effect, chimpanzees might be capable of seeking vengeance just as people do because
of their prodigious memories for ideas and events, which is limited to
more advanced species. Sulking may even be unique to a few primates
and it suggests the increasing similarity between the intellectual capacities
of species closer to us on the evolutionary tree. This would also suggest
that there is much greater similarity between people and chimpanzees in
the experience of emotions than would apply, say, between people and
dogs.

Although biology imposes a great many of the conditions on which
emotions depend, it does not explain all the variety and complexity of
emotion, as will be evident when we examine the role of culture in human emotion next.

What of Culture and Emotion?

We live in a complex web of social relationships, which shape how we
think, feel, and act. As we grow up, we learn about specific rules from
intimate family ties, religious and ethnic groups, and the local communi-
ties in which we live, which in turn, are a part of nations. We tend not
to realize how elaborate and complex the rules and conventions are that
govern our social behavior. Though barely conscious of them, we follow
these rules on streets, buses, subways, and trains, at weddings, funerals, in
school classes, and with members of the opposite sex. Social rules keep
our immediate social world relatively stable and predictable.

The way rules and conventions operate is not precisely the same from
one group to another. Nor is the subjective world exactly the same for
different groups living within the same society. An African-American or
Asian living in an urban ghetto sees the social environment quite differently from the affluent white living in a suburb. The same religion can be
experienced differently by factory workers, merchants, millionaires, farm
sharecroppers, forest loggers, intellectuals, and other groups.

If this is true within our multicultural society, imagine the differences in outlook among the diverse cultures of the world—Japanese, Chinese, Filipino, or Vietnamese, Eastern European, Egyptian Muslim, Coptic Christian, Indian Hindu. People from these cultures grow up with somewhat different value systems, patterns of goal commitment, and beliefs about themselves and the world which, in addition to the actual events of their lives, are prime factors shaping their emotions.

The same sort of diversity applies to individuals as well. We have different experiences with the people who are influential in our childhood, such as parents (who are two quite different individuals), teachers, and peers. And all these diverse influences help to create unique social worlds, which each of us perceive and define differently. Culture, too, provides the meanings on which our transactions with other people depend.[18]

We must now examine how our emotions are influenced by culture, which does so in the two distinctly different ways we have come across before.[19] First, it influences appraisal by defining the significance of what is happening for a person's well-being. This significance, in turn, determines the emotion that will be *aroused*. Second, culture informs us about how the emotion should be *controlled and expressed* once it has been aroused. Let us look at the ways cultural influences work more closely.

How Culture Influences the Arousal of Emotions

A culture provides the basis for the appraisal of a provocation. It defines what is a demeaning offense (for anger); an existential threat (for anxiety); a violation of a moral proscription (for guilt); the evidence that one is adored (for love); the events that enhance one's ego-identity (for pride); the ways we have failed to live up to an ego-ideal (for shame); the nature of an altruistic gift (for gratitude); and so on, for each of the other emotions and their dramatic plots.

As usual, anger, anxiety, and shame provide good illustrations. Culture communicates the consensual meaning for appraising whether or not another person's actions constitute a demeaning offense. Should a particular criticism from a friend, teacher, or whomever be considered an insult or an altruistic gift to be appreciated? What kinds of criticism should we consider insulting? Is it appropriate to react to the criticism, or to some other act, with anger as opposed to anxiety or shame?

In Japan, social criticism is even more offensive to people than it is in the United States. One reason is that Japanese children become highly sensitized to the way they are viewed by the group and the society. They spend very little time separated from their mothers, who communicate anxiety about the world outside the family and make prodigious efforts to create and preserve closeness between them and the child. The Japanese mother sensitizes the child to avoid feelings of loneliness and to manage these feelings through closeness to and dependence on the mother.

The ultimate aim is to create a child who will be embedded in the social group or community rather than being autonomous. The Japanese child wants much more than the U.S. child to please the mother and be at one with her. In contrast, mothers in the United States emphasize autonomy and independence on the part of the child. They readily offer criticism and freely display anger. The ultimate aim is to foster self-reliance, individualism, and toughness.

In stories in which there is conflict between the wishes of an individual and the welfare of the family or community—for example, when there is social pressure on a couple to give up their love to conform to social rules—the two cultures differ in interesting ways. Individual values are apt to triumph in the stories of Western cultures, while community values triumph in those of Japan.

Although there is some ambivalence in both cultures, these stories usually end with the Japanese couple giving up their relationship and ultimately conforming. To the Japanese, there is a sense of rightness about this. In the West, in contrast, the lovers resist the family's wishes; we have a sense of rightness about this, and enjoy the triumph of the individual (or the couple) over society.

The result, however, may be the tragedy of star-crossed lovers, who must die as they defy the society, as Shakespeare's *Romeo and Juliet* and Leonard Bernstein's *West Side Story* poignantly illustrate. We are saddened because Romeo and Juliet almost pull off their daring plan. The audience wants them to defy their feuding families. In Japan, there are also star-crossed lovers, but the tragedy here is that the couple must suffer or sacrifice themselves, giving each other up in the interest of family and community or kill themselves. The Japanese audience wants them to conform to their world.

As a result of its cultural heritage and the childrearing practices that enforce it, the Japanese child grows up being far more sensitive to how the community reacts compared with the child in the United States, whose values are more individualistic. Criticism by the Japanese mother is far more devastating to the Japanese child who is not accustomed to it compared with similar criticism by a mother in the United States.

The Japanese child is more likely to feel shame and less likely to feel anger than a child in the United States. The relationship between anger and anxiety are also reversed in the two cultures. Being anxious seems more acceptable to the Japanese self-image, while anger is tolerated less; in contrast, anger seems more acceptable and anxiety less so to the self-image of a person growing up in the United States.

What is criticized is also different in these two cultures. For example, if you are Japanese and fail in school, criticism for lack of effort is almost never expressed, but, if it were, it is particularly devastating and likely to result in shame, while criticism for lack of ability is not. On the other hand, if you are a child in the United States and fail, criticism for lack of ability is more devastating than criticism for lack of effort. In the United States, we often use lack of effort as an excuse for failure, a way of saving face. Lack of ability in a competitive and individualistic society like ours is a prescription for failure; it is inescapable. In a society like that of Japan, more devoted to the community than to the individual, a person of meager ability still has a place.

How Culture Influences the Control and Expression of Emotion

Many of the emotional differences observed in different cultures have to do with what happens after an emotion has been aroused rather than with the arousal itself. Every culture maintains values and rules about how an emotion should be controlled and overtly expressed. We learn them as a result of growing up and living within a culture, and this makes us different in certain respects from those of a different culture. Because societies have an important stake in how anger, sadness, guilt, shame, and pride are dealt with, these emotions provide excellent examples of these values and rules in the shaping of our emotions.

Let us begin with the Yanomamö people of Venezuela, which is among the most aggressive and angry of all the cultures anthropologists have studied. The Yanomamö seem to prize anger and aggression. They are extremely warlike, and practice infanticide to keep their population below 80 in number. When the food supply is reduced, intense competition and frustration develop in the group, and release is sought in warfare with an enemy group.[20]

How are we to understand this extreme behavior? How, in fact, can we understand any differences between cultures? Part of the explanation arises from the physical circumstances in which a people live, the available resources, the population pressures on those resources, the type of contact with other peoples, and so on. However, some differences are probably just the result of chance. To put the Yanomamö approach to anger in context, let us look at another culture that approaches anger very differently.

Many of the things we know about negative cultural attitudes toward anger come from the research of cultural anthropologist Robert Levy, who made an intensive study of the Tahitians.[21] In Tahiti, displays of anger are met by gossip, coolness, and instructions about how to handle it. As a people, they are very wary of this emotion. If it is felt, anger is apt to be masked by a smile rather than expressed overtly. Here is Levy's distillation of the Tahitian outlook, which is in marked contrast to that of the aggressive Yanomamös.

> Doctrines about anger and violence . . . lead to [the following] strategies for coping with anger: try not to get into situations which will make you mad. Don't take things seriously, or withdraw if possible. If someone else is mad at you, try not to let it build up. If you do get angry, however, express it by talking out your anger, so that things can be corrected and you will not be holding it in. Express your anger, if possible, by verbal rather than physical means. If you use physical means try to use symbolic actions, not touching the person. If you touch him, be careful not to hurt him.

It is interesting to compare Levy's observations about the Tahitian attitude toward anger with the attitude of our own society. They resemble each other in important ways. We are a society given to considerable aggressiveness and anger, though we are also ambivalent about these reactions.

The outlook toward aggression and anger also differs among groups within our society. For example, middle-class values treat the physical display of anger as less tolerable than its verbal display. In the working class, and some ethnic groups—Latino, for example—it is considered macho to threaten physical attack to support one's position. If threats are not acted out, social status and self-esteem are thought to be undermined by what appears to be physical cowardice, an unwillingness to fight.

On the whole, values about anger and aggression in the United States are well expressed in Western movies. These values are described by Professor of English Jane Tomkins, who uses the plot of the movie *Shane* to illustrate them. The outlook seems comparable to what Levy found in Tahiti. Even if you have never seen this movie, you will find it familiar. In an essay titled "Fighting Words,"[22] Tomkins describes the plot sequence of *Shane*, which she considers typical of many Westerns.

> [This] sequence reproduces itself in a thousand Western novels and movies. Its pattern never varies. The hero, provoked by insults, first verbal then physical, resists the urge to retaliate, proving his moral superiority to those who are taunting him. It is never the hero who taunts his adversary; if he does, it's only after he's been pushed "too far." And this, of course, is what always happens. The villains, whoever they may be, finally commit an act so atrocious that the hero *must* retaliate in kind. At this juncture, the point where provocation has gone too far, retaliatory

violence becomes not simply justifiable but imperative: now we are made to feel that *not* to transgress the interdict against violence would be the transgression. The feeling of supreme righteousness in this instance is delicious and hardly to be distinguished from murderousness. I would almost say they are the same thing.

And when the hero finally retaliates, the audience cheers, either quietly or in a collective outburst of hoorays and clapping with pleasure, showing how much it shares in the value system being portrayed.

In Tahitian culture, while anger is responded to warily, it still remains in the forefront of consciousness. There are many words for anger and shame, as there are in our own culture. And yet there is little consciousness of sadness (which includes longing and loneliness) and guilt. These emotions are either ignored or disguised, and there are few words for them. Tahitians recognize severe grief or lamentation, but they describe the experience of sadness and the loss that produces it as fatigue, sickness, or some other kind of bodily distress. In other words, sadness and guilt are downplayed, but anger and shame remain an important concern for Tahitians.

This poses an interesting psychological problem in the cultural analysis of emotions. Considering the Tahitian way of dealing with loss in which the reaction to it is described as fatigue or illness rather than sadness, it is difficult to know whether Tahitians fail to experience sadness or cover it up with another word—in this case, illness. Actually, there are four logical possibilities: They may be (1) reacting with sadness but labeling it as illness; (2) experiencing sadness but denying it; (3) reacting with no emotion (though this seems inconsistent with their bodily symptoms); or (4) reacting with an emotion other then sadness which, for argument's sake, might be called illness.

The first possibility seems the most reasonable—namely, they feel sad but call it something else, perhaps to deny the culturally proscribed idea. But emotions are not games we play with words; they are real states of mind and body, which occur when we experience, say, irrevocable loss or a demeaning offense. People may control the overt manifestation of an emotion and the label used to indicate its meaning, or even deny the presence of the emotion altogether. However, regardless of how it is labeled or whether it is denied, the emotion will occur.

In sharp contrast to the Tahitians are the Utku-Inuit Eskimos who have been described by cultural anthropologist Jean Briggs in a book titled *Never in Anger*. According to Briggs, the Utku do not feel, much less express, anger.[23] Unlike the Tahitians, the Utku do not talk much about anger and regard it is reprehensible. This example seems—on the face of it, given Briggs's interpretation—to be about the arousal of the emotion in the first place rather than its regulation. But we must be wary about accepting the interpretation that anger is absent among these people. The lack of common words for anger, and the fact that they don't talk about it, does not necessarily mean that anger is not felt. It may be that anger to the Utku is similar to sadness among the Tahitians—the emotion goes underground and is transformed, but is present nonetheless.

Indeed, it is necessary to separate surface behavior from the feelings and mental processes that lie beneath, perhaps unknown to both actors and observers. Only an effort to study the motives, beliefs, and appraisals that might operate below the surface can resolve the issues of whether and to what extent Briggs's title, *Never in Anger*, is apt. The issue is no less than the momentous one of whether culture can overcome biology in the arousal—as opposed to the regulation—of an emotion.

What should make us suspicious of Briggs's interpretation is that the Utku do recognize anger in foreigners, and some anthropological observations suggest that they do sometimes feel annoyed, even hostile. They squeeze their children so hard on the grounds of loving them that their offspring become apprehensive about aggression. They display a form of violence as well. For example, they readily beat their dogs in the name of discipline, perhaps as a displacement of their anger. And on occasion they seem to get as "heated up" as we do. [24]

In effect, it is not so much that they do not experience anger, but that they are very selective about the person or animal toward whom it is directed. This case more likely serves as an example of how cultural values shape the *expression* of anger rather than proving the absence of the arousal of that emotion.

Our final example of the role of culture in emotion comes from a classic study of mental illness in Irish-American and Italian-American families. [25] This research, unusual in that it is about a cultural contrast within Europe and America, focused on the emotional patterns displayed by male schizophrenic patients as a result of their different cultural backgrounds.

Observations were made of sixty male schizophrenic patients in a mental hospital in New York City. Their ages ranged from 18 to 45. The two cultural groups were comparable in education and socioeconomic status. Both groups were Catholic, had been hospitalized at about the same time, and were composed of first-, second-, or third-generation Americans. They differed only in whether their cultural background was Italian or Irish.

At the time of the study, Irish mothers usually were the dominant and controlling influence in the family. In the Irish family, sexual activity was subordinated to procreation, celibacy was encouraged, sexual feelings were considered sinful and a source of guilt, courtship was drawn out and lacked intensity, and marriage for males was typically delayed for a long time, probably for economic reasons. In contrast, the Italian family had a dominant father rather than a dominant mother. Sexuality was not only acceptable, but was cultivated as a sign of healthy maleness. Expressive acting out of feelings was encouraged, whereas in the Irish family they were inhibited.

Given these sharp cultural differences, we should expect to find considerable differences in the emotional patterns displayed by the two groups of schizophrenic patients. This was indeed the case. The Irish male was far more inhibited than the Italian and more beset by anxiety and guilt. Irish males felt greater anger toward female family members than the Italian males, though these feelings were largely inhibited in the Irish group. Italian males were far more emotionally expressive and overtly angry than the Irish, but they directed their anger at the male parent and did not express anger at female family figures.

These observations provide a striking instance of the influence of culture. Not only was anger expressed differently in these two European cultures, but the culture also influenced those toward whom the anger was directed. Roughly the same amount of anger was found in both the Irish-Americans and Italian-Americans, but anger was more readily expressed by patients of Italian origin than by the patients of Irish origin. The anger was also directed at different family members.

Culture and the Individual

We must not forget that individuals within a culture differ greatly from each other in all sorts of ways, including the emotions they typically experience and how they are controlled and expressed. This means that the effects of culture—though substantial—are not monolithic. The larger culture's values and meanings do not necessarily become adopted as firmly in all persons.

Each of us as individuals experiences formative influences that are distinct from the cultural norms in which we live. These influences depend on the particular parents, relatives, and peers we encounter as we are growing up. We have unique personal experiences that shape our beliefs and goal patterns. In some societies—such as our own—there are apt to be a number of subcultures, each with divergent outlooks, each contributing to variability among individuals. One cannot, therefore, reliably predict what an individual will be like, but only the patterns that may be supported in that society.

Putting Biology and Culture Together

We come now to the bottom line of this analysis of biology and culture, which has the purpose of reconciling them as influences on emotional development. The important conclusion is that biology forms some essential features of the emotion process since it is an adaptation that aids our survival. Culture, on the other hand, teaches us the meaning of the social situation that arouses each emotion and whether and how the emotion is expressed.

Biology influences the particular emotion that will arise from particular meanings in the form of the core relational themes, or dramatic plots, which we have looked at for each emotion. We are, in effect, constructed in such a way that we all experience a number of types of human relationships. This makes it almost inevitable that we will sometimes be slighted, be made uneasy about uncertain threats, violate cultural norms, enjoy affection, be triumphant in a struggle, appreciate the plight of another person, and so on.

Once a particular appraisal has been made, a given emotion will follow. If the personal meaning we have constructed about what has happened is that we have been demeaned, the emotion we are impelled to experience is anger; if it is an existential threat, we will react with anxiety; if it is the enhancement of our ego-identity, we will feel pride; and so on for each of the emotions. The connection between relational meanings and the emotion we react with is a property of our biology.

Biology also sets in motion the pattern of physiological changes, which is an important part of the complex emotional response. Changes in the brain and in the hormones that circulate in the blood have profound effects on the tissues throughout the body, thereby affecting the physical resources available to us for confronting emergencies.

Culture (also the "cultures" of our individual lives) influences the goals and beliefs that lead to the personal stakes and relational meanings we construct in appraising what is happening. Cultures tell us when to feel demeaned, what is an ambiguous threat, what is a proper source of pride, and so on. A particular emotion will only be aroused if we make the appraisal that is biologically linked with it. But once we have made that appraisal, it is inevitable that the emotional reaction ordained by our biological heritage will occur.

This means that we may react to the same situation differently on the basis of our particular cultural or subcultural background, or our individual life experience. The rules are clear; if two individuals both make different appraisals in the same situation, they will each experience a different emotion. And if both individuals make the same appraisal in different situations, they will each experience the same emotion.

The two major influences on our emotions, biology and culture, enter into every emotion we experience, as well as into the control of its visible expression. It could be no other way, since we are biological *and* social animals, and our survival and well-being are tied to our emotional reactions. These reactions motivate efforts to cope when we are in danger, when we must deal with harms and losses, and when we experience the benefits of a favorable event in our lives.

We turn now to the logic of our emotions—that is, to the link between emotion and reason—and confront some of our misconceptions about what emotions are really all about.

10

The Logic of Our Emotions

FOR THOUSANDS OF YEARS in the Western world, we have believed that emotion is an unpredictable response to life's events, incompatible with intelligent judgment. We speak disparagingly of making decisions based on emotions, which are said to be a property of lower animals, while reason is claimed to be characteristic of advanced and intelligent beings like ourselves. When people react with emotion, we say they are regressing and displaying their primitive, animal natures. And these are not just our ideas; they have been handed down from the Ancient Greeks and have come to dominate Western ways of thinking, and are still taken for granted by most of us.[1, 2, 3]

This way of thinking about emotion and reason can be observed repeatedly. To offer one recent illustration, the respected and distinguished American diplomat George F. Kennan wrote in a personal diary dated December 9, 1992, a comment about President Bush's decision to send Marines to Somalia to deal with the widespread starvation and chaos that was rampant there. The comment reveals a remarkably farsighted anticipation of the quagmire that later developed in that country, as well as the tendency to contrast emotion and reason. Kennan's comment was published in the *New York Times* on September 30, 1993, on its Op Ed page. It read in part:

> There can be no question that the reason for [the public's] acceptance [of the decision] lies primarily with the exposure of the Somalia situation by the American media, above all, television. . . . But this is an emotional reaction, not a thoughtful or deliberate one. . . . [It was] occasioned by the sight of the suffering of the starving people. It is one which was not under any deliberate and thoughtful control.

The problem with this statement is that it pits emotion against reason even though the emotion charged with being the basis of the public acceptance—sympathy for a starving people—is itself the result of reason, albeit not the reason Kennan would like to have seen employed. It was, he believes, a poor judgment. But it is incorrect to see this reaction as any more emotional than if the decision had been not to do anything. In an otherwise well-reasoned diary comment, it is a careless—but common—usage to suggest that when we make bad decisions, they are based on emotion, but when we arrive at good decisions, they are based solely on reason.

Nowadays psychologists concerned with emotion are beginning to think that this view is quite false—that, in fact, emotions always depend substantially on reason. The purpose of this chapter is to suggest that there is no emotion without thought or reason, and that our emotions are really products of the way we personally construe what is happening in our lives, which is expressed in the idea—formally developed in Chapter 7—that emotion depends on an appraisal of personal meaning. Without meaning, without appraisal, there is no emotion.

The Ancient Greek word for emotion was passion. Only in modern times has the word emotion been substituted for passion. In contrast with passion, reason was said by Greek thinkers to be a voluntary activity of the self-directed mind. Unlike other beasts, reason permits us to plan and control what we do. The same is said about will, a concept that was emphasized in Catholic Church doctrine in the Middle Ages.

What is important here is that we have culturally inherited notions about reason and will that subjugate and belittle our emotional reactions. We say animals live by emotion. In contrast, reason and will are said to represent the highest development of the mind, and they keep our primitive emotions in check. To be good—or in one of the modern incarnations of goodness, to be healthy—requires that we exercise strong controls over our emotions.

To make sense of the role of reason in emotion, it would help us to make a very important distinction about the sequential nature of the emotion process. There are two stages in that sequence.

In Stage 1, *arousal*, an emotion is generated when a person with certain goals and beliefs about self and world makes the appraisal that what is happening is harmful, threatening, or beneficial. This appraisal depends on reason, though the reasoning may be far from accurate.

In Stage 2, *the control of emotion*, we decide on the best course of action. Once an emotion has been aroused, whether and the way it is expressed are usually controlled in the light of what it does to our relationships with others. As we have pointed out, the uncontrolled expression of an emotion may create much harm to a relationship.

So the second stage of the emotion process involves what we do to avoid harmful social consequences through the process of coping. This may involve inhibiting the action tendency that the emotion produces or transforming it in some way to make it useful, safe, and palatable to others. Not everyone is in good control of their emotional impulses, but the control or lack of control is an important feature of our emotional lives. In effect, we use reason not only in the arousal of an emotion—Stage 1— but also in the control of the way it is expressed—Stage 2. Reason plays a part in both stages.

We are singleminded when we experience strong emotions, and this can lead us to act foolishly. Destructive rage or fear must be controlled by drawing on knowledge about the social realities being faced, which means that reason often turns out to be in conflict with the emotional impulse. This was the most important theme of the Ancient Greeks, and it remains one of the solid principles of the relationship between emotion and reason today. What is different about our present view is that reasoning or thinking is an integral part of emotion from start to finish.

When we are beset with the powerful impulses generated by a strong emotion, effective control of emotion is not easy to achieve. Some persons are unable to control their impulses, which creates serious problems of social living. Others are overcontrolled; they regulate their emotions too much.

Ancient Greek thought, which became medieval and Euro-American thought, failed to distinguish between the two stages of emotion. In Western culture, the idea of an opposition between emotion and reason was emphasized, and it was extended mistakenly to the entire emotion process—the arousal as well as its regulation. In effect, we came to believe that emotions and reason were in opposition, one the enemy of the other. What was forgotten was that the very arousal of emotion depends on reason.

Needless to say, the ancient idea that reason is opposed to emotion has had profound consequences for our courts of law and jurisprudence. That emotion, once aroused, can make us unreasonable—in Stage 2, which has to do with the control of the emotion—has strongly influenced our criminal justice system.

We punish "crimes of passion" less severely than we do crimes that are premeditated, malicious, and cold; the latter are regarded as unjustified and deserving of the most severe punishment. The person's intent (implying will) in an assault or a murder is a very important factor in judging the crime and the punishment suitable for it.

Crimes of passion are to some extent excused, as if to imply that people who commit them couldn't help themselves because they are in the grip of animal passion. Overcome by intense emotions, people may experience a "diminished capacity" to control their impulses, which is only natural—or so the argument goes. Moreover, we can understand crimes of passion and perhaps be sympathetic to those who commit them, even as we deplore their actions.

Crimes are also excused in jurisprudence on the basis of insanity (a legal, not a clinical term). Insane people—that is, those who "cannot tell right from wrong"—are said to be unable to judge the consequences of their actions and, therefore, to control them. Here the Stage 1 principle— the dependence of emotional arousal on reasoning about the significance of what is happening for our well-being—is drawn on, as well as the Stage 2 principle that people who are mentally sound regulate their emotional expressions in light of the conditions being faced. In the eyes of the court, the inability to reason adequately mitigates the seriousness of the crime enough to reduce the sentence or to put the perpetrator in a mental hospital rather than a prison.

Historical Reversals of the Classical Tradition

Few traditions remain unchallenged over the course of history, and this applies to the elevation of reason over emotion. There have been numerous attempts throughout Western history to reverse Ancient Greek and medieval ideology and make reason subordinate to emotion rather than the other way around. As a matter of fact, emphasis on the primacy of emotion or, alternatively, on the primacy of reason, comes and goes in cycles, like an historical pendulum. In periods of romanticism, emotion is said to hold the ultimate human truth, but in periods in which rationality is the dominant outlook, emotion is held accountable to reason.

The *romanticism* of the late eighteenth and early nineteenth centuries is a case in point. It was a shortlived period, but more recently (e.g., in the 1960s) romanticism again emerged in certain social circles. There are many ways to speak about romanticism, but we would define it as an outlook that greatly values and admires human creativity, wisdom, goodness, lofty ideals, diligence, and perseverance. The romantic believes we can, by the reach of the mind, overcome—one could say transcend—the bleak realities of existence.

In the romantic tradition, Rousseau urged people to get back to nature and repossess the emotional animal they are.[4] The worship of nature was, for a while, an influential ideology. Rousseau and others who adopted this romantic view were not saying that emotions should be unregulated, but that they are valuable and should not be altogether suppressed.

Before the heyday of romanticism, the dominant outlook was shaped by what has been called the *Age of Reason,* or to use its other name, the *Enlightenment.* In the early eighteenth century, there was great optimism about the capacity of disciplined knowledge and intellect to improve human well-being. Science began to flourish, as it had in earlier times during the Renaissance in Italy and Northern Europe.

In the nineteenth and twentieth centuries, the emphasis on science continued to grow. Science had come to mean close observation and disinterested reason applied to the task of advancing human knowledge. The dominant metaphor for biological creatures, including people, became mechanistic. And the mind was said to work much like a computer. Indeed, the hope is still held out that highly complex intelligence rivaling or exceeding that of humans could be programmed into computerized robots.

Modern science was, in effect, a reaffirmation of classical and eighteenth-century rationalism, a search for the basic rules that help us understand all creatures and objects in the world. Scientists and the public alike believed that knowledge could be used to teach people to manage their lives more effectively. And in many ways it has.

Today we are somewhat less sanguine than in the past about the benefits of science, and about the huge strides we have made in technology, which have transformed life in both good and bad ways. This is a time of doubt and cynicism about the neutrality of scientists and their ability to improve the condition of humankind.

If you are middle-aged or older, you will remember the resurgence of romanticism in the 1960s. Perhaps as a reaction against rationalism and science, the counterculture movement in the United States returned once again to the earlier romantic ideology about the proper place of emotion in our lives. The counterculture displayed an obsession with getting in touch with one's feelings. It was said that feelings had been so subordinated to reason and societal rules that most people had ceased to be adequately aware of and responsive to them. Indeed, among all creatures, humans are probably the most emotional.

If we subordinate our emotional natures to intellect and social control, so it was claimed, we then become merely intellectual machines—not unlike Mr. Spock of *Star Trek* fame. It is interesting that Dr. Leonard McCoy represented the emotional man in the TV series and Captain Kirk the measured leader and effective fighting man who culled insights from both officers. In one telling episode, Kirk, using human emotion and argument, defeats an alien computer that had run amok.

The counterculture also presumed that when emotions are suppressed the conflicts that bring them about remain active in the mind, leading to neurotic conflicts. Since we may be unaware of the suppressed emotions, only psychotherapy could help us gain insight about our real motives and emotional makeup.

Readers who were moviegoers in those days may remember the amusing 1968 film with Peter Sellers entitled *I love you, Alice B. Toklas*. Sellers, a conservative lawyer, "freaks out" and has an affair with a free-spirited young woman who turns him into a "hippie." The movie satirizes the tenet of the counterculture that we should abandon the social and intellectual constraints that purportedly distort a person's true emotional nature. If you have not seen this movie and it is replayed on television, we hope you will be able to see it, and, if you have, perhaps you will enjoy it all the more by viewing it in the context of history.

Romanticism reverses the Ancient Greek belief in the primacy of reason over emotion. Instead of emphasizing that our lives should be dominated by reason, it said that emotion should be the dominant feature of our lives. This, incidentally, remains a tenet of some modern psychotherapies that consider emotions to be valuable in living day to day and adapting to changing circumstances.

However, regardless of which is said to be primary, emotion or reason, both outlooks—romanticism, which venerates emotion, and its opposite ideology, which venerates reason—still treat each as separate concepts, as if one could occur without the other. Our position in this book is that emotion depends on reason, and that there is no way to separate them. To do so fails to recognize the role of reason in the arousal of the emotions.

Rationality in Human Affairs

You might wonder why the question of rationality or reason is important in a book about emotion. The idea of rationality is crucial for several reasons.

First, since emotions are aroused by an evaluative judgment—what we refer to as an appraisal—about the significance of what is happening for our well-being, we will never be able to understand how emotions come about without examining the reasoning that lies behind them.

Second, to view emotion as irrational is a way of denigrating emotion as not to be trusted when, in reality, emotion is an important resource that helps us survive and flourish. It is probably not going too far to say that reason may hold our emotions in check, but often in constructive ways the emotions hold reason in check. There is something of a balance between them. If not, there lies madness.

Life without emotion would also be an exercise in boredom. One psychologist, R. Dreikurs, put it this way:[5]

We may easily discover the purpose of emotions when we try to visualize a person who has no emotions. His thinking ability could provide him with much information. He could figure out what he should do, but never would he be certain as to what is right and wrong in a complicated situation. He would not be able to take a definite stand, to act with force, with conviction, because complete objectivity is not inducive to forceful actions. This requires a strong personal bias, an elimination of certain factors which logically may contradict opposing factors. Such a person would be cold, almost inhuman. He could not experience any association which would make him biased and one-sided in his perspectives. He could not want anything very much and could not go after it. In short, he would be completely ineffectual as a human being.

Third, emotions are an extremely important source of knowledge about ourselves and of information about how we are faring in our lives. We—as well as others—can learn from our emotions. When we feel angry, for example, this tells us about how we are evaluating and coping with the conditions of our lives. In effect, if we did not realize it before, we learn from the anger that we have been offended by someone, and perhaps even about the particular vulnerability that has led us to react in this way. And so on, for each of the other emotions. The messages that our emotions provide are critical to our well-being.

Fourth, the quality of our emotional lives is often a source of distress and dysfunction, for which we may seek psychotherapy. If our emotions are out of sync with the realities of our lives, we need to discover the errors of reasoning that have created the problem. We deal with psychotherapy for emotional distress and dysfunction in Chapter 13.

Finally, our emotions usually seem plausible to us because we always have our own personal reasons for what we do and how we feel about it—whether or not the reasons are sound or wise. In other words, the emotions have their own implacable logic, their own life, which makes sense if we know the personal reasons that lie behind them. Even the mentally impaired, who may reason badly, have reasons for their mistaken judgments and feelings. Paranoid patients who think certain people are trying to harm them look crazy, but their anger, anxiety, or fright follows a logic of its own.

For example, if you believe someone is trying to harm you, it is logical for you to be angry, anxious, or frightened. The paranoid's judgment that the other person is dangerous may be erroneous, but there is a sensible link between that judgment—once it is made—and the emotional reaction. So it is essential that we struggle with the ambiguous concept of rationality before we draw conclusions about the logic by which emotions are aroused.

Unfortunately, we can get little help about how to distinguish rationality—which is defined as thinking based on reason—from irrationality. The problem is to distinguish "right thinking" from "wrong thinking." There is no durable standard for doing so that works in all situations, even though people are constantly talking about rationality and irrationality. Yet we know, too, that some ways of thinking are unwise or unrealistic and get people into trouble. The dilemma can be seen more clearly if we examine some of what academic scholars and the populace think about rationality.

Ideas About Rationality

There is no agreement among philosophers and scientists about what is rational and irrational, as is evident by the vigorous debates about this question that continue to take place.[6]

A person's goals and thoughts in decision making are often quite complex and hidden. They need to be explored systematically and with care if they are to be identified. People who go to gambling casinos usually think of gambling as entertainment, expect to lose an affordable amount, and regard losing as paying their dues for the amusement of taking a chance. It is an oversimplification to regard what they do in these situations as irrational because they buck the odds or end up with a poor outcome. Perhaps a better example of irrationality would be the compulsive gambler who constantly loses everything; this is a state of mind that we think of as a sickness.

Another issue of importance has to do with the values underlying the definition of what is rational. For the economist, and many psychologists too, rationality means maximizing the chances of success in getting what one wants and minimizing loss. The economic view of rationality assumes that self-interest is the driving force behind all rational human decisions.

Because this seems to us to be a very narrow position, we want to raise a number of rhetorical questions that express our doubts. If people were always rational in the egoistic sense, why would they sacrifice for their children or make altruistic political decisions about the funding of education or other social services, even though they have no children, or when their children are grown? Isn't it equally rational—though a different kind of rationality—to renounce the things that people always want and never have enough of, as the Ancient Greek Stoics and the Buddhists have recommended. Why do people exhibit concern about less fortunate people, and even volunteer their time and resources to help them? Is it irrational to do so? Do we really believe that idealism is irrational and selfishness rational?

We should perhaps be questioning whether it is rational, wise, or socially desirable to strive entirely for the purpose of maximizing our selfish individual wants.[7] The economic view of rationality ignores other values, such as fairness, compassion, and justice. Maximizing what we want as individuals is apt to be accomplished at the expense of the society and community.

What kind of world would it be if there were no room for self-sacrificing idealism or loyalty? One could answer that we would have just the kind of world we already have in which famine, self-centeredness, tribalism, meanness, hatred, murder, and genocide are widespread and perennial. Societies that are constructed on more community-centered values emphasize a very different kind of rationality.[8]

The point is that there are a number of different values about what determines rational action, based on different premises about what constitutes the good life. They are collective versions of the divergent values, goals, and beliefs individuals bring to their social and work lives which, in turn, influence their emotions. Reviewing these different values makes it all the more clear that we use the term rationality to criticize and be dismissive of any view about what is rational other than our own.

Many expressions in the English language imply irrationality. Folly or foolishness, lack of prudence, poor judgment, being illogical, unreasonable, and crazy thinking are some examples. These expressions can be applied both to Stage 1 of the emotion process—its arousal—and to Stage 2—its control, in recognition of the social situation being faced. We use the way people react to judge the match between the reaction and the social circumstances.

With respect to Stage 1, when we see a person reacting with an emotion that doesn't make sense to us, because it doesn't seem to fit the realities of the situation, we consider the emotion irrational or crazy. With respect to Stage 2, when people react so intensely with an emotion that they do harm to themselves, this too seems irrational. For example, when a person explodes in wrath—seemingly unable to hear what other people are saying—that person seems out of touch with reality.

Logic and reason are defined quite differently by philosophers, logicians, and mathematicians than they are by life scientists. A geometric or trigonometric theorem can be tested for its validity by outcomes that flow inexorably from a theorem. That is why we can put up buildings that do not fall down. However, reasoning in medicine, social behavior, and personal decisions involve such complexity, ambiguity, and large numbers of variables—some of them hidden—that logic works quite differently in these fields; among other things, the reasoning cannot be as precise and definitive.

There are two very different issues we can bring to our effort to evaluate how well people reason. First, we can examine the *process* of reasoning—that is, the use of logical rules of thought in solving problems, which also reveals the way we feel about these problems Second, we can examine the *outcomes* of this process—for example, how well the decisions or choices we make work in helping us to attain our goals or to what extent our emotions fit the conditions of our lives.

In the social and biological sciences, judging the outcomes of our decisions is relatively simple compared with judging the reasoning process, because we can easily observe when outcomes are counterproductive. Judging the reasoning process, on the other hand, is far more difficult because we must examine the reasons that underlie the decisions people make. If we consider the person's private reasons, we would find that most often the person has reasoned logically, given his or her goals and beliefs, even if the outcome is poor.

The person who explodes in wrath seems irrational because this emotional reaction has led to personal or social harm. The wrath should have been controlled or suppressed. It might not occur to us as observers, however, that the most important goal of that wrath is to repair a severely impaired ego, which blinds the person to any other consideration. For that person, it was unthinkable not to explode in wrath even though it might result in serious harm, an aspect of the situation that was never even considered.

Simply to label the reaction as irrational, or an equivalent of irrationality—mental illness—is not very useful in helping us understand what has happened. It might have been more useful to know what was of primary importance to that person. What happened looks crazy to us, but the person is not crazy. When we explore such events with the person afterward, and express perplexity, the person may say "If you were in my shoes, you would feel (or do) the same." And this might be true.

It may be a truism, but in our dealings with other people we should try to see the event from the other person's perspective. The emotions experienced and expressed by others are reasonable from their standpoint—even if foolish or destructive—and if we understand the predicament of the person, the reasonableness of an emotional response might be more evident.

Psychopathology, incidentally, was a fashionable—but unproductive—way to rationalize the actions of Hitler and the German Third Reich. But it is not enough to say that the madness of World War II was the result of human emotion. The people of Germany regarded their country's mission—the goals and beliefs that powered their destructive assault on the world—as perfectly rational and in their own interests. They blamed it—in part—on the punitive terms of the Treaty of Versailles that were put into play right after World War I and created a disastrous economic inflation, then an equally disastrous deflation.

The process and the outcome of the Nazi ideology was terrifying. Everyone who was not pure Aryan—whatever that meant—was blamed for the nation's problems, especially certain groups, such as the Jews, Gypsies, and homosexuals. The Jews especially were marked for extermination. Ironically, today under difficult economic conditions and with unstable societies around the globe, we are again witnessing an outbreak of similar ugliness in many parts of the world, including Germany with its skinheads and their attacks on foreigners. To the credit of modern Germans, there is widespread anxiety and revulsion over this lunacy. To this must be added the brutality of ethnic murder (the euphemism is ethnic cleansing) in Bosnia, once part of Yugoslavia.

With these recent events as backdrop, it may be hard to convince you that judging rationality is mostly a waste of time. And yet we would be wiser not to try to judge what is rational or irrational in some abstract sense, but to try to understand why people make the decisions they do. We are too ready to label anything we don't understand as pathological or sick. Instead of blaming mental illness for what looks irrational, we need to discover what lies behind the actions and reactions—for example, particular personal goals and beliefs—and how and why the judgments underlying decisions are erroneous or counterproductive. Only then can we better understand what the causes of these judgments have to do with the emotions we observe.

It will help if we turn now to why deviant and erroneous judgments are made, and folly is rampant,[9] without explaining them away by simply calling them irrational.

Sources of Erroneous Judgment

We consider several sources of erroneous judgment here, and many more may exist. We look at brain damage, mental retardation, and psychosis; lack of knowledge; personal beliefs about how things work; ambiguity in the information on which a judgment is based; inattention or paying attention to the wrong things; and coping by avoidance or denial. Let's look at each of these more closely.

Brain Damage, Mental Retardation, and Psychosis

For persons who are *brain damaged*, judgment may be impaired, sometimes severely. Aging persons with Alzheimer's disease reach the tragic point at which they do not know who they are and are no longer able to recognize loved ones whom they have lived with all their lives. As we observe them in their tragic confusion, their emotions make no sense to us, yet they do make sense within the person's frame of mind and beliefs.

People who are *mentally retarded*— especially when the retardation is severe—lack basic knowledge and are unable to engage in complex reasoning, though they may do some things adequately or even spectacularly, as in those relatively rare persons described as autistic who are idiotsavants, an evident oxymoron which in French means wise fools.

Psychosis is the clinical term for severe mental illness. Its central feature is disordered thinking and emotion. Schizophrenic patients hear voices or see things that are not there, and act as though these hallucinations are real. Paranoids believe they are Jesus Christ, Napoleon, the president of the United States, or that others are plotting to harm or kill them. The legal term for this kind of disorder is insanity, the lay term is crazy, the technical term is psychosis.

The emotions of psychotic persons seem crazy too, because they don't seem to add up. In clinical work, mental health has long been viewed as requiring the unity and integrity of reason and emotion, and any major dissociation between them as a sign of true madness.

People in all three of these mentally impaired groups are likely to reason badly about many things, including the significance of social relationships. This is why their emotions seem off base. When they feel angry, frightened, sad, guilty, ashamed, proud, and so forth, it makes little sense to others. They have their own reasons for the way they feel, and the reasons are unique to them as well as unrealistic to us. But given their reasons, their actions and reactions flow logically from them. If you believed someone was trying to kill you, wouldn't you be frightened or angry?

Lack of Knowledge

We cannot be expected to make correct judgments, or draw valid conclusions about what is happening if we lack the necessary knowledge— whether technical or commonsensical—on which such judgments are based. A large proportion of errors of judgment are linked to a deficiency in knowledge, whether in individual persons or in those who act in the name of society.

Throughout history, illnesses have been treated medically by methods that seem absurd in light of today's knowledge. For example, it was common until fairly recently to draw large amounts of blood from a sick person. Called bloodletting, this procedure was often done with the aid of leeches. Ironically, leeches are now once again in demand for use in lowering blood pressure. And to consider another example, before the nineteenth century, mental patients were chained, beaten, or plunged into ice cold baths as treatment. Our knowledge was inadequate and our medical practices reflected this. But given what was believed to be known, the practice was sensible.

And so it seems quite possible that many of the things we do today to cure or prevent illness will seem absurd tomorrow in the light of what will be learned. Perhaps we will discover that new drug treatments will work far better than surgery in particular ailments. We have already learned that radical mastectomies for breast cancer before the tumor has spread—long a recommended practice—are no better at preventing recurrence of the disease than the less invasive lumpectomies.

If our reasoning is faulty because we lack knowledge, then our emotions too will be out of touch with reality and seem so to observers who are better or differently informed. Lack of knowledge may lend an aura of unreality to our emotional lives, just as a mental disorder plays havoc with our grasp of reality. But lacking the essential facts in a situation is not irrational, it is merely ignorance. Thus, we might fly off the handle because we have drawn the wrong conclusion about what the appearance of a situation tells us.

Personal Beliefs

People have imperfect models of the world, and their beliefs about how things work are not always on the mark. All or most of us draw on faulty assumptions about the way things are. We live in accordance with unique and even shared illusions. (See Chapter 8.) Perhaps we believe that the world has singled us out for pain, that the good are rewarded and the bad punished, that we are unloved or unlovable, that God watches over us as individuals, that we deserve punishment for moral transgressions, that we should have received more from life, that our country never acts deceitfully in the world, and so on. These beliefs serve as powerful influences on how we reason. Therefore, some of the emotions we experience make little or no sense to others who do not share these beliefs, and may even surprise us when we are unaware of the beliefs that underlie our reasoning.

For example, even when the social conditions we face are reassuring and should make us feel secure, we may react with anxiety because we actually believe we are threatened. Even when conditions seem to other people to be friendly and supportive, we may react with anger because we think we have been demeaned. Even when there is no evident reason for self-blame, we may experience guilt because we assume we have acted badly. Even when there seems good reason for rejoicing, we may experience sadness or depression because we believe we have actually suffered a loss.

It is as if we are reacting to a world quite different from the one that is observed by others. It may be unwise for us to make these troublesome assumptions, which cause deviant—and often erroneous—conclusions about what is happening to us. However, since we have made them, we respond accordingly in a manner that seems to others to be out of touch with reality.

Differences in the beliefs people have about themselves and the world arise from diverse personal backgrounds. Although we all share common beliefs, in a multicultural society each of us has acquired some of our outlooks from our subculture and our unique life histories. They are not necessarily faulty or based on psychopathology because they deviate from the beliefs of others. We can also be right even when everyone else thinks we are wrong.

Suppose you are a white North American, say, of Italian background. You are likely to appreciate and enjoy the celebration of the discovery of America on Columbus Day. Because your family was able to immigrate here, perhaps from an oppressive society, you are now a citizen of a free and prosperous country. Columbus Day has for you a positive aura.

However, if you are an American Indian from one of many tribal subcultures, or if you resent Spain's conquest of the New World and share the view that it led to the cruel decimation of the Aztec, Mayan, and Inca civilizations, you take no pleasure from this holiday. Perfectly sound people view events from many different perspectives—sometimes opposite ones—and this variation should not necessarily be regarded as an error of reasoning.

Because the conditions of our lives are construed differently, the emotions we experience vary in the same social situations. Those who observe emotions different from their own will be perplexed because they have made other assumptions about what is happening. To understand these emotions requires that the observers put themselves in the shoes of the person being observed.

Ambiguity

One of the most common sources of error in judgment is an ambiguous situation in which it is difficult to make a definitive judgment. There is insufficient data or the available facts don't add up and we have to guess, to reason by the seat of our pants, so to speak. To make an educated guess, we must draw on this or that set of facts, on our past experience, or on our prejudices.

There is normally a high degree of ambiguity about what other people are thinking, feeling, and intending. To help us resolve the ambiguity, we may take what they say about their feelings at face value—making the assumption that they are honest or informed about their inner life. Or, if we do not trust them or believe that they have poor insight about themselves, we discount what they say.

It is easy to be wrong in the assumptions we make in ambiguous social situations. Our beliefs about how things work play an important role in our actions and reactions. Errors of judgment under conditions of ambiguity are not irrational; we make the best judgment we can, given what we believe.

When the conditions of life are ambiguous, there is apt to be great variation in the emotions that different people feel in the same situation. For example, when having a biopsy to evaluate a suspicious growth, the patient is apt to have no clue about the likely outcome. The situation is ambiguous. One patient awaits the report in great anxiety, virtually certain that the news will be bad, while another is confident the growth will prove benign. Only if the diagnosis is cancer will the latter patient begin to worry.

In a complex social world, the personal and social issues in which we have a stake are apt to be ambiguous, which is why we argue about them. We are likely to regard conclusions opposite from our own as foolish or irrational. As we have said, to speak of irrationality in such instances does not lead to better understanding.

Inattention or Looking at the Wrong Things

Although emotions are reasonable in the way they are aroused, once an emotion has been aroused, the reaction can get in the way of effective thinking.[10] Most of us have had an experience in which a strong emotion seems to have impaired our ability to think clearly.

This often happens because our attention is misdirected by the emotion. Emotions, especially negative ones such as anger and anxiety, signify something important—perhaps a major emergency. This deflects our attention from what we have been trying to do and makes us focus on the emergency. We are so busy paying attention to the emergency itself that we fail to understand all that is happening.

Consider, for example, patients who must be told by a physician that they have an inoperable cancer. Wise physicians realize that it might be better to take up the treatment options later. It would be better to give such patients time to digest the terrible news rather than provide advice that comes at the wrong time and leaves them incapable of absorbing it.

In the shock and distress of the discovery, patients are apt not to hear what is said, or to distort what they hear. The mind is elsewhere; it is not irrational.

In complex situations, there is so much to pay attention to that we have to decide what is important and what is unimportant. This is a major source of error in judgment—we pay attention to the wrong things. We may be inattentive and miss the observation that is crucial to a correct judgment because we are in the middle of something else that commands our attention. Beliefs about ourselves and the world direct our attention to what is supposedly important. When these beliefs are faulty, our judgment about what is important, and how it should be viewed, is likely to be in error.

Finally, our attention may also be purposely misdirected by someone who wants to fool us. Magicians use misdirection to create most of their illusions. They locate the right card in the deck by a trick, such as palming it, but disguise what they are doing by getting us to look in the wrong place. White-collar criminals disguise a crooked transaction by concealing it and getting us to look at what is not suspicious. Politicians who want us to believe that a sagging economy is really improving cite evidence selectively and try to keep our attention away from information that contradicts their statements. We fail to see what is going on under our very eyes.

Coping by Denial and Avoidance

When an emotion is very strong, it may also lead us to disavow the realities of the situation by *denial*. (See Chapter 8.) This is an important form of coping. If we want very much to believe something, we may believe it in spite of evidence to the contrary. In so doing we might be trying to make ourselves feel better in the short run, but pay dearly for the disavowal of reality in the long run.

For example, people who inhale cigarettes may recognize that it is dangerous from a health standpoint, but they will often convince themselves that the warning does not apply to them. Indeed, it might not, and they can cite examples of long-lived, profligate smokers, which is an effort to justify the denial of the danger.

We have known a number of people who have continued to smoke cigarettes even after they were ill with emphysema, a serious lung disease, or after a cancerous lung has already been surgically removed. Surely there is a strong element of denial in this kind of decision, which will almost certainly make the disease much worse and shorten life.

The emotional distress that comes from realizing that we are engaging in a life-threatening risk by smoking can also be reduced somewhat by refusing to think about it—in other words, by *avoidance*. Many people who smoke realize that they might be better off if they quit—so that they are not denying the danger—but they avoid thinking about it.

Is this kind of judgment, which draws on denial or avoidance, irrational? No, as we see it, though it does entail major risk. Like gamblers, these persons have made a bet whose statistical odds could readily be calculated, but are difficult to apply to any single individual. One should say that they have made an imprudent choice, not an irrational one.

Most smokers these days recognize the dangers, but many decide that the bad fate won't happen to them. It has been shown in research that smokers who currently smoked and were not trying to quit believed that they were less vulnerable to health risks from smoking than the typical smoker.[11] In other words, they are denying the danger of what they are doing to their health.

The Implacable Logic of the Emotions

Before closing this chapter, allow us to point up what it means to say that emotions follow an implacable logic on the basis of what we have said thus far. We restrict ourselves here to just the arousal of emotion, though a similar analysis can be made for its control.

To grasp the logic of an emotion, to see it in action, requires that we examine how the things people want (their goals), what they believe (their assumptions), and their evaluation of what is happening lead them to experience an emotion. We must, in effect, examine the logic—or we should say psycho-logic—the underpinnings of emotional arousal.

Somewhat oversimplified, the basic logic of an emotion is as follows: We want something and, because having it is not assured, we make efforts to attain it. If we succeed or make good progress toward what we want, we will experience a positive emotion; we have been benefitted. If we fail, we will experience a negative emotion; we have been harmed. If no important goal is at stake, there will be no emotion; there is no harm or benefit.

The arousal of an emotion normally follows the rule that we will feel whatever is appropriate considering the fate of our goals in the situation we are facing. The implacable logic, which means it is seldom or never violated, is that emotion flows inexorably from an *appraisal* that we have been harmed or benefitted in a particular way. Appraisal involves intelligence and reasoning.

Although the process may get out of hand and result in impaired thought and foolish action, emotions are aroused by a pattern of reasoning that is based on the fate of goal commitments, which are judged to be at stake in an encounter. The judgment may be unwise, even foolish and counterproductive, but given the goals and beliefs on which it is based, the emotion aroused is always rational, in the light of what a person wants and believes.

When all is said and done, if human emotion were not dependent on reasoning or thought, we could never make sense of anyone's emotions. If we know someone's emotional state, we should be able to reason backward to the conditions that must have been responsible—namely, goals, beliefs, an event that provokes the emotion, and the particular appraisals of personal harm or benefit. And if we know a person's goals, beliefs, and appraisals, then using the logic of emotion, we should be able to predict with reasonable accuracy how that person will react when faced with relevant events that could provoke the emotion again.

This gives us a powerful tool for understanding and managing a person's emotions. It is, in effect, the knowledge that psychotherapists use in helping patients with distressing and dysfunctional emotions. But when all is said and done, we are all psychologists trying to guess each other's intentions and emotions. All of us know that emotions reveal the "hot spots" in another individual's life.

Let us proceed now to psychological stress in Chapter 11 and consider how it is related to the emotions.

III

PRACTICAL IMPLICATIONS

11

Stress and Emotion

FROM TIME TO TIME in previous chapters we have used the word stress. This is a word familiar to everyone—even more familiar than emotion. Our intent in this chapter is to provide an account of stress so that you can see how stress and emotion are related.

We have always enjoyed what psychotherapist Ethel Roskies said, with biting but accurate sarcasm, about the modern penchant for elevating stress, and stress management, to a human problem of major proportions. She wrote the following about self-help stress manuals:[1]

From its humble origins as a laboratory term in the 1950s, stress has now become a shorthand symbol for explaining much of what ails us in the contemporary world, invoked to explain conditions as diverse as nail biting, smoking, homicide, cancer, and heart disease. From an anthropological perspective, stress serves the same purpose in modern society as ghosts and evil spirits did in former times, making sense of various misfortunes and illnesses that otherwise might remain simple random games of chance.

It would be un-American to accept a new cause for disease without seeking to cure or control it. Thus, it is not surprising that the ranks of self-help manuals have recently been joined by books devoted to teaching us how to manage stress. Among the array of do-it-yourself guides to increasing sexual pleasure, building the body beautiful, and unlocking hidden mental and emotional capacities is a new crop of manuals devoted to taming the killer stress. . . . Although the sales pitch varies from threats of dropping dead to promises of maximum well-being, all are dedicated to the premise that the individual can avert or diminish the potential harm of stress by using new, improved coping strategies.

Historical Origins

Stress is a comparatively modern word; it first received widespread professional attention after World War II. As more and more biological and social scientists came to regard stress as important, the public too began to pay attention.

The word stress was used occasionally and unsystematically as early as the fourteenth century to mean hardship, straits, adversity, or affliction. In the seventeenth century it first achieved technical importance when a prominent physicist-biologist, Robert Hooke,[2] sought to help engineers design man-made structures. Bridges, for example, must carry heavy loads and resist buffeting by winds, earthquakes, and other natural forces, which could destroy them. Therefore, an important and practical engineering task is how to design them to resist these loads.

Hooke's analysis greatly influenced the way stress is thought of in physiology, psychology, and sociology. Stress came to be defined as an environmental demand on a biological, social, or psychological system, which is analogous to the load that a bridge might carry.

Hooke was especially interested in the characteristics of metals that would make them vulnerable to deformation or breakage as a result of a load. Wrought iron, for example, is soft and flexible and easily worked; it bends but does not break. Cast iron, on the other hand, is hard and brittle and breaks easily. So the right type of metal had to be used for the kind of load it would carry. This idea turns out to have practical value for psychologists too, since the ability of metals to withstand loads is like the ability of people to resist stress. In the case of people, we use the word resiliency, or its opposite, vulnerability.

During World War I, emotional breakdowns had been explained neurologically rather than psychologically. They were attributed to "shell shock," which implied the vague but erroneous notion that the pressure produced by the noise of exploding shells could produce damage to the brain. During World War II, there was great interest in stress because soldiers often "broke down" emotionally in military combat. The breakdown was referred to as "battle fatigue" or "war neurosis," which implied a psychological explanation.

The military brass worried about stress during World War II because it would often lead men to become demoralized and to hide from the enemy and fail to fire their own weapons. Military leaders also worried about the high proportion of men who had to be removed from military duties because of stress disorders. They wanted to know how to select men who would be stress resistant, and how to train them to cope effectively.

This motivated a growing body of research on these problems in which one of us (RL) became personally involved.

After World War II, it became evident that stress was also relevant to many ordinary life events, such as marriage, growing up, going to school, taking exams, being ill, and so forth. These experiences, like military combat, could result in psychological distress and dysfunction.

Interest in stress as a cause of human distress and dysfunction blossomed in the 1960s and 1970s, and continues to be strong. What we have learned is that we all need some stress to mobilize our efforts to deal with common human problems. Stress is a natural response to life's demands and not all bad, and its negative side is probably overemphasized.

It soon became apparent that, because there were large individual differences in vulnerability, the effects of stress could not be easily predicted. What was a major demand or adversity to one person was not to another. Moreover, some people showed improvement in performance under stress, some showed impairment, and still others showed no evident effect. So it became necessary to discover the psychological characteristics that would explain why some people were more vulnerable to stress than others.

Stress as a Special Person-Environment Relationship

The person-environment relationship that brings stress about is a subjective imbalance between demands that are made on people and their resources to manage these demands. Depending on the degree of imbalance, we experience more or less stress.

Imagine a doctor's scale in which the weight of your body is balanced on one side against metal bars of known weight on the other. Weights are added or subtracted until the scale is level, which means that you and the weights are evenly balanced; this tells you how much you weigh at that moment. Analogously, when the environmental demands become too great for the person's resources, the implicit scale is not in balance and it tilts toward the environmental side. The greater the imbalance, the higher the stress.

When the person's resources exceed the environmental load, stress is low or absent. The demands seem to be easily managed and the person feels confident about handling them. However, when the person's resources are much more substantial than the demands, there is apt to be insufficient demand—or too little stress—and boredom occurs which, ironically, is experienced as noxious or stressful. For each individual there is an optimal level of stress. Below that level, the person is bored; above it, the person feels too much pressure.

The subjective sense of imbalance between demands and resources varies with the nature of the demands and the resources available to the person. Some demands are far more difficult to manage than others, so they may be stressful for most of us. And while some people cannot handle even mild demands; others can readily master severe ones.

Normally, most of us feel fully on top of the demands of living. However, in the ordinary course of our lives, there are apt to be times when our usual coping ability is weakened, because we are ill, fatigued, or have had too much to handle for too long.

To offer an illustration, after falling asleep quickly, many people awaken at 3 or 4 A.M. and begin to ruminate about what they have to cope with the next day. They may spend a few hours with all sorts of tasks floating around in their heads, unable to turn them off. Still tired or sleepy in these early morning hours, the demands seem more than they can handle. The unbidden thoughts keep intruding in their minds until they eventually fall asleep just before the alarm rings—or so it seems.

As soon as these people awaken fully and get started with breakfast and other activities, these twilight concerns now seem quite manageable. With their physical resources mobilized, it is difficult to understand why what they had to do had seemed so overwhelming earlier. The answer is that, still weary and fuzzy from being half asleep in the middle of the night, their coping resources also seemed inadequate. Notice that the scale analogy is again helpful: the amount of stress is not defined by the demands alone, but by the demands in relation to resources for coping with them, both being subjectively defined.

Two Types of Stress: Physiological and Psychological

When we are exercising vigorously or competing in sports, our body is under stress because of the physical demands we are making on it. Some of the signs of this are a strong sense of effort, sweating and fatigue, a rapid heartbeat, and an increase in blood pressure. If we make the necessary measurements, we would find that stress hormones are being poured into the bloodstream by the adrenal glands that, in part, cause these bodily changes. We are undergoing *physiological stress* but not necessarily psychological stress, especially when we are having fun.

The physiological changes produced by exercise are adaptive reactions by our bodies to physical demands. They are the physiological counterpart of the process of coping with psychological stress. The body is mobilizing to manage the physical demands, just as the mind is mobilizing to manage psychological demands. After the mobilization, which uses up physical resources, we need rest and recuperation during which the physiological balance is restored. This imbalance also applies when we are facing any physiologically noxious environmental condition, such as heat, cold, or starvation.

The bodily reactions that are generated by physical stress can also be generated for psychological reasons, without the physical exertion. Feeling angry, anxious, frightened, envious, jealous, or the like, will result in many of the same bodily changes as those that stem from physical demands. Their basic cause is psychological. They are reactions to various types of stress. So we refer to these bodily reactions, and the purely psychological events that result in them, as *psychological stress*.

Both sources of stress—physiological and psychological—are often combined in the same situation. Thus, we can experience the emotions of anger or anxiety when our aims are threatened in competitive sports, and joy—even though physically exhausted at the end of a competitive race—because we won. Exercise is always physiologically stressful, but emotions, which have purely psychological causes, are not inevitable when we engage in physical exertion, such as jogging, playing ball, and gardening.

Although psychological stress and physiological stress overlap in their neurochemical effects on the body, they produce somewhat different patterns of hormonal reactions. If the two are separated, it is also discovered that each kind of physiological stress, for example, exercise, fasting, heat, and cold, has its own special hormonal signature.[3] The same can be said for the hormonal output of different kinds of psychological stress. We must not confuse these types of stress because they are brought about by different conditions, have their own distinctive neurochemistries, and certainly involve different kinds of psychological reactions.

Though we may want to measure its physiological effects, the type of stress we are talking about in this chapter is psychological. In the future, when we use the word stress by itself—as in the heading below—we are referring only to psychological stress. When we want to talk about physiological stress, we will always use the appropriate modifying adjective.

Kinds of Psychological Stress

Although psychological stress can be thought of as a continuum from none to little to too much, three kinds can also be distinguished: harm, threat, and challenge. One major difference between them has to do with the meaning that an individual constructs about an encounter with the world, which is distinctive in all three. In other words, we have made quite different appraisals in each.

Harm refers to an event that has already occurred in which damage has been done. Harms can be of many different kinds. For example, we may have failed to prepare adequately for an upcoming demand, such as a job interview, a public performance, or a school exam. We may have made a fool of ourselves socially and damaged our relationships with people who are important to us.

A harm that is irrevocable or cannot be prevented is also called a loss. Death of a loved one is a case in point. All we can do is grieve, find ways of accepting the loss with grace, and move on. In other instances, the harm is not necessarily permanent, and we can do something about it. For example, we might try to overcome harm to our reputations by subsequently being more effective, or we can try another job interview with new resolve, with the potential benefit of having learned from the earlier negative experience.

Threat is probably the most common source of psychological stress. It arises when we are exposed to a harm that has not yet happened but is possible, likely, or inevitable in the near future. We worry about what is going to happen and try to figure out what it will be like, when it will happen, and what we might do about it. If we can anticipate what is going to happen, we can prepare for it and sometimes either prevent harm or loss, or mitigate its severity.

Challenge consists of events that are appraised as opportunities rather than occasions for harm. Like threat, challenge mobilizes the person to struggle against obstacles, which is why it is stressful. The difficulty contributes to the challenge. If the task were too easy, we would not experience much enthusiasm for tackling it.

In addition to the differences in appraised meaning, another important contrast between threat and challenge is that, when we are threatened, we are apt to feel anxious and act in a self-protective way. Threat creates a negative and distressing message about ourselves and the world about us. Our concerns shrink from dealing vigorously with what seems manageable, as we do when challenged, to one in which we need to defend ourselves against potential harm. The preoccupation with the harm that might occur weakens the verve with which we tackle the problem, narrows the scope of our attention, and undermines our performance.

When challenged, however, we are expansive, our thoughts flow easily and effortlessly, and we are confident about what must be done. We are keen to pit ourselves against the obstacles that stand in the way of opportu-

nity. Unlike threat, challenge is a delightful, exhilarating, and often pro-
ductive experience.

So you can see that harm, threat, and challenge differ in three ways—
first, in the appraisal that brings them about; second, in the way we feel;
and third, in the way we function. We would all much prefer situations
of challenge to those of harm and threat.

Situations determine to some extent whether we experience threat or
challenge. Some situations, such as when we are being criticized, make
many of us feel threatened, while others, such as an opportunity to shine,
make many of us feel challenged. Differences in personality—for example,
lack of self-confidence and the expectation that others will be malevolent
toward us—also lead some people to feel threatened much more frequently
than others, and such people may seldom feel challenged. Others with a
more positive sense of themselves and the world show the reverse pattern—
seldom threatened but often challenged.

Post-traumatic Stress Disorders (PTSD)

Being traumatized is feeling helpless against the overwhelming onslaught
of demands that greatly exceed one's resources. A trauma also undermines
cherished meanings on which the person's sense of well-being depends.

How this works can be illustrated with a disturbed mental condition
known as *post-traumatic stress disorder*. Patients with PTSD usually suffer
from severe and prolonged anxiety, which is the most obtrusive emotion
experienced in their response to trauma. In addition, however, chronic
anger, guilt, and depression are also common.

The emotion of anger in traumatized persons tells us that they blame
another person or a social institution for the terrible thing that has happened to them. Guilt tells us that these persons blame themselves for what
has happened, or for surviving when others did not. Depression tells us
that those traumatized despair of ever restoring a sense of well-being and
commitment to living. Long after the traumatic event—sometimes for the
rest of their lives—patients with PTSD may experience recurrent, unbidden, and intrusive images of the horror of their experience and make efforts—often unsuccessful—to avoid thoughts of what has happened.

The most recent *Diagnostic and Statistical Manual* of the American
Psychiatric Association defines the traumas commonly experienced by patients with PTSD as follows.[4]

The individual has experienced an event that is outside the range of usual
human experience . . . e.g., serious threat to one's life or physical integ-

rity; serious threat or harm to one's children, spouse, or other close relatives or friends; sudden destruction of one's home or community; or
seeing another person who has been, is being (or has recently been),
seriously injured or killed as a result of an accident or physical violence.

Think, for example, of a sexually and physically abused child, or a
boy who sees the rape and bloody knife murder of his mother by an in-
truder—who by luck barely escaped the assassin's attempt to kill him too.
Imagine being the only survivor of an automobile crash in which you
viewed the bloody dismemberment of your family. These are situations
that are so terrible that they are almost unimaginable. We would prefer
not to think of them.

One of us (RL) once treated a college student who, when he was a
young teenager, returned home from school to find his widowed mother
hanging dead in the hall closet. That morning, after an altercation, he
had angrily said to her "I wish you were dead." Depressed and despairing,
his mother had granted him his wish. In addition to being an expression
of despair about her life, the suicide was also a hostile retaliation for his
impulsive comment and her impression that he didn't care about her.

Like Tom Sawyer's dream in which he was an observer at his own
funeral—with everyone crying and saying what a wonderful boy he had
been—the mother's suicide undoubtedly expressed the same lonely wish
that he would be sorry after she died. The assaultive act, and the horror
of the discovery, left the boy permanently victimized, suffering from severe, chronic anxiety and guilt, and unable to function to his capacity. He
later left the university still quite dysfunctional.

Although most traumas are of the severe variety, and we can understand the disturbed reaction very easily, trauma can occur simply because
a person is especially vulnerable and is overwhelmed by conditions that
others can readily handle. In other words, some people are traumatized by
events—for example, rejection by a lover or a criticism of one's work or
personality—that others would consider occurrences that they must learn
to take in their stride.

There are numerous sources of such vulnerability. For example, when
people have a very strong goal commitment, they might feel threatened
when things fail to go their way. Yet failure in a situation in which their
goal commitment is weak would not engender significant threat. They
may urgently need to be loved, admired, or successful, perhaps too much
so. Another source of vulnerability is a lack of confidence in one's resources for attaining what one wants. Still another is the belief that the
world is hostile and dangerous so that the slightest sign an encounter will

turn out negatively is promoted into a disaster. These personal sources of vulnerability often arise from earlier life experiences. We saw examples of this in the case studies of emotional distress and dysfunction in Chapters 2 to 6.

What often happens following extreme traumatic situations is that the sudden and unexpected danger, the brutality, the suffering, the terror, and the closeness of a meaningless death thoroughly undermine the person's protective assumptions about life. Whether a child or an adult, the world can no longer be viewed as benevolent, meaningful, or controllable, and the person is overwhelmed, which is what trauma is all about. Only the reestablishment of a viable set of beliefs on which a commitment to life can be based can restore what has been destroyed.

Most instances of psychological stress involve life struggles that are nowhere near as extreme as those leading to traumatic stress disorders. Garden-variety stresses are those in which demands merely tax our coping resources: trauma represents demands that exceed our resources and, therefore, overwhelm or traumatize us. Most of us experience recurrent stress and dislike it, but are not overwhelmed.

Common Examples of Stress

Stress is to be found in an almost unlimited variety of the circumstances in which we live and function. We experience stress even in normally pleasant situations such as vacations. The circumstances of stress are mainly of two types—life events, which are uncommon, but when they occur have a profound impact on our state of mind, and daily hassles, which are very common and sap our goodwill.

Life Events

One of the first efforts to measure stress systematically consisted of a list of life events,[5] which has since been often published in magazines and newspapers. It was based on the idea that major changes in our lives are inherently stressful because they disrupt our usual patterns, involve personal losses, and require major readjustments. These events have been rated and ranked by large numbers of people as to the severity of the adaptational demands they impose, providing data on a public consensus about how stressful they are. Death of a spouse is ranked number 1, divorce number 2, and marriage number 7. Even events, such as marriage, which we think of as positive, can be stressful. We hasten to add that many major life events are missing from this list—for example, the death of one's child. And other events, which may not seem so stressful, can take their toll—for instance, having to put one's dog to death because of a terminal disease.

Although it has been possible to obtain a consensus about the stressful impact of life events, based on what the average person says about them, large individual differences are found in the impact of these events. For example, the impact of death of a spouse depends on a variety of conditions that influence the personal meaning of the event.

If the relationship with the spouse has been largely negative, the psychological loss is apt to be less severe than it would be in a long-standing positive relationship. Exceptions to this rule are instances in which the loss is severe mainly because of the feelings of anger and guilt over the negative relationship, which the death promotes.

How the person died is an important consideration. It might have been the result of a sudden accident, which is very traumatic, or after a long, painful, lingering illness, and so might be almost welcome. The psychological impact may also be less—though not by any means always—in the case of a very old person for whom death was expected compared with someone who was still in the prime of life.

As we emphasized in discussions of the emotions, there are two main reasons individuals differ in how major life events will be responded to. One is the way the event is appraised. The same event for one individual may be catastrophic but only mildly damaging for another. The second reason for individual differences is the way the event is coped with. Some people do much better than others in adjusting to the loss, or the threats posed by it, because their coping resources are more substantial.

Allow us to illustrate this further with divorce. The stress of an impending divorce is different depending on whether or not children are involved, and whether you are the person who sought and initiated it rather than the other way around. Much also depends on what happens after the divorce; in the subsequent process of coping, the person's psychological state is in flux.

Many divorces are successful in that one individual—or both—ultimately adopts a new life pattern that works as well or better than the old one. However, many result in continuing and longstanding distress and dysfunction because the person fails to cope adequately with the loss. If we evaluate the adjustment very soon after the stressful life event, we may obtain a picture of considerable dysfunction, but later on, the person may seem quite sound. Conversely, some who seem to be doing well early on may be in trouble later.

Daily Hassles and Positive Experiences

The potential for seemingly minor hassles to be stressful is substantial. These daily hassles include misplacing or losing things, troublesome neighbors, social obligations, inconsiderate smokers, concerns about money, health, or alcohol, fixing meals, cleaning house, one's physical appearance, problems with aging parents, difficulties with coworkers or supervisors, and countless others.[6]

People differ greatly in how many hassles they experience during a day, a week, or a month. They also rate some hassles as very intense and others as weak. Having a large number of intense daily hassles over a long period of time can be an indication that people are not doing well in managing their stress from day to day. Research tells us that people with large numbers of daily hassles in their lives show more emotional distress and other psychological symptoms than those whose level of hassles is relatively low.[7] It may be that, for some, all demands are perceived as hassles, but for others, they are accepted, even laughed off as part of life.

Some hassles are more central to an individual than others. Central hassles go to the heart of an individual's special vulnerabilities; they deal with matters that are personally important. Though they may seem minor to others, they are major to the person experiencing them. They recur often in a person's life and produce long-lasting distress, even after the provoking incident has disappeared.[8] The recurrence is a sign that such a person seems again and again to repeat the same mistake, making the same negative construction of what is happening in different situations, or if the meaning had been correctly appraised, consistently magnifying its importance.

For example, a minor slight, which others would easily shrug off— another person fails to show interest in what one is saying at a social gathering—may be ruminated about for days or weeks. People like this who are particularly vulnerable can't get what they take as a slight out of their minds. A hassle like this could impair the way such people function in social relationships or at work, and the tendency to react this way could even be harmful to their health. Hassles that are central seem to be more damaging to emotional equanimity than ordinary hassles.

There is a close connection between stressful life events and daily hassles. Stressful life events affect us, in part, through the daily hassles they produce. Loss of a spouse through death or divorce again provides a good example. In both kinds of loss, loneliness and having to assume the tasks the lost person took care of are daily stresses that continue well after the initial stressful event. Loneliness and sexual frustration are also common to both kinds of loss.

However, the death of a spouse and divorce each produce very different daily hassles. For example, if the loss is the result of death, there is no
necessary implication—as there may be in divorce—that we have failed in
the relationship, or that the other person has rejected us. In divorce, however, the other person continues to live—often in the same community—
and it may be necessary to communicate with the divorced partner in
dealing with the children. So although the daily hassles created by these
two forms of loss overlap, many are different and some of them—such as
feeling rejected, that one is a failure at marriage, or having to deal with
the spouse in issues related to child care—may have chronic and recurrent
psychological effects that are very disturbing.

One of the puzzles about daily hassles is whether they are more tolerable and less damaging when they are balanced by positive, uplifting experiences that make us feel good. Examples of what we have called positive
experiences—in stress research they have also been referred to as uplifts—
include liking our fellow workers and being liked in return, being with our
children in a pleasant activity, eating out, travel, having free time, being
complimented, and even getting a good night's sleep. The same individual
may experience many hassles, but also many positive, uplifting experiences.[9]

Do these positive experiences overcome the negative consequences of
hassles? One would certainly think so, just as good social relationships
tend to buffer the negative effects of stress. However, evidence about this
has so far been inconsistent.

Stress at Work and in the Family

Psychological stress tends to be most prominent in the activities and settings in which we spend the most time and have the strongest commitments—namely, work and family.

The different kinds of stress[10] found at *work* can be classified into a
number of categories: One is work overload, such as too much to do in
the time available, having too many interruptions at the job, constantly
having to meet deadlines, and having to defer what is important because
of other duties.

A second category is role ambiguity, such as not knowing what your
responsibilities are, the priorities of the job, the amount of authority you
have, and having little feedback about how you are doing.

A third is future uncertainty, such as not knowing about your future
job tenure, feeling that there is little you can do to influence things, and
uncertainty about the future of the company—hence your job security.

Other sources of work stress include lack of authority over your job, conflicts within the organization about how things should be done, unpleasant coworkers, and technical difficulties in doing your job as a result of technological change. This list does not exhaust all the sources of stress at work, which differ from individual to individual, but it provides illustrations of the situations that most frequently provoke psychological stress in the work setting.

Sources of stress in the *family*, which center on what is happening at home, also vary in kind. Some focus on spousal conflict, such as over the control of money, sex, the expression of affection, and childrearing patterns.

The care and disciplining of children is another major source of stress in the family, which is troubling not only for the parents but for the children as well. Competition within the family is also a source of stress for the children as well as for their parents.

Although not as frequently studied as divorce, decaying spousal relationships can be a source of family stress. There are good reasons for believing that a severely troubled spousal relationship can be even harder on the marital partners and the children than divorce.

Families differ greatly in the way they are organized and function, which results in differences in the main sources of stress. Today, nontraditional families are proliferating, especially single-parent families in which a person must, if they are not to live on welfare, work for a livelihood in addition to the standard spousal task of having to care for children and a household.

Especially important today in a large proportion of marriages are conflicts about the balance between work and household obligations. These are quite prominent in families in which both husband and wife work outside the home. When this is the case, there are apt to be heavy demands on both wife and husband. Who is to cook and clean, and how often? Who is to attend to and discipline the children? The resolution of these conflicts in the family may be managed well or badly.

The troubles of a working couple often center on contrary values and commitments on the part of husbands and wives. For the husband, a prime commitment is typically made to career, which leads to the downplaying of intimate relationships. Women commonly—though not always by any means—consider family relationships and intimacy of prime importance and, frustrated by a husband's indifference to their emotional needs, may want to confront the problem, which the husband may seek to avoid. A frequent pattern is for the husband in such a confrontation to stonewall or sulk when pressed, since his primary interest at home is apt to be peace and harmony. The result is often a failure of communication and deep frustration on the part of both.[11]

Among the most interesting problems of stress at work and in the family are the occasions in which the spheres of home and workplace overlap. Work stress can intrude on the family, and conflicts at home can interfere with functioning at work. Some husbands and wives are skillful at keeping them separate, seldom or never allowing stresses in one arena to enter the other. Work problems are laid aside on coming home, and home problems are isolated from work involvements. We need to learn more about how this separation of spheres is accomplished in successful cases.

But when work or family stresses are especially powerful and psychologically damaging, separating them may become difficult or even impossible. In Chapter 2, we saw an example of a husband whose job was endangered taking part in an angry confrontation with a wife who felt that he was inattentive.

Stress as a Subjective State

Modern theories of stress draw on a view that was described in Chapter 7, The Nuts and Bolts of Emotion. This view is often referred to as a subjective approach, and it centers on how an individual construes what is happening. You will remember that the two central concepts of this view are *appraisal*, in which the person evaluates the significance of events for personal well-being, and *coping*, in which that person tries to manage harms, threats, and challenges.

One major problem with doing research on psychological stress is that it is difficult to create stress in the laboratory so that it can be carefully studied as it occurs. If one tries to study it in natural settings, it is usually over before we can make observations. We must then depend on what the person reports afterward about what happened. However, memory is fallible and subject to all sorts of defensive distortions. And if we cannot be present at the time of the stressful experience, we cannot measure the physiological changes that have occurred as a result of stress.

To study psychological stress as naturally as possible, one of us (RL) used stressful movies to induce responses from the college students being studied.[12] Movies permit us to be right on the spot when a person is exposed to stress so we can measure the reactions. Movies draw on the natural tendency of people to empathize with the troubles of others portrayed in the story (see Chapter 6).

During the movies, RL and his colleagues continually monitored changes in heart rate and the resistance of the skin to an electric current, both of which react strongly under stress. Heart rate rises sharply and involuntarily under stress. The electrical resistance of the skin drops substantially because of the increased action of the sweat glands under stress. We would also periodically ask participating subjects—who saw the movie individually while sitting in a comfortable chair—to rate how much stress they were experiencing at different points during the film.[13]

One of our favorite movies for use in stress research was a black-and-white commercial film, which was made to train men in a woodworking shop to be more conscious of dangers and safety procedures. The movie begins with a stressful film sequence in which a man named Slim is impaled by a wooden board that accidently flies from a circular saw into his abdomen. He dies writhing on the shop floor. After this dramatic opening episode, a foreman steps forward to give a lecture about the need for greater care for safety purposes, and Slim is shown before the accident accumulating wood chips around his work bench and acting in an otherwise careless fashion. He is to be an object lesson about the need for safe shop practices.

In another accident in the same film, it is evident that a worker by the name of Armand, who is using a milling machine, is missing the middle finger of his right hand. The foreman-instructor points out that Armand understands how important it is to be careful, because he had lost that finger in an accident. Then the viewer is shown a flashback scene in which his hand is intact. The viewers now know they are about to see the accident happen. As Armand's hands move closer and closer to the blades of the milling machine, viewers become increasingly anxious about what they are about to witness. Suddenly, as expected, Armand's finger is cut off, blood seems to spurt as he holds his finger in pain and consternation, and the scene ends.

Watching this movie is quite stressful for most viewers, and there are marked changes in heart rate and skin resistance, as well as reports of considerable distress. The researchers wanted to examine how the kind of appraisal made about what is happening in the movie determines the level of stress produced by it. So special orienting passages were created, which were played before subjects watched the movie to influence their appraisal of these events.

There were three different kinds of orienting passage, each with a different message, and a control or comparison condition in which the movie was played as it was originally made without the orienting passage. Imagine yourself seated in an easy chair—hooked up electrically to measure your physiological reaction—about to watch a movie that has been identified as stressful.

In the first condition, which was created for the purpose of comparison with the orientation passages, there was nothing to listen to before you watched the movie. If you were one of the subjects in this condition, you would view the movie without any orientation passage to influence how you interpret the events shown. This was the *control* condition.

If you were in a second group of subjects, the researcher first plays the orientation. You hear that the events to be portrayed in the movie never actually took place but were simulated by skilled actors. This is the *denial* condition. It was designed to provide some reassurance against the upcoming stressful scenes—in other words, to influence the viewer's appraisal toward a more benign interpretation. The denial statement is, of course, true because no one could have been ready and waiting with a camera to film relatively infrequent accidents; they had to be enacted.

And if you were slated to listen to the third orientation passage, you were told about the interesting strategies that are being used for training people to avoid accidents. This is the *distancing* condition. It was designed to help the viewer gain psychological distance from the distressing events by making a purely intellectual analysis of them. This is something like what physicians or scientists do when they examine the sources of human misery and try to understand them, rather than being personally involved and emotionally reactive. (Distancing as a coping device was discussed in Chapter 8.)

In a fourth orientation passage, the terrible pain and distress experienced by the people you are about to see are described. This is the *trauma* condition. It was designed to emphasize the main sources of psychological stress and, therefore, to increase the degree of stress on the part of the viewer.

What happened is that the manipulated appraisals of the meaning of what was seen in the movie dramatically affected the intensity of the stress reactions. Compared with the control condition in which there was no special instruction, the *denial* and *distancing* conditions both lowered the levels of stress—physiologically and subjectively. Heart rate and skin resistance, as well as the subjective ratings of stress level, showed much lower levels throughout the film, especially during the accident scenes. The *trauma* condition substantially increased these levels compared with the *control* condition. Though all subjects watched the same movie, its appraisal, and therefore the stress levels experienced, had been changed.

Now another experiment was tried using the section of film in which Armand's finger is cut off in flashback scenes. The researchers took the entire episode of Armand's accident out of the movie, and by careful cutting and splicing created two movie versions of the episode—a long version in which the viewer waited 18.75 seconds before the accident happened, and a short version in which the viewer only waited 6.67 seconds. The long wait was referred to as the *suspense* condition, and the short one as *surprise.* Some of the subjects saw the long version and others saw the short version.

One main question was whether it made any difference how long subjects had to wait for the anticipated accident. Which do you think would be more stressful—surprise or suspense? A second question had to do with the point in the finger amputation scene at which the stress level would be highest. What do you think?

Responding to the first question, the physiological changes produced by the accident never reach the stress levels in surprise (the short version) that they did in suspense (the long version). In other words, surprise produces far less stress than suspense. This is similar to the experience we have when the dentist decides to give us a shot of novocaine. Quick as a flash he has the needle in our mouth before we can work up much anxiety. If he took longer, we might have enough time to realize that this is going to be a very unpleasant experience, and some patients might decide to leave the dentist's office in anxiety over the shot.

With the second question, one might have expected that viewing the scenes in which the finger is cut off would be the most stressful part of the movie experience. Not so. The entire buildup of stress takes place before the viewer sees the finger being cut off. At the point at which the dreaded event happens, stress levels are already beginning to come down. It is not seeing the accident that is so terrible, but the anticipation of seeing it that is much worse than the reality.

As an aside, how suspense works presents a number of fascinating psychological questions. For example, this film episode with Armand seems to be more stressful to watch than unexpectedly seeing Slim impaled on a board flung from the circular saw. No doubt it was the suspense that accounts for this. But are all instances of suspense alike? In the episode with Armand, we know more or less what will happen to Armand but he doesn't, which adds another dimension to the psychological stress. We can anticipate the catastrophe that Armand will suffer. We empathize with Armand, which gives this episode a special poignancy. Other instances of suspense involve no such foreknowledge.

Suspense can take a number of interesting psychological forms, and moviemakers who use it to heighten a drama, like Alfred Hitchcock did, usually have strong intuitions about how to manipulate these forms of suspense in the interest of arousing emotions in their audiences. In the research we have been describing, the degree of stress can be objectively ascertained, providing possible explanations of why Hitchcock was so successful.

But let us return to the length of time a person must wait for something ominous to happen. There is much more to this than meets the eye.

The time periods in which people awaited a damaging event in this film study—even in the suspense condition—are very short, too short for much coping to occur. More time than this may be needed to do what is necessary psychologically to cope with the stress.

We might note, parenthetically, that subjects could have chosen to close their eyes so as not to see the accident. This is a form of coping that many people use when a movie scene is more than they think they can handle. Nevertheless, curiosity about what is going to happen next is a very strong impulse, as is the social context of the experiment, in which you relate to the experimenter who expects you to keep your eyes open. No subjects in this research actually closed their eyes. Instead, subjects coped by reasoning about what was happening to them.

To reason about what is happening in an attempt to cope should take much more time than a few seconds. The experimenters wanted to know how much time is necessary for emotion-centered coping to occur when we are waiting for something bad to happen. So one member of the Berkeley Stress and Coping project[14] designed a very different kind of experiment. Subjects, all volunteers, were threatened with an electric shock and then tested individually. They sat in a chair with a clock directly in front of them, and were told they would receive a strong and painful electric shock in a certain amount of time.

The waiting time was flashed on a screen in front of them. It read "Shock in ____ seconds" and they could watch the clock to tell how close in time it was to the moment when they would receive the shock. Some subjects had to wait 30 seconds, others 1 minute, 3 minutes, 5 minutes, or 20 minutes. Actually, no shock was ever given. Just anticipating it was enough to create stress. At the end of the experiment, subjects were told all about the experiment and its purposes, and questioned about what they had thought about during the waiting period.

As in previous research, subjects were hooked up to instruments that measured their heart rates and skin resistances. The results of the different waiting periods proved fascinating. The main finding was that if you waited only 30 seconds or 1 minute, the level of stress was high, but it was lower for the 3- and 5-minute wait. When you wait for 20 minutes, however, the stress level goes up again, starting to climb after about 7 or 8 minutes of waiting.

The reason for these differences has to do with what subjects thought about during the waiting periods. In the 30-second and 1-minute wait, subjects had enough time only to assimilate the idea that they were going to receive a painful shock. As one subject put it, "There was not enough time to think of much of anything."

However, those who waited for 3 and 5 minutes had lots of time to think reassuring thoughts about the upcoming shock, and these thoughts were realistic. They said to themselves: "I have been shocked before and it wasn't really bad; it's waiting for it that is the hard thing." Or, "I can see that the shock is produced by a battery operated inductorium, which I'm sure cannot produce much pain." Or, "I am certain that a university professor would not be allowed to really hurt me; it can't be so bad." In effect, if they had enough time to analyze the situation, subjects would reappraise it as not so bad. So, thinking back to the distinction between surprise and suspense, if the suspense is long enough, a new process, coping, comes into play. In the movie study, however, 18-odd seconds was not long enough to provide this opportunity to cope.

What did subjects think, however, in the 20-minute waiting period in which stress levels were again high? Why is waiting a fairly long period of time more stressful than waiting a modest period? The findings suggested that a long wait seemed to add an ominous significance to the upcoming shock. The meaning of the situation was changed and subjects began to have second thoughts that made reassurance difficult or impossible. They would think that anything one has to await inactively for so long could not be minor. In effect, the long waiting period undermined reassuring thoughts or reappraisals about the way things would work out.

In all these studies, and many more, again and again one could see that it is the way a person appraises what is happening, rather than the realities themselves, that determines the stressful impact. In emotion too, thinking is the powerful agent that influences both the kind and the degree of emotion and the potential for coping. Research such as this provides the modern chapter and verse for Shakespeare's intuition expressed in *Hamlet:* "For there is nothing either good or bad but thinking makes it so." (See Chapter 7.)

Psychological Stress and the Emotions

Stress is a far simpler idea than emotion in that it is commonly measured in one-dimensional terms. Even when it is treated, as we have, as being more complex—that is, as being of three kinds, harm, threat, and challenge—it is still a simple idea compared with emotion. Missing from the concept of stress is a concern with the many different emotions that can flow from a stressful relationship with one's environment. In the film studies just described, one knows only that appraisal lowered or raised the *degree of stress*, but nothing about whether the reaction was one of a possible *fifteen emotions*—for example, anxiety ("I will experience pain"), anger ("That SOB professor"), shame ("What if I act badly?"), pride ("I'm tough"), and so forth.

The problem here is that up to now we have been speaking as though psychological stress and the emotions are separate, independent topics. You may already have sensed, however, that the two topics are intimately connected. Stress, for most of us, calls forth distressing emotions— namely, the nasty emotions of anger, envy, and jealousy, the existential emotions of anxiety, guilt, and shame, and the emotions brought about by unfavorable life situations, which include relief, hope, and sadness.

By looking at the cases in Chapters 2 to 6, we were able to examine the emotions experienced in stressful encounters and the rich information that comes from identifying the many different kinds of situations and personal meanings that fall within the rubric of stress. That is why this book is about the emotions, within which the topic of stress is properly placed. Personal meanings underlie both stress and emotion, but fifteen different emotions greatly enlarge the range of these meanings and are far more instructive about the individual who experiences them.

The emotions we experience, including the stress emotions, tell us much about ourselves. We can learn from them about the goals and beliefs that remain active over a lifetime, and the appraisals we repeatedly make in our struggles to understand and adapt to the world. They also reveal the coping strategies we favor in dealing with the conditions that arouse these emotions, and with their personal and social implications.

In the next chapter we take up whether emotions, the relationships that arouse them, and how we cope are harmful or beneficial to our health.

12

Emotions and Our Health

A MAJOR REASON FOR SCIENTIFIC and professional interest in the emotions (and stress, too) is the conviction that our emotional lives can promote either health or illness. Although the distinction between illness and disease is not a technical one, we often reserve the term illness for temporary, functional ailments and symptoms, such as respiratory infections from which we usually recover, pain, distress, depression, and lack of energy. Disease, on the other hand, refers to structural damage to tissues, such as the clogging of arteries with cholesterol-based plaque (arteriosclerosis) and cancer. The words ailment and disorder, which are also commonly used, are ambiguous with respect to this distinction.

Two key questions provide the main themes of this chapter. The first is whether or not emotions cause illness and disease. Assuming a yes answer to the first question, the second question has to do with how emotions affect health—in other words, the psychological and physiological mechanisms that are involved.

Can Emotions Cause Illness and Disease?

What sort of evidence favors the belief that emotions play a causal role in illness? The issues surrounding this belief are interesting, perplexing, and provocative. We will first try to give you a sense of what has been discovered about emotional factors in four kinds of ailments: psychosomatic disorders, infections, heart disease, and cancer, before addressing the psychological and physiological mechanisms that could explain the effects. Too many studies have been published in recent years to review them all here, but we can consider some representative ones.

Psychosomatic Disorders

An ailment is referred to as psychosomatic when it is the result of stress. These ailments are also called stress disorders. Psychosomatic refers to bodily symptoms that have psychological causes, hence the union of *psycho* with *soma* (body) in the combined term psychosomatic.

Certain ailments have traditionally been recognized as being psychosomatic because they are especially responsive to stress. Gastrointestinal distress of all kinds, such as indigestion, everyday bellyaches, and bowel problems are by far the most common of all bodily ailments linked to stress.

Recognizing that some ailments have genetic and constitutional origins as well as psychological ones, the classic list of psychosomatic ailments— which means the way medical researchers have thought about them— includes colitis (frequent diarrhea, perhaps punctuated by constipation), ulcers (lesions in the stomach or duodenum), migraine (severe headache with nausea), tension headaches, and several other ailments whose status as psychosomatic is more complex and less certain, such as hypertension (high blood pressure), asthma (acute difficulty in breathing), and a number of skin disorders.

As will be evident shortly, the list can be greatly expanded to the universe of illnesses and diseases because today we have reason to believe that any ailment can be affected by stress emotions. For example, in recent research it has been shown that under conditions of stress herpes can break out in an individual who carries the virus. In some instances stress exacerbates an ailment even when its main cause is not psychological. In other instances, psychological stress is considered a primary cause.

From about the 1920s to the 1950s, the dominant outlook toward these disorders was psychoanalytic.[1] Each psychosomatic illness was said to result from a particular type of intrapsychic conflict, which expresses itself in a particular pattern of symptoms.

A psychoanalyst by the name of Franz Alexander[2] is usually credited with being the major pioneer of the psychoanalytic approach to psychosomatic disorders. D. T. Graham,[3] a research-oriented psychologist, later presented an influential analysis of psychosomatic disorders that centered on attitudinal conflicts about which the individual is usually unaware. Some examples of these attitudinal conflicts are feeling humiliated for ulcerative colitis, constantly endangered for essential hypertension, and not getting what one feels entitled to, or owed, for duodenal ulcer. Although his account overlaps with that of Alexander, Graham's version is clearer and more concrete, and so we use it to illustrate the psychoanalytic approach.

The fundamental principle of Graham's theory is expressed in two ideas: First, that each psychosomatic disorder is part of a specific emotion; and, second, that each emotion has its own unique physiological components, which help to explain how the bodily symptoms are brought about. To test these fundamental principles, Graham had psychiatrists identify the basic attitudinal conflict of numerous psychosomatic patients from selected segments of recorded interviews that had been obtained earlier by other psychiatrists. None of the psychiatrists—neither the original interviewers nor the psychiatric judges—knew the specific hypotheses that linked the attitudinal conflicts with each disorder.

The task of the judges was to guess what each patient's disorder was from the attitudinal conflict they identified in the interview segment. The judges were able to do this correctly—that is, as hypothesized by Graham from the theory—more often than by chance. In effect, there appeared to be an ulcer personality, a colitis personality, an asthma personality, and so on, each with its own particular attitudinal conflict.

Because of methodological difficulties, however, the evidence that was accumulated over many years was often contradictory, and left many residual doubts among professional workers with a scientific bent. As early as the 1950s, the assumption that each disorder had its own specific psychological cause had begun to be increasingly challenged. A contrary position became widely accepted—that *any* conflict or source of stress produced common physiological changes that could, if prolonged, lead to illness.[4] But it was still necessary to explain why people got different ailments as a result of stress, and some people seemed immune to these ailments even when their stress levels were high.

The revised explanation was that the victims of psychosomatic ailments had either been born with vulnerable organ systems, or acquired them over the course of their lives. Stress was said to produce the irritable bowel seen in colitis only in persons whose lower intestinal tracts (i.e., the large colon) were vulnerable, regardless of the nature of the attitudinal conflict that might have been responsible for the stress. Similarly, gastric pain and ulcers would occur under stress only in persons whose upper gastrointestinal tracts (i.e., the stomach and duodenum) were vulnerable, and so on, for each of the other psychosomatic disorders, such as headaches, hypertension, asthma, and skin problems.

In recent years, the term psychosomatic has been expanded, as we noted, to mean that *any* illness or disease—not just those originally called psychosomatic—could have emotional causes or be aggravated by stress emotions.[5] This reasoning has empowered widespread research efforts to track down the emotional factors operating in infectious illnesses, heart disease, and cancer.

These research efforts are centered on a discipline still commonly referred to as psychosomatic medicine, but alternatively called behavioral medicine or health psychology. These disciplines are all predicated on the principle that certain lifestyles, emotional ones included, are hazardous to health, and that illness and disease can be in some degree controlled and even prevented by changing one's lifestyle. The story of cancer patient Alice Epstein, which we presented as an example of hope in Chapter 4, illustrates an effort to change what was regarded as an illness-producing lifestyle. In our discussion, we ignore diet, exercise, smoking, and drinking, which are among the most important lifestyles of interest to health psychology in favor of only one lifestyle factor—namely, the emotions.

Infectious Illnesses

Interest in the role of emotional factors in infections, such as colds, flu, mononucleosis, and so forth, got a major shot in the arm—no pun intended—with our growing awareness and knowledge of the *immune process*, which has long been known to defend our bodies against germs and other harmful agents. But how does it do this? The first breakthrough came many decades ago when the so-called white blood cells were recognized as a mainstay of the body's army of infection fighters. But as a result of vigorous research, it is now known that the immune system is much more complex than had been earlier supposed. For example, we recognize a number of separate but interrelated components of the immune system, including lymphocytes (white cells), T-cells, B-cells, and a number of types of leucocytes, which engulf and kill bacteria, all of which work together to fight diverse illnesses and diseases.

Although our understanding of the immune system and how it works is far more sophisticated today than it was years ago, many mysteries remain. We need not examine the details of this system to understand that the most obvious way emotion might contribute to infectious illness is by its effects on the immune process.[6] Some of the hormones secreted in the presence of stress emotions impair or weaken the immune process by reducing the available number of disease-fighting components, such as lymphocytes (white cells), thereby leaving us more vulnerable to infection. Others probably restore or strengthen the immune process, but we are less sure about this.

Many studies of the effects of stress on the immune system have recently appeared and show that prolonged stress weakens the ability of the immune system to fight infection. It has been demonstrated, for example, that lonely students have a poorer immune response to infection than those who are not lonely. Also those who have been grieving over the death of a loved one display weakened immunity. Although other explanations are possible, this could be why many people die within a year or so of their spouse's death.

And it has been shown that the coping style of patients who are HIV positive influences the immune system and, therefore, how soon they are likely to develop full-blown AIDS. Patients with passive coping style (i.e., accepting and cooperative), which was followed over the previous year, had lower lymphocyte counts, which means that their immune system is weaker than patients with an active coping style (i.e., confident and forceful).[7]

But what are the steps leading from stress and coping to illness? Can we trace the behavioral factors that have an impact on the immune system? If we were setting up a study to look at these steps, how could we begin?

A first step might be to evaluate whether stress emotions actually result in *hormone changes*. One study of male Swedish high school students did just this.[8] Students who were exposed to an exam, a stressful event, were rated by their teachers according to how academically ambitious they were. The findings revealed that the extremely ambitious boys did secrete more adrenaline in this stress situation than other boys in the same class who took the same test. What is particularly interesting in this study is that boys who cared less about succeeding academically were not under as much stress from the exam, and secreted less adrenalin, than those who cared greatly. We can conclude that the ambitious boys were under more stress, which increased levels of adrenaline in the blood, and which, if prolonged, could compromise the effectiveness of their immune system to fight illness.

But how can we know whether stress results in changes in the *immune system*. This is a second step in the analysis. Some research has been performed to address this question with nonhuman primates. In one recent study, for example, the social behavior of monkeys was observed over a period of 26 months.[9] The scientists were particularly interested in how the monkeys initiated and sustained a comfortable social relationship with another monkey. Only some of these relationships were stable and therefore supportive. Others were unstable, which would arouse the stress of social rejection. T-cell immune activity was also observed—these T-cells metabolize bits of the invading germs, then become sensitized to recognize it as the enemy, and finally kill and eat the invaders.

It was found that stable affiliations with other monkeys enhanced T-cell immune activity, while unstable affiliations—for example, the breaking up of a relationship—suppressed immune system activity. On the basis of these data, we can't say whether this suppression also led to increased illness, but most researchers are confident it would.

But can the stress emotions increase the risk of infectious illness—a third research step? Such an effect was demonstrated in a study of West Point Cadets who had contracted infectious mononucleosis, the so-called student's illness.[10] The researchers found that students who became ill showed a distinctive combination of high academic motivation and poor academic performance compared with those who did not become ill. Evidently, the stress of doing badly when you want very much to do well increases the risk of getting infectious mononucleosis. By the same token, if you don't care very much, your level of stress is not as great, and you are not as likely to become ill. Unfortunately, these researchers did not look at the immune process or the stress hormones that might have influenced it.

A fourth step is illustrated by a striking recent study by Sheldon Cohen and his colleagues showing that stress emotions can both weaken the immune process and increase the likelihood of a rhinovirus infection—the common cold.[11] A large number of men and women in good health were tested for the amount of stress experienced during the past year. Then they were exposed to a cold virus, which was introduced into their nasal passages.

A direct relationship was found between the amount of stress to which an individual had been exposed, the incidence of colds, and changes in the immune system. The high-stress subjects got infected more readily than the low-stress subjects, and the immune system was weakened in those who had the rhinovirus in their bloodstreams, proving they had been infected. In effect, the more stress reported, the more likely subjects were to have contracted the common cold as a result of the exposure to the rhinovirus. Although this study did not examine hormonal patterns, it is one of the strongest bits of experimental evidence that infectious illness and immune system changes are influenced by stress.

Unfortunately, research in the area of infectious illness has been fragmented, so our knowledge remains less secure than one might wish. It would be far more revealing if all four variables we have been looking at in this book—stress emotions, hormones that are generated by stress (such as adrenaline, noradrenaline, and the corticosteroids), the immune system, and coming down with an infectious illness—had been combined in the same study.

As matters stand now, we know some powerful but separate facts that are not fully connected—namely, that stress emotions increase the secretion of certain hormones, that they weaken the immune system, and that this weakness can increase the likelihood of infectious illness. When all four variables are combined one day in the same research, the proof of these relationships, which have long been suspected, and the knowledge of how they work, will be even more solid.

Heart Disease

Because those of us in the industrial world live longer than we used to, heart disease is the leading cause of death. What is encouraging to those who have been working to reduce or prevent death from heart attacks is the extraordinary fact that the death rates from heart attacks, which rose precipitously from 1920 to 1960, have sharply declined ever since. It is difficult to analyze why the rates have fallen, but the change is often interpreted as the positive consequences of altered lifestyles, such as different diets, more exercise, and a reduction in smoking. However, this interpretation is still largely conjecture. What role does emotion play in all this?

There are at least three reasons for thinking that emotions have something to do with cardiovascular diseases. First, stress emotions increase the level of low-density blood cholesterol, which is said to be one of the primary causes of blockage of the arteries supplying blood to the heart. This blockage is a major factor in heart attacks, as well as other diseases.

Second, stress emotions result in maladaptive coping behaviors that are, in themselves, damaging to the heart and its surrounding blood supply. For example, to the extent that people under stress smoke more, fail to eat enough, eat excessively, follow a poor diet, or drink in excess, they are at increased risk of heart disease and heart attacks.

Third, stress emotions result in powerful hormones, such as adrenaline, being sent into the bloodstream, markedly increasing heart rate and blood pressure. Coupled with a diseased cardiovascular system, these demands on the heart could subject a person to acute cardiovascular crisis under stress, which could provoke sudden death. This has generated a large amount of attention from those who believe that stress emotions could be important both in heart disease and heart attacks.

The idea that a stressful lifestyle contributes to heart disease is an old one in medicine. In the nineteenth century, a distinguished physician, Sir William Osler, made the following comment[12] about Jewish businessmen, who seemed to him to epitomize those most vulnerable to heart disease for emotional and lifestyle reasons:

> Living an intense life, absorbed in his work, devoted to his pleasures, passionately devoted to his home, the nervous energy of the Jew is taxed to the utmost, and his system is subjected to that stress and strain which seems to be a basic factor in so many cases of angina pectoris [pain resulting from the narrowing of the arteries serving the heart].

In this early document, we can recognize the pattern we now call the *type A personality*, an idea that has gained much recent attention in research and in the media. What Osler said about Jewish businessmen, many of whom he saw as patients, certainly applies to us all. Although enthusiasm for the original version of the type A-heart disease link has waned in recent years, it is worth discussing at some length because it has been a mainstay of psychological approaches to heart disease. It also illustrates some of the research problems on stress emotions and disease. And as we will see shortly, new ideas about this link have been emerging that seem more promising to many scientists than the original version of the type A personality.

Modern interest in type A individuals began with two cardiologists, Meyer Friedman and Ray Rosenman,[13] whose work originated in San Francisco in the 1950s. They divided their heart patients into type As and type Bs. Type As are said to be characterized by an exaggerated sense of time urgency, competitiveness, and hostility. Type Bs display the opposite pattern, having a more relaxed outlook on life. The types were identified from interviews in which the focus of attention of the researchers was centered more on the style with which questions were answered—for example, the tendency to interrupt often or be argumentative—than on the content of the answers.

This interview approach was later converted into a questionnaire by a psychologist interested in lifestyles and health, C. David Jenkins.[14] He and his collaborators characterized the coronary-prone behavior pattern by the same three qualities that had been proposed by Friedman and Rosenman—time urgency, competitiveness, and hostility. This pattern could be revealed in subjects' answers to their questionnaire.

Questions about *time urgency* focus on what you would do—for example, if someone is late for an appointment. Would you sit and wait, walk about while waiting, or carry reading materials with you to get something done while waiting. The last choice, especially, illustrates a sense of impatience and time urgency. Other questions have to do with whether most people consider you *hard driving and competitive* or relaxed and easygoing. Still other questions ask about tendencies toward *hostility*, though our preference is to speak of anger.

One well-known study used this assessment approach with several thousand men who were followed for eight and a half years. Although certain anomalies were present in the data, the findings provided some confirmation—both for the interview measure and the questionnaire—that type A men had a substantially greater likelihood of coronary heart disease than type Bs. Later studies suggested that women too were similarly vulnerable. However, several later prospective studies failed to confirm the earlier findings on the type A-heart disease connection. We do not know the reasons for this failure to confirm, but it was a blow to what many had considered an important advance in our knowledge.

On the positive side, while not focused on heart disease per se, a number of experimental studies provided indirect evidence that type As react to stress emotions differently than type Bs and in ways that seem consistent with type A theory. In one such study, type A college students, who were asked to exercise to the limit of their capacities, reported feeling less fatigue than type Bs, which is consistent with the idea that type As drive themselves harder, even to the point of denying fatigue.

And on the basis of a number of other experiments, the same researcher[15] suggested further that type As are driven to maintain control and mastery in stress situations, but in uncontrollable situations they become resigned more quickly than type Bs to the absence of control. This pattern of reaction could have important effects on the hormones secreted under stress and presumably make the type A person more vulnerable to cardiovascular disease. Although ardent adherents of the type A concept can still be found, in the light of continuing research, doubts have been raised about the validity and utility of the proposed type A-heart disease relationship.

A new way to think about the type A phenomenon is to focus on a different key ingredient that might be responsible for the increased cardiovascular risk. It has been suggested, for example, that pressure of a job that is frustrating and a source of distress, rather than time urgency, is the causal factor. This may explain why people who love their work and its pressures might not be at risk.

The most recent hypothesis, and one that is currently generating much enthusiasm, is that the emotional cause of heart disease is *anger*, which had not been emphasized in the original type A concept. To evaluate this, the tendency to become angry was separated from the other type A characteristics and studied on its own. A considerable body of research has suggested that anger is conducive to heart disease. Here too, however, the evidence is mixed. Some studies have found that it is not the intensity of anger that causes the problem but its frequency.[16] In other words, people who are often made angry may be the ones at risk.

But is the culprit anger or how the anger is managed by the person? It has been proposed that the suppression of anger is the key psychological contributor to heart disease. In one study,[17] interview data were obtained on how people would handle work-related anger. Blood pressure was sampled several times during the interview. Those studied showed three kinds of coping styles: anger directed toward oneself ("Just walk away from the situation that provoked the anger"), anger directed toward the person who has acted offensively ("Protest to him directly"), and reflective ("Talk to the offending person about it after he has cooled down").[18]

What is salient in all these diverse coping styles is the centrality of personal meaning—which generates anger in the first place. People construct the meaning of socially offensive confrontations and these must be studied if we are to understand anger and heart disease. To react with anger, as we have seen, is to appraise situations as demeaning.

Personal meaning is also involved in coping with anger when it has been aroused. For example, to inhibit the expression of anger is to appraise overt anger as dangerous or reprehensible, especially when it involves a direct attack on another person. To cope with a provocation to anger with reflection and to be careful about its expression implies that the person believes that aggression should be avoided in the interests of finding a more sensible and civilized solution.

Clearly, in much of this research, inhibiting anger appears to be desirable for health rather than undesirable, and the failure of controlling anger seems to be associated with illness. This is what we implied in Chapter 2 about the failure of Freud's boiler analogy, which suggested, incorrectly, that we need to release anger lest it build up. Nevertheless, some theorists still believe that bottling up anger is dangerous for our health.

These research areas have revealed interesting emotional and coping possibilities for understanding disease, especially heart disease. Unfortunately, however, in all this research on anger, little attention has been paid to individual differences in the way meanings are ascribed to social encounters, meanings that affect the arousal of anger and its control.

The growing ferment about the role of anger and its control in cardiovascular disease is reflected in the growing volume of research, which ultimately could resolve some of these problems. Research psychologist Charles Spielberger and his colleagues, as well as research physician Redford Williams,[19] have published extensive research on this problem. Both have developed scales for the measurement of anger to facilitate this research.

In any case, we are left with a puzzle. There is ample evidence that the stress emotions, including anger, seem to play a role in heart disease. It all seems very sensible and promising. However, although most media accounts are gung-ho about this idea, the research findings are not fully consistent and many measurement problems remain that have not been adequately resolved. We regard the issue as still problematic in firmly establishing the connection between personal styles and heart disease, the emotions that might create harm or benefit to health, and the physiological mechanisms involved.

Cancer

Cancer is the second highest cause of death in the United States, which justifies the considerable effort being made to prevent and treat it. And, like heart disease, its incidence increases with age. Cancer consists of a number of related diseases, each defined by the type of tumor and the body organ that is attacked—for example, lung, breast, stomach, colon and rectum, bladder, or prostate—and it is not clear whether these diseases are united as to cause or if each is distinctive. Most preventive efforts are directed at environmental causal agents such as smoking, drinking, and diet. As in the case of heart disease and infectious illness, our concern here is limited to emotional factors.

Social scientists have generally approached emotional factors in cancer with the idea that there is a cancer-prone personality, and there are several theoretical candidates. One simple one is that emotionality could be an *indirect* cause of cancer by leading the person to smoke or drink excessively. We saw a similar hypothesis with respect to heart disease.

Another theory is that people who tend to suppress their emotions are more prone to cancer than others. The suppression is, presumably, a *direct* cause by virtue of the way it might affect hormonal activity.

Several studies have supported this possibility, but for every study that is supportive, other studies have produced opposing results. In order to view the evidence supporting the hypothesis that emotional patterns can increase the risk of cancer, we consider here only a few of the studies suggesting that emotional suppression contributes to the disease.

In one such study, a group of women who were admitted to a hospital for a biopsy (a test for cancer) because of a suspicious lump in the breast were evaluated with respect to personality factors that might be relevant to whether they had a positive or negative biopsy.[20]

One group of these women, 40% of the original sample, was found to have a malignancy; in the rest, the lump was benign. Before these biopsy results were known, the researchers had assessed the tendency to suppress emotions to see if these traits would predict who had the cancer and who did not. It was found that women who tended to suppress or deny emotions such as anger were more likely to have the breast cancer than those who did not.

In another study,[21] a sample of males who were free of any diagnosed medical condition were given personality tests at a Veterans Administration hospital. Ten years later, they were divided on the basis of their medical records into those who had developed a cancer and those who had not. The cancer group was found to have suppressed their emotions prior to the onset of the disease, as inferred from the personality tests. Here, too, the evidence suggested that emotional suppression may have something to do with cancer proneness.

As an aside, it is also notable that studies of the inmates of homes for the elderly have also found evidence that those who were compliant, well-adjusted, and uncomplaining did not live as long—regardless of the cause of death—as those who were argumentative and discontented.

Taking both the cancer studies and those made on the longevity of the elderly together, it seems that showing distress and being resistive and demanding are somehow associated with longer survival than suppressing negative emotions and being pleasant and compliant. A problem here is that one cannot say whether the difference has to do with the actual experience of emotions or with their social expression. We, the authors, are personally attracted to these findings because we tend to be easily angered and have always loved the Dylan Thomas poem urging us to "rage, rage, against the dying of the light." We are also reminded of the sardonic but ambiguous saying that only the good die young.

In a different series of studies,[22] it was found that terminal cancer patients who became depressed and withdrew from social contacts died sooner than patients who maintained active contacts with friends and relatives. These two groups of patients did not differ in the severity of the disease when initially observed. So it would seem that emotional and coping factors play a role in how long terminal cancer patients survive. We don't know why this should be. But it is possible that people who feel they have nothing to live for simply give up and fail to engage in life-sustaining activities, such as eating, rousing oneself to get out of bed, protecting oneself against injury, and so forth.

In a very systematic and unusual exploration of coping with breast cancer, Edgar Heim, a Swiss research psychiatrist, and a number of colleagues have focused not on survival as an index of patient adaptation, but on psychological and social adjustments that cover a wide range of adaptive goals on the part of patients, family, and health-care providers.[23]

The question they investigated is how the patient manages the psychological and medical problems imposed by the illness, such as regaining a sense of well-being, restoring and preserving emotional balance, adjusting to or restoring body integrity after mutilation or loss of body functions, mastering external threats—particularly if the illness becomes terminal—and preserving a meaningful quality of life whatever the circumstances.

These researchers observed that adjustment and the coping strategies employed by patients differ considerably depending on the stage of the cancer. Adjustment tends to be poorest several months after surgery but improves with time as strategies of coping are learned for dealing with cancer-induced problems. These strategies are very responsive to the changing demands of the illness. In other words, there is no fixed pattern of coping, but the coping strategy depends on the circumstances being faced.

On the basis of the emotional state of patients and how they manage the adaptational tasks imposed by the illness, Heim and his colleagues regard "good coping" as seeking and perceiving social and emotional support and the cultivation of an attitude of stoical acceptance of the illness. This pattern is associated with efforts at realistic problem analysis and head-on efforts to tackle the problems brought on by the illness. "Poor coping," on the other hand, goes with resignation and fatalism, combined with an attitude of passive avoidance, which may include the denial, isolation, or suppression of emotional distress.

These researchers also note that a connection between attitudes and coping strategies has been observed in many studies. Again and again, withdrawal, depression, and the suppression of emotional distress prove to be a damaging strategy. In contrast, actively trying to address a host of problems and maintaining favorable social relationships sustains patients and, in other studies at least, seems to favor longer survival.

Evidence like this encourages us to think that emotionality—and the appraisal and coping process related to it—is indeed a factor in health and illness. This applies even to the most deadly of diseases, such as heart disease and cancer. Nevertheless, because of conflicting evidence, the causal significance of emotion and coping continues to be hotly debated

Most studies are flawed in some way, which creates nagging doubts about their conclusions. Some of those cited here, such as those of Heim and his colleagues, have the important strength that the data about emotion were obtained before the existence of serious illness became known. That is, such studies are prospective and the effects of emotion were predicted in advance. However, most studies are merely correlational—all the measurements are typically made at the same time—rather than over a period of time—which makes it difficult to prove a cause. This is a problem we address in more detail shortly.

Still another reason for doubt about the role of emotion and coping is that the measurement of emotion itself—and its expression—leaves something to be desired. This adds fuel to the debate among those who are true believers about the emotion-cancer connection and those who are doubting Thomases.

Given the state of the art of this kind of research, it might be helpful now to explore why it is so difficult to prove the connection between emotion and illness or disease, much less be confident about the mechanism that might account for it. Let us digress a moment here to consider the scientific problem we face when proving a cause of illness or disease.

How a Possible Cause of Illness Can Be Proved

To help us understand how scientists could prove that emotions cause illness, we might turn briefly to the famous microbe hunters of the nine-teenth century, before it was known that tuberculosis and other diseases were caused by germs.

When Louis Pasteur proved that tuberculosis was caused by a germ, he injected guinea pigs with large doses of tuberculosis bacteria. All the animals became infected and died. A comparison group of guinea pigs not so injected remained healthy, leaving little doubt that the TB germ was the cause of the disease. To prove causality, it must be demonstrated that the illness occurs only if the causal factor—in this case, the germ—was present before the illness occurred, and this means that if it was not pres-ent the illness did not occur.

Today we know that the idea of a single external cause, such as a germ, is oversimplified; the presence of the germ does not always cause the illness. Whether or not it does depends on the amount of the germ one is exposed to, the type of animal species studied, and the physical condition of each animal. Some species and individuals are immune to tuberculosis, apparently because they have antibodies against it in their immune system; others are vulnerable when their physical condition is poor—that is, when their resistance is low—but not when their physical condition is good. Guinea pigs are sitting ducks for many infections, in-cluding tuberculosis.

Pasteur was evidently clever in using a vulnerable species to prove the germ theory. People are vulnerable, but not nearly as much as guinea pigs. We have to be in poor condition to contract a disease that, in the case of TB, will tend to disappear with the advent of better diet, rest, and proper living conditions. Many epidemiologists who study world patterns of disease believe that it is mainly improved living conditions that have reduced the frequency and severity of tuberculosis, as well as many other illnesses. Tuberculosis is on the rise again, probably because of an increase in poverty, AIDS, and the development of bacterial strains resistant to an-tibiotics.

So the cause of illness is not quite as simple as we once thought; it requires both a vulnerable individual and exposure to a large quantity of germs to make us ill. If we live in an urban center, we are exposed to many people who carry the germs, but most of us do not become ill. Nevertheless, even though the tuberculosis bacterium will not necessarily cause tuberculosis in a robust individual, Pasteur's experiments erased any doubt that infection with the tuberculosis germ was necessary for the dis-ease to occur.

Let us now apply this reasoning about how the role of germs was demonstrated to whether emotions can cause illness. To make a strong case, as Pasteur did, we would need to show that a particular emotional pattern was present in target persons just prior to developing a given illness. In addition, it would be necessary to have a control (comparison) group, which never showed the emotional pattern and did not become ill. Such a finding would be comparable to Pasteur's proof that bacteria caused tuberculosis.

This is much more difficult to accomplish in the case of emotional causes than it is in the case of germs. Because emotions are not so easily identified and manipulated, their study creates a much more ephemeral problem than germs, which can be seen under a microscope and readily manipulated in a laboratory.

Emotions as Causes—Special Problems

A number of problems that are unique to the emotions and other psychological processes make methodologically impeccable research very difficult to accomplish. We will briefly enumerate four main problems.

First, many powerful causal agents produce illness. One of these is genetic influences, which have an impact on vulnerability. The risk of getting certain cancers, for example, seems to run in families. Another consists of constitutional factors that emerge at birth or later in life, which are affected both by inheritance and conditions in utero or during birth. Environmental toxins, especially early in life, are another cause of illness. Long-term lifestyles, such as smoking, alcohol, drug abuse, and engaging in high-risk behaviors are also causal factors. All these agents have such a large effect on whether we suffer illness, and live or die, that they dwarf the emotions as causes, making the role of emotion in illness all the more difficult to isolate.

Second, to show a causal link between emotion and illness requires a change in the health status of the people we are studying. To imitate the Pasteur type of proof requires that the causal agent not be present initially, but, when it is present, illness follows. There has to be a change in health status from health to illness to identify a prior cause.

However, health is quite stable for most people in our affluent society, though we periodically develop minor, short-lived infections, or have ups and downs in the symptoms of stress disorders, such as colitis and ulcers. When we are very young we are more subject to infection and accidents, and when we are old—perhaps because of weakening of the immune system—there is an increase in chronic ailments such as arthritis, cardiovascular disease, cancer, and so forth. But in the relatively long middle period of our lives, health is pretty stable. We need to study people who were healthy but are now ill, and people who were ill but recover. This would make it possible to observe major health changes and find the responsible causal agents.

To do this, however, is easier said than done. Most of the time, all we can do is show a correlation between an emotional pattern and an illness. We identify a group that does not display the pattern and show that few of its members have the illness; and we identify a group that does display the pattern and then show that many of its members have the illness. This produces evidence that is suggestive, but not proof.

Third, it is illogical to suggest that a single, short-lived emotional episode can produce long-term disease, though it might temporarily increase susceptibility to illness and disease. We are built to be able to experience a modicum of emotion without harm, but not to experience intense emotions chronically. Many of us notice that when we are traveling abroad, or after we get home, we seem to be susceptible to respiratory infection and wind up with a severe cold, hacking cough, or flu. One reason for this is that, even when we enjoy it, travel can result in sustained stress, both physical and psychological, and our resistance to infection is then lowered.

If it is possible for stress emotions to produce cardiovascular disease, cancer, diabetes, and so forth, it would require a long, sustained period of emotional distress to do so. It also takes years for arteriosclerosis (hardening of the arteries) to develop into a dangerous condition. Oncologists (cancer specialists) believe that a cancer has probably been growing undetected for a long time before it is discovered. One theory suggests that the emotional origins of breast cancer might well have occurred as much as 20 years earlier, for example, when the woman's hormonal patterns in the process of sexual maturation—which are often cited as a contributing cause—were changing in puberty.

Studying the emotional lives of people continuously for five, ten, or twenty years is not very practical. A more practical alternative may be to sample a person's emotional pattern for a short period at time, say, when that person is 30 years old. We would have to assume that this pattern is stable and will continue. If that person is restudied at age 50 after the presence of target diseases, such as breast cancer, becomes evident, we might be able to infer that the disease is associated with the particular emotional pattern—and its effects on hormonal activity—that was observed earlier.

Fourth, Pasteur had laboratory animals available to him, which made it possible for him to inject lethal germs into them. This can't be done with people if we want to study the effects of the emotions. It is difficult to arouse the full range of emotions in our psychological laboratories. Efforts have been made to generate anger by insulting subjects, or anxiety by exposing them to threats. These experimental efforts, however, are apt to founder on the ethics of experimentation with human subjects, and on the difficulties of manipulating human emotions because of individual differences in susceptibility.

Even if we could legitimately manipulate human emotions, we would find that we have generated not one emotion—say, anger, which is what we wanted to study—but several different emotions in different individuals. Some people would get angry as we intended, but others would feel anxious, perhaps guilty, or experience more than one emotion at the same time. Having limited control over the emotions that we want to study restricts us to the study of emotions as they occur in nature and to rely on descriptions of recent emotional experiences. This kind of research is less precise than was possible in Pasteur's—and others'—pioneering experimentation with germs.

Although these problems are not insurmountable, understanding them helps us appreciate how difficult and costly it is to pursue research that would unequivocally demonstrate the role of the emotions in health and illness.

Ways Emotions Could Affect Health

We have already hinted at some of the ways emotions can affect health. There are three. (1) A person copes with stress emotions in ways that are directly damaging to health. (2) Powerful stress hormones that disturb the body's immune functioning are produced and secreted, thereby creating illness or disease. (3) Hormones resulting from positive emotions, such as relief, happiness, pride, and love, might be produced and secreted, which could promote bodily equanimity and thereby protect against illness and disease or help cure it.

Coping Processes That Damage Health

Certain strategies of coping with stress emotions can be destructive to health and our body's normal functioning by *distorting the painful realities*. We discussed some of these in Chapter 8 on coping. Imagine having symptoms of a heart attack, such as chest pain late in the evening after a large dinner. The symptom is ambiguous. You have heard that it could signify a heart attack. Fishing around for some explanation for the discomfort, you find a reassuring answer and interpret the pain as indigestion caused by the heavy meal you have just eaten. If you are subject to attacks of indigestion, this explanation is reasonable, but not certain.

In interpreting the pain as indigestion, you could be engaging in a denial of the threatening possibility of a heart attack. In any case, you delay seeking medical help. If you are correct, you go to sleep and the pain will probably be gone by the next morning. If you are incorrect, the pain may get worse, coupled with breathing difficulty, which suggests you are having a heart attack from which you might die if not helped. The first minutes and hours of a heart attack are the most dangerous and the need for emergency medical help at this time often greatest.

As you may remember from Chapter 8, some men try to prove that the symptoms being experienced do not arise from a heart attack. They do pushups or run up several flights of stairs—extremely dangerous actions— on the premise that being able to do this proves they couldn't be seriously ill. In the same vein, women postpone a medical checkup for a breast lump, perhaps denying that it could be important. Coping by denial can sometimes endanger one's life.

It is difficult to blame someone for not taking potentially dangerous symptoms seriously. These are difficult decisions. To seek medical inter- vention could be costly and it is certainly time consuming to go through the tests needed to determine your medical condition. If there is a serious health problem, your life will be changed substantially. The procedures are also embarrassing or dehumanizing to many people, and waiting for test results can cause much anxiety.

People differ greatly in how they respond to such situations. Some are overly concerned about every pain and symptom; others fail to worry even when they should. Denial as a style of coping may buy immediate peace of mind, perhaps at the expense of ignoring a future danger. A vigilant style of coping, which focuses on the sources of danger, adds to anxiety because such persons worry about everything that might happen. How- ever, vigilant coping protects them against a bad outcome when there are practical measures to prevent it.

We note in passing that the modern preoccupation with health drives vigilant people up the wall and leaves them constantly anxious when they could be indulging themselves and enjoying life. Hardly anything we do today to indulge ourselves in traditional ways is considered safe any more. In the past, people could, and did, enjoy rich foods and drink without anxiety—cholesterol wasn't measured or thought about.

Some forms of coping lead to illness, disease, and premature death because they do *direct harm to the body*. Earlier in this chapter we pointed to cigarette smoking, abuse of alcohol and drugs, overeating or under- eating (as in anorexia), and excessive risk taking as potentially harmful coping strategies. The harm done by these pathogenic patterns of behavior—statistically speaking—is so evident that the case for their role in illness and disease need not be argued.

The evidence suggests that to some extent risky habits are associated with heightened levels of stress in an individual. When stress is high, there is an increase in smoking, drinking, eating disorders, and risk taking. It is as if such persons are saying to themselves "I am under such great pressure that I need to be good to myself and not tackle the difficult task of regulating these bad habits." People who do this obtain short-term gratification from these activities but are not taking long-term risks into account.

Stress Hormones, Illness, and Disease

Stress emotions, such as anger, anxiety, guilt, shame, sadness, envy, and jealousy, generate powerful hormones, which are sent coursing through the bloodstream to influence the way our organs function, speeding up some functions and slowing down others. One could say, somewhat poetically perhaps, that the mind talks to the body through the emotions and the effects of these hormones.

The distinguished stress physiologist, Hans Selye, showed that two main types of corticosteroids are secreted by the outer portion of the adrenal glands. When we are injured, for example, or in psychological emergencies, the first hormones to appear have inflammatory effects on the tissues. This is why we become swollen—with attendant pain—when we break a bone or are stung by a bee. Inflammation is one of the body's defenses against noxious agents; it helps to isolate the area for healing to occur. Other steroids, which are anti-inflammatory, enter the bloodstream later and help bring down the swelling.

Selye referred to the inflammatory hormones as catabolic; they use up the body's resources. The anti-inflammatory hormones are anabolic; they restore the resources that have been drawn on so that our bodies can get back to normal. If catabolic activity is sustained too long, or is too severe, we grow ill or become diseased and perhaps die. The body's defenses—especially when they overreact to the noxious agent—are capable of doing us in as well as helping us survive.

This appears to be what happens in a severe allergic reaction. The body overreacts to a foreign substance, which may not be as dangerous as the defense mounted against it. A bee sting or piece of crab eaten by a person who is severely allergic to it can create severe swelling and blockage of the windpipe so that the person cannot breathe. This acute reaction is called anaphylactic shock; the person's life signs reach a very low point, and if adrenaline is not administered quickly, the person may die.

Notice that these examples refer to physical trauma, but the same could be said about psychological emergencies that arouse intense emotions such as anger or fright. Powerful hormones in such emotions are also secreted, with the same effects that Selye is describing. Selye's analysis deals with the body's mobilization for any reason—whether because of physical injury or psychological threats—and the bodily disequilibrium the mobilization causes, as if the specific condition producing stress doesn't matter.

However, as we saw earlier, specific links between an emotion and psychosomatic disorders were proposed by psychoanalytic theorists, and recently by those who see anger or its control as especially conducive to heart disease, and sadness and depression as conducive to cancer. Many scientists concerned with emotion and health take the theory of emotional specificity—that each disorder has its own emotional cause—quite seriously, even though the psychoanalytic explanations are no longer widely accepted. This is a major source of argument among those whose interests center on understanding the relationship between emotion and illness. Unfortunately, the argument has not yet been resolved.

Positive Emotions and Health Versus Illness and Disease

Until now we have emphasized the stress emotions but not the positive emotions. It is possible, however, that while the stress emotions generate catabolic or destructive hormones, the positive emotions generate other hormones that serve to maintain health and well-being.

The most famous illustration of this idea is the extraordinary and well-publicized experience of Norman Cousins. Cousins was the influential editor at the *Saturday Review* who was hospitalized with a presumably fatal collagen disease called ankylosing spondylitis. His physician told him that he had one chance in 500 to recover. He was expected to die.

Viewing the hospital setting as "no place for a person who was seriously ill,"[24] Cousins set out to control his treatment actively by avoiding the toxic psychological aspects of serious illness as much as possible. Influenced by Walter Cannon and Hans Selye, two pioneers in stress physiology, he made the assumption that he was suffering in part from adrenal exhaustion after a stressful foreign meeting he had been attending. As he put it, he needed to restore the homeostatic wisdom of his body that had been disrupted by frustration and suppressed rage. The task, he thought, was to substitute positive emotions for stress emotions insofar as he could. About this he wrote:

> The inevitable question arose in my mind: What about the positive emotions? If negative emotions produce negative chemical changes in the

body, wouldn't the positive emotions produce positive chemical changes? Is it possible that love, hope, faith, laughter, confidence and the will to live have therapeutic value? Do chemical changes occur only on the downside?

With the cooperation of his doctor, Cousins did two main things: First, he went off certain medicines, such as aspirin, which might have harmful effects on a collagen disorder—a disease of the connective tissues—and he took large quantities of vitamin C. Second, he initiated a plan to create distracting laughter from TV programs, such as *Candid Camera*, and amusing books on humor, which were read to him. This increased the periods in which he experienced a positive mood and greatly improved his ability to sleep without pain.

Evidence of improvement in his physical condition began to show up, and eventually he was able to leave the hospital and return to work. Year by year, his physical mobility improved. The disease seemed to have been tamed. Cousins—impressed with his experience and convinced that positive emotions deserved substantial credit for his recovery—later took a job at UCLA as a professor of medicine to pursue this line of thought about the role of positive emotions in health.

He lectured widely throughout the world about his experience, and what has since been referred to as *holistic medicine*. This outlook gives primary attention to the patient as a whole person, rather than focusing narrowly on particular diseases, as traditional medicine tends to do. From that time until he died many years later, he extolled the capacity of the human mind and body to regenerate, and the chemistry—as he put it—of the will to live.

What are we to make of Cousin's remarkable story? Although the odds were heavily against it, maybe he was the one in 500 who would recover—in effect, the rare case. After all, it is possible to get a straight flush in poker or win a multimillion dollar lottery against astronomical odds. Even Cousins recognized that a single case cannot provide scientific proof.

Other stories like this with different diseases provoke a similar interpretative dilemma. You will recall the story of Alice Epstein, who had a terminal cancer, with death appearing imminent (which we described in Chapter 4 in our discussion of hope).[25] Epstein describes herself as having a cancer-prone personality. She undertook psychotherapy with both her psychologist husband and another practicing psychotherapist, and abandoned parts of the medical treatment prescribed for her. Her advanced cancer, which was highly visible in X rays and other scanning procedures, and was extensive throughout her body, gradually disappeared. Her husband, a tough-minded personality psychologist whose forte is research, is convinced that a major change of personality is what cured her, though he also understands the doubts of others about the psychological basis of the cure.

In these stories, we, the authors, worry—as Norman Cousins seems to have when he wrote his account—about misleading people who are desperately seeking a way out of their deadly diseases. The risk of abandoning useful treatments for an improbable cure is a serious one, and many people make very unwise decisions along these lines. On the other hand, a substantial number of people—some medical, some not—are believers and offer various brands of uplifting psychological help to cancer sufferers.

Aside from occasional narratives about individuals who have survived for a long time, or seem to have had a temporary or even permanent remission from a disease—which is really not terribly rare—there is no credible evidence that psychological factors have caused their diseases, nor that psychotherapy has cured them. Generally, those who offer undoctrinaire therapeutic solutions do not perform the research that would be necessary to support or refute their convictions. Yet in the absence of the necessary research, the possibility cannot be ruled out.

Summing Up

Is it plausible that emotions play a causal or contributory role in illness and disease? The answer is yes, especially in the realms of traditional psychosomatic disorders and infectious illness. The hormones produced by stress emotions have been shown to produce *psychosomatic disorders*, to affect the immune system, and to result in infection. We think that a yes answer in these instances is quite reasonable given the research available.

Could this apply to *heart disease?* Again, the answer has to be affirmative because the hormones produced by stress emotions have been shown to affect bodily processes that increase the likelihood of heart attack and its physiological causes. How much of a cause emotions are, however, is more problematic.

The case for *cancer* is more difficult because its causes go back so far in time, perhaps 20 years. Most cancer specialists believe that the origins of this disease are usually far in the person's past, before the disease becomes evident. This means that, many years before the appearance of the malignant growth, bodily processes could be affected by stress disorders and the hormones they produce. The problem is to distinguish what happened in the formative years of the cancer from what is happening after the cancer has appeared and is too far advanced to cure by methods used today. There is some evidence, too, that how the person copes with the disease may make a difference in its rate of progression even when it is terminal, and in how soon death occurs.

Remember also that most diseases are influenced by many factors, not just one. Genetic factors seem to play a role as well as a person's style of life with respect to diet, smoking, alcohol abuse, and so on. It may be unrealistic to suggest that emotional patterns are a primary cause of cancer, and more reasonable to suggest that they contribute to it along with a number of other factors.

Does each type of illness or disease have its own specific emotional cause? We don't know, but it is one of the widely believed hypotheses. Could stress emotions increase the likelihood of any kind of illness and disease, the specific disease being the result of the particular constitution of the individual, as in the vulnerable organ hypothesis? We don't know, but this hypothesis also has thoughtful adherents.

Is it plausible that positive emotions—which are certainly good for morale or one's psychological sense of well-being—also offer protection against disease or increase the likelihood of positive physical health? We must say yes here as well. Could they work as a form of treatment? This also is plausible, but plausibility is not proof, nor does it provide us with the detailed knowledge of how the emotion-health link works.

Alas, neither Cousins's nor Epstein's provocative personal accounts offer the evidence we need, and little systematic research is being done to put these accounts to the test. Like many other problems of great import for human well-being, we must hope that, armed by plausible theories and provocative anecdotes, answers will be forthcoming in the next generations of social and biological scientists. In the meantime, we will just have to wait and see and be wary of undocumented claims.

13

When Coping Fails—
Psychotherapy Offers
a Solution

IN THIS CHAPTER, we explore psychotherapy as a way of dealing with dysfunctional and distressing emotions. People seek professional help for their emotional problems when they feel miserable, when their hopes and ambitions are blocked or interfered with by these problems, and when their own efforts have not ameliorated their pain and suffering. They may have tried other sources of help, looking to friends, family, or clergy, but the problems remain daunting. This is an age-old story, going back to ancient shamans who, with potions and potent ideas consistent with their cultural traditions, sought to cure emotional problems and the physical symptoms often accompanying them.

A person confronts several major obstacles when deciding to seek professional help for emotional problems. The first and most serious is that many people believe, erroneously, that seeking help implies that they are mentally ill, and so they feel ashamed. Another is reluctance to disclose their troubles to anyone. Still another obstacle is lack of funds or readily available qualified professionals, which is compounded by the lack of knowledge about who is qualified as a psychotherapist. Finally, there often is doubt about receiving sound help and whether the specific treatment will help.

What Goes Wrong with Our Emotions

We must now turn to the distinction made earlier between emotional arousal as a result of appraisals of what is happening—Stage 1 of the emotion process—and the control of emotion through coping—Stage 2.

What goes wrong in the *arousal* stage is that conflicts or mismatches occur between how we appraise events and what the environment is actually like. Let us illustrate. We believe we have been offended and feel angry, but no offense was intended. We believe we are endangered and feel anxious, but there is no danger. We believe we have failed to live up to an ego-ideal and feel ashamed, but the failure is only in our minds and not in reality as other people see it. We believe that our ego-identity has been enhanced by what we have done and feel proud, but have no realistic grounds for this feeling. And so on, for each of the emotions.

The opposite kind of mismatch occurs when we make an erroneous appraisal that we are not harmed or threatened. We fail to see an offense and do not feel angry but should because there was a provocation. We do not think we are threatened and don't feel anxious, but there really is danger. We have acted immorally but do not feel guilty because we have rationalized the action as proper or as someone else's fault. We do not see that our ego-identity has been enhanced by what we have done and don't feel proud, but others view what has happened as a testament to our sterling character. And so on, for the other emotions.

What goes wrong in the *control* of emotion is that there is a mismatch between the way we act out our feelings and what the situation calls for. We feel angry, but need to inhibit the anger in the interests of our long-term good. We feel angry and need to express the anger but do not, which misleads the other person about how we feel. We feel guilty, and need to apologize or atone in some way, but do not. And so on, for the other emotions.

Why should these mismatches occur? The reasons are many. One of the most common is that people have goal commitments and beliefs that lead them to misjudge the situations they face. Engaging in wishful thinking, they make unrealistic appraisals, either with respect to the arousal of an emotion, the choice of the emotion, or the social consequences of expressing it.

And they do this consistently in a wide variety of social situations, with each individual having a distinctive personal signature, so to speak, in the meanings that are constructed and the emotional patterns displayed. For example, some people acquire an exaggerated need to be approved, loved, and appreciated by others. They see themselves as being unloved or unappreciated. Others view the social world as malevolent and themselves as inadequate to deal with it.

These particular patterns may have begun in childhood, but they are manifest in adulthood in reactions that do not fit the circumstances. Overprotective and unduly solicitous parents may have pushed such persons in this direction by portraying them as dependent on parental protection for their safety. Underprotective parents may force their children to deal with the world before they have developed the necessary skills, leaving them to sink or swim, which often increases their fearfulness and dependency. In consequence, they overreact to even the slightest sign of disapproval. They are vulnerable to anxiety, guilt, or shame, especially if they see themselves as inadequate and a failure, and blame themselves for whatever happens.

In such persons, the four main components of our mental life—reason, motivation, emotion, and action—are in conflict. For example, what they do or feel is not what they want or believe is appropriate. Instead of operating with integrity, their minds are divided. They are at war with themselves, fragmented like Humpty-Dumpty, going this way and that, without the parts working together in a consistent direction. The components of mind must be integrated to allow them to function effectively, given who, what, and where they are.

Since what is in the mind has much to do with how people act, the most serious lack of integrity is when mind and action are divorced. A divided mind cannot get the person to act in a consistent and realistic way, especially over the long haul when one needs to plan for the future and to actualize goals and beliefs. Such individuals want to act prudently, but because of their inability to cope effectively, they act impulsively and out of short-term interests, which gives them only momentary pleasures. These people are unable to carry out their life desires, and they are constantly in trouble emotionally, which makes their lives miserable.

Can We Change Our Emotional Makeup?

The premise of all efforts to fix troubled emotional patterns is that we have the power to alter the way we see things, act, and react. Although we realize it is difficult to change these patterns, those of us who deal with them professionally share the conviction that it is possible.

Some changes are easier to accomplish than others. When our troubled emotions result from lack of knowledge or skill, people can sometimes be taught techniques to help themselves. For one reason or another, the troubled person has never learned what to think and do in the face of life changes that create chronic or recurrent distress and dysfunction. Their problems are not the result of deep emotional troubles, but of a lack of knowledge or skill to cope effectively.

Consider, for example, someone who is struggling with traumatic life conditions, such as serious illness, death of a loved one, divorce or separation, or loss of a job. These conditions create new demands on the victimized person. Learning how to deal with these demands will help to ameliorate the anger, anxiety, guilt, shame, or periodic depression, which the inability to deal with the new demands has created. The necessary changes are well within the power of the person to make if that person wants to.

Coping with the loss of a loved one through death, divorce, or separation is a case in point. Consider the advice given in the form of what has been called survival manuals for women alone.[1] Some of these manuals provide useful information and advice on the important concrete issues that must be dealt with—often for the first time—such as handling money and credit, travel, maintaining the car, managing the children and work together. In addition, there is also advice about more complex and diffuse issues, such as loneliness and sexuality, and the cultivation of social skills needed to cope with them.

Men, too, when confronted with this kind of situation could profit from information and advice. They also may not have the knowledge and skill to deal with the new demands, such as cooking for themselves, handling their finances—which their wives may have done for them during the marriage. Initiating and maintaining social relationships have typically been a woman's function in the home and, without supportive social networks, many men are at a loss.

Since one feature of the stress that follows divorce or bereavement is an overpowering feeling of inadequacy about doing what must now be done, such manuals usually provide inspirational thoughts and reassurances designed to bolster readers' feelings of adequacy. To believe that one is capable of managing these demands can motivate sustained coping efforts, helping to overcome dysfunctional and distressing emotions following the traumatic loss.

But it is especially difficult to produce therapeutic changes after a traumatic loss in a person with long-standing emotional problems. Conflicts underlying their problems make it more difficult to learn new ways of relating to the world. Since troubled persons are often not aware of these conflicts, they fail to understand the reasons for many of their disturbed reactions, and deal with them ineptly. Their mistakes are the result of consistent but faulty ways of viewing themselves and others and inappropriate ways of coping, which are brought about by faulty appraisals of what is happening. Such persons commonly repeat these mistakes without recognizing what they are doing.

In persons with exaggerated needs to be approved or loved, whatever produces their feelings remains unconscious. They are unaware of the developmental origins of these exaggerated needs and the role they play in their emotional lives. They know only that they experience great distress in their social relationships, not why. Therefore, the emotions experienced are more difficult to control or change than they are in persons merely lacking required knowledge and skill. The hidden agendas keep getting in the way of learning how to cope.

Long-standing emotional patterns involving unconscious conflicts, hidden goals and assumptions, and sources of anxiety that originated early in life can complicate and obstruct the learning that will facilitate change. The problem then shifts from simple education and training to the more traditional therapeutic goals of personality change. Without outside help to guide the search for the truth, the person may not be able to overcome the deeply ingrained emotional patterns that have become resistant to change. Such persons must discover the personal meanings that shape their emotions and their inept ways of coping. They must learn to recognize what they have been doing wrong to have a good chance of changing their emotional lives. These are usually the major tasks of psychotherapy.

We are about to proceed with a therapeutic case history of a young woman who has a difficult time getting her mother to accept her as an autonomous and adequate adult. However, before going ahead with it, we want to show concretely how another person with whom one has a strong emotional involvement can play communication games and fail to hear emotional messages, which frustrate the best efforts to communicate reasonably. We saw the following interchange in a recent article in a scientific journal.[2] The journal authors begin by quoting from a popular book.[3]

> "Today is promising, tremendously promising. . . .
>
> I go to meet my mother. I'm flying. Flying! I want to give her some of this shiningness bursting in me, siphon into her my immense happiness at being alive. Just because she is my oldest intimate and at this moment I love everybody, even her.
>
> 'Oh, Ma! What a day I've had,' I say.
>
> 'Tell me,' she says. 'Do you have the rent this month?'
>
> 'Ma, listen . . .' I say.
>
> 'That review you wrote for the Times,' she says. 'It's for sure they'll pay you?'
>
> 'Ma, stop it. Let me tell you what I've been feeling,' I say.
>
> 'Why aren't you wearing something warmer?' she cries. 'It's nearly winter.'
>
> The space inside begins to shimmer. The walls collapse inward. I feel breathless. Swallow slowly, I say to myself, slowly. To my mother I say, 'You do know how to say the right thing at the right time. It's remarkable, this gift of yours. It quite takes my breath away.'
>
> But she doesn't get it. She doesn't know I'm being ironic. Nor does she know she's wiping me out. She doesn't know I take her anxiety personally, feel annihilated by her depression. How can she know this? She doesn't even know I'm there. Were I to tell her that it's death to me, her

not knowing I'm there, she would stare at me out of her eyes crowded with puzzled desolation, this young girl of seventy-seven, and she would cry angrily, 'You don't understand! You have never understood!' "

Each of us can readily understand and empathize with the daughter's frustration in this interchange. It beautifully illustrates how communications can go haywire between people in close relationships.

A Therapeutic Case History

Before talking about psychotherapy and describing the therapeutic process, it will be instructive to look at a concrete clinical example. Although no dialogue is given here between the woman who is a patient in treatment and her mother with whom she has a troubled relationship, you might imagine the interchanges that are so troubling to her in light of the brief vignette just quoted.

The example is that of a young woman of 25, in therapy because of chronic anxiety and guilt, who was pregnant and close to the time of delivery. She also suffers from a tendency to asthma, which commonly surfaces under conditions of stress. Her mother tells her on the telephone that she is going to visit her daughter to help her before and after the delivery. This news greatly alarms the daughter. Her mother is a very domineering woman who, the daughter is sure, will be a very disruptive emotional presence, both in her relationship with the new baby and with her husband. The patient knows that her mother will keep telling them what to do and will not allow them to learn for themselves.

The daughter tells her mother on the phone that she would rather she didn't come right away, that she and her husband want to manage by themselves in the beginning, but they would love a visit later on. The mother is offended and this reaction generates much guilt and anxiety in her daughter, leading to a mild attack of asthma that required a period of medication. The mother insists on coming, seeming to imply that without her presence the daughter will prove inadequate for the important tasks of motherhood. Despite her desire to avoid what she knows will be a very stressful visit, the daughter is unable to hold firm. Her protestations are mild and unpersuasive, and the visit appears inevitable.

In prior therapeutic sessions, the daughter has spoken frequently of problems with her mother, especially about feelings of guilt and anxiety when, in her efforts at independence, she has opposed her mother. She has sought many times to get her mother to accept her independence and to allow her to make her own mistakes. Inevitably, she capitulates to her mother's wishes and is smothered.[4]

In therapy, she has learned much about her particular family dynamics. There is her sister's struggle against her mother's domination and the anger it fosters, her father's gentility and passivity, and her own chaotic feelings about these complex emotional relationships.

Her sister is five years older, and grossly overweight. The mother has had a terrible relationship with the older daughter, nagging her constantly about her weight to no avail. Highly intelligent and competitive, the older girl is thought of in the family as an unstable person, argumentative and unattractive, difficult to live and work with, and unappealing to most men. Our patient sees her as deviant and oppositional as a result of this long history of struggle with the mother, a person who has become a pariah in the family.

In contrast, our young patient is good looking and popular, and as bright as her sister, though she has some doubts about this. She is open and socially graceful, but viewed by her parents as a delicate flower, vulnerable and needing nurturing and protection. The sisters are often compared by the parents, the younger one—our patient—viewed as having everything in her favor; the older one regarded as having poor life prospects, which were actually borne out in later years. The contrast is no secret. This pattern has led to competitive hostility on the part of the older sister toward the favored younger one. The resentment is shared by both, but is much more muted in the patient, who feels sorry for her sister and guilty about her own social success.

The father has never sided with the older daughter against the mother, nor has he offered her any real protection. So he was also a great source of disappointment and ambivalence. Within the family, the older daughter could never win. The father was too mild-mannered and accepting to provide much help against the domineering mother. Though beloved by both daughters, he was henpecked at home and seldom played an important role in family decisions.

When the very limited financial resources of the family were needed to send the girls to college, there was only enough money available for one. It was given to the older sister. The parents felt that she needed the education more, since she had poor prospects without it. This decision added to the younger sister's resentment. But it did not make the older sister feel any more appreciated, because she recognized the denigration that was implied.

Our patient struggled with considerable guilt about her resentment of her older sister, partly fueled by anger about the college decision. On the one hand, she knew she was favored by her parents. On the other hand, she would have benefitted by an advanced education. Feelings of resentment toward her older sister made the patient feel both guilty and anxious.

The overpowering mother was a source of great emotional ambivalence in our patient. Whenever she struggled against her mother's domination and overprotection, which was not very often, she felt guilty about undermining her mother. She was also anxious lest her opposition lead to disapproval and perhaps even rejection. She saw opposition to her as a danger to what seemed like powerful maternal protection against outside dangers and hostile forces. In a word, she was in great conflict about achieving independence, which she wanted, and going against her mother to live autonomously. This was the patient's central problem.

When the patient married, it was to a somewhat controlling man like her mother, a man she loved and respected. And so both her husband and mother struggled to control her, leading to recurrent wariness and irritability between husband and mother. Their conflict distressed her greatly. She needed badly to become her own person. Nor did she like being a pawn in the struggle between her mother and husband.

The early years of her marriage were punctuated by efforts to resolve the struggle. The fact that she had identified much more with her mother than her father produced strong wishes to exercise control in her marriage. Her father was lovable but not someone to emulate. Her mother felt disappointed in the man she had married and often treated him contemptuously.

But first our patient had to confront her mother and make independence and autonomy work without endangering the positive side of their relationship. This recognition and the distress it caused, more than anything else, had led her to enter therapy.

She was especially troubled whenever she felt hostility to her mother, and she sensed that she had difficulty overcoming her dependency. But she was only dimly aware of her own fears of being disapproved by her mother, and of the basis for her guilt. She was cheerful and competent on the outside, but struggled with a sense of inadequacy on the inside. The therapy had begun to teach her about her conflicts and how they affected her life decisions. She wanted to change her emotional life.

Now, with the imminent birth of her own baby, she is facing a situation that epitomized the task of freeing herself from maternal control. She seemed unable to tell her mother in a convincing way that she did not wish her to visit and take over, and she feared the conflict between her mother and her husband.

During therapy she had begun to see more clearly what had happened to her in her family conflict. She had gained insight and realized that to become independent from both her mother and her husband, and autonomous as an individual, she had to prevent her mother's visit. Since she was not yet ready to proceed gung-ho along the route to autonomy, it would not be wise to accept this visit. She still had too much psychological work to do to be able to manage the stress of face-to-face confrontation, which she believed she would lose.

In spite of her emerging insight about what was needed, she still suffered great guilt and anxiety in confronting her mother about the prospective visit. How could she let her mother down when the relationship between her mother and her older sister was so crushing to her mother? To prevent the visit seemed like a rejection. And to do so was to risk retaliation from this powerful woman. In effect, she had to work through what she had learned about herself and about what she wanted, and to force herself to deal with it successfully, in spite of the emotional distress this would inspire.

In her telephone conversations with her mother, she had tried to state her wishes, with the overwhelmingly stubborn and insensitive response that should have been expected. She had rehearsed what she would say over and over. The mother had insisted she was coming, so the first conversation ended in failure, distress, and confusion.

She examined what had happened in her next therapy session, with the therapist reflecting her ambivalent feelings. Playing back the spoken record to the patient, so to speak, was designed to help her hear what she was saying. It was also necessary to relate it to her past struggles so she would understand what was going on.

Knowing that she must be more firm, the patient tried again in her next phone call to get her mother to desist. This time she protested more forcefully, but the mother now acted out the role of victim. She expressed distress that her daughter did not want to allow her to enjoy her first grandchild. The altercation produced terrible emotional distress and another attack of asthma. The phone call ended without resolution, and she was sleepless for days, ruminating almost constantly about what had happened, and rehearsing again what she should have said.

In a subsequent phone call, which she initiated shortly thereafter, the daughter reiterated with great anxiety her wish not to be visited and her need to cope with the baby and post-pregnancy on her own, but leaving open the possibility of a later visit. Fortunately, the mother grew adamant and angry, forcing the daughter into the choice of either capitulating totally or sticking to her guns. She could not back down now. With much more force than usual, she left no door open for the mother to come at this time, expressing her own frustration and anger openly. Never before confronted with such firmness, the mother backed down.

As you might imagine, the daughter's state of mind after this confrontation was a mixture of gratification over having won the day, as well as guilt and anxiety. Her husband tried to be supportive and wisely avoided attacking his mother-in-law. When the baby came, attention was temporarily diverted from the confrontation with her mother, and the demands and joys of the new life took over.

Six months after the arrival of the baby, our patient invited her mother to visit. When she came it was a difficult experience, but it passed without a crisis. The daughter began to consolidate her newfound power over herself, and gradually worked out a more autonomous pattern with her husband, punctuated with occasional discomfort when she visited her parents or when her parents visited her.

For years thereafter, the struggle with guilt and anxiety over the conflict between dependence and independence recurred, both with the mother, the sister, and husband. But the first potent step had been taken on the road to applying what she had learned in therapy to her life and relationships. As a finale, she began to experience a better and more realistic appreciation of her mother and father. She learned to manage the recurrences of guilt and anxiety without excessive distress and dysfunction. She continued to have periodic asthmatic attacks, though these seemed less severe than they had been.

One must not imagine that problems such as these completely disappear. Emotional change is often desirable, but it is not easy and is apt to take a toll. Such change is also slow and grudging, but when it is successful, the original distress gradually comes under control. As in successful grieving, emotional residuals, such as the recurrent anxiety and guilt when she acted against her mother's and husband's wishes, and those of others, remained to be dealt with. But what had been learned—in this case, dysfunctional emotional patterns—can also be unlearned, which is the rationale for psychotherapy in the first place.

We are now ready to examine some of the main ways in which psychotherapy is practiced and the role of emotion in different therapies. We first consider what might be referred to as insight-centered therapy, which has its origins in Freudian psychoanalysis, followed in recent years by the emergence of shorter, cognitive therapies. Then we examine other types of therapy and how they work.

Insight-Centered Therapies

The dominant intent of most psychotherapies has always been to help patients achieve insight about the causes of their troubles on the premise that understanding what has gone wrong is necessary to making successful changes in a patient's emotional life. Although psychotherapy did not begin with psychoanalysis, it was greatly influenced by the ideas of Freud and other psychoanalytic thinkers at the turn of the century, who followed and modified his pioneering efforts.

Psychoanalysis

Psychotherapy became a major industry in Europe and the United States in the 1920s, 1930s, and 1940s under the impact of Freudian theory and its strategy of treatment. Although this form of treatment has lost favor, modern psychotherapeutic practice owes much to psychoanalysis, and psychotherapy in general continues to blossom. Freud's earliest psychological interests began with *hypnosis*, which he studied with Charcot in Paris. Hypnosis helped patients to ventilate unconscious sources of distress, and uncovering them allowed the therapist to learn what had hitherto been hidden from view.

In the early days, Freud's theoretical emphasis was on bringing blocked and hidden urges to the surface. This could certainly be done with hypnosis. Using the now discarded metaphor of dammed-up energy in a boiler ready to burst, the new therapy centered on releasing the blocked urges that caused the pent-up energy. Soon, however, Freud came to realize that more than release, or *catharsis*, as it was called, was required. The problem with hypnosis was that patients remained largely passive when they needed to struggle actively to understand the nature and origins of their troubles, rather than merely following the suggestions of a hypnotherapist. This understanding is called *insight*. Psychoanalysis literally means making an analysis of the psyche.

Freud's key assumption was that psychologically troubled people failed to recognize the conflicts that lay behind their distress because the conflicts had been distorted by ego-defenses that kept them out of awareness. So patients acted and emoted on the basis of conflicting motives they did not understand.

The task of therapy should be to make these conflicts, and the urges and fears that powered them, conscious so that they could be dealt with in more effective ways. If the patient could understand what was going on, it should be possible to change the maladaptive reactions—in other words, to cope more effectively with the emotional conditions of life. Ideally, patients would learn why they keep making the same mistakes, and how to act and react differently.

To facilitate insight, the treatment should uncover memories of the past, especially of early childhood events that were traumatic, proscribed urges, and family struggles, which Freud regarded as the sources of emotional problems. A strategy was needed to promote this self-understanding, and Freud developed the technique of *free association* in which patients were asked to say anything that came into their minds without self-censorship. Free association became a primary feature of psychoanalytic treatment. The discovery of the truth was often resisted by the patient because remembering and viewing what had happened was filled with threats to the ego-identity that the patient had constructed.

An emotional relationship develops between the patient and the therapist, termed *transference*. Transference refers to redirecting childhood attitudes about parents toward the therapist who is now serving as a kind of parental figure on whom the outcome of treatment depends. In effect, the therapist came to be viewed in a way that was literally similar to how the patient viewed the most salient parent. And with this increasing dependency on the therapist, the patient could be motivated to overcome the natural resistence to exposing the hidden conflicts that were threatening.

The analysis of this relationship with the therapist, and of childhood emotional relationships, provided further insight about what had gone wrong. It revealed love, hate, and ambivalence. To encourage this exploration, the therapist avoided criticizing patients, provided acceptance and reassurance, and allowed them freely to find their way through the maze of conflicting thoughts and feelings characteristic of their past and, whenever possible, to draw new conclusions about what it all meant.

Even insight, however, is not quite enough. Merely to know intellectually what is going on does not produce therapeutic change. There has to be *emotional insight*, which means that it is necessary for the patient to relive troubled emotional experiences.

The hard-won insight ultimately has to be tried out by acting and reacting in new ways to life situations that are troubling. The success of psychoanalysis depends on adequately *working through* the problems of living, trying out new ways of thinking and acting by applying the new understanding about what has gone wrong. This is apt to be an arduous, often frustrating, and distressing process. Real emotional change does not come easy.

In classic psychoanalytic treatment the patient sees the therapist three to five times a week, for an hour a session, over a number of years. A lengthy and expensive process, it offers no certainty that it will lead to correction of the emotional problems that had brought the patient for help in the first place.

Because exploring the developmental sources of the present emotional dysfunction is so time consuming and expensive, many therapists began to question the need for so much attention to the distant psychological past. They began to shorten the process with less emphasis given to childhood and more emphasis on the way the past influences the present. A number of modifications to the Freudian approach to treatment emerged, some of which came to be referred to as neo-Freudian psychoanalytic therapy.[5]

Psychoanalysts still practice either traditional, Freudian methods, or they use these modifications. Today psychoanalysis, which had once dominated the field of therapy, has more or less lost favor and briefer therapies are now more the rule. Nevertheless, some of its major themes still dominate the outlook of most therapies—most notably the belief that emotional distress and dysfunction are the result of wishes, needs, and ways of thinking about which troubled people are unaware because ego-defenses have distorted how they understand themselves. The search for insight and its use in working through dysfunctional ways of relating to the world still remain centerpieces of the therapeutic process.

Cognitive Therapy

Ironically, the approach to treatment known as cognitive therapy first arose as a protest, called *behaviorism*, against the mentalistic concepts of psychoanalysis, with its emphasis on an unconscious but influential mental life. The protest was part of a phase in American academic psychology from roughly 1920 to the 1970s. During this period, speculation about what was going on in the mind was distrusted because it was believed to be refractory to scientific study.

This distrust of inferences about mental activity led to an emphasis on what could be directly observed—namely, a person's behavior—rather than what a person is thinking and feeling, hence the term behaviorism. What must be done from a behaviorist standpoint is to get people to behave differently by helping them unlearn old patterns and acquire new ones.

Scientific fads and fashions change. So in the 1970s and beyond, cognitive psychology, which emphasized that what people think is the basis of the way they act and feel, began to displace behaviorism. Its outlook shaped the approach to the emotions that you have seen in this book. Cognitive therapy is now one of the main approaches to clinical work throughout the world.

Cognitive therapists believe that therapy works because it changes a person's ways of thinking about problems of living. People acquire expectations about what will happen from having experienced the positive or negative consequences that follow events. This is what learning is said to be all about—that is, the acquisition of expectations. To change emotions, a person has to change expectations. This way of thinking is still anathema to behavior therapists, who prefer to avoid subjective language and concepts about the mind.

Although they resisted the idea for a time, cognitive therapists inherited the psychoanalytic principle that insight and working through are required for a patient to change emotionally. However, like earlier modifications of Freudian psychoanalysis, cognitive therapy is focused much more on the present than the past. Cognitive therapists do not see the necessity of discovering and reviewing what happened in childhood.

Cognitive therapists also reject much of the baggage of psychoanalytic theory, such as the emphasis on biological urges (instincts) and the idea that clinical symptoms arise from dammed-up psychic energy. The basic premise of cognitive therapy is simply that what we think—which includes what we want and expect—is the source of our emotional troubles.

Therefore, the mission of cognitive therapy is to change dysfunctional ways of thinking so that the person can relate more effectively and with less emotional distress to the world. A variety of treatment strategies are employed to help patients learn how their emotional lives have been distorted by faulty appraisal and coping processes.

Most cognitive therapy encounters consist of a series of conversations between a patient and a therapist. The conversations are controlled, in part, by the clinician's therapeutic strategy, by the patient's story, and by the need to know what has gone wrong. This overlaps substantially with what psychoanalysts do in their "talking cure," and is the way most therapists work.

Patients arrive in the therapist's office and are asked what brought them there. They present their complaints and what they see as their problems of living, and describe their symptoms and their emotional distress. The therapist probes for examples of important emotional encounters. If anxiety is the problem, the therapist asks about the events that made the patient feel anxious, and so on, for the other emotions.

This helps to provide a picture of the patient's emotional pattern—for example, an exaggerated tendency to deny threats or seek emotional distance from them—and the thoughts, beliefs, and personal goals that could help to explain the pattern. Chronic or recurrent emotional distress is always at the heart of psychotherapy because it is one of the best indicators of social relationships that have gone sour, and the personal meanings that lie behind them.

The therapist also needs to know about what the patient wants to accomplish in therapy, and whether the problem reflects a short-term crisis—precipitated, say, by a loss—or a long-term pattern of dysfunction. In due time, an agreement is established between the therapist and patient about the goals to be sought in the therapeutic sessions.

If what the patient wants is not realistic, the therapist indicates what is reasonable to try to accomplish. Often the patient's view of the problem needs to be redefined, and this may take much time. A great deal depends on the problem that has brought the patient to the therapist in the first place and on the particular strategies employed by the therapist. However, in all types of treatment, there is a need to forge an appropriate set of expectations, to make an evaluation of what has gone wrong, and to examine how the problem manifests itself in the patient's life.

Let us examine a few of the key themes of cognitive therapy as it is conceived by practicing professionals today. There are many versions of this type of therapy, so we must limit ourselves to just a few of the most prominent ones.

One of the earliest cognitive therapies was developed in the 1960s by Albert Ellis. It is called *Rational-emotive Therapy*,[6] and is still going strong. Ellis assumes—as we do—that the construal of a situation is more important in determining a person's reactions than the objective situation. Beliefs about oneself and the world shape the emotions, as we have maintained in this book. Ellis zeros in on how emotional problems arise from incorrect thinking.

Ellis tries to get his patients to abandon the *irrational beliefs* that are said to get the patient into trouble emotionally. The treatment is designed to help patients think more clearly and flexibly, so that they will feel appropriately and act in ways that are less self-defeating.

Irrational beliefs fall into three major categories: (1) I must do well and win approval, or else I am a rotten person; (2) others must treat me considerately and kindly in precisely the way I want or they should be severely damned and punished; and (3) conditions under which I live must enable me to get what I want comfortably, quickly, and easily, and to get nothing I don't want.

The thinking involved in emotional disturbances, says Ellis, is also inherently self-defeating. There are four common types of such thinking: (1) awfulizing; (2) I can't-stand-it-itis; (3) self-worthlessness; and (4) other unrealistic overgeneralizations from a bad experience.

Ellis acknowledges that some *negative feelings*, such as sorrow and annoyance, are appropriate when one's goals are blocked. Others, such as depression and anxiety, are inappropriate because the premises on which they are based make negative life conditions even worse. Some *positive feelings*, such as love and happiness, are appropriate when one's goals are realized. Others, such as grandiosity, are inappropriate because they are based on faulty premises. Although they make people feel good in the short run, sooner or later they lead to conflict with others and to ill-considered risk-taking behavior. All goals are appropriate even when they are not easily fulfilled, but absolutistic commands (you *must* do this or that) are inappropriate and self-sabotaging.

The therapeutic task is to determine which irrational beliefs are at the root of a patient's troubles, and to convince the patient to abandon them. If patients can see how beliefs create irrational expectations, they can more easily change their faulty thinking and thus the troubling emotions that stem from these beliefs. Patients are taught to question what seems to make them overly upset and ask themselves: "Why *must* I do something well? Where is it written that I am a bad person? Where is the evidence that I can't stand this or that?" And so on.

Overlapping considerably with Ellis is the approach of Aaron Beck,[7] whose therapeutic work on depression and anxiety is also well known. Beck believes that depressed patients share five negative and distorted ways of thinking about themselves, the world, and their future. These distortions encourage the emotions of anxiety and depression, which are very troubling emotions if they are chronic.

The distorted ways of thinking include (1) *selective abstraction*, in which a person ignores contradictory and better evidence, thus forming conclusions on the basis of an isolated negative detail; (2) *arbitrary inference*, in which a negative appraisal is made in the absence of evidence; (3) *overgeneralization*, in which a negative conclusion is drawn from a single event and inappropriately applied to dissimilar situations; (4) *magnification* (sometimes referred to by the colorful term catastrofication), in which the significance of a negative event is overestimated or magnified; and (5) *all-or-none thinking*, in which a person thinks in absolutes—anything is either good or bad, mostly the latter. Notice how similar these ideas are to Ellis's about irrational beliefs and incorrect thinking.

As with Ellis, the therapeutic task set by Beck is to help the patient give up these damaging beliefs, which are considered responsible for the recurrent anxiety or depression. As in most other modern cognitive therapies, emotional insight on the part of the patient is the key to change. In depression, for example, one sees one's situation as hopeless. So to overcome the tendency to be depressed, patients must discover the core errors of thinking that contribute to their recurrent patterns of faulty thinking and compel them to repeat the same dysfunctional emotional patterns.

Some qualification is in order here. For people who are depressed for good reasons—for example, someone whose physical condition has rapidly or severely declined with sudden illness—help with their depression requires that they learn to make the best of it, and that significant, positive possibilities of commitment and enjoyment in what remains of the precious gift of life are still available to them. Again one has to say, easier said than done.

However, in this kind of pattern, therapy cannot address faulty thinking—they have good reason to feel bad—as much as to help them see that life is short, that feeling like a victim does not go very far in producing satisfaction, that depression is counterproductive, and that other alternative ways of managing might improve their lives despite their poor health. And so we are still talking about changing ways of thinking.

Two friends of ours fit this pattern, one who—seemingly a healthy and vigorous man—has had recent bypass surgery for clogged coronary arteries and suffered a distressing series of side effects from the surgery that required several additional operations that have over a year's time left him in pain, unable to eat to sustain his weight and strength, depleted his energy, and rendered him barely able to work, which had always been a major feature of his life. The other is a young woman in her thirties who, probably as a result of poor medical treatment, has become totally blind and who is angry and depressed about her condition.

If treatment could help both these victims of a bad fate take advantage of the possibilities available to them, then unhappy future years might be turned around. This cannot happen if they remain preoccupied with their victimization and fail to develop the motivation to cope by seeking available alternatives. Then all that is left is for their families and friends to sympathize, which is worth something and certainly justified, but is an inadequate substitute for doing the best these unlucky persons can to take their life in hand to the extent possible.

Although they are also concerned with how emotion is aroused by ‘lty reasoning, other cognitive therapists center their attention mainly ‑ development of coping skills. One such approach is the stress‑ ‑ training program of Donald Meichenbaum.[8] Patients are made aware of their negative self-image and self-statements. They are helped to learn what happens in problem situations, urged to cultivate positive self-statements, and learn ways of dealing more effectively with stressful situations.

Meichenbaum—along with others—uses the term *cognitive restructuring* to identify the aim of the treatment. The patient comes to construe things differently and in a more functional way.[9] Cognitive restructuring has a meaning similar to our use of the term reappraisal.

Inoculation training, as defined by Meichenbaum who originated it and Ray Novaco[10] who has used it with police, refers to the acquisition of new knowledge and coping skills for handling anticipated stressful confrontations. Often police contact with a criminal escalates into a violent confrontation. Police recognize that this escalation to violence is unprofessional and undesirable, especially if they helped provoke it, and they want to avoid allowing this to happen again. The training is said to inoculate them, as it were, against future failure. Novaco has also trained probation counselors to deal with anger and aggression in their clients.

The program has three phases, which can be illustrated by its use with the police officers. First, information is provided to groups of officers about the way stress works and how distressing emotions are aroused. In this educational phase, members of the group also talk among themselves about difficult situations they have experienced, and about their failures and successes in handling them. The group is also given a number of self-statements to help them control counterproductive thoughts and actions. For example, they remind themselves to slow down and not to get their dander up when a criminal aggravates them. Second, the handling of possible confrontations is rehearsed. Third, what has been learned is tried out in real-life situations, and evaluated in later group sessions.

What is striking in this kind of training program is that, in the educational phase, police learn about and discuss undesirable emotional reactions they have had to stressful confrontations. It may come as a surprise to them, for example, how much anger the criminal can arouse in them, and how easily their tendency to get angry is manipulated by criminals. Their ego-identity may be easily threatened by an effort to get their goat. Because they can lose their cool easily, the confrontation often escalates into violence, which requires force to control.

The process of gaining insight about their emotional problems and their contribution to professional failures helps them understand their mistakes. Without this insight, it would be difficult for them to prevent similar mistakes in the future.

This method illustrates what we said earlier about psychological processes arising from within the person that promote dysfunctional emotions and get in the way of learning necessary coping skills. The problem is not merely to obtain information, but to acquire insight about one's own emotions, which are operating in the encounter. When disruptive conflicts and faulty appraisals are the sources of the dysfunctional emotions, especially when one is unaware of their basis, simple skills training to handle situations differently, such as getting information from directories or speaking up in a group, is easily undermined.

A fine example of how deeply ingrained personality traits can defeat a person who tries to learn certain skills is the effort to train women to overcome a lack of assertiveness in social situations. Although these assertiveness training programs are thought of primarily for women, not all men are assertive and many could also gain from such a program. With the modern feminist interest in becoming more assertive in school and work, many women have participated in such programs. The assumption is that lack of assertiveness in women is acquired by growing up with traditional role models, most of which regard women as properly supportive rather than competitive and dominant in social relationships. The training program is designed to teach participants how to be assertive without being hostile.

There is a fascinating study that demonstrates that women participating in such programs must learn much more than merely saying the right words. After completing the training, the success of women trainees was rated while they demonstrated what they had learned. While they followed directions appropriately in these demonstrations, observers nevertheless rated many of them as nonassertive.[11] Their well-ingrained expressive pattern of deference overshadowed their words and deeds, and observers saw through the surface behavior to these ingrained patterns. These women needed to make deeper changes in attitude to play assertive roles convincingly. Skills training is not always enough in the absence of more fundamental change. This is the basic assumption of all insight therapies.

Non-Insight Therapies

The main alternatives to insight therapy are based on the belief that undesirable habits—including dysfunctional emotions—are conditioned and deconditioned. The reader should consider conditioning to be a technical word for learning. Let us look at learning-centered therapies to illustrate this approach.

Learning-Centered Therapies

Two kinds of conditioning are practiced in learning-centered therapies, technically referred to as classical and instrumental conditioning. In *classical conditioning*, emotions, such as anger and anxiety, are aroused, and they are paired with some neutral stimulus, which will then elicit these emotions when the stimulus is again presented.

Let us say that in our past we became fearful in the presence of a stranger with a moustache, to be a bit fanciful about the conditioning of fear. Later, when we see men with moustaches, we tend to become fearful. For such learning to occur, fear and moustaches need to be paired a number of times; however, if the emotions involved are intense enough, as in a traumatic episode, one incident in which the pairing occurs may be enough to establish the mental association between the neutral stimulus (a moustache) and the emotional response (fear) with which it was paired. The person may or may not be aware of the pairing, though awareness facilitates learning because one can verbalize the expectation that has been learned.

This kind of learning was first discovered accidentally many years ago by a Russian physiologist, Ivan Pavlov (1849–1936). Pavlov put dogs in a harness to study salivation and digestion, and he noticed that saliva flow was affected not only by the food that was placed in the dog's mouth, but also by just the sight of the food. The salivary response to food is innate, but it had become conditioned to the sight of the food.

In his experiments, Pavlov also found that a stimulus—for example, a bell tone—would lead the dog to salivate if an association had been established between the salivation and a stimulus that originally could not elicit it. In Pavlov's experiments, the bell tone could not originally bring forth salivation. But, of course, food did. So if the bell tone could get associated with salivation, the dog would now salivate to the once neutral bell tone. By inadvertently discovering a learning principle of great significance, Pavlov became one of the most influential psychologists of all times.

Others demonstrated later that emotions, such as fear, can be learned in this way too. We use the term fear rather than fright or anxiety here because this is the way the emotion has usually been labeled by conditioning theorists, despite our preference for the terms anxiety and fright (see Chapter 3).

An experiment that is relevant to the conditioning of fear, which was very well known in the 1920s, was described in many psychology textbooks for several generations. In the experiment, a male infant named Albert was conditioned to be afraid of white rats and other furry animals because a white rat had been present in a fear-inducing situation.[12]

A loud noise was used as the fear-inducing stimulus, which was paired with the sight of the white rat. Later, when the rat was present without the frightening noise, the child would react with fear. It had learned to associate the fear with the rat. The essence of this kind of conditioning is that a stimulus, which—like the bell tone in Pavlov's research—is normally not itself capable of producing fear (the white rat),[13] is made to provoke the fear when it has been repeatedly paired with another stimulus (the loud noise), which naturally arouses it.

This experiment quickly led to the important therapeutic idea that unwanted emotions could be unlearned or deconditioned in the same way as when they had been learned. As an example, a psychiatrist named Joseph Wolpe[14] created a procedure in which the fear-inducing stimuli for a given patient are presented in graded degrees from neutral or mild fear-inducing to progressively stronger fear-inducing ones. Only when the patient does not react with fear to a mild stimulus does the therapist proceed to the next stronger one. The presence of some familiar, reassuring object or activity, such as eating a tasty food, facilitates the deconditioning of fear to these fear-inducing stimuli.

The second type of conditioning is technically called *instrumental conditioning*. This is a different arrangement of stimulus conditions that also facilitates learning. Instrumental conditioning is the way we usually train animals to do what we want. For example, when we teach a dog to "stay" or "come" on command, the dog must, for its own reasons, first perform the action we desire, at which point we give a signal or command. The dog eventually learns to associate performing the action with the command, which then becomes the instrument for generating the desired action. It learns to do this because we have rewarded it after the action by a bit of food or a warm display of affection, which is a reward it wants.

An unwanted emotion can be conditioned in the same way to an action that normally would not provoke it if the action is followed by an aversive or unpleasant event, such as a punishment. When the connection between the action and the emotion has been well established, we perform the action and then experience the emotion. Thus, when we express anger, we have learned that the other person—say, a parent or boss—is apt to retaliate with anger, which could be dangerous. So our expression of anger leads us also to feel anxious, lest the retaliation occur. This connection between anger and anxiety can be thought of as an example of the instrumental conditioning that can take place between an action and a threat.

An important theoretical change in the way we understand the process of conditioning took place in the 1970s, which led to the rise of the cognitive therapies. We now understand that what is learned is an *expectation* of a harmful or beneficial consequence in the presence of an action or a conditioned signal.

Pavlov's dogs learned that a previously neutral stimulus, such as a bell tone, will lead to a reward, such as food, or a punishment. The cognitive interpretation is that they learned an expectation. A dog that comes on command has learned the expectation that it will be rewarded by food or approval from its master. People who are made anxious when they express anger expect punitive retaliation for it.

Cognitive therapists conceive of learning as the acquisition of an expectation of some harm or benefit. This is, in effect, what is meant by an appraisal of the significance of an event for one's well-being; the appraisal is not only an evaluation, but it also draws on or creates an expectation of what is to happen. To eliminate the emotional response if it is unwanted, the person must be taught to reappraise the conditions that have in the past led to the unwanted emotion—in other words, the evaluation and the expectation of what will happen have been changed.

Relaxation, Meditation, Hypnosis, and Biofeedback

A number of simple procedures, though not based on insight or changed expectations, can help with anxiety and other distressing emotions. The oldest and simplest procedure is the systematic practice of *relaxation*, which is an effort to make the body, which has been aroused by an emotion, calm down. In progressive relaxation, for example, one tenses and then relaxes each of the body's major muscle groups in sequence in order to relax.

A related technique is *meditation*, which imitates practices developed by the Buddhists. As advocated by the distinguished cardiologist Herbert Benson of the Harvard Medical School, it is a simple practice that is followed for 10 to 20 minutes once or twice a day. In Benson's version, the practice of meditation does not contain any religious connotations.[15]

The patient chooses a word or brief phrase, such as "one," which is said over and over again while sitting quietly in a comfortable position, eyes closed, muscles relaxed, and breathing slowly in a regular rhythm. If other thoughts come to mind, the patient should not be concerned but keep returning to the meaningless word or phrase in an effort to shut out disturbing thoughts. At the end of the meditation period, the patient sits quietly for a few minutes before making the transition back to ordinary activity. One gets better at this exercise with practice.

It is plausible that relaxation and meditation practices, which have been known for a very long time, can help some people to reduce debilitating stress. However, as we noted in Chapter 12, there is much to be learned about them before we can tell who might benefit, under what conditions, and how much.

One of the strengths of this kind of procedure is that it is unlikely to do much harm. Another strength is that it can be done without professional intervention, at home, though often practitioners serve as guides to its use. One of its weaknesses is that it does not go to the heart of what is troubling the person, nor provide any insight about the causes of personal anxiety.

Hypnosis is still used today in psychotherapy. Its traditional use in insight therapy was to expose hidden conflicts, which can then be more systematically explored in a fully conscious state. As such, hypnosis is an adjunct of insight therapy.

It is also used because it is a state of high suggestibility, and suggestions made under hypnosis, say, to quit smoking or to be mentally at ease, can help some people overcome unwanted dependencies and lower tension states and their physiological concomitants. Hypnosis is also sometimes used to decrease the frequency of headaches and the intensity of their pain, to control the severity of asthmatic attacks, which are exacerbated by anxiety about not being able to breathe, and in the control of anxiety itself.

As in the case of relaxation and meditation, this use of hypnosis does not go to the heart of the patient's trouble or provide insight by uncovering the causes of the trouble, and so it must be considered a superficial treatment and, perhaps, useful as an adjunct to insight-centered treatments.

Finally, a procedure known as *biofeedback* has many present-day professional adherents. It is used to reduce the frequency or intensity of tension headaches and other physiological symptoms of emotional distress. The patient is hooked up to electronic instruments that measure heart rate, skin resistance, or muscular activity whose tension one wishes to reduce. The frontalis muscle that runs across the brow and is implicated in tension headaches is a common biofeedback target.

The task of biofeedback is to get the patient to bring under voluntary control these normally automatic responses of the body. The method depends on providing visual or auditory recordings of changes in physiological activity. These changes are transformed into readings on a visual or auditory monitor, which the patient watches. Information about the physiological reaction is, in effect, fed back to patients so that they can see when they are controlling it. Certain ways of thinking are conducive to relaxing and others are not, so if patients hit upon doing something that makes a difference, they can learn to have some limited control over bodily reactions, which are normally not under voluntary control.

No one really knows what patients actually do or think to change their physiological activity, and there is controversy about whether significant control of these physiological states is consistently possible. One theory is that the control is indirect—that is, it is produced by the thoughts and actions that patients engage in while monitoring changes in their physiological states.[16] Biofeedback may be another illustration of the importance of the way a patient construes what is happening, which is having an impact on the emotions and their physiological correlates. Like the other methods in this section, the treatment is superficial in that it doesn't direct the patient to the psychological causes of bodily tension, but rather to the control of its physiological symptoms.

Emotions in Psychotherapy

Therapeutic approaches differ in the way emotions are regarded. All therapists consider emotions important, both as sources of distress and dysfunction, and as object lessons about what has gone wrong in patients' lives. They embrace emotions as a key therapeutic tool. Two therapeutic pioneers in examining the role of emotion in psychotherapy, Leslie S. Greenberg and Jeremy D. Safran,[17] have expressed the principle as follows:

> Unless we grapple with the role of emotion in therapy, our understanding of the human change process will remain hollow, missing some of the vital elements of what makes psychotherapy a potentially powerful change process.

Following Freud, *psychoanalysts* first conceived of emotions as symptoms of the blockage of innate urges (or unsatisfied goals). The therapeutic cure was to purge the dammed-up tension, a process often referred to as catharsis. Catharsis occurs when, in talking about what was bothering them, patients ventilate frustrations and distress, expressing feelings that had been repressed. This was said to purge them of the poisons disturbing their lives, much like a laxative rids us of the unneeded products of our digestion.

Freud later substituted the idea that in people with serious emotional disturbances, which he referred to as neurosis, the problem is that a threatening urge has been repressed. The defense, not the blocked urge, is the problem because it deceives the person about what is really taking place. With this shift came a new way to view psychotherapy that did not depend on catharsis. The newer emphasis on uncovering the defense and gaining insight led to the realization that catharsis or release of dammed-up energy is not what is important in therapy.

Unfortunately, associating emotions with dammed-up energy gave them mainly a pathological connotation in psychoanalytic thought. As we have seen, this is wrong because emotions are adaptive outcomes of both gratified and blocked goals. When they are the result of inappropriate appraisals and coping processes they become dysfunctional—therefore, pathological—and must be set right. The focus should be on how a person appraises what is happening and how this appraisal is counterproductive, leading to ineffective ways of coping.

To treat an emotional problem that is the result of ego-defenses, the patient's defenses need to be exposed, which could lead to insight about the blocked urges and allow the faulty appraisals and coping processes to be consciously changed. But the insight has to be tested by action-centered emotional confrontations—what we earlier referred to as working through. Only by living out distressing emotional experiences and trying new ways of coping could fundamental changes take place within the person.

Behavior therapists make little mention of the way a person evaluates what is going on in the process of deconditioning unwanted emotions. To work, therapy must create a confrontation between the patient and the sources of emotional distress. Before treatment, these sources were avoided.

The therapeutic task is to unlearn what has been learned so one can perform an action or be in the presence of a fear-inducing object without fear. The patient must discover in this confrontation between events and distressing emotions that what is painful will not follow. The patient who could not contradict her mother had to learn, for example, that the anticipated disaster would not befall her if she followed her own dictates and, in doing so, angered her mother. Fearful people must learn that their fearful expectations are wrong. To learn this, they must stop avoiding an action, such as driving across a bridge to a nearby city—which always generated fear—and perform the act whose consequences they fear. This makes it possible to discover that they will not be harmed, say, by driving across the bridge. Therapy provides the opportunity to make this discovery and to draw on it in making changes in the way we live. Notice that the discovery could just as well be called insight. The following quotation from one pair of behavior therapists expresses this idea.[18]

> Anxiety disorders are continuous attempts to avoid confrontation with fear-evoking cures. . . . Indeed, if neurotics are avoiders who fail to recognize and/or retrieve discomfort-evoking information about themselves or their environment, psychotherapy might be construed as providing a setting in which *confrontation* with such information is promoted so that changes in affect [emotion] can occur. [Italics added]

Cognitive therapists consider distressing and dysfunctional emotions the result of the personal meaning constructed about negative events. Their therapeutic commitment is to change these personal meanings and the ways of thinking that foster them. However, the therapy is not merely an intellectual exploration of the problem but includes experiencing the emotions connected both with the old, pathological ways of thinking and the new, more realistic ways.

This theme of working through the problem is expressed in what cognitive therapists say about the union of emotions and reason, which is another way of speaking of emotional rather than intellectual insight. For example, in their discussion of stress inoculation, psychotherapists Donald Meichenbaum and Roy Cameron[19] write about the use of self-statements in therapy as follows (shades of Emil Coue's litany, "Every day in every way I am getting better and better").

> It is important to understand that [self-statements] are not offered as catch-phrases or as verbal palliatives to be repeated mindlessly. There is a difference between encouraging the use of a formula or psychological litany that tends to lead to rote repetition and emotionless patter versus problem-solving thinking that is the object of stress inoculation training. Formula-oriented thoughts that are excessively general tend to prove ineffective.

Cognitive therapist Albert Ellis[20] makes a related point about the unity of thought, emotion, and motivation:

> RET (Rational-emotive therapy) assumes that human thinking and emotion are not two disparate or different processes, but that they significantly overlap and are in some respects, for all practical purposes, essentially the same thing. Like the two other basic life processes, sensing and moving, they are integrally integrated and never can be seen wholly apart from each other. . . . Instead, then, of saying that "Smith thinks about this problem," we should more accurately say that "Smith senses-moves-feels-THINKS about this problem."

And, turning the direction of the relationship between reason and emotion around slightly, the progenitor of another cognitive therapy, Aaron Beck, points out that emotional catharsis without thinking and understanding is also not enough to produce change.[21]

> [Some] type of intellectual framework is important if the cathartic . . . or emotional experience is to have a therapeutic effect. It is apparent that people go through catharsis and abreactions . . . continuously through-

out their lives—without any benefit. What seems to be offered within a therapeutic milieu is the patient's ability to experience simultaneously the "hot cognitions" [highly emotional thoughts] and to step back, as it were, and to observe this experience objectively. . . . When therapy is effective the essential components are the production of "hot cognitions" . . . within a therapeutic structure and the opportunity to [check the reality of] these cognitions—whether the therapist is employing psychoanalysis, behavior therapy, [or] cognitive therapy.

There exists still another brand of insight therapy we have not yet mentioned. It is called experiential-existential therapy, which centers on the meanings of life, which may be lost or have never adequately been explored by the patient.[22] This kind of therapy looks a lot like psychoanalysis, except that it is focused mainly on the failure to have constructed or sustained the fundamental meanings on which a good life is based.

Experiential-existential therapists see emotion as a key to what has gone wrong and, as in the counterculture of the 1960s, they assume that people in trouble need to get in touch with their emotions. The task of the patient is to become more aware of the personal meanings that are signaled by these emotions and become more responsive to them. The experience and expression of emotion are said to be necessary for change to occur in this therapeutic approach.

So there is remarkable agreement among diverse schools of psychotherapy. All agree that avoiding painful emotions prevents people from understanding what is going on in their lives. Whether anxiety, anger, guilt, or shame are involved, confrontation with emotions and the situations provoking them is necessary for insight and change to occur. In all the therapies, a union is assumed to exist between emotion and reason, a convergence of belief that thinking patterns lay the groundwork for the emotions, and that patients must unite them in living and experiencing rather than trying defensively to isolate one from the other.

Treatment involves actions, feelings, thinking, wanting, and a sense of the social environment to eliminate the conflicts between these components of mind. Feeling without thought does not help in this; thought without feeling, action, or the motives that sustain life won't help either. All these diverse but interdependent psychological activities must be brought together and integrated by the person for sufficient integrity of the mind to be achieved in treatment. This is the way emotional change is made possible.

14

Final Thoughts

IN OUR INTRODUCTION we emphasized two themes. The first is that emotions are a product of personal meanings that depend on what is important to us—in other words, our commitments—and what we believe about ourselves and the world in which we live. The second is that each emotion has its own dramatic plot or story, defined by the personal meanings we give to an experience. To understand our emotions requires that we know these plots. Throughout the book we have elaborated on these themes, enlarged them, and looked at additional issues and features of emotions, providing case histories to concretize what we have been saying.

Now we return to these themes to pull together some of the main lessons revealed from our exploration of the emotions. It is impressive to see that clinicians engaging in psychotherapy recognize how important emotions are in the daily lives of their patients (Chapter 13). And it is no coincidence that writers and playwrights are also correct in seeing that how well or badly we are doing in our lives is reflected in our emotions—which are, in turn, centers of satisfaction, distress, and dysfunction. Therapists try to get patients to examine their emotions and the situations that arouse them in order to highlight what has gone wrong—as well as right—in their lives. However, even without undergoing therapy you can achieve some of the same benefits that psychotherapy makes possible by applying the lessons of this book to your own lives. Let us turn to some of the main lessons you might want to remember and ponder.

Passion and Reason Cannot Be Disentangled

Society has traditionally managed to separate passion and reason—heart and head—as it were. You should now see that this is not the way emotions work at all, both when they are aroused and when they are being controlled in social intercourse. Emotions always depend on reason and the two cannot be separated in nature, except for purposes of analysis. This is the first and most important lesson to be learned, and it has powerful implications for understanding and coping with our emotional lives.

We must cease the long-standing habit of thinking of emotions as irrational or having nothing to do with the ways we think. Quite the contrary, evaluations of what is happening in our daily lives, and their long-range, existential implications, constitute primary causes of every emotion we experience. To know why we feel any emotion requires that we understand the personal meaning that we have derived from the life encounter that brought the emotion about. Appraisal is the technical word we have used throughout this book to refer to these evaluations. Appraisals also shape the ways we cope with the events that arouse emotions and how we control the expression of emotions themselves.

In addition, what we do to cope with emotional situations in our lives and how this action matches the circumstances we must deal with are important for our effectiveness in managing routine as well as highly stressful tasks of living. And the accuracy and wisdom of the appraisals on which coping depends have much to do with our physical and psychological health, including our sense of well-being or ill-being.

Emotions Depend on Our Personal Histories

Although we have much in common with each other as a result of our shared inheritance as human beings—for example, our physical and psychological capacities and the things we need to survive and flourish—there are also great individual differences in our biological and psychological makeup. Some people are tall, others short; some are thin, others fat; some are energetic, others phlegmatic. Some are born colicky and are irritable and highly strung; others are born calm and cheerful; some are bright, lively, and talented; others dull. These and other variations in the basic equipment with which we have to function have an important impact on our emotions.

The same extensive variation also exists in our personal life histories. We live in different regions of the country, speak different dialects or have different accents, belong to different subcultures, races, and religions, have different parents, go to different schools, have been taught by different teachers, raised with different siblings, and so on. Some are poor, others well-to-do. Some have parents who are divorced or have lost one or both parents at an early age. Some parents can be cold and demanding, indifferent, insensitive, or even abusive, and other parents are warm, intelligent, and nurturing.

All these variations, both in biology and social experience, have much to do with individual differences in our emotional patterns. As we develop from childhood into adulthood, we learn different things about the nature of life and how to live it. Although we have many of the same goals, some of them are more important for some than for others. There are people for whom achieving success is the most important goal in life, while for others having warm, friendly social relationships is most important and achievement means little.

People also acquire different beliefs about themselves and the world. They learn different styles of appraising and coping. They undergo different stresses they must cope with, and from which they learn how to manage. Some of these differences arise from the happenstance of their placement in the world and from early life decisions they made about education, occupation, marriage and family, and place of residence.

This variation means that each individual will emerge with a somewhat distinctive pattern of emotion, and to understand it you must know two things about yourself in contrast with others. First, you have acquired a distinctive set of values and goal commitments, as well as beliefs about yourself and the world in which you live. Second, the actual environment in which you live, which is unique to you, creates its own particular demands on your resources, provides its own constraints on how you might live and act, and affords different opportunities.

Although the rules about the emotion process are common to us all, the juxtaposition of your own particular personality with the particular environments you encounter, with their changing demands, constraints, and opportunities from day to day and over your lifetime, make your emotional pattern distinctive. Your environment—especially your social environment, which means the people you deal with—is constantly changing over your lifetime, and you too are changing. Emotions are sensitive to these changing juxtapositions and, as we have said many times, present a useful index of how things are going in your life.

To illustrate the variety of change in our lives, it is obvious, for example, that what you wanted and believed as a child was different from what it is today, whether you are young, middle-aged, or old. In your youthful days, you had to decide your direction in life and to make choices relevant to that decision. In middle age, personal concerns involve an ongoing job or career, raising children, and improving financial security for the future. In old age, for most people, work and career are no longer paramount, but health and sustaining activities are. The important point here is that these different goals, ways of thinking, environmental pressures and opportunities, the struggles one must engage in, and one's sense of the present and future, betoken different patterns of emotion and ways of coping with life's struggles at different stages of life and as the world changes.

People Actively Shape Their Lives

Another telling observation we can make is that people do not sit idly by waiting for things to happen to them. Rather, they seek out situations that favor the attainment of their goals, try to avoid those that lead to frustration, and struggle to deal with whatever must be faced. Some of us may be more conscious of these choices than others. But they are clearly choices we must make throughout our lives.

A baby who cannot crawl or walk is stuck wherever it is placed and cannot move to where it will be more comfortable, safe, or engaged. A caretaker must move it to change its physical and psychological circumstances. It is not passive, however, since it can cry, look away, smile in contentment, and in a growing number of ways communicate its plight. As it grows older, it becomes more competent in dealing with its environment. And by the time we are adults, we have acquired a rich variety of physical and psychological resources for addressing our needs and coping with the conditions that must be faced.

In making choices in our lives, we are constantly appraising the implications of what is happening, what we are doing, how we are reacting, and how others react or will react, in order to play the cards we have drawn in life as effectively as possible. This process of appraising (and reappraising) goes on all the time, even when we are not conscious of the personal meanings we construct, and it directs how we play these cards.

Although often we cannot do much to change the way things are, those who manage well actively strive to change what they can when things go badly, prepare for what must be faced, and make the best of things as they are when nothing can be done. What is remarkable in all this is that, even under very difficult or destructive circumstances, most people manage somehow to hold together and retain a favorable view of life. Our lot as humans is to strive and work, to experience pleasure and perhaps some happiness, as well as to experience loss, pain, and suffering. Emotions attend all these conditions of life.

Making Sense of Our Emotions

A fourth lesson we may draw is that each emotion has its own unique plot, comprised of appraisals that reveal particular personal meanings.

Anger has its own dramatic scenario, as does anxiety, guilt, pride, love, and so on.

Knowledge of what the plot is for each emotion provides a powerful tool for understanding ourselves and others, as we intimated in our introduction. We learn these stories and begin to appreciate them when we are very young. Because there is an implacable logic to each of the emotions we experience, if we know the logic we can decipher the emotional patterns we, our loved ones, and our enemies alike, experience and display.

So, for example, when we feel angry, or when we see that someone else is angry, we can comprehend what brought it about. In the case of anger, we know that an event, happenstance, or person's action or inaction was construed as an insult to the ego. And for each emotion, we can usually piece together a meaningful plot.

By now, it should be clear that, as humans, we can read these plots in our own lives and others. They are themes that recur in our everyday lives and, because of the way we are built, we use emotions in ourselves and others as powerful clues to the meanings we attach to experience.

And it bears repeating that we are the most emotional animal in the jungle. Our faces, our postures, the quality of our voices, our language, and our actions are wrought with emotion. Taking what we know of evolutionary theory, we can only gather that this emotional life helps us adapt to a changing environment. Emotions allow us to remain responsive to that environment and flexible in the way we respond. And as we said before, emotion and reason do not work separately, but in tandem. They are, in fact, inseparable. And if, indeed, there is a major disparity between passion and reason, or heart and mind, we are either being dishonest or suffering from mental illness.

Arousal and Control of an Emotion Are Different Stages in the Emotion Process

Still another lesson we should learn is that the arousal of an emotion is, in part, only the first stage in the emotion process, a stage apart from the expression of the emotion. Sometimes we feel angry, for example, and recognize clearly what has made us so. We blame another person for the slight we have experienced, which explains our anger. However, this doesn't mean that we must act out the emotion by a counterattack. The aroused emotion does not need to become a full-blown emotional episode.

A second stage (though the distinction between stages should not sound too neat since both combine as parts of the whole emotion process) involves what to do about the aroused emotion and the situation that provoked it. This stage is what we have called coping throughout this book. Every emotional situation calls for coping, which must take into account how others are likely to respond to what has happened and to the emotion we display.

We may think, "This person deserves to be put down a peg or made to see the error of his ways." Or "I wonder what the other person will think, or others who might be watching, if I express anger or lash out in rage? Will the other person retaliate? Should I be ashamed of my loss of control?" And even when feeling happy or proud, it may be prudent or kind to inhibit its expression—prudent because a person less well off might want to punish us for our good fortune, kind because the other person may be suffering from a loss and our happiness may add insult to injury.

It is probably easier to control what we do in an emotional encounter than to control the initial arousal of an emotion. To a great extent, biology shapes the emotional reaction to the personal meaning we construe from a situation. If we are slighted, we feel anger; if we sense the presence of an uncertain threat, we feel anxious; if we are using our resources well to advance our goals, we feel happy; and so on.

Yet these connections between personal meanings and the emotions that are aroused are not totally fixed or predetermined, and the emotion aroused can be changed. We have seen that we can change emotions by coping in a number of ways. We can sometimes select our life situations to physically avoid unwanted outcomes and the emotions they arouse. We can deal with negative situations by not thinking about them—at least until they can no longer be avoided—or by distracting ourselves by pleasurable activities. We can to some extent choose careers on the basis of our own needs, personal resources, and dispositions, and sometimes we have the option of changing jobs.

And we must not forget the great power we can have over negative emotions, such as anger, by reappraising what is happening in benign rather than emotionally disturbing terms. We can make excuses for the person who might have angered us so that we don't feel the expectable anger. In fact, we can learn to think this way about certain people and situations so habitually that there would be little or no need for anger, envy, or jealousy.

And when we are caught up in an emotion whose arousal cannot be prevented but may be socially dangerous, we can suppress its expression. An important part of our adaptation consists of recognizing in advance how other people will react to our actions. Despite what has long been thought, suppression—say, of verbal or physical aggression when we are angry—is not necessarily bad for us on any given occasion, though chronic or recurrent suppression might be. But not because a bottled-up emotion might explode. Suppression of the emotions keeps us from learning about ourselves. And just because we control the expression of an emotion does not mean that we fail to experience it. Emotions are a natural feature of our psychological experience, and we should pay attention to them.

In this connection, growing up in certain cultures also helps to shape our appraisals in such a way that the arousal of an emotion and the task of coping with it are made either easier or more difficult, depending on the social rules and values of the culture. Regardless of culture, however, the emotions we experience depend on what we have learned to want and to believe, as well as the meanings we have learned to appraise in a situation. We need not be victims of our emotions but can do much to shape and change them, if we understand what arouses them and how they affect others.

Understanding and Changing Our Emotional Patterns

Not all emotional patterns should be changed. Emotions express the realities of our lives and are a normal and important aspect of living. But a final lesson we can draw is that if we don't like the emotional patterns that seem to hold sway over our lives, by understanding the rules that bring them about we can change the way we are reacting. We may still feel the same emotion, but we can cope better with the emotional episode.

To produce change requires that we do two things, as we saw in the psychotherapeutic case examples presented in Chapter 13. First, we must systematically pay attention to our daily emotions, especially those that are unwanted and get in the way of what we consider to be a good life. Anger, anxiety, guilt, shame, envy, and jealousy are among those that give people the most problems. If we have the courage and persistence to pay attention, we can begin to see the typical patterns we experience and display in our emotional reactions.

We learned, for example, that although they can be useful as ways of coping, under some circumstances repressing emotional impulses, denying them, or developing the coping style of distancing oneself from them, can create difficulties. When we remain unaware of what is happening to us, fooling ourselves about these realities, our decisions in life may be in error and sometimes even self-destructive.

Second, we must also pay attention to the thoughts we engage in before and during these emotions. These thoughts express how we view what is happening, the goals that are important to us, the beliefs that contribute to the personal meanings that aroused the emotion, and the significance of the environmental pressures and opportunities that we have to deal with.

And when the reasons for an emotion seem obscure, we must be ready to challenge ourselves to discover what is going on. Perhaps we haven't paid close enough attention. When it is important enough to do so, we can learn to overcome this inattention, which could lead to an understanding of ourselves that has previously not seemed possible.

Probably the most important reason why we remain unaware of the reasons for many of our emotional experiences is that we would rather not know the truth, since it violates our cherished views of who we are and what we are like. We would often rather fool ourselves about our wishes and beliefs because they impugn the picture of ourselves that we want to maintain. We spend a great deal of our energy protecting this self-image, justifying our actions and reactions.

We also spend a great deal of energy trying to fool others into believing an idealized portrait of ourselves, presenting ourselves as supremely honest, strong, self-directed, decent and concerned about others, smart, and so on. We do this even though we might doubt the authenticity of this self-image, but we often fall for the same line about ourselves we try to present to others. This defensiveness, both with others and ourselves, defeats a valid understanding of who we truly are. It often takes considerable courage to seek and accept the truth about our strengths and weaknesses.

In many of the case studies presented in this book, lack of attention to and insight about thoughts and emotions, and their relationship, made it difficult or impossible for the people we described to have a sound understanding of their emotions, especially those reflecting troubled relationships with others.

However, you must not believe that discovering the truth and changing an emotional pattern are out of reach. Psychotherapy is one way to seek the truth with the help of an experienced professional. But the use of your own basic intelligence and knowledge about how emotions are aroused and controlled, particularly the logic that applies to each of the emotions, can help you make sense of your emotions even without professional help. To do this requires not only courage but strong motivation to look into your social relationships, and the capacity to be introspective about the way you think and feel.

When what seems to be happening emotionally in particular situations is obscure, sit down quietly and ask yourself why you felt the emotion you did, and why it recurs. Try to identify the personal meaning you bring to the occasion, and go on from there. When you are angry, for example, something must have happened to make you feel slighted. What could it have been? And if you find yourself angry much of the time, you are either in a life situation that is chronically demeaning or you have personal vulnerabilities that lead you to react inappropriately with anger. The same kind of reasoning applies to each of the other emotions.

You can utilize the same exercise in reasoning about others who are important to you—a son, daughter, or spouse who is repeatedly angry, or anxious, or guilty, or jealous. The emotional patterns they display reveal recurrent meanings—wrongheaded or not—that they bring to events in their lives. We pinpointed these meanings in the case stories we presented throughout the book.

In light of what you have read here, we hope that you will have come to regard the emotions as complex, but not the inscrutable or irrational phenomena that you might have once thought. Quite the contrary, if you can grasp the meanings that bring them about, you may come to understand your emotions and control them. It is our wish that reading this book has added to your understanding and perhaps has offered you some insight into how your emotions influence the quality of your life.

Notes

Chapter 2. The Nasty Emotions

1. Lerner, M. J. (1970). The desire for justice and reactions to victims. In J. McCauley & L. Berkowitz (Eds.), *Altruism and helping behavior.* New York: Academic Press.

2. The short story, "counterparts," from James Joyce's *Dubliners*, is about an inadequate man who, with little to be proud of, is downtrodden by his social experiences throughout the day, and returns home and beats up his small son when he discovers the further indignity that his wife has left him no supper.

3. Tavris, C. (1989). *Anger: The misunderstood emotion.* 2nd ed. New York: Simon & Schuster.

4. For an interesting account of the history of attitudes toward anger in the United States, see Stearns, C. Z., & Stearns, P. (1986). *Anger: The struggle for emotional control in America's history.* Chicago: University of Chicago Press.

5. Freud, S. (1930). *Civilization and its discontents.* London: Hogarth Press. (First German edition, 1930). Freud, S. (1959). Thoughts for the times on war and death. *Collected Papers*, Vol. 4 (translation by Joan Riviere). New York: Basic Books. (First German edition, 1915). Freud, S. (1959). Why war? In J. Strachey (Ed.), *Collected papers*, Vol. 5. New York: Basic Books. (First German edition, 1932).

6. See, for example, Lore, R. K., & Schultz, L. A. (1993). Control of human aggression: A comparative perspective. *American Psychologist, 48*, 16–25.

7. Bugental, J. F. T. (1990). *Intimate journeys: Stories from life-changing therapy.* San Francisco: Jossey-Bass. Quotes on p. 106.

8. See Smith, R. H.. H., Kim, S. H., & Parrott, W. G. (1988). Envy and jealousy: Semantic problems and experiential distinctions. *Personality and Social Psychology Bulletin, 14*, 401–409, for discussion and research on the language of these emotions.

9. For a scholarly, modern research account of envy and jealousy, see Salovey, P. (Ed.). (1991). *The psychology of jealousy and envy.* New York: Guilford; and of jealousy, see White, G. L., & Mullen, P. E. (1989). *Jealousy: Theory, research, and clinical strategies.* New York: Guilford.

10. Taylor, S. E., Lichtman, R. R., & Wood, J. V. (1984). Attributions, beliefs about control, and adjustment to breast cancer. *Journal of Personality and Social Psychology, 46*, 489–502.

11. Schimmel, S. (1992). *The seven deadly sins: Jewish, Christian, and classical reflections on human nature*. New York: The Free Press. Quote on p. 62.

12. Tov-Ruach, L. (1980). Jealousy, attention, and loss. In A. O. Rorty (Ed.), *Explaining emotions* (pp. 465–488). Berkeley: University of California Press.

13. Freud, S. (1922). Some neurotic mechanisms in jealousy, paranoia and homosexuality. *Standard Edition*, XVIII. London: Hogarth, p. 223.

14. This concept was used by Klein, M. (1957/1975). *Envy and gratitude and other works* (1946–1963). London: Hogarth Press.

Chapter 3. The Existential Emotions

1. See, for example, Baumeister, R. F. (1991). *Meanings of life*. New York: Guilford; also Lazarus, R. S., and Averill, J. R. (1972). Emotion and cognition: With special reference to anxiety. In C. D. Spielberger (Ed.), *Anxiety: Current trends in theory and research* (Vol. 2, pp. 242–282). New York: Academic Press.

2. Lifton, R. J. (1983). *The broken connection: On death and the continuity of life*. New York: Basic Books.

3. See, for example, Tillich, P. (1959). The external now. In H. Feifel (Ed.), *The meaning of death* (pp. 30–38). New York: McGraw-Hill. Also May, R. (1950). *The meaning of anxiety*. New York: Ronald.

4. Becker, E. (1973). *The denial of death*. New York: The Free Press.

5. Lifton, R. J. (1983). *The broken connection: On death and the continuity of life*. New York: Basic Books. Quotes on p. 66, footnote; p. 70 is the father-daughter dialogue.

6. For research on children's insecure reactions to their mothers' withdrawal, see Ainsworth, M. D. S., Blehar, M., Waters, E., & Wall, S. (1978). *Patterns of attachment*. Hillsdale, NJ: Erlbaum; also Ainsworth, M. D., & Bowlby, J. (1991). An ethological approach to personality development. *American Psychologist*, 46, 333–341.

7. See Shweder, R. A. (1991). The astonishment of anthropology. In R. S. Shweder (Ed.), *Thinking through cultures: Expeditions in cultural psychology* (pp. 1–23). Cambridge, MA: Harvard University Press.

8. Zahn-Waxler, C., & Kochanska, G. (1990). The origins of guilt. In R. S. Thompson (Ed.), *Nebraska symposium on motivation, 1988*. Lincoln: University of Nebraska Press.

9. Hoffman, M. L. (1982). Development of pro-social motivation: Empathy and guilt. In N. Eisenberg (Ed.), *The development of pro-social behavior*. New York: Academic Press.

10. Adler, A. (1927). *The practice and theory of individual psychology*. New York: Harcourt.

11. Wicklund, R. A. (1975). Objective self-awareness. In L. Berkowitz (Ed.), *Advances in experimental social psychology* (Vol. 7). New York: Academic Press.

12. Ohbuchi, K., Kameda, M., & Agarie, N. (1989). Apology as an aggres-

sion control: Its role in mediating appraisal of and response to harm. *Journal of Personality and Social Psychology, 56,* 219–227.

13. For other discussions of shame, see also M. Lewis (1992). Shame, the exposed self. New York: The Free Press; and Scheff, T. (1989). Socialization of emotions: Pride and shame as causal agents. In T. Kemper (Ed.), *The sociology of emotions.* Albany: SUNY Press.

14. Lewis, H. B. (1971). Shame and guilt in neurosis. New York: International Universities Press; also Lewis, M. (1992). *Shame: The exposed self.* New York: The Free Press, for a less technical treatment.

Chapter 4. Emotions Provoked by Unfavorable Life Conditions: Relief, Hope, Sadness, and Depression

1. Epstein, A. H. (1989). *Mind, fantasy and healing: One woman's journey from conflict and illness to wholeness and health.* New York: Delacourt Press. Quote on p. xxv.

2. Some modern sources are Breznitz, S. (1986). The effect of hope on coping with stress. In M. Appley & R. Trumbull (Eds.), *Dynamics of stress* (pp. 295–306); and Stotland, E. (1969). *The psychology of hope.* San Francisco, CA: Jossey-Bass.

3. Averill, J. R., Catlin, J. G., & Kyum, K. C. (1990). *The rules of hope.* New York: Springer-Verlag. Quotation on p. 3. I have drawn on their account of the history of ideas substantially.

4. See, for example, Erikson, E. H. (1963). *Childhood and society.* 2nd ed. New York: Norton.

5. Marris, P. (1975). *Loss and change.* Garden City, NY: Anchor Books.

6. See, for example, Gilbert, P. (1992). *Depression: The evolution of powerlessness.* New York: Guilford.

7. For a psychoanalytic answer, see Weiss, J. (1952). Crying at a happy ending. *Psychoanalytic Review, 39,* 338. Weiss, J. (1986). Part I: Theory and clinical observations. In J. Weiss, H. Sampson, & the Mount Zion Psychotherapy Research Group (Eds.), *The psychoanalytic process: Theory, clinical observation, and empirical research.* New York: Guilford. Silberschatz, G., & Sampson, H. (1991). Affects in psychopathology and psychotherapy. In J. D. Safran & L. S. Greenberg (Eds.), *Emotion, psychotherapy, and change.* New York: Guilford.

8. See Doka, K. J. (1989). *Disenfranchised grief: Recognizing hidden sorrow.* Lexington, MA: Lexington Books.

Chapter 5. Emotions Provoked by Favorable Life Conditions: Happiness, Pride, and Love

1. See, for example, Diener, E. (1984). Subjective well-being. *Psychological Bulletin, 95,* 542–575.

2. Actually, well-being is closer to a mood than an acute emotion, since it refers to how we are doing existentially. However, when people are asked to make

the judgement, it is mainly an intellectual task and they are not apt to be engaged in a real feeling as they would be in a mood state.

3. See Scheier, M. F., & Carver, C. S. (1987). Dispositional optimism and physical well-being: The influence of generalized outcome expectancies on health. *Journal of Personality, 55,* 169–210.

4. Isen, A. M. (1970). Success, failure, attention and reaction to others: The warm glow of success. *Journal of Personality and Social Psychology, 15,* 294–301.

5. Sedikides, C. (1992). Mood as a determinant of attentional focus. *Cognition and Emotion, 6,* 129–148.

6. Lazarus, R. S., & Launier, R. (1978). Stress-related transactions between person and environment. In L. A. Pervin & M. Lewis (Eds.), *Perspectives in interactional psychology* (pp. 287–327). New York: Plenum. See also Lazarus, R. S., & Folkman, S. (1984). *Stress, appraisal, and coping.* New York: Springer.

7. Hume, D. (1957). *An inquiry concerning the principles of morals.* New York: Library of Liberal Arts.

8. For an interesting and systematic set of data and psychological analyses on unrequited love, see Baumeister, R. F., & Wotman, S. R. (1992). *Breaking hearts: The two sides of unrequited love.* New York: Guilford.

9. Reiss, I. L. (1990). *An end to shame: Shaping our next sexual revolution.* Buffalo, New York: Prometheus.

Chapter 6. The Empathic Emotions: Gratitude, Compassion, and Those Aroused by Aesthetic Experiences

1. For one of the rare discussions of gratitude, see Klein, M. (1957/1975). *Envy and gratitude and other works* (1946–1963). London: Hogarth Press.

2. Schaefer, C., Coyne, J. C., & Lazarus, R. S. (1982). The health-related functions of social support. *Journal of Behavioral Medicine, 4,* 381–406.

3. Fascinating research on this type of stress and social support has been published by Mechanic, D. (1962). *Students under stress: A study of the social psychology of adaptation.* New York: The Free Press. Reprinted in 1978 by the University of Wisconsin Press.

4. Stuhlmiller, C. M. (1991). An interpretive study of appraisal and coping of rescue workers in an earthquake disaster: The Cypress collapse. Doctoral dissertation in Nursing Science, University of California Medical School, San Francisco, CA.

5. For some recent but incomplete discussions of this, see Walters, K. S. (1989). Aesthetic emotions and reality. *American Psychologist, 44,* 1545–1546; also Frijda, N. H. (1989). Aesthetic emotions and reality. *American Psychologist, 44,* 1546–1547.

6. For example, Clynes, M. (1977). *Sentics: The touch of emotions.* Garden City, NY: Anchor/Doubleday, for research that supports this idea.

7. Clark, K. (1970, p. 95). *Civilisation.* New York: Harper & Row.

8. Jung, C. G. (1960). Symbol formation. In H. Read, M. Fordham, & G. Adler (Eds.), *The collected works* (Vol. 8, pp. 45–61). (Trans. from the German

by R. F. C. Hull.) New York: Pantheon (copyright held by Bollinger Foundation, Inc.).

Chapter 7. The Nuts and Bolts of Emotion

1. Erikson, E. H. (1950/1963). *Childhood and society.* 1st and 2nd eds. New York: Norton.

2. James, W. (1890). *Principles of psychology.* New York: Holt.

3. Mahl, G. F. (1953). Physiological changes during chronic fear. *Annals of the New York Academy of Sciences, 56,* 240–249.

4. Klos, D. S., & Singer, J. L. (1981). Determinants of the adolescent's ongoing thought following simulated parental confrontations. *Journal of Personality and Social Psychology, 41,* 975–987.

5. Horowitz, M. J. (1976). *Stress response syndromes.* New York: Jason Aronson.

Chapter 8. Coping and the Self-Management of Emotions

1. See Lazarus, R. S., & Folkman, S. (1984). *Stress, appraisal, and coping.* New York: Springer.

2. Pennebaker, J. W. (1989). Confession, inhibition, and disease. In L. Berkowitz (Ed.), *Advances in experimental social psychology* (Vol. 22, pp. 211–244). Orlando, FL: Academic Press. See also J. W., Colder, M., & Sharp, L. K. (1990). Accelerating the coping process. *Journal of Personality and Social Psychology, 58,* 528–537.

3. Tavris, C. (1989). *Anger: The misunderstood emotion.* New York: Touchstone.

4. Ellis, A. (1962). *Reason and emotion in psychotherapy.* New York: Lyle Stuart.

5. Speisman, J. C., Lazarus, R. S., Mordkoff, A. M., & Davidson, L. A. (1964). The experimental reduction of stress based on ego-defense theory. *Journal of Abnormal and Social Psychology, 68,* 367–380. See also Lazarus, R. S. (1964). A laboratory approach to the dynamics of psychological stress. *American Psychologist, 19,* 400–411.

6. Freud, A. (1936). *The ego and the mechanisms of defense.* New York: International Universities Press.

7. Susan Langer has written about the illusion of control in Langer, S. (1975). The illusion of control. *Journal of Personality and Social Psychology, 32,* 311–328.

8. Cohen, F., & Lazarus, R. S. (1973). Active coping processes, coping dispositions, and recovery from surgery. *Psychosomatic Medicine, 35,* 357–389.

9. Levenson, J. L., Kay, R., Monteferrante, J., & Herman, M. V. (1984). Denial predicts favorable outcome in unstable angina pectoris. *Psychosomatic Medicine, 46,* 25–32.

10. Levine, J., Warrensburg, S., Kerns, R., Schwartz, G., Delany, R., Fontana, A., Gradman, A., Smith, S., Allen, S., & Cascione, R. (1987). The role of denial in recovery from coronary heart disease. *Psychosomatic Medicine, 49,* 109–117.

11. Lazarus, R. S. The costs and benefits of denial. In S. Breznitz (Ed.), *The denial of stress* (pp. 1–30). New York: International Universities Press.

12. Lazarus, R. S. (1984). The trivialization of distress. In B. L. Hammonds & C. J. Scheirer (Eds.). *Psychology and health.* 1983 Master Lecture Series (Vol. 3, pp. 121–144). Washington, DC: American Psychological Association.

13. Hackett, T. P., & Weisman, A. D. (1964). Reactions to the imminence of death. In G. H. Grosser, H. Wechsler, & M. Greenblatt (Eds.), *The threat of impending disaster.* Cambridge, MA: MIT Press, pp. 300–311.

14. Collins, D. L., Baum, A., and Singer, J. E. (1983). Coping with chronic stress at Three Mile Island: Psychological and biochemical evidence. *Health Psychology, 2,* 149–166.

Chapter 9. How Biology and Culture Affect Our Emotions

1. Sociologists are also interested in emotion, and explain these variations on the basis of the social structure within a society, which has to do with the social roles we play, such as father, worker, wife, lover, and child, and social stratifications, such as social class. I have ignored social structure in my discussions to avoid complicating my discussion too much, though it is important in the study of emotion.

2. Darwin, C. (1859). *The origin of species.* London: J. Murray.

3. Darwin, C. (1872/1965). *The expression of the emotions in man and animals.* New York: Appleton. (1965, Chicago: University of Chicago Press.)

4. See, for example, Domjan, M. (1987). Animal learning comes of age. *American Psychologist, 42,* 556–564.

5. Eibel-Eibesfeldt, I. (1989). *Human ethology.* New York: Aldine de Gruyter. Quote on p. 19.

6. MacLean, P. D. (1949). Psychosomatic disease and the 'visceral brain.' Recent developments bearing on the Papez theory of emotion. *Psychosomatic Medicine, 11,* 338–353.

7. Tinbergen, N. (1951). *The study of instincts.* London: Oxford University Press.

8. Cannon, W. B. (1939). *The wisdom of the body.* 2nd ed. New York: W. W. Simon (First edition, 1932).

9. This idea was encouraged by Tomkins, S. S. (1962, 1963). *Affect, imagery, consciousness* (Vols. 1 and 2). New York: Springer. Tomkins greatly influenced the empirical research of two of his students, Paul Ekman and Carrol Izard. See Ekman, P. (1971). Universals and cultural differences in facial expressions of emotion. In J. K. Cole (Ed.), *Nebraska symposium on motivation,* 1971 (pp. 207–283). Lincoln: University of Nebraska Press; and Izard, C. E. (1971). *The face of emotion.* New York: Appleton-Century-Crofts.

10. Ekman, P., Friesen, W. V., & O'Sullivan, M. (1988). Smiles when lying. *Journal of Personality and Social Psychology, 54,* 414–420.

11. Plutchik, R. (1991). Emotions and evolution. In K. T. Strongman (Ed.), *International review of studies on emotion* (Vol. 1, pp. 37–58). London: Wiley. Quote on p. 41.

12. Plutchik, p. 42.

13. From Lorenz, K. (1963). *On aggression.* Translated by Marjorie Kerr Wilson. Orlando, FL: Harcourt Brace Jovanovich.

14. Cannon, W. B.

15. Selye, H. (1956/1976). *The stress of life.* New York: McGraw-Hill.

16. Plutchik, quote on p. 41.

17. Hebb, D. O., & Thompson, W. R. (1954). The social significance of animal studies. In G. Lindzey (Ed.), *Handbook of social psychology* (pp. 532–561). Cambridge, MA: Addison-Wesley. Quote on p. 554.

18. See Shank, R. C., & Abelson, R. B. (1977). *Scripts, plans, goals and understanding.* Hillsdale, NJ: Erlbaum.

19. See Lutz, C., & White, G. M. (1986). The anthropology of emotions. *Annual Review of Anthropology, 15,* 405–436.

20. Vayda, A. P. (1968). Hypotheses about functions of war. In M. Fried, M. Harris, & R. Murphy (Eds.), *War: The anthropology of armed conflict and aggression* (pp. 85–91). Garden City, NY: The Natural History Press.

21. Levy, R. I. (1984). Emotion, knowing, and culture. In R. A. Shweder & R. A. LeVine (Eds.), *Culture theory: Essays on mind, self, and emotion.* Cambridge, England: Cambridge University Press.

22. Tomkins, J. (1989). "Fighting words." *Harpers Magazine,* March, pp. 33–35.

23. Briggs, J. L. (1970). *Never in anger: Portrait of an Eskimo family.* Cambridge, MA: Harvard University Press.

24. Solomon, R. C. (1984). Getting angry: The Jamesian theory of emotion in anthropology. In R. S. Shweder & R. A. LeVine (Eds.), *Culture theory: Essays on mind, self, and emotion* (pp. 238–254). Cambridge, England: Cambridge University Press.

25. Singer, J. L., & Opler, M. J. (1956). Contrasting patterns of fantasy and motility in Irish and Italian schizophrenics. *Journal of Abnormal and Social Psychology, 53,* 42–47.

Chapter 10. The Logic of Our Emotions

1. The story of how this came about is told by James Averill, a psychologist with long-standing interest in the emotions. See Averill, J. R. (1974). An analysis of psychophysiological symbolism and its influence on theories of emotion. *Journal for the Theory of Social Behavior, 4,* 146–190; see also Averill, J. R. (1982). *Anger and aggression: An essay on emotion.* New York: Springer-Verlag.

The original word for emotion was "passion." It comes from the Greek *pathos* and the Latin *pati,* from which we also get passive and patient. Passion expresses the idea of being involuntarily (passively) gripped, seized, or torn by emotion. We are said to be possessed by powerful forces that are too strong to be suppressed.

2. See also Gardner, H. M., Metcalf, R. C., & Beebe-Center, J. G. (1937/1970). *Feeling and emotion: A history of theories.* Westport, CT: Greenwood Press.

3. Much later, in the eighteenth century, the distinction was made between the voluntary nervous system, consisting of the striate muscles of the body whose movements we could "willfully" control, and the involuntary nervous system, whose activities were automatically regulated by homeostatic mechanisms that worked like a thermostat, and could not be directly influenced by conscious intent. Regulation of body temperature, sugar in the blood, heart rate and blood pressure, and so forth, are examples of nonvoluntary or autonomic nervous system activities.

4. Clark, K. (1970). *Civilisation.* New York: Harper & Row.

5. Dreikurs, R. (Ed.). (1967). *Psychodynamics and counseling.* Chicago: Adler School of Professional Psychology.

6. Fox, R. (1992). Prejudice and the unfinished mind: A new look at an old failing. And commentaries. *Psychological Inquiry, 3,* 137–152.

7. This position has been engagingly explored by Shweder, R. A. (1987). Comments on Plott and on Kahneman, Knetsch, and Thaler. In R. M. Hogarth & M. W. Reder (Eds.), *Rational choice: The contrast between economics and psychology* (pp. 161–170). Chicago: University of Chicago Press.

8. In making this critique of the economic view of rationality, we note that a group of academics in the United States has been, in the words of the *London Financial Times*, "trying to launch a new kind of economics: a set of theories more likely to promote a kinder, gentler America than the free market doctrines of the 1980s." An effort is being made to recruit social scientists from many disciplines, including psychology. See the *London Financial Times*, Tuesday, April 2, 1991, pp. 15–16.

9. Historian Barbara Tuchman calls much of history the march of folly.

10. See, for example, Lazarus, R. S. (1991). *Emotion and adaptation.* New York: Oxford University Press, for a treatment of the effects of stress emotions on thought.

11. McCoy, S. B., Gibbons, F. X., Reis, T. J., Gerrard, M., Luus, C. A. E., and Sufka, A. V. W. (1992). *Journal of Behavioral Medicine, 15,* 469–488.

Chapter 11. Stress and Emotion

1. Roskies, E. (1983). Stress management: Averting the evil eye. *Contemporary Psychology, 28,* 542–544. Quote on p. 542.

2. See an account by Hinkle, L. E., Jr. (1973). The concept of "stress" in the biological and social sciences. *Science, Medicine & Man, 1,* 31–48.

3. Mason, J. W., Maher, J. T., Hartley, L. H., Mougey, E., Perlow, M. J., & Jones, L. G. Selectivity of corticosteroid and catecholamine response to

various natural stimuli. In G. Serban (Ed.), *Psychopathology of human adaptation*. New York: Plenum.

4. American Psychiatric Association. (1987). *Diagnostic and statistical manual of mental disorders*. 3rd ed., revised. Washington, DC: APA.

5. Holmes, T. H., & Rahe, R. H. (1967). The social readjustment rating scale. *Journal of Psychosomatic Research, 11*, 213–218.

6. See Lazarus, R. S. & Folkman, S. (1989). *Manual for the study of daily hassles and uplifts scales*. Palo Alto, CA. Consulting Psychologists Press.

7. Lazarus, R. S. (1984). Puzzles in the study of daily hassles. *Journal of Behavioral Medicine, 7*, 373–389.

8. Gruen, R., Folkman, S., & Lazarus, R. S. (1989). Centrality and individual differences in the meaning of daily hassles. *Journal of Personality, 56*, 743–762.

9. Lazarus & Folkman, 1989.

10. Dewe, P. (1991). Measuring work stressors: the role of frequency, duration, and demand. *Work & Stress, 5*, 77–91.

11. See Gottman, J. M., and Levenson, R. W. (1992). Marital processes predictive of later dissolution: Behavior, physiology, and health. *Journal of Personality and Social Psychology, 63*, 221–233; also Gottman, J. M. (1993). The roles of conflict engagement, escalation, and avoidance in marital interaction: A Longitudinal view of five types of couples. *Journal of Consulting and Clinical Psychology, 61*, 6–15.

12. This research is accurately summarized in Opton, E. M., Jr. & Lazarus, R. S. (1966). The use of motion picture films in the study of psychological stress: A summary of theoretical formulations and experimental findings. In C. Spielberger (Ed.), *Anxiety and behavior* (pp. 225–262). New York: Academic Press; and in Lazarus, R. S., Averill, J. R., & Opton, E. M., Jr. (1970). Towards a cognitive theory of emotion. In M. Arnold (Ed.), *Feelings and emotions* (pp. 207–232). New York: Academic Press. I have taken some liberties with the exact details of the research in order to present a more readable account.

13. In the account of this research, we have brought together a number of studies instead of describing a single one in order to summarize what we did. This distorts some of the details of individual studies but not the main findings and conclusions. For actual details, see Speisman, J. C., Lazarus, R. S., Mordkoff, A. M., & Davison, L. A. (1964). The experimental reduction of stress based on ego-defense theory. *Journal of Abnormal and Social Psychology, 68*, 367–380; also, Lazarus, R. S., & Alfert, E. (1964). The short-circuiting of threat by experimentally altering cognitive appraisal. *Journal of Abnormal and Social Psychology, 69*, 195–205.

14. Folkins, C. H. (1970). Temporal factors and the cognitive mediators of stress reaction. *Journal of Personality and Social Psychology, 14*, 173–184; see also Monat, A., and Lazarus, R. S. (1976). Temporal uncertainty, anticipation time, and cognitive coping under threat. *Journal of Human Stress, 2*, 32–43, for a related experiment.

Chapter 12. Emotions and Our Health

1. See Lipowski, Z. J. (1977). Psychosomatic Medicine in the seventies: An overview. *American Journal of Psychiatry, 134,* 233–244, for a historical account.

2. Alexander, F. (1950). *Psychosomatic medicine.* New York: Norton.

3. Graham, D. T. (1962). Some research on psychophysiologic specificity and its relation to psychosomatic disease. In R. Roessler & N. S. Greenfield (Eds.), *Physiological correlates of psychological disorder.* Madison: University of Wisconsin Press. Quote on p. 237.

4. Selye, H. (1956/1976). *The stress of life.* New York: McGraw-Hill.

5. Weiss, J. H. (1977). The current state of the concept of a psychosomatic disorder. In Z. J. Lipowski, D. R. Lipsitt, & P. C. Whybrow (Eds.), *Psychosomatic medicine: Current trends and clinical applications.* New York: Oxford University Press.

6. See Jemmott, J. B., & Locke, S. E. (1984). Psychosocial factors, immunological mediation, and human susceptibility to infectious diseases: How much do we know? *Psychological Bulletin, 95,* 78–108, for a review. Also Glaser, R., Kiecolt-Glaser, J. K., Bonneau, R. H., Malarkey, W., Kennedy, S., & Hughes, J. (1992). Stress-induced modulation of the immune response to recombinant hepatitis B. Vaccine. *Psychosomatic Medicine, 54,* 22–29, for an example of some technical research.

7. Goodkin, K, Fuchs, I., Feaster, D., Leaka, J., & Rishel, D. D. (1992). Life stressors and coping style are associated with immune measures in HIV-1 infection—A preliminary report. *International Journal of Psychiatry in Medicine, 22,* 155–172.

8. Bergman, L. R., & Magnusson, D. (1979). Overachievement and catecholamine excretion in an achievement-demanding situation. *Psychosomatic Medicine, 41,* 181–188.

9. Cohen, S., Kaplan, J. R., Cunnick, J. E., Manuck, S. B., & Rabin, B. S. (1992). Chronic social stress, affiliation, and cellular immune response in nonhuman primates. *Psychological Science, 3,* 301–304.

10. Kasl, S. V., Evans, A. S., & Niederman, J. C. (1979). Psychosocial risk factors in the development of infectious mononucleosis. *Psychosomatic Medicine, 41,* 445–466.

11. Cohen, S., Tyrrell, D. A. J., & Smith, A. P. (1991). Psychological stress and susceptibility to the common cold. *New England Journal of Medicine, 325,* 606–612.

12. Cited in Hinkle, L. E., Jr. (1977). The concept of 'stress' in the biological and social sciences. In Z. J. Lipowski, D. R. Lipsitt, & P. C. Whybrow (Eds.), *Psychosomatic medicine: Current trends and clinical implications.* New York: Oxford University Press.

13. See Friedman, M., & Rosenman, R. H. (1974). *Type A behavior and your heart.* New York: Knopf.

14. Jenkins, C. D., Rosenman, R. H., & Zyzanski, S. J. (1974). Prediction of clinical coronary heart disease by a test for the coronary prone behavior pattern. *New England Journal of Medicine, 290,* 1271–1275.

15. Glass, D. C. (1977). *Behavior patterns, stress and coronary disease*. Hillsdale, NJ: Erlbaum

16. Keinan, G., Ben-Zur, H., Zilka, M., & Carel, R. S. (1992). Anger in or out, which is healthier? An attempt to reconcile inconsistent findings. *Psychology and Health, 7*, 83–98.

17. Harburg, E., Blakelock, E. H., & Roeper, P. J. (1979). Resentful and reflective coping with arbitrary authority and blood pressure: Detroit. *Psychosomatic Medicine, 41*, 189–202.

18. In my opinion, the most readable and useful book on the subject of anger and its management for laypersons is Tavris, C. (1982). *Anger: The misunderstood emotion*. New York: Touchstone.

19. See, for example, Spielberger, C. E., Krasner, S. S., & Solomon, E. P. (1988). The experience and control of anger. In M. P. Janisse (Ed.), *Health psychology: Individual differences and stress* (pp. 89–108). New York: Springer Verlag; Spielberger, C. D., Jacobs, G., Russell, S., & Crane, R. J. (1983). Assessment of anger: The state-trait anger scale. In J. N. Butcher & C. D. Spielberger (Eds.), *Advances in personality assessment* (Vol. 2, pp. 159–187). Hillsdale, NJ: Erlbaum; and Williams, R. & Williams, V. (1993). *Anger kills: 17 strategies for controlling the hostility that can harm your health*. New York: Time Books/ Random House.

20. Greer, S., & Morris, T. (1978). The study of psychological factors in breast cancer: Problems of method. *Social Science and Medicine, 12*, 129–134.

21. Dattore, P. J., Shontz, F. C., & Coyne, L. (1980). Premorbid personality differentiation of cancer and noncancer groups: A test of the hypotheses of cancer proneness. *Journal of Consulting and Clinical Psychology, 48*, 388–394.

22. Weisman, A. D., & Worden, J. W. (1975) Psychosocial analysis of cancer deaths. *Omega: Journal of Death and Dying, 6*, 61–75.

23. Heim, E. (1991). Coping and adaptation in cancer. In C. L. Cooper and M. Watson (Eds.), *Psychological, biological and coping studies* (pp. 198–235) London: Wiley; also Heim, E., Augustiny, K. F., Blaser, A., Burki, C., Kuhne, D., Rothenbuhler, Schaffner, L., & Valach, L. (1987). Coping with breast cancer—A longitudinal prospective study. *Psychotherapy and psychosomatics, 48*, 44–59.

24. Cousins, N. Anatomy of an illness (as perceived by the patient). (1976). *The New England Journal of Medicine, 295*, 1458–1463. Quotes pp. 49 and 52.

25. Epstein, A. H. (1989). *Mind, fantasy, and healing: One woman's journey from conflict and illness to wholeness and health*. New York: Delcorte Press.

Chapter 13. When Coping Fails—Psychotherapy Offers a Solution

1. See, for example, Yates, M. (1976). *Coping: A survival manual for women alone*. Englewood Cliffs, NJ: Prentice-Hall, as one of many examples.

2. Hatfield, E., Cacioppo, J. T., & Rapson, R. L. (1993). Emotional contagion. *Current directions in psychological science, 2*, 96–99.

3. Gornick, V. (1987). *Fierce attachments*. New York: Simon & Schuster.

4. Isn't "smothered" a striking word in this context! It links "mother" with not being allowed to breathe. It is noteworthy that early psychoanalytic pioneers in psychosomatic medicine regarded the conflict between wanting independence and fearing it as the psychological basis of asthma.

5. One school of neo-Freudians took root in Chicago and was dominated for a time by the ideas of Karen Horney; see Horney, K. *The neurotic personality of our times*. New York: Norton. Other neo-Freudians, who deviated sharply from many of the Freudian concepts, included now famous figures who had earlier belonged to the Freudian group. They were Jung, C. G. (1916). *Analytic psychology*. New York: Moffat, Yard; Adler, A. (1927). *The practice and theory of individual psychology*. New York: Harcourt; Sullivan, H. S. (1953). *The interpersonal theory of psychiatry*. New York: Norton. Today there are additional offshoots too numerous to mention that have gained prominence in psychoanalytic thought.

6. Ellis, A. (1962). *Reason and emotion in psychotherapy*. New York: Lyle Stuart. See also Ellis, A., & Grieger, R. (Eds.). (1977). *Handbook of rational-emotive therapy*. New York: Springer; and Bernard, M. E., & DiGiuseppe, R. (Eds.). (1989). *Inside rational-emotive therapy*. San Diego, CA: Academic Press.

7. Beck, A. T. (1976). *Cognitive therapy and the emotional disorders*. New York: International Universities Press. See also Beck, A. T., & Emery, G., with Greenberg, R. L. (1985). *Anxiety disorders and phobias: A cognitive perspective*. New York: Basic Books.

8. Meichenbaum, D. (1977). *Cognitive-behavior modification: An integrative approach*. New York: Plenum.

9. See also Goldfried, M. R., & Goldfried, A. P. (1975). Cognitive change methods. In F. H. Kanfer & A. P. Goldstein (Eds.), *Helping people change*. New York: Pergamon. Also Goldfried, M. R. (1980). Psychotherapy as coping skills training. In M. J. Mahoney (Ed.), *Psychotherapy process: Current issues and future directions*. New York: Plenum.

10. Novaco, R. W. (1979). The cognitive regulation of anger and stress. In P. C. Kendall & S. D. Hollon (Eds.), *Cognitive-behavioral interventions: Theory, research, and procedures*. New York: Academic Press. See also Novaco, R. W. (1980). Training of probation counselors for anger problems. *Journal of Consulting Psychology*, 27, 385–390.

11. McFall, R. M., & Twentyman, C. T. (1973). Four experiments on the relative contribution of rehearsal, modeling and coaching to assertion training. *Journal of Abnormal Psychology*, 81, 199–218.

12. See Watson, J., & Rayner, R. (1920). Conditioned emotional reactions. *Journal of Experimental Psychology*, 3, 1–14. See also Watson, J. B., & Watson, R. R. (1921). Studies in infant psychology. *Scientific monthly*, 13, 493–515. Also Jones, M. C. (1924). A laboratory study of fear: The case of Peter. *Pediatrics Seminar*, 31, 308–315.

13. A white rat could create fear in an adult who believed it carried germs and liked to bite people; however, this belief itself is conditioned.

14. Wolpe, J. (1958). *Psychotherapy by reciprocal inhibition.* Stanford, CA: Stanford University Press.

15. Benson, H. (1984). *Beyond the relaxation response.* New York: Times Books. See also Benson, H. (1978). *The relaxation response.* New York: Avon.

16. Andrasik, F., & Holroyd, K. A. (1980). A test of specific and nonspecific effects in the biofeedback treatment of tension headache. *Journal of Consulting and Clinical Psychology, 48,* 575–586. See also Lazarus, R. S. (1975). A cognitively oriented psychologist looks at biofeedback. *American Psychologist, 30,* 553–561.

17. See Greenberg, L. A., & Safran, J. D. (1989). Emotion in psychotherapy. *American Psychologist, 44,* 19–29.

18. Foa, E., & Kozak, J. J. (1986). Emotional processing of fear: Exposure to corrective information. *Psychological Bulletin, 99,* 20–35. Quote on p. 20.

19. Meichenbaum, D., & Cameron, R. (1983). Stress inoculation training: Toward a general paradigm for training coping skills. In D. Meichenbaum & M. E. Jaremko (Eds.), *Stress reduction and prevention.* New York: Plenum Press. Quote on p. 141.

20. Ellis, A. (1984). Is the unified-interaction approach to cognitive-behavior modification a reinvention of the wheel? *Clinical Psychology Review, 4,* 215–218. Quote on p. 216

21. Beck, A. T. (1987). Cognitive therapy. In J. Zeig (Ed.), *Evolution of psychotherapy.* New York: Brunner/Mazel. Quote on p. 32

22. See Bugental, J. F. T. (1990). *Intimate journeys: Stories from life-changing therapy.* San Francisco: Jossey-Bass, for an example of experiential-existential therapy.

Index